Chapter-wise
Topical Objective
Study Package
for

CBSE 2022 Class 12 Term I

Biology

Corporate Office

DISHA PUBLICATION

45, 2nd Floor, Maharishi Dayanand Marg,
Corner Market, Malviya Nagar, New Delhi - 110017
Tel : 49842349 / 49842350

Typeset by Disha DTP Team

www.dishapublication.com

Books & ebooks for School & Competitive Exams

www.mylearninggraph.com

Etests for Competitive Exams

Write to us at **feedback_disha@aiets.co.in**

Contents

1. Sexual Reproduction in Flowering Plants

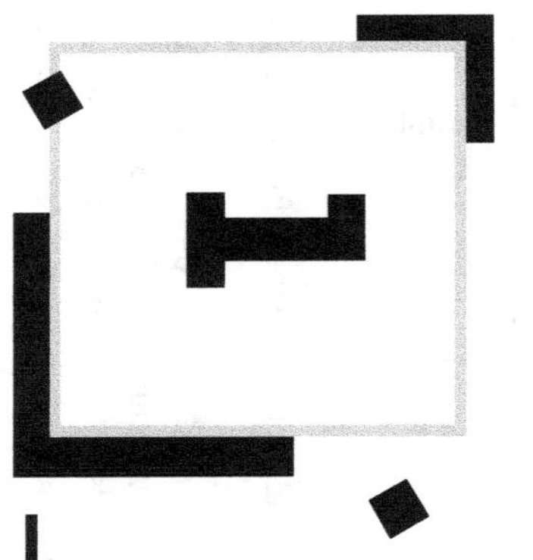

Sexual Reproduction in Flowering Plants

Pre-fertilization Changes
Formation of flower and its component, stamen and pistil are pre-requisite for fertilization

Pollination
Process of transfer of pollen grain from anther to stigma.

Post-fertilization changes
Formation of endosperm, development of embryo, seed formation and then fruit is formed.

Microsporogenesis
In this process, pollen grains are formed from pollen mother cell through meiosis.

Megasporogenesis
In this process, megaspore mother cell is form and undergoes meiosis and form 4-haploid cell and later embryo sac is formed.

Embryo
It is formed from syngamy.

Endosperm
It is formed by double fertilization.

Self pollination
Pollination at the same flower or genetically similar flower eg-wheat, barley, etc.

Cross-pollination
Transfer of pollen from the flower of one plant to the stigma of the flower of another plant.

Autogamy
Transfer of pollen from anther to stigma at some flower.

Geitonogamy
Different flower of same plant.

Abiotic agencies
Anemophilly by wind Hydrophilly by water.

Biotic agencies
(Entomophilly i.e. by insects. By Bats (Chiropterophily), By snails (Malacophily) By Birds (Ornithophily)

Topic 1   Pre-Fertilization Events

Sexual reproduction is the formation of new individuals through the meiotic gamete formation and their subsequent fusion during fertilization. Sexual reproduction is also called Amphimixis.

Flowers are the most fascinating organs in plants found only in angiosperms i.e., plants in which seeds are enclosed within fruit. Flowers and their parts are responsible for sexual reproduction in angiosperms and all flower bearing plants reproduce sexually. The colour, fragrance, modification in shape of flower ensure its sexual reproduction. Fruits and seeds are the end products of sexual reproduction. Sexual reproduction in plants includes microsporogenesis, megasporogenesis, pollination, fertilization, embryogensis and seed formation.

FLOWER

Flowers are highly modified shoots, bearing nodes and modified floral leaves, which are meant essentially for sexual reproduction in plant. The flower is commonly borne on short or long stalk called the pedicel it has upper swollers region known is receptacles or thalamus or torus. Flowers, usually have four different kinds of floral members arranged in four whorls (i.e., calyx, corolla, androecium and gynoecium).

Parts of the Flower

A typical flower has four different kind of whorl. These are

(i)   **Calyx** – Consists of number of green leafy sepals. It is the outermost whorl.

(ii)   **Corolla** – Consists of a number of usually bright coloured petals and is the second whorl in the flower.

(iii)   **Androecium** – This is the male whorl and consists of stamens and each stamen can be regarded as modified leaf (microsporophyll) that consists of filament and anther. The anther may contains two-four microsporangia that produce a large number of pollen grains.

(iv)   **Gynoecium** – It is present in the centre of the flower and is the female reproductive whorl. Its unit is called carpel. Each carpel is made up of '3' parts — ovary, style and stigma.

Ovary is the swollen basal part of the carpel that encloses ovules and each ovule encloses embryo sac containing egg. Stigma is the receptive part of carpel whereas style is the tubular structure that joins stigma & ovary. Thus, androecium & gynoecium are the two innermost whorl of flower in which sexual reproduction take place. Anther bears spores in sporangia and ovary contains ovules which bear embryo-sac with egg.

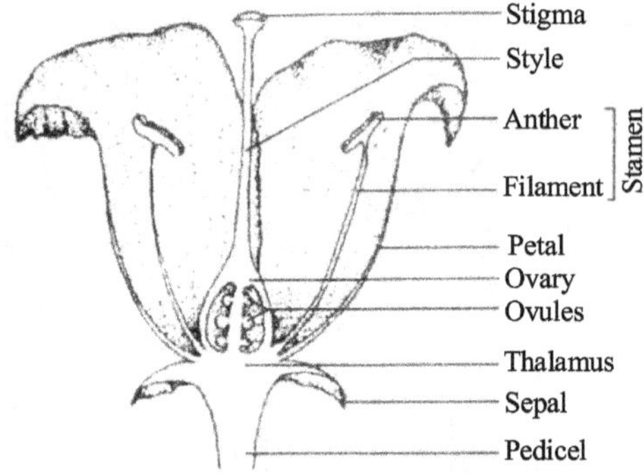

Fig. : L. S. of Flower
Table : Some important flowers

1.	Ornamental		2.	Social and Cultural values	
	Helianthus annus	Sunflower		*Michelia champaca*	Champa
	Lochnera rosea	Periwinkle		*Polyathia longifolia*	Ashok
	Nerium indicum	Oleander		*Brassica campestris*	Mustard
	Hibiscus rosa-sinensis	China rose		*Cassia fistula*	Amaltas
	Cherianthus	Wall flower		*Acacia nilotica*	Babul
	Lilium	Lily		*Oryza sativa*	Rice
				Rauwolfia serpentina	Sarpgandha

Functions of a Flower

(i) Flowers are modifications of shoot to perform the function of sexual reproduction. The fertile leaves become microsporophylls (stamen) and megasporophylls (carpels) which bear anthers and ovules respectively. The anthers produce pollen grains and the ovules possess eggs.

(ii) Flowers of most of the angiosperms are shaped variously to help diverse modes of pollination.

(iii) Flowers provide seed for germination of pollen, development of pollen tube, formation of gametes and fertilization.

(iv) The ovary part of the carpel gets transformed into fruit and the ovules are transformed into seeds after fertilization.

(v) Some floral parts like calyx and various modifications in ovaries help in the dispersal of fruits and seeds.

The process of fertilization starts much before the actual fertilization takes place. Formation of flower and its component parts stamen and pistil, are pre-requisite for fertilization.

Stamen

Stamen is the male reproductive unit of angiosperms consists of anther, connective, and filament. The long and slender stalk called as filament and the terminal structure is known as anther. Typically, angiospermic anther is bilobed and dithecous i.e., each lobe has two theca. The bilobed structure of the anther is tetra sporangiate (four sporangia). In transverse section, it appears as four sided tetragonal structure consisting of two microsporangia in each lobe. Microsporangia develops into pollen sac filled with pollen grains within each pollen-sac there is a fine, powdery or granular mass of cells called the pollen grains or microspores. Pollen grains are produced in large quantities in pollen sacs. The number, form, and length of stamen varies from species to species.

Microsporangium

A typical microsporangium usually appears circular in outline with sporogenous tissue at the centre surrounded by four layers of different kinds of cells.

Each microsporangium is surrounded by four layers that are as follows :

(i) **Epidermis** – It is single layer Protective in function.

(ii) **Endothecium** – Cells posses bands of callose and help in dehiscence of anthers at maturity.

(iii) **Middle layers** – Cells are crushed or where persistent contain starch and other reserve material to be consumed by the growing microspore mother cells.

(iv) **Tapetum** – Single celled innermost layer surrounding the sporgenous tissue, having dense cytoplasm and are multinucleated. Its main function is to provide nutrition to the developing microspore mother cells and pollen grains. In tapetal cells, nuclear division is not followed by cell division hence, binucleate or multinucleate condition is achieved. It secretes callose enzyme which dissolves callose substances by which 4 pollens of a pollen tetrad are united, hence seperating microscopes or pollens of a tetrad. Tapetum secretes ubisch bodies which gets covered with sporopollenin and so increase thickness of exine.

Tapetum is of two types – amoeboid and sectetory. In amoeboid or plasmodial tapetum, the inner and radial walls break down at an early stage and these cells are free in microsporangia. In secretory or glandular tapetum, the tapetum remain as such throughout. Pollen kitt is the outermost oily, thick, sticky, coating of pollen grains, mainly composed of lipids and carotenoids. It is secreted in case of Entomophily.

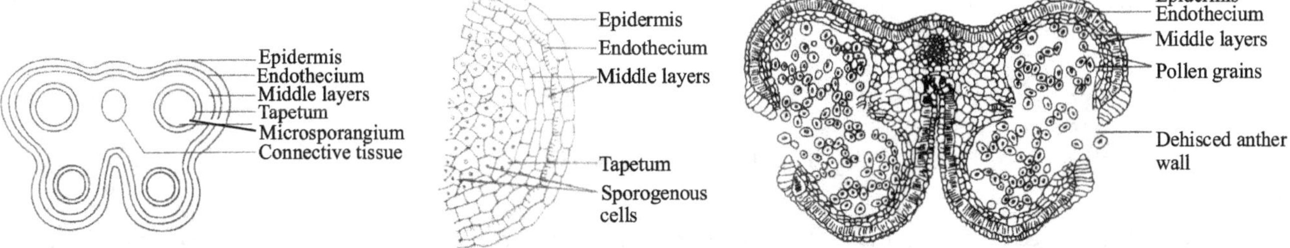

Fig. : T. S. of mature anther   **Fig. : A portion of enlarged microsporangium**   **Fig. : T.S. of a dehisced anther**

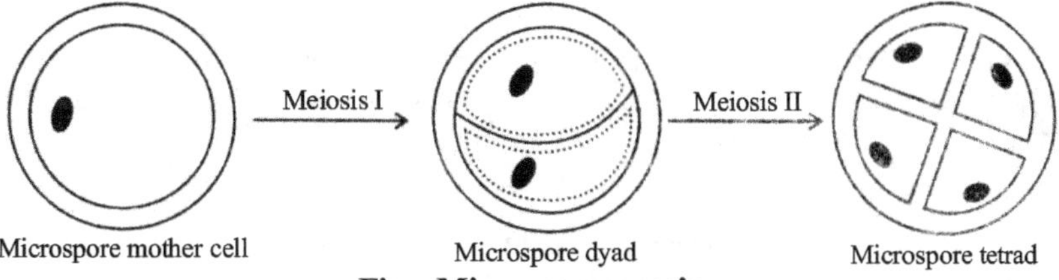

Fig. : Microsporogenesis

Microsporogenesis

This is the process of formation of microspores or pollen grains, from a pollen mother cell through meiosis is micro sporogenesis Each cell of sporogenous tissue serve as microspore mother cell (MMC). These MMCs undergo meiosis and form microspore tetrad and become haploid, microspores or pollen grains. As anthers mature microspores of the tetrad separate from each other and develops into pollen grains. Each microsporangium contains numerous pollen grains which are released after dehiscence of anther wall.

Isobilateral tetrads are formed in monocots. Tetrahedral tetrads are formed in dicots. One microspore is formed from one pollen mother cell, e.g., cyperaceal. In member of asclepiadaceae and orchidacea all the pollens of an anther lobe are packed in a bag like structure called pollinium-pollinia of two adjacent anthers together form a translator. Polyspory is the occurrence of more than 4 spores in a pollen tetrad, e.g., cuscuta reflexa when 4 pollens do not separate and remain in tetrads it is known as compound pollen.

Dehiscence of anther

The mature anther dries up. The sterile strip present between the two pollen sacs of each anther lobe disintegrates to form a single cavity. Therefore, the mature anther has only two cavities or the cal, with one the ca in each lobe. With the loss of water the differently thickened dead cells of endothecium contract from their outer thin walls. As a result the endothecium shortens and ruptures the anther. Lobe wall in the region of stomium.

Dehiscence of anther is of 4 types–

(i)   Longitudinal dehiscence (*e.g. Datura*).

(ii)   Transverse dehiscence (*e.g. Ocimum*).

(iii)   Porous dehiscence (*e.g. Solanum*).

(iv)   Valvular dehiscence (*e.g. Beberis*).

Pollen Grains

Within each "pollen sac" there are fine powdery granular mass of cells called pollen grains. These are male reproductive bodies of a flower. Generally these are spherical, measuring 20-25 micrometres in diameter. Pollen grains consist of outer "exine" and inner "intine". **Exine** is tough, cutinized layer often with spinous outgrowth but sometimes smooth. Exine is composed of sporopollenin which is resistant to physical and biological decomposition. It protect the pollens from environmental extremes. Spropollenin is absent in the pollen grains of *Zostera*. Thin areas of the exine are called germ pore or germ slits. At these pores, sporopollenin is absent. **Intine** is thin, delicate, cutin and cellulosic layer lying internal to exine. Pollen grains in pine are provided with two distinct wings. When pollen grains germinate, intine grows out into tube called pollen tube, through germ pore present on exine.

Mature pollen grain contains two cells – a large, nucleated **vegetative cell** which is irregular in shape with abundant food reserve and a small spindle shape **generative cell**. In most of the angiospermic species, pollen grains are shed at two-celled stage while the others shed them at three-celled stage.

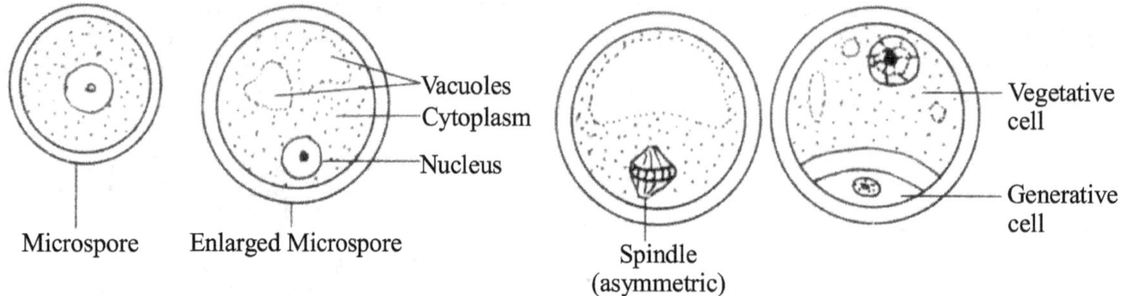

Fig. : Development of Pollen grain

Pollen allergy

Pollen grains of many species are the cause of severe allergies and respiratory problems, like - asthma and bronchitis. *Parthenium* or carrot grass is a well known pollen allergen. It entered India as contaminant with imported wheat but has spread in all parts of the country. *Chenopodium, A Maranthus Sorghum, Cynodon* are other common sources of pollen allergy.

Pollen products

The pollen grains especially the ones collected by bees are being used for a variety of purposes like nature cure, cosmetics and as food supplements. Pollen grains are believed to be rich in nutrients (protein 7–26%, carbohydrates 24–48%, fats 0.9–14.5%). They are taken as tablets or syrups to enhance performance of athletes and race horses.

Pollen viability

Viability period of pollen grains varies from species to species like in cereals (rice & wheat), it is 30 minutes while in some plants they may be viable for months e.g., Rosaceae, Leguminaseae. It however, depends upon environmental conditions of temperature and humidity. Viability of pollen grains can be retained for longer duration by keeping them in liquid nitrogen (–196°) in pollen banks for later use in plant.

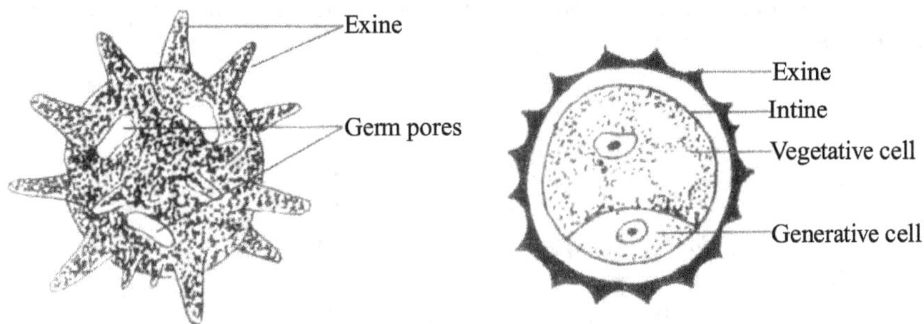

Fig. : Pollen grain

Gynoecium (Pistil)

Gynoecium represents the female reproductive whorl of the flower. It is composed of one or more carpels or pistils. Each pistil is a unit of gynoecium comprising ovary, style and stigma. Gynoecium may be comprised of one or more carpel. The carpels are modified leaves which bear ovules and also called megasporophylls. Carpels can be of two types:

Monocarpellary – When gynoecium comprises of single carpel.

Multicarpellary – When gynoecium consists of more than one carpel.

If there are more than one carpel and they are fused then called "**syncarpous**" (united carpels) or when carpels lie free from each other then called "**apocarpous**" (fused carpels). Each carpel consists of three parts i.e; Stigma, Style and ovary. The stigma is the terminal end of the style upon which the pollen grain falls and is generally Knob-Like and Sticky. The style is the slender projection of the ovary and bears stigma at its terminal end. The surface of the style may be smooth or covered with hair. In many cases these hairs collect the pollen grains. The swollen basal part of the pistil which is single or many chambered, is termed **ovary**. The ovary contains one or more roundish or oval, egg-like bodies, known as ovules which are attached to the placenta. Each ovule contains a large oval cell known as the embryosac. The ovary give rise to the fruit and ovules give rise to seeds.

There may be one or more than one ovules in an ovary.

Ovary with single ovules – Sunflower, mango, paddy and marigold.

Ovary with many ovules – Pea, water melon, mustard and water lily.

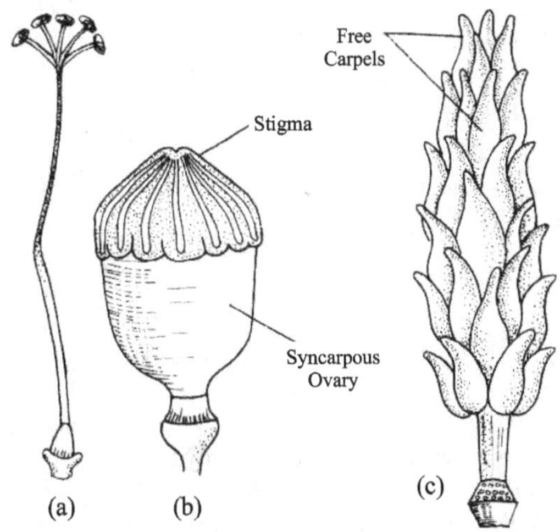

Fig. : Gynoecium.
(a) A syncarpous pentacarpellary pistil of *Hibiscus*. (b) A syncarpous multicarpellary pistil of *Papaver*.
(c) A syncarpous multicarpellary gynoecium of *Michelia*.

Megasporangium (Ovule)

An Ovule is a female megasporangium where the formation of megaspore takes place. The various parts of an ovule are :-

(i)   **Funiculus:** It is a small stalk like structure which represents the point of attachment of the ovule to the placenta of the ovary.

(ii)   **Hilum:** It is the point where the body of the ovule is attached to the Funiculus.

(iii) **Integument:** Integuments are outer layers surrounding the ovule that provide protection to the developing embryo.

(iv) **Micropyle:** It is a narrow pore formed by the projection of integuments. It marks the point where the pollen tube enters the ovule at the time of fertilisation.

(v)   **Chalaza:** It is the basal swollen part of the nucellus (opposite the micropylar end) from where the integuments originate.

(vi) **Nucellus:** It is a mass of parenchymatous tissue surrounded by integuments from the outside. Nucellus provides nutrition to the developing embryo.

(vii) Embryo sac: The embryo sac or female gametophyte is located inside the nucellus. An ovule generally has a single embryo sac formed from a megaspore through meiosis.

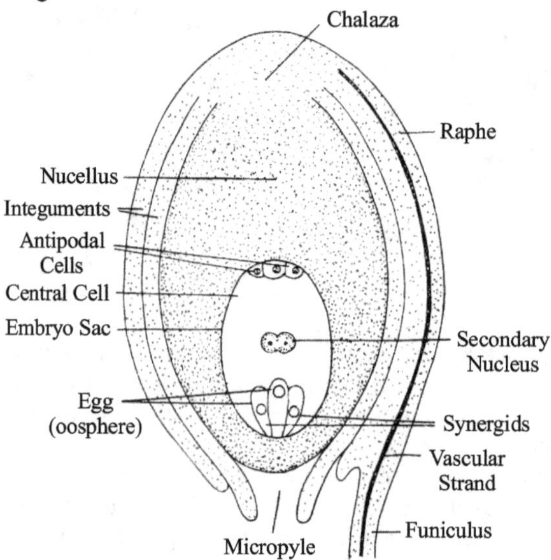

Fig. : Structure of a typical ovule (anatropous ovule) prior to fertilization

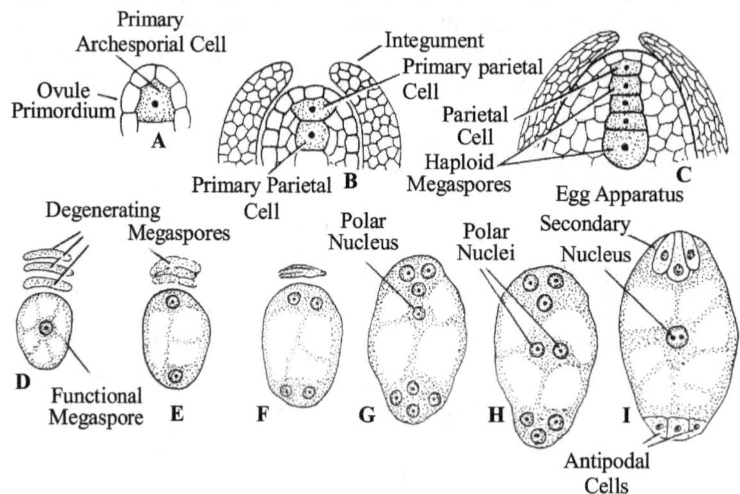

Fig. : Development of embryo sac

Types of ovules in relation to integuments are -

Unitegmic : Ovule with a single integument, *e.g.*, synpetalous or gamopetalous dicotyledons.

Bitegmic : Ovule with two integuments as in polypetalous (Archichlamydeae) dicotyledons and monocotyledons.

Aril : This is a collar-like outgrowth from the base of the ovule and forms third integument. Aril is found in litchi, nutmeg, etc.

Caruncle : It is formed as an outgrowth of the outer integument in the micropylar region. Caruncle is common in the ovules of Euphorbiaceae. *e.g.*, Castor (*Ricinus*).

Ategmic : In some parasites like *Loranthus, Viscum, Santalum* etc., there is no integument. Such an ovule is called ategmic.

Types of ovules in relation to shape and orientation.

(i)   Orthotropous or Atropus : The micropyle, chalaza and funicle are in straight line. This is most primitive type of ovules, *e.g.*, Betel, *Piper, Polygonum*.

(ii)   Anatropous : The body of the ovule is completely inverted (turn at 180° angle) so that micropyle and hilum come to lie very close to each other, *e.g.*, 82% of angiosperm families.

(iii) Hemianatropous : Ovule turns at 90° angle upon the funicle or body of ovule is at right angle to the funicle, *e.g.*, *Ranunculus*.

(iv)   Campylotropous : Ovule is circled more or less at right angle to funicle. Micropylar end is bent down slightly, *e.g.*, in members of *Leguminosae* and *Cruciferae, Capsella*.

(v)   Amphitropous : Curvature of ovule is more and embryo sac becomes curved like horse shoe, *e.g. Lemna, Poppy, Alisma*.

(vi)   Circinotropous : The ovule is initially orthotropous but becomes anatropous due to unilateral growth of funicle. The growth continues till the ovule once again becomes orthotropous. As a result funicle completely surrounds the body of the ovule, *e.g.*, *Opuntia* (prickly pear).

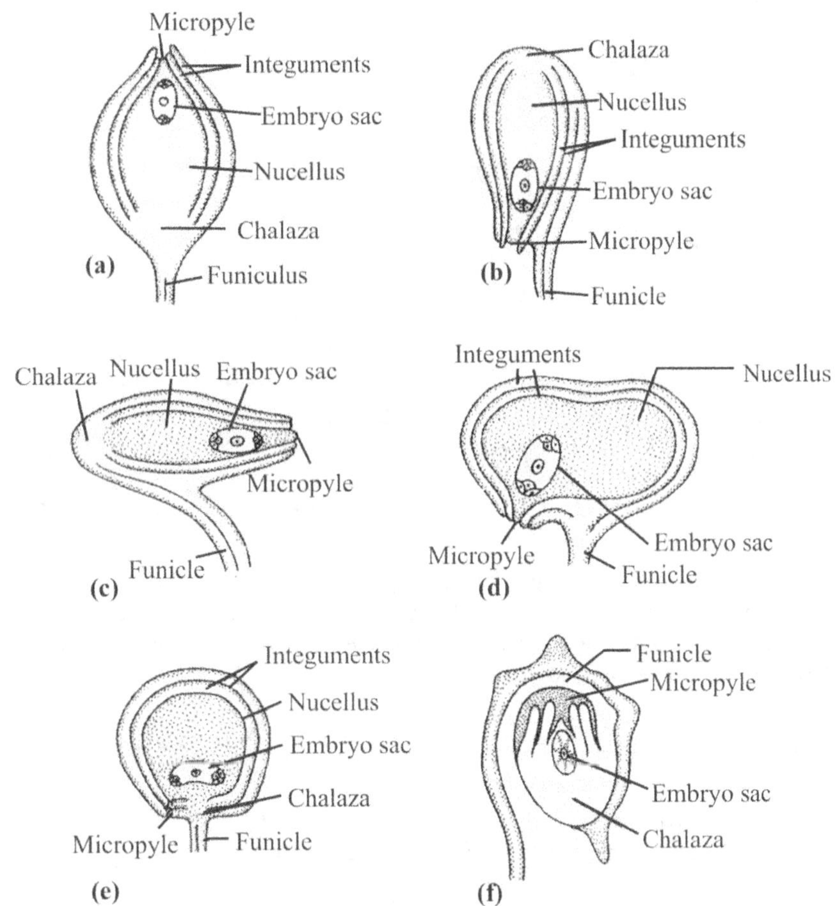

Fig. : Different forms of the ovule in longitudinal section (a) Orthotropous, (b) Anatropous, (c) Hemianatropous, (d) Campylotropous, (e) Amphitropous, (f) Circinotropous

Megasporogenesis

The process of formation of megaspore from megaspore mother cell (MMC) is known as **megasporogenesis**. Single MMC with dense cytoplasm and a prominent nucleus gets differentiated from nucellus near the micropylar region as a primary archesporial cell. This MMC undergoes meiosis to form '4' haploid cells called **megaspores**. In majority of flowering plants, only one megaspore is functional while the other three degenerate.

Female gametophyte (Embryo sac)

Megaspore is the initial cell or beginning of female gametoplyte orembryo sac.

Out of the four haploid megaspores, either few of them degenerate or all take part in embryo sac formation. Depending upon the number of megaspores taking part in formation of female gametophyte, it is classified into following 3-types :

(i)   **Monosporic type** – When only one megaspore undergoes division to form female gametophyte while other three degenerates. All nuclei are genetically identical.

(ii) **Bisporic type** – When two-nuclei take part in the development of female gametophyte.

(iii) **Tetrasporic type** – When all the four nuclei take part in female gametophyte development.

Formation of the embryo sac:

The female gametophyte develops from a single functional megaspore. This megaspore undergoes three successive mitotic divisions to form 8-nucleated embryo sac. The first mitotic division in the nucleus of the functional megaspore forms two nuclei. One nucleus move towards the micropylar end, while the other nucleus move towards the chalazal end. This result into 2-nucleate embryo sac.

Two more sequential mitotic nuclear divisions at their respective ends i.e. at the micropylar and chalazal end of the embryo sac result in the formation of the 4-nucleate and later the 8-nucleate stages of the embryo sac. These divisions are strictly free nuclear, i.e. nuclear divisions are not followed immediately by cell wall formation.

After the 8-nucleate stage, cell walls are laid down leading to the organization of the typical female gametophyte or embryo sac.

Six of the 8 nuclei get surrounded by the cell wall and remaining two nuclei called polar nuclei are situated below the egg apparatus in the large central cell.

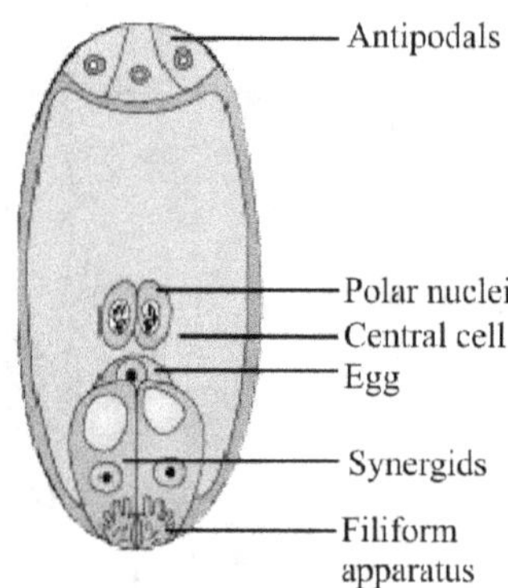

Fig. A diagrammatic representation of the mature embryo sac.

$$\text{Functional Megaspore} \xrightarrow{\text{Mitosis}} \text{'2' Nuclei} \xrightarrow{\text{Mitosis}} \text{'4' Nuclei} \xrightarrow{\text{Mitosis}} \text{'8' Nucleate Embryo sac}$$

A mature embryo sac consists of egg apparatus, synergids and antipodals.

Egg apparatus

It consists of two synergids and one egg cell lying at the micropylar end. Synergids bear prominent structure called **'filiform' apparatus** which are finger like projections. Synergids guide the path of pollen tube towards the egg, help in obtaining nourishment from the outer nucellar cells and also function as shock absorbers during the penetration of pollen tube into the embryo sac. Cytoplasm of egg is inactive, rich in ribosomes, and contains plastids.

Central cell

Two polar nuclei form the central cell. These two polar nuclei fuse to form single diploid secondary nuclous or definitive nucleus.

Antipodals

Three cells present at the chalazal end constitute antipodals. Thus, a typical mature embryo sac of angiosperm is 7-celled, 8 nucleate structure i.e., 3 antipodal cells, 3-egg apparatus cells and one central cell (2 polar nuclei).

Practice Exercise-1

Multiple Choice Questions

1. The functions of tapetum is to
(a) dehiscence of anther
(b) produce pollen grains.
(c) provide nourishment to the developing pollen grains.
(d) store and protect pollen grains.

2. Egg apparatus consists of
(a) egg cell and antipodal cells.
(b) egg cell and central cell.
(c) egg cell and two synergids.
(d) egg cell and one synergid.

3. In a fertilized ovule, n, $2n$ and $3n$ conditions occur respectively in
(a) antipodal, egg and endosperm.
(b) egg, nucellus and endosperm.
(c) endosperm, nucellus and egg.
(d) antipodals, synergids and integuments.

4. Pollen grains are preserved as fossils because of the
(a) Presence of cellulose & pectin
(b) Presence of sporopollenin
(c) Presence of lignin
(d) Presence of cellulose

5. After penetrating stigmatic and stylar tissue the pollen tube usually grows down towards the egg cell because
(a) the egg cell attracts pollen tube
(b) it grows under the influence of ovum
(c) it has no other passage to follow
(d) the filiform apparatus of synergids attract the pollen tubes

Match the Following

6. Match the items given in column-I with those given in column-II and chose the correct option given below.

	Column-I		Column-II
A.	Tapetum	I.	Irregular in shape with abundant food reserve
B.	Exine	II.	Acts as nutritive layer
C.	Pollenkit	III.	Thick, rigid protective layer
D.	Vegetative cel l	IV.	Involve in the formation of microspores
E.	Sporogenous	V.	Oily and sticky layer, tissue help in pollination.

(a) A – II; B – III; C – V; D – IV; E – I
(b) A – I; B – III; C – II; D – IV; E – V
(c) A – II; B – III; C – I; D – IV; E – V
(d) A – II; B – IV; C – V; D – I; E – III

Assertion & Reason Questions

DIRECTIONS (Qs. 7-10) : *Each of these questions contains an assertion followed by reason. Read them carefully and answer the question on the basis of following options. You have to select the one that best describes the two statements.*

(a) If both Assertion and Reason are correct and the Reason is a correct explanation of the Assertion.

(b) If both Assertion and Reason are correct but Reason is not a correct explanation of the Assertion.

(c) If the Assertion is correct but Reason is incorrect.

(d) If both Assertion and Reason are incorrect.

7. **Assertion:** Cells of the tapetum possess dence cytoplasm and generally have more than one nucleus.
   Reason: The anther and the filament are attached together with the help of connective.

8. **Assertion:** All the four microspores are attached together with the help of callose layer which is dissolved after sometime by callase enzyme.
   Reason: All the five types of microspore tetrads are found in a plant named *Aristolochia elegans*.

9. **Assertion:** The megasporangia, commonly called ovules arise from placenta.
   Reason: The number of ovules in an ovary may be one as in wheat, mango etc. to many as in papaya, watermelon and orchids.

10. **Assertion:** The process of formation of megaspores from megaspore mother cell (MMC) is called megasporogenesis.
    Reason: Ovules generally differentiate a single megaspore mother cell (MMC) in the micropylar region of the nucellus.

Very Short Answer Questions

11. Name the parts of the flower that form the calyx.
12. Which is the most resistant organic material ?
13. Circinotropous type of ovule is found in which plant.
14. How many megaspores are formed by meiosis of megaspore mother cell ?
15. What is process in which anther is removed ?

Short Answer Questions

16. With the help of labelled diagrams, depict the stages of a microspore maturing into a pollen grain.
17. What is the significance of patterns and designs over pollen grains ?
18. How the pistil recognizes the pollen grain before accepting it ?
19. Write short note on pollen products?
20. What do you understand by pollen or nector robbers.

Topic 2   Pollination

The process of transference of pollen grains from anther to the stigma of a pistil is known as pollination. This process of pollination occurs only in gymnosperms and angiosperms. Pollination in angiosperms generally takes place at 2-called stage (rarely 3-celled stage) of microspores or pollen i.e; vegetative cell and generative cell. If the pollen grains are transferred to the micropyle of the ovule directly, the pollination is called direct pollination eg. gymnosperms. Since the ovules are enclosed in the ovary in angiosperms, the pollination is called indirect pollination.

Pollination that occurs in closed flowers is called cleistogamy. Cleistogamous flowers do not expose their reproductive parts. Anther and Stigma lie close to eachother. Pure autogamy occurs since there is no chance of cross-pollination. Cleistogamy is the most efficient floral adaptation for promoting self-pollination. eg. *Viola mirabilis and Oxalis autosella.*

Pollination occurs in opened flower, which expose their sex org ans, it is called chasmogany and the flowers are called chasmogamous flowers. Majority of angiosperms have chasmogamous flowers. e.g. *Catharanthus, Mirabilis.* Pollination is facilitated by various factors like wind, water, insects, birds and animals.

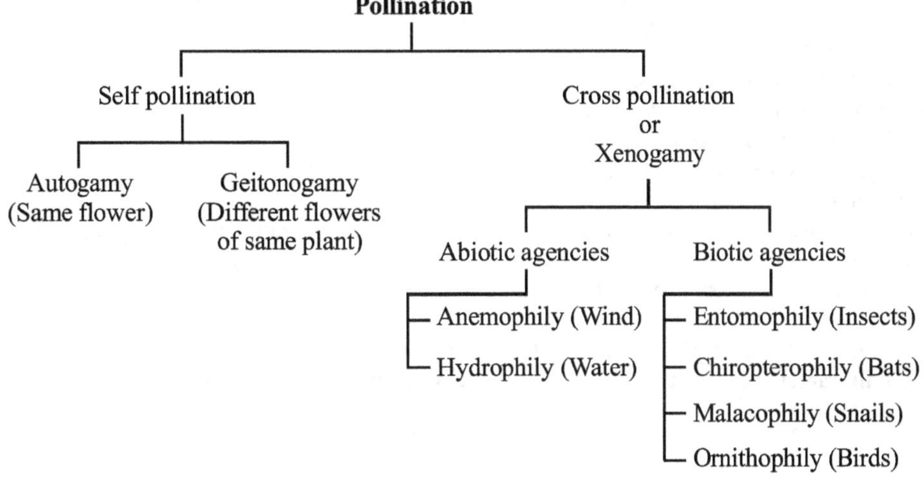

Self-Pollination or Autogamy

Transfer of pollen grains from anther to stigma of same flower or genetically similar flower is called self pollination. It occurs always in crops with bisexual flowers, *e.g.* wheat, barley etc. Self pollination is a rule in cleistogamous flower. It is of two types — autogamy and geitonogamy.

(i)   **Autogamy** is a kind of pollination in which the pollen from the anthers of a flower are transferred to the stigma of the same flower.

(ii)   **Geitonogamy** is a kind of pollination in which the pollen from the anthers of one flower are transferred to the stigma of another flower borne on the same plant. It usually occurs in plants which show monoecious condition (unisexual, male and female flowers are borne on the same plant). Geitonogamy involves two flowers but these belong to the same parent plant.

       Advantages of self pollination : Pollen grains are not wasted and the purity of the generation is maintained.

       Disadvantages of self pollination : New and healthier varieties are not formed. It results in weaker progeny, producing weaker seeds and plants.

Cross Pollination or Xenogamy

Cross pollination involves the transfer of pollen grains from the flower of one plant to the stigma of the flower of another plant. It is also called *xenogamy*. It is performed with the help of external agency.

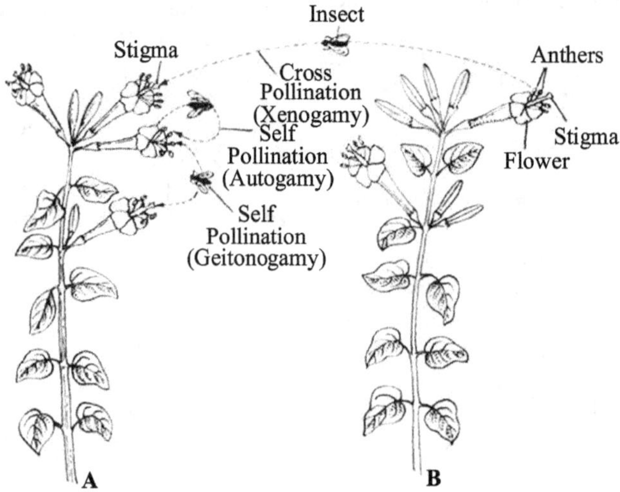

Fig. : Self and Cross-pollination

Dichogamy, dicliny, herkogamy, heterostyly and self sterility are the main reasons or adaptations for cross pollination in bisexual flowers.

(i)   **Dichogamy** – Maturation of male and female sex organs occurs at different times in a bisexual flowers, *e.g.*, Cruciferae family.

(ii)   **Herkogamy** – Male or female sex organs themselves prove as a barrier to prevent self pollination, *e.g.*, *Cyprepedium*, Orchids.

(iii) **Dicliny or Unisexuality** – Effectively prevents self-pollination. Presence of unisexual flowers in plants that prevents self pollination, *e.g.*, Castor, Maize and Papaya.

(iv) **Heterostyly** – Presence of styles of different heights in flower of many plants to prevent self-pollination, *e.g.*, *Primula vulgaris, Oxalis.*

(v)   **Self sterility (self-incompatibility)** – Plants in which pollen from same flower is incapable of bringing about fertilization, due to the presence of similar self sterile gene, *e.g.*, Tobacco, Potato.

Advantages of cross pollination are-

(i)   It increases the adaptability of offsprings.

(ii)   It induces genetic recombination and hence variation in progeny.

(iii) Plants produced are more disease resistants.

(iv) New and more useful varieties are produced.

Disadvantages of cross pollination are-

(i)   It is highly wasteful method because the plants are able to produce a number of devices for helping the pollen grains to use external agencies for transport.

(ii)   In nature cross pollination is a better method of pollination because-it avoids recessive lethal or harmful genes to become homozygous.

(iii) it produces healthier plants due to phenomenon of hybrid vigour.

(iv) it keeps the variability and hence adaptability of the race interact so that an adverse environment does not destroy the species.

Table : Difference between self pollination and cross pollination

	Self Pollination	Cross Pollination
1.	It is the process of deposition of pollen grains from anther of a flower to the stigma of the same or genetically similar (another flower) of the same plant.	It is the process of the deposition of pollen grains from anther of a flower to the stigma of a different flower of another plant.
2.	Externally pollinating agency is not required.	External pollinating agency is required like wind, water, bird etc.
3.	It results in the production of pure line homozygous offsprings.	It results in the production of zygotes with higher degree of heterozygosity.
4.	It is achievable only in those plants which produces bisexual flowers or have monoeious conditions	It is possible in all unisexual plants which are dioecious. It may also occur in plants which produces bisexual flowers.
5.	Examples-Wheat, rice, pea, tomato citrus etc.	Examples- Maize, bajra, cab bage, cauliflower, apple, banana, papaya etc.

Agents of Pollination

The expressin of relationship between the agents and structure of flower is called pollination mechanism. For cross pollination, agent is a must. The spreading of pollen grains from platn to plant in cross pollination takes place through biotic agencies (living agencies) or through abiotic agencies (non living agencies).

(i) **Abiotic agencies :** for cross pollination on include non living components for pollination such as wind ad water.

(ii) **Biotic agencies :** for cross pollination include living agents for pollination.

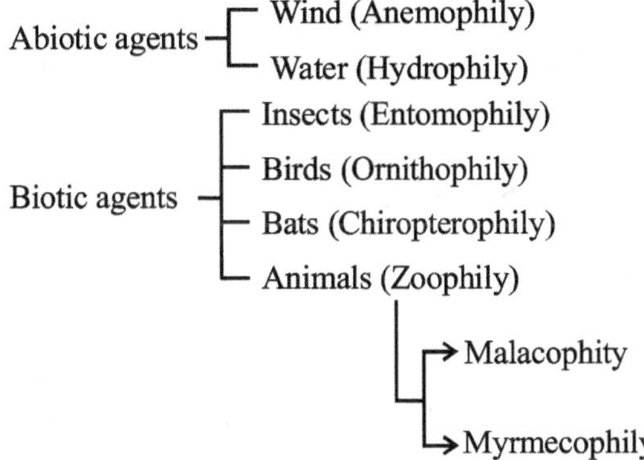

Anemophily : The pollination taking place by means of wind in known as an Anemophily. In this type pollen grains reach the stigma through winds. Lots of pollen grains are formed as compared to the number of ovules available for – pollination. Pollen are small, light, smooth, dry, non sticky ad unwettable Female reproductive organ i.e., stigma is large and feathery for trapping the wind-borne pollen grains. Wind pollinated flowers have few ovules or even one ovule in the ovary, because the chances of pollination is rare. e.g., A tassel of maize gives rise to 20-25 million pollen grains.

Hydrophily : Pollination with the help of water is called hydrophily. Pollination by water rare in nature. Floral envelop of these plants are highly reduced or absent. Thus, exposing stamen and stigma and favour hydrophily Pollination can occur within water, e.g., *Zostera, Ceratophyllum* or on the surface of water, e.g., *Vallisneria*. In *Vallisneria* (ribbon weed), female flower reaches on the surface of water and assumes horizontal position due to elongation of its stalk, male flowers or pollen grains are released on to the surface of water. They are carried passively by water currents & some of which eventually reach to the stigma. Both wind & water pollinated flower do not need to attract insect or birds thus, they are not very colourful and do not produce nectar. Pollen grains of most of the water pollinated species are coated by mucilage that protects them from wetting.

Entomophily : Pollination by insects like bees, wasps, butterflies and flies etc. Bees are responsible for over 80% of all pollination done by insects. Plants pollinated by insects are colourful with fragrance and abundant nectar which attracts insects. Apart from search for nectar insects also visit flower to lay eggs. e.g., *Amorphophallus* – moth deposit its eggs within the ovary of this flower and the flower in turn gets pollinated by young moth. There are some insects which consume pollen from male organs and nectar from female flower without facilitating pollination. Such insects are called as **pollen or nectar robbers**.

Ornithophily : Pollination of flowers by birds is called Ornithophily. Ornithophillous Flowers are large size brightly colourful and rich in nectar. Humming birds are the most common group of flowers visiting bird in America. Honey creepes are common pallinators in Africa and Asia. E.g., *Calcistemon* (Bottle brush), *Erythrina* (Coral Tree).

Chiropterophily: Pollination of flowers via means of bats is called chiropterophily. Chiropterophilous flowers are dull coloured with fruity odour, having abundant nectar and pollen grains.
E.g., *Kigelia pinnata* (Sausage tree), *Anthocephalus* (Kadam tree).

Malacophily : Pollination by snails and slugs is called malacophily. This type of pollination is seen in some water plants such as *Lemma* and in some members of family *Poaceae*.

Myrmecophily : It is the pollination of flowers by means of ants- eg; members of family *Mimosaceae* (Aceacia, babool, kikar etc.)

Outbreeding Devices

Majority of flowers are bisexual, hence self pollination is a common phenomenon. Plants are modified variously to ensure cross-pollination :

(i)   **Self sterility (self-incompatibility)** – Plants in which pollen from same flower is incapable of bringing about fertilization, due to the presence of similar self sterile gene. e.g., Tobacco, Potato.

(ii)   **Dichogamy** – Maturation of male and female sex organs occurs at different times in a bisexual flowers. e.g., Cruciferae family.

(iii)   **Herkogamy** – Male or female sex organs themselves prove as a barrier to prevent self pollination. e.g., *Cyprepedium*, Orchids.

(iv)   **Dicling or Unisexuality** – Effectively prevents self-pollination. Presence of unisexual flowers in plants that prevents self pollination. e.g., Castor, Maize and Papaya.

(v)   **Heterostyly** – Presence of styles of different heights in flower of many plants to prevent self-pollination. e.g., *Primula vulgaris*.

Pollen-Pistil Interaction

All the events from landing of pollen-grains on stigma till pollen tube enters ovule are termed as **pollen-pistil interaction**. It is not always that right type of pollen grains will fall on stigma or even if the desired pollen interacts with stigma, it may be incompatible. Pistil and pollen mutual chemical secretions determine the compatibility of pollen grains. If incompatible is there, then either germination of pollen grain is inhibited or pollen tube abort in style, but if compatible pollen tube reaches the style it causes fertilization. Indepth analysis of pollen-pistil interaction, can help in development of hybrids and in overcoming incompatibility.

Pollen grain germinates on the stigma to produce a pollen tube through one of the germpores on its surface.

Pollen tube grows through the style towards the ovary.

If the pollen grain is released at the two celled stage (i.e., vegetative and generative cells) then generative cell divides meiotically to produce two male gametes, but when pollen grain are released at 'three'-celled stage then two male gametes are already present.

Pollen tube after reaching the ovary enters into the ovule through micropyle & enters one of the synergids through filiform apparatus.

Significance of Pollination

(i)   Pollination is a means of taking the male gametoplyte.

(ii)   Pollen-pistil interaction determines the suitability of pollen for carrying out the process of sexual reproduction.

(iii)   It has freed the seed plants from the dependence on external water during fertilization.

(iv)   It can be manipulated to produce pure lines as well as desired varieties.

Double Fertilization

Fusion of male and female gametes is called **fertilization**. The phenomenon of fertilization was first reported by Strasburger (1884) in *Monotrapa*. In the cytoplasm of the synergid, pollen tube releases the two male gametes. After reaching ovary, the pollen tube enters the ovule. Pollen tube may enter the ovule by any one of the following routes :

(i)   **Porogamy :** When the pollen tube enters the ovule through micropyle, it is called porogamy. It is the most common type, *e.g., Lily*.

(ii)   **Chalazogamy :** The entry of pollen tube into the ovule from chalazal region is known as chalazogamy. Chalazogamy is less common, *e.g., Casuarina, Juglans, Betula*, etc. It was first observed by *Treub* (1981) n *Casuarina*.

(iii)   **Mesogamy :** The pollen tube enters the ovule through its middle part *i.e.*, through integument (*e.g., Cucurbita, Populus*) or through funicle (*e.g., Pistacia*).

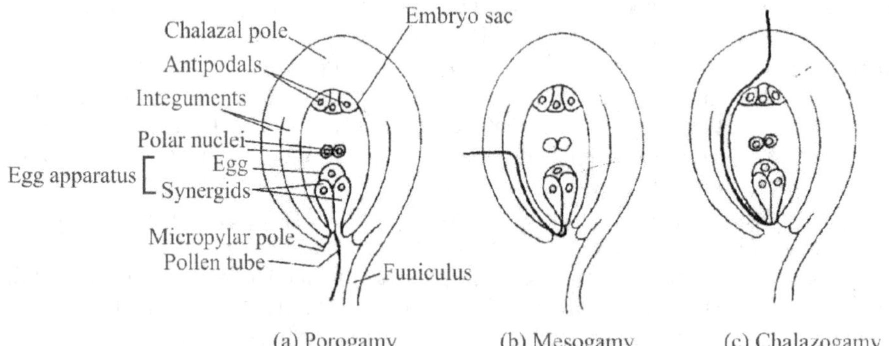

Fig. : Various routes of pollen tube entry into the ovule

One of these male gametes fuses with egg to form diploid zygote (2n) while the other fuses with two polar nuclei of the central cell to produce triploid primary endosperm cell (PEC) (3n). Since, the latter involves fusion of three haploid nucleus, therefore it is called **triple fusion**. In some angiosperms, two types of fusion occur in the same embryo sac "syngamy" leading to the formation of zygote & "triple fusion" forming primary endosperm cell, this phenomenon is called "**double-fertilization**". The unique characteristics of angiosperms is the participation of both male gametes in the act of fertilization. One male gamete fuses with the egg to form the diploid zygote. The diploid zygote finally develops into embryo.

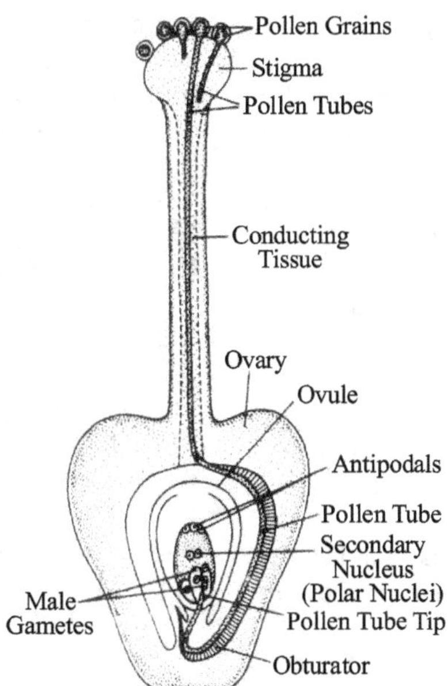

Fig. : Fertilization in an angiosperm through porogamy

Artificial hybridization

Dusting of pollen from a chosen plant on to the stigma of the selected plant artificially for obtaining commercially superior varieties is called artificial hybridization.

Process involved in artificial hybridisation :

(i)   Anthers are removed before dehiscence from bisexual flowers by using forceps, this phenomenon is called **emasculation** but if flower is unisexual emasculation is not required.

(ii) Now, the flower containing only stigma is covered with butter paper, this is called **bagging**, which is done to prevent contamination of stigma from other pollens.

(iii) When the bagged stigma attains receptivity, it is dusted with pollens of desired plant.

(iv) Flowers are again rebagged and fruits are allowed to develop that contain seeds of hybrid variety.

Practice Exercise-2

Multiple Choice Questions

1. Unisexuality of flowers prevents
- (a) geitonogamy but not xenogamy.
- (b) autogamy and geitonogamy.
- (c) autogamy but not geitonogamy.
- (d) both geitonogamy and xenogamy.

2. An advantage of cleistogamy is that
- (a) it leads to greater genetic diversity.
- (b) seed dispersal is more efficient and wide spread.
- (c) each visit of pollinator brings hundreds of pollen grains.
- (d) seed set is not dependent upon pollinators.

3. Which of the following statement is **incorrect** about emasculation?
- (a) During emasculation process, stigma is removed.
- (b) Emasculated flowers are bagged in order to prevent self-pollination.
- (c) Emasculation is an outbreeding device to promote cross-pollination..
- (d) It is one of the steps for artificial hybridization.

Match the Following

4. Match the biotic agent of cross pollination given in column-I with their feature given in column-II and select the correct answer using the codes given below.

Column-I		Column-II
A.	Zoophily	I. Pollination by birds
B.	Ornithophily	II. Pollination by insects
C.	Entomophily	III. Pollination by bats
D.	Chiropterophily	IV. Pollination by animals

- (a) A – III; B – II; C – I; D – IV
- (b) A – I; B – II; C – III; D – IV
- (c) A – IV; B – I; C – II; D – III
- (d) A – IV; B – II; C – I; D – III

5. Match column I with column II and select the correct option from the given codes.

Column-I		Column-II	
A.	Anemophily	(i)	Grasses, Date palm
B.	Hydrophily	(ii)	Rose, Jasmine
C.	Entomophily	(iii)	Butea, Bignonia
D.	Ornithophily	(iv)	Vallisneria, Ceratophyllum

- (a) A-(i), B-(iv), C-(ii), D-(iii)
- (b) A-(i), B-(iv), C-(iii), D-(ii)
- (c) A-(ii), B-(iii), C-(i), D-(iv)
- (d) A-(ii), B-(i), C-(iii), D-(iv)

Assertion & Reason Questions

DIRECTIONS (Qs. 6-9) : *Each of these questions contains an assertion followed by reason. Read them carefully and answer the question on the basis of following options. You have to select the one that best describes the two statements.*

(a) If both Assertion and Reason are correct and the Reason is a correct explanation of the Assertion.

(b) If both Assertion and Reason are correct but Reason is not a correct explanation of the Assertion.

(c) If the Assertion is correct but Reason is incorrect.

(d) If both Assertion and Reason are incorrect.

6. **Assertion:** Pollination by water is quite abundant in flowering plants and is found in about 300 genera, mostly dicotyledons.
   Reason: All aquatic plants use water for pollination.

7. **Assertion:** In some species floral rewards are in providing safe places to lay eggs.
   Reason: The pollination by birds is called malacophily or malmacophily.

8. **Assertion:** Majority of insect pollinated flowers are large, colourful, fragment and rich in nectar.
   Reason: To sustain animal visits, the flowers how to provide rewards to the animals

9. **Assertion:** Pollination guarantee the transfer of the right type of pollen.
   Reason: The pistil does not have the ability to recognise the pollen, whether it is of the right type d of the wrong type.

Passage/Case Based Questions

DIRECTIONS (Qs. 10-11) : *Read the following passage and answer the question the follow.*

In group discussion during laboratory class, the process of seed formation in flowering plants was being discussed. One student pointed out that pollution is a major step involved in seed formation. Another student asked how the pollination occur in plants present in water. The teacher explained the process of pollination to solve their queries.

10. What is pollination? Name the two types of pollination.

11. Give an example of plant where pollination occur in presence of water.

Very Short Answer Questions

12. What is the type of pollination, when a bird pollinates a flower ?

13. What is geitonogamy ?

14. What is chiropterophily ?

15. What are the adaptations that favour self-pollination ?

15. Give example of a plant in which pollination occur with the help of bat.

Short Answer Questions

17. What are the characteristics of wind pollinated flower ?

18. Differentiate between autogamy and geitonogamy.

19. What are the advantages and disadvantages of self-pollination ?

20. Differentiate between entomophilous flowers and hydrophilous flower.

21. Write a short note on pollen allergy.

22. How does pollination differ from fertilization?

23. Mention the reasons due to which wind pollinated flowers are not visited by insects.

24. Name any one example of bat pollinated flowers and mention the important characteristics of such flowers.

25. What is Pollenkitt?

Topic 3   Post-Fertilization Events

Soon after pollination, the flower begins to fade. It is sometimes accompanied by sudden increase in respiration and ethylene production. The petals stamen and style wither away. The calyx may persist and even show growth as in physalis ad Dillenia. Other changes which takes place are endosperm formation, embryoe development, seed formation ad fruit formation. The events of endosperm and embryo development, maturation of ovules into seeds and ovary into fruit, are collectively termed as post fertilization events.

Endosperm

As an consequence of triple fusion in which male gamete with the secondary nuclears, atriploid structure called **primary endosperm nucles (PEN)** is formed that divide by mitotic divisions and forms a mass of nutritive cells called endosperm.

Endosperm is the nutritive tissue which provides nourishment to the embryo in seed plant. It also protects the embryo from mechenical injury. Primary endosperm cell undergoes continuous division without being immediately followed by cell wall formation leading to the formation of a large number of nuclei. This forms a **free-nuclear endosperm.** Later these free nuclei are followed by cell wall formation and endosperm becomes cellular. On the basis of development, endosperm are of 3 types– cellular, nuclear and helobial.

In some plants, endosperms lack free nuclei stage, these are called as **cellular endosperms** (e.g. *Datura Petunia*) and where free nuclei are present, these are called as **nuclear endosperms** e.g. maize, wheat, rice etc. In the helobial type of endosperm development, the endosperm is intermediate between cellular and nuclear types. The division of primary endosperm nucleus is followed by wall formation and as a result two chambers, micropylar and chalazal chambers, are formed. Helobial type of endosperm development is prevalent in monocotyledons. *e.g., Erumurus.*

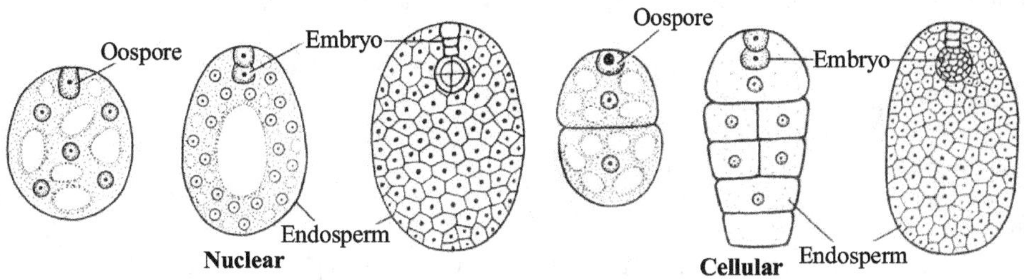

Fig. : Types of endosperm

Endosperm may be completely consumed by developing embryo before it matures (e.g. beans and peas) or it may persist in the mature seed and used up during seed germination, e.g., coconut. Endosperm is usually triploid in majority of the plants, while the highest ploidy is noted in *Arum maculatum*. Endosperm protects the embryo from mechanical injury and provides nutrition to the developing embryo.

Embryo

Zygote formed after fertilization of egg cell secretes a cellulose wall around itself. In dicots, after formation of some endosperm, zygote elongates and divides into upper and lower cell. The lower one lying toward micropyle further divides in one direction into a row of cell called suspensor. The upper cell towards the antipodal end is called embryo cell. The first cell of the suspensor often enlarges and acts as haustorium or absorbing organ while its terminal cell called hypophysis cell, divides giving rise to the apex of the radicle. The upper cell or embryo cell enlarges and divides repeatedly to form eight cells that are arranged in two tiers – **epibasal** (terminal) and **hypobasal** (near the suspensor). The former form two cotyledons and the plumule in dicots and one cotyledon in monocots. The latter form the hypocotyl except its tip. Subsequent divisions give rise to globular heart-shaped embryo.

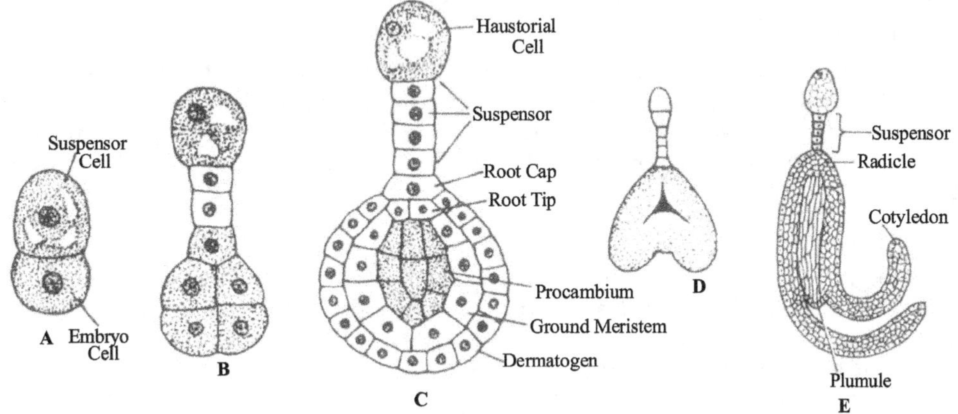

Fig. : Stages in the development of a dicot embryo :
A. Division of zygote into suspensor and embryo cells. B. Formation of suspensor and embryo octant.
C. Globular embryo showing regions of radicle, procambium, ground meristem and dermatogen,
D. Heart-shaped embryo

Typically, dicotyledonous embryo consists of an embryonal axis and two cotyledons. Portion of embryonal axis above cotyledon is **epicotyl** while below it is **hypocotyl**. Epicotyl terminates in plumule while hypocotyl terminates in radicle. Plumule gives rise to the shoot while radicle gives rise to root tip. Dicotyledonous plants have two cotyledons while monocotyledonous plants have only one cotyledon. A mature embryo in monocotyledons has a single cotyledon called **'scutellum'**. At lower portion of scutellum, portion of embryonal axis has the radicle, which bears apical meristem and root cap at the lower end. The radicle and root cap is enclosed in coleorhiza, which is the undifferentiated lower part of the proembryo. The portion of embryonal axis above the level of scutellum is epicotyl. It comprises of shoot apex with some leaf primordium enclosed in a hollow follicular structure, the **coleoptile**.

Seed

Seed is a fertilized ovule. Seed is the final product of fertilization in angiosperm and acts as a main propagative unit in plants. Ovules mature into seed and simultaneously ovary develops into a fruit. Transformation of various units of ovary during seed formation.

Ovary wall	–	Fruit wall
Ovary	–	Fruit
Integuments	–	Seed coats
Outer	–	Testa
Inner	–	Tegmen
Ovule	–	Seed

During seed formation, endosperm is consumed in varying amount by the developing embryo depending on this seed it may be albuminous or non-albuminous.

(i) **Albuminous** – Seed contains some endosperm that acts as food storage tissue.
e.g., Dicots – castor, poppy, custard apple.
Monocots – cereals, millets, sugarcane.

(ii) **Non-albuminous** – Seeds that are devoid of endosperm.
e.g., Dicots – gram, pea, bean, mustard, mango.
Monocots – orchid, alisma.

(iii) **Perisperm** – In some seeds, remain of nucellus are present which is called perisperm. e.g. blackpepper & beet, As the seed matures seed coat hardens, seed becomes dry and becomes dormant. Under favourable conditions, the period of dormancy gets over, oxygen and moisture enter the seed through micropyle (small pore or the seed coat) and seed germination occur.

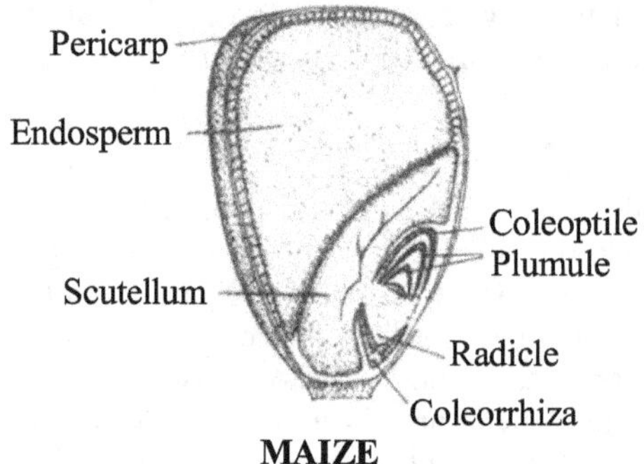

Fig. : Structure of Maize seed

Advantages of Having Seed

Seeds can remain dormant for many years and germinate on return of favourable conditions. Reproductive process is not dependent on water. Seeds have sufficient food reserves to initiate embryo development and seedling development till the photosynthesis process is initiated. Hard seed coat also protects the embryo from environment extremes. Since seeds are the product of sexual reproduction it promotes diversity. Seeds have better adaptive strategies for dispersal to new habitats & help the species to colonise in other areas.

FRUITS

After fertilization ovary begins to grow and gradually matures into fruit. As fruits are products of flowers and therefore they occur only inflowering plants. The wall covering the fruit is called penicarp, it consists of three. It consists of three parts :

(i) **Epicarp :** called the skin of fruits.

(ii) **Mesocarp :** middle fleshy and pulpy part.

(iii) **Endocarp :** Innermost portion that surrounds the seeds.
True fruit : Normally it is a ripe ovary that grows into the true fruit, e.g, cucumber, tomato, coconut.
False fruit : When floral parts other than ovary particularly thalamus or even calyx form part of the fruit, e.g., apple, cashewnut, strawberry. Fruits can also be classified into three main groups:

(i) **Simple fruits :** A simple fruit develops from syncarpous(fused) ovary.

(ii) **Aggregate fruit :** develops from apocarpus (free) ovary.

(iii) **Composite fruit :** develops from a complete inflorescence.
The fruit may be dry as in groundnut, mustard. etc.
Parthenocarpic fruit : In some plants, ovary may grow into fruit without fertilization, e.g., Oranges, watermelon, banana, grapes. Parthenocarpy can occur naturally but sometimes it may be induced artificially by using hormones.

APOMIXIS AND POLYEMBRYONY

Apomixis is the production of seed without fertilization. The normal process of cell cycle involving meiosis and fertilization is called **amphimixis.** There are several ways of development of apomictic seeds. In some species the diploid egg cell is formed without reduction division & develops into the embryo without fertilization. In some species the nucellar cells surrounding the embryo sac start dividing, protrude into the embryo sac & develop into embryos. Some apomictic plants are citrus, cactaceae, grasses, *Parthenium,* etc. Apomixis provides possibility of indefinite multiplication of specially favourable biotypes, without loosing their productivity due to segregation.

Polyembryony is the state of occurrence of more than one embryo in a seed, e.g. onion and groundnut. Polyembryony may be formed by cleavage of zygote or formation of embryo by the cells of the embryo sac other than egg usually synergids or by development of more than one embryo sac within the same ovule. Polyembryony is practically important because genetically uniform parental type seeding are obtained from nuclear embryos.

Practice Exercise-3

Multiple Choice Questions

1. Which of the following is an example of false fruit?
(a) apple and pear   (b) strawberry
(c) cashewnut   (d) All of these

2. In a seed of maize, scutellum is considered as cotyledon because it
(a) protects the embryo.
(b) contains food for the embryo.
(c) absorbs food materials and supplies them to the embryo.
(d) converts itself into a monocot leaf.

3. The phenomena of Amphimixis in plants involes.
(a) from stem cutting
(b) without the fusion of gametes
(c) fusion of two different gametes to form zygote
(d) from root cutting

4. Which one of following is an example of parthenocarpic fruit.
(a) Apple   (b) Persimmon
(c) Cashew   (d) Latermelon

5. Seed coat is not thin, membranous in
(a) coconut   (b) groundnut
(c) gram   (d) maize

Assertion & Reason Questions

DIRECTIONS (Qs. 6-9) : *Each of these questions contains an assertion followed by reason. Read them carefully and answer the question on the basis of following options. You have to select the one that best describes the two statements.*
(a) If both Assertion and Reason are correct and the Reason is a correct explanation of the Assertion.
(b) If both Assertion and Reason are correct but Reason is not a correct explanation of the Assertion.
(c) If the Assertion is correct but Reason is incorrect.
(d) If both Assertion and Reason are incorrect.

6. **Assertion:** Most zygote divide only after certain amount of endosperm is formed and this is an adaptation to provide assured nutrition to the developing embryo.
Reason: Embryo develops at the chalazal and of the embryo sac, where the zygote is situated.

7. **Assertion:** Non-albuminous seeds have no residual endosperm as it is completely consumed during embryo development.
Reason: Albuminous seeds retain a part of endosperm as it is not completely used up during embryo development.

8. **Assertion:** Apomixis is a form of asexual reproduction that mimics sexual reproduction.
Reason: Occurence of more than one embryo in a seed is referred as polyembryony.

9. **Assertion:** In the most common type of endosperm development, the PEN undergoes successive nuclear division to give rise to free nuclei and this stage of endosperm development is called free-nuclear endosperm.
Reason: The coconut water from tender coconut is cellular endosperm and the surrounding white kernel is the free nuclear endosperm.

Very Short Answer Questions

10. What is micropyle?
11. Define syngamy.
12. What is the function of endosperm ?
13. How many nuclei are taking part in double fertilization ?
14. Define adventive embryony.

Short Answer Questions

15. Why is banana called a parthenocarpic fruit? Give two examples of parthenocarpic fruits developed by horticulturists.

16. Differentiate between dicot seeds & monocot seeds.

17. If the chromosome number of a plant species is 16, what would be the chromosome number and the ploidy level of the (i) microspore mother cell and (ii) the endosperm cells?

18. In the adjacent figure of a typical dicot embryo, label the parts (1), (2) and (3). State the function of each of the labelled part.

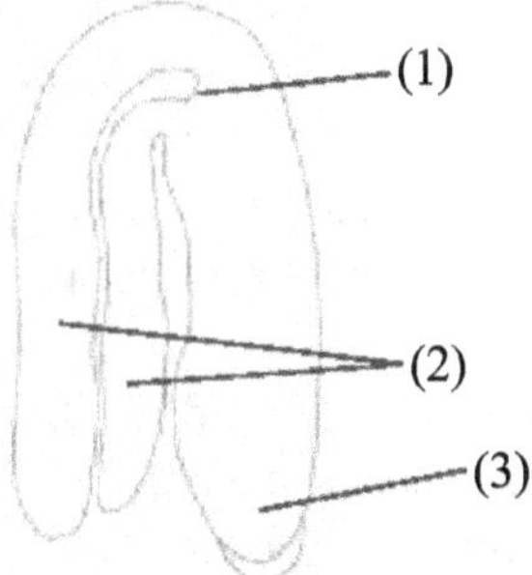

19. What is polyembryony? Give two reasons of polyembryony.
20. What is the importance of seed in agriculture ?
21. What is the difference between true fruit and false fruit ?
22. What is the advantage of parthenocarpy ?

Important Tips & Formulae

- A flower is a specialised organ which is meant for sexual reproduction in the angiosperms.
- Flowers are modified condensed shoot. A typical flower is consists of four main parts such as sepals (calayx), petals (corolla), stamens (androcieum) and carpels (gynocieum).
- **Structure of microsporangium:**
  - (i) **Epidermis:** It is the outer protective layer that provides protection to pollen.
  - (ii) **Endothecium:** It lies beneath the epidermis and is single layered. The cells of endothecium are uninucleated and vacuolated. So, the cells contains bands become radially elongated. The endothecium helps in dehiscence of anthers.
  - (iii) **Middle layer:** This layer is rich in reserve food material such as starch. These reserve food materials are consumed by growing microspore mother cell.
  - (iv) **Tapetum:** The cells of tapetum produce Ubisch bodies that help in the development of pollen grains. The Ubisch bodies helps in the ornamentation of microspore wall. Sporopollenin is secreted by tapetum cells. It also provides nourishment of the developing pollen grains.
- Each cell of the sporogenous tissue is capable of giving rise to a microscope tetrad and each microspore is a potential pollen or microspore mother cell (PMC).
- Inside each microsporangium, several thousands of microspores or pollen grains are formed and are released with the dehiscence of anther.
- Pollen grain has two layers such as the hard outer layer is called **exine** and inner layer is called **intine**.
- Exine is made of sporopollenin and is an organic solvent which is resistant to biological and chemical decomposition.
- Pollen grains are preserved as fossils because of the presence of sporopollenin.
- Exine has prominent aperture called germ pores where sporopollenin is absent.
- Intine is a thin and continuous layer that is made up of cellulose and pectin.
- The vegetative cell is bigger and has abundant food reserve as well as a large irregularly shaped nucleus.
- The generative cell is small and floats in the cytoplasm of the vegetative cell.

- Carrot grass or Parenthemium that come to India as a contaminant with imported wheat causes pollen allergy in humans.
- Pollen grains are rich in nutrients and are used as food supplements by athelets and races horses to increase their performance.
- Pollen grains are stored for many years in liquid nitrogen (-196 °C) and can be used as pollen banks in crop breeding programmes.

Female Reproductive Part:

- The functional megaspore develops into female gametophyte or embryo sac. The method of embryo sac formation from a single megaspore is called **monosporic development**.
- The nucleus of the megaspore divides into two four and eight daughter nuclei. So, the six nuclei are surrounded by cell walls and are organised into cells and remaining two nuclei are called **polar nuclei** that are situated below the **egg apparatus** in the large central cell.
- Three cells are grouped together at the micropyle end to form egg apparatus that consists of two cells known as **synergids** or one egg cell.
- The synergids have special cellular thickenings at the micropylar tip called **filiform apparatus**. It helps in guiding the pollen tube towards the synergids. Three cells are located at the chalazal end and are called the **antipodals**.
- Hilum is the junction between ovule and funicle and nucellus have abundant reserve food material.
- Plants such as *Oxalis*, *Viola* and *Commelina* produce two types of flowers.
- Chasmogamous flowers are similar to the flowers of other species with exposed anthers and stigma.
- Cleistogamous flowers do not open at all and are autogamous.

Types of pollination:

- **Anemophily** is an abiotic means of pollination by winds in which pollen grains of anemophillus flower are light, small and dusty. Stigma is hairy, feathery or branched to catch the wind born pollen grains
- **Hydrophily** is the mode of pollination through water. Hydrophily is of two types such as epihydrophily that takes place over the surface of water for example *Vallisneria* and such plants are pollinated inside the water for example *Najas* and *Zoostera*.

- Entomophily is the mode of pollination through insects. Pollen grains of entomophilus flowers are oily and sticky for example *Clematis.*
- Ornithophily is the mode of pollination by birds. Common examples of birds pollinated plants are Bombax, Erythrina and so on.
- Chiropterophily is the mode of pollination by bats and such flowers open only at or after dusk with the anthers dehiscing at the same time.
- Such flowers are large, dual coloured and have strong scent for example: *Kigella* and *Adansonia.*
- **Emasculation:** It is a method of artificial hybridisation in which the anther is removed from the flower bud before the anther dehisces.
- **Bagging:** This method of hybridisation involves the covering of emasculated flowers by using butter paper to prevent contamination of its stigma with unwanted pollen.
- Monocotyledonous embryo is consists of one cotyledon whereas dicotyledonous embryo is consists of two cotyledonous embryo consists of two cotyledons as well as embryonal axis.

- The part of embryonal axis is present of the level of cotyledon is called epicotyl which terminates at the shoot tip called *plumule.*
- The part below the level of cotyledons is called *hypocotyl.*
- Non-albuminous seeds have no residual endosperm as it is completely consumed during embryo development.
- Albuminous seeds retain part of endosperm.
- The residual, persistant nucellus is the *Perisperm*
- True fruits are develops only from the ovary for example: lemon and water.
- The oldest is that of a lupine, *Lupinus arcticus* excavated from Arctic Tundra. The seed germinated and flowered after an estimated record of 10,000 years of dormancy.
- A recent record of 2000 years old viable seed is of the date palm, *Phoenix dactylifera* discovered during the archeological excavation at King Herod's palace near the Dead Sea.

NCERT Questions

1. Name the parts of an angiosperm flower in which development of male and female gametophyte take place.

Sol. Anther and ovule are the parts of angiospermic flower where development of male and female gametophytes takes place respectively.

2. Differentiate between microsporogenesis and megasporogenesis. Which type of cell division occurs during these events? Name the structures formed at the end of these two events.

Sol. Differences between microsporogenesis and megasporogenesis are as follows –

	Microsporogenesis		Megasporogenesis
1.	The process of formation and differentiation of pollen grains from microspore mother cells by meiosis is called microsporogenesis.	1.	The process of formation and differentiation of megaspores from megaspore mother cells by meiosis is known as megasporogenesis.
2.	Pollen grains are produced in the anther which is a broader knob like fertile part of the stamen.	2.	Ovules (which are the future seeds) are formed in the ovary.
3.	All the four pollen grains that are formed from microspore mother cell are functional.	3.	Only one out of the four megaspores is functional.

Each microspore mother cell and megaspore mother cell contain two sets of chromosomes and are therefore diploid. The diploid megaspore mother cell and microspore mother cell enlarges and undergo *meiosis* to produce, four haploid cells called megaspores and microspores respectively.

The chromosome number is reduced by half and therefore megaspores & microspores are haploid.

Microsporogenesis and megasporogenesis give rise to pollen grains and embryo sac respectively. Pollen grain is the male gametophyte and embryo sac represents the female gametophyte.

3. Arrange the following terms in the correct developmental sequence : Pollen grain, sporogenous tissue, microspore tetrad, pollen mother cell, male gametes.

Sol. Sporogenous tissue – pollen mother cell – microspore tetrad – pollen grains – male gametes.

4. With a neat, labelled diagram, describe the parts of a typical angiosperm ovule.

Sol.

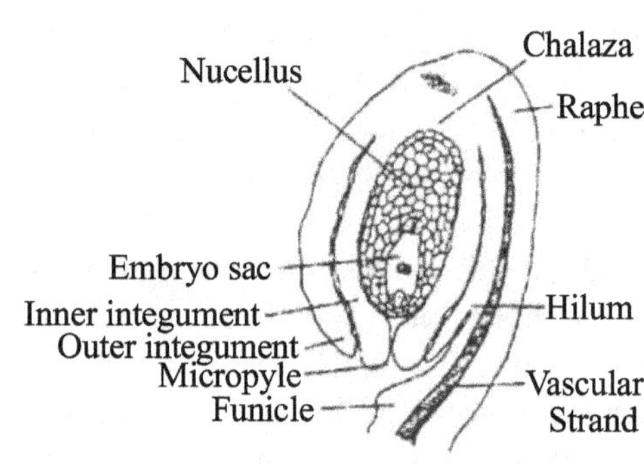

Fig. Longitudinal section of a mature anatropous ovule

A typical angiospermic ovule is a small structure which is formed in the ovary. Ovule first develops as a projection on the placenta and composed of multilayered cellular tissue called the nucellus. The hypodermal cell of the nucellus enlarges and transformed into megaspore mother cell. This cell undergoes meiosis to produce four haploid cells only one of which develops & forms embryo sac (female gametophyte) other three degenerate. An ovule may be surrounded by one or two protective layers called integuments, leaving a small opening at one end termed as micropyle which acts as passage for the entry of the pollen tube into the ovule. Thus, a typical ovule consists of a fully developed embryo sac with the nucellus and integuments. The place of junction of intequnerts and nucellus is called chalaza. In inverted ovule (most common type), the stalk or funiculus is attached to the main body of ovule for some distance to form a ridge like structure called raphe. In the nucellus of ovulue, a large oval cell is present at micropylar end, which is known as embryo sac (female gametophyte), developing from megaspore.

5. What is meant by monosporic development of female gametophyte?

Sol. In many flowering plants, only one out of the four megaspores enlarges and develops into female gametophyte or embryo sac. The other three megaspores degenerate. This type of embryo sac formation is called as monosporic type of development.

6. **With a neat diagram explain the 7-celled, 8-nucleate nature of the female gametophyte.**

Sol.

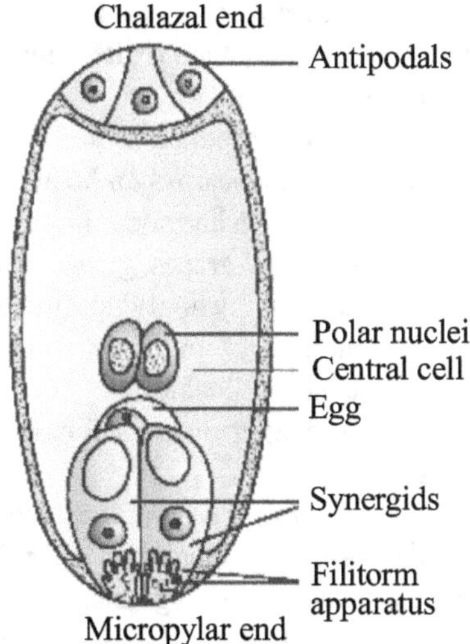

Fig. A diagrammatic representation of the mature embryo sac.

Embryo sac (or female gametophyte) is formed by three successive mitotic divisions that take place in the nucleus of megaspore.

The nucleus of the functional megaspore divides meiotically to form two nuclei which move to the opposite poles, forming the 2-nucleate embryo sac. Two more sequential mitotic nuclear divisions result in the formation of the 4-nucleate and later the 8-nucleate stages of the embryo sac. After the 8-nucleate stage, cell walls are laid down leading to the organisation of the typical female gametophyte or embryo sac. Six of the eight nuclei are grouped together at micropylar and chalazal end and form the egg apparatus and antipodals respectively. The large central cell left over with two polar nuclei. Thus, a typical female gametophyte consists of 7 cells with 8 nucleus.

The central cell is the largest cell of the embryo sac. It has a highly vacuolate cytoplasm which is rich in reserve food and golgi bodies. In the middle, the cell contain two polar nuclei which often fuse to form a single diploid secondary or fusion nucleus. Thus all the cells of the embryo sac are haploid except the central cell which becomes diploid due to fusion of polar nucli.

7. **What are chasmogamous flowers? Can cross-pollination occur in cleistogamous flowers? Give reasons for your answer.**

Sol. Chasmogamous flowers or open flowers in which anther and stigma are exposed for pollination. eg., catharanthus, Mirabilis.

Cross-pollination cannot occur in cleistogamous flowers. These flowers remain closed thus causing only self-pollination. In cleistogamous flowers, anthers dehisce inside the closed flowers. So the pollen grains come in contact with stigma of same flower. Thus there is no chance of cross-pollination, e.g. *Oxalis, Viola.*

8. **Mention two strategies evolved to prevent self-pollination in flowers.**

Sol. Continued self-pollination decreases the vigour and vitality of a particular race. Thus, flowering plants have developed many devices to discourage self-pollination and to encourage cross-pollination.

Dichogamy and self-sterility are two most common devices that ensure cross-pollination.

Dichogamy – Maturation of anther & stigma at different times in a bisexual flower prevent self-pollination. Self-sterility (or self-incompatibility) - Due to the presence of self-sterile gene in some flowers, pollen grains do not germinate on the stigma of that flowers. e.g.- tobacco, potato.

9. **What is self-incompatibility? Why does self-pollination not lead to seed formation in self-incompatible species?**

Sol. When the pollen grains of an anther do not germinate on the stigma of the same flower, then such a flower is called self-sterile or incompatible and such condition is known as self-incompatibility or self-sterility.

The transference of pollen grains shed from the anther to the stigma of the pistil is called pollination. This transference initiate the process of seed formation. Self-pollination is the transfer of pollen grain shed from the anther to stigma of pistil in the same flower. But in some flower self-pollination does not lead to the formation of seed formation because of the presence of same sterile gene on pistil and pollen grain.

10. **What is bagging technique? How is it useful in a plant breeding programme?**

Sol. Covering the emasculated flowers by a bag of suitable size or butter paper is known as bagging. This technique is mainly used in artificial hybridization. Plant breeders often use this technique to prevent the contamination of stigma of the flowers from unwanted pollen grains.

11. **What is triple fusion? Where and how does it take place? Name the nuclei involved in triple fusion.**

Sol. Fusion of second male gamete with the two polar nuclei located in the central cell to form the triploid primary endosperm nucleus (PEN) is called triple fusion or vegetative fertilization.

This process takes place in the embryo sac. After reaching the ovary, pollen tube enters into the embryo sac from the micropylar end. After penetration, the tip of the pollen tube ruptures releasing the two male gametes. The one male gamete fuses with the egg to form the diploid zygote. This process is called syngamy and the other male gamete fuses with the two polar nuclei to form the triploid primary endosperm & this process is known as triple fusion. These two events of fertilization constitute the process of double fertilization.

12. **Why do you think the zygote is dormant for sometime in a fertilized ovule?**

Sol. Fertilized egg which is known as zygote after a period of rest develops into embryo. Most zygotes remain dormant till certain amount of endosperm forms. They do so, to provide assured nutrition to the developing embryo.

13. **Differentiate between:**
    (a) **hypocotyl and epicotyl**
    (b) **coleoptile and coleorrhiza**
    (c) **integument and testa**
    (d) **perisperm and pericarp.**

Sol. (a) The region of the embryonal axis between the radicle and the point of attachment of the cotyledons is called the hypocotyl (below the cotyledons) whereas the portion between the plumule and cotyledons is called the epicotyl (above the cotyledons).

(b) The plumule is surrounded by a leaf-like covering called the coleoptile whereas the protective covering of radicle and root cap is called coleorrhiza.

(c) Each ovule is surrounded by one or two protective layers called integuments, leaving only a small opening at one end called the micropyle whereas the outer seed coat is called the testa and inner seed coat is tegmen.

(d) Periplasm is the residual, persistent nucellus whereas pericarp is the wall of the fruit.

14. **Why is apple called a false fruit? Which part(s) of the flower forms the fruit?**

Sol. Botanically ripened ovary is called a true fruit. The fruits in which thalamus and other floral parts develop alongwith the ovary are called false fruits. For example - apple, strawberry, cashew etc. In apple the main edible portion of the fruit is the fleshy thalamus.

15. **What is meant by emasculation? When and why does a plant breeder employ this technique?**

Sol. Emasculation is the removal of stamens mainly the anthers from the flower buds before their dehiscence. This is mainly done to avoid self-pollination. Emasculation is one of the measures in the artificial hybridization. Plant breeders employ this techniques to obtain an overall superior variety.

16. **If one can induce parthenocarpy through the application of growth substances, which fruits would you select to induce parthenocarpy and why?**

Sol. Parthenocarpy is the production and development of seedless fruits. Parthenocarpy can be induced through, the application of growth harmones Important fruits like banana, papaya, orange-grapes, guava, watermelon etc. can be made seed less by applying growth substances as they are economically important fruits and if made seed less will be more valuable.

17. **Explain the role of tapetum in the formation of pollen-grain wall.**

Sol. Tapetum is the innermost layer of the microsporangium. The tapetal cells are multinucleated and polyploid. They nourish the developing pollen grains. These cells contain ubisch bodies that help in the ornamentation of the microspores or pollen grains walls. The outer layer of the pollen grain is called exine and is made up of the sporopollenin secreted by the ubisch bodies of the tapetal cells. This compound provides spiny appearance to the exine of the pollen grains.

18. **What is apomixis and what is its importance?**

Sol. Apomixis is a mode of asexual reproduction that produces seeds without fertilization, e.g.- some species of asteraceae and grasses. This method is important in hybrid seed industry. Hybrids are extensively cultivated for increasing productivity. But the main drawback is that the hybrid seeds are to be produce every year because the seeds of the hybrid plants do not maintain hybrid characters for longer period due to segregation of characters. This can be avoided if apomixis can be introduced in hybrid seeds. For this reason scientists are trying hard to identify genes for apomixis.

Past year Exercise

Multiple Choice Questions

1. Self-pollination is fully ensured if
(a) the flower is bisexual
(b) the style is longer than the filament
(c) the flower is cleistogamous
(d) the time of pistil and anther maturity is different

Very Short Answer Questions

2. An anther with malfunctioning tapetum often fails to produce viable male gametophytes. Give one reason.

3. A bilobed, dithecous anther has 100 microspore mother cells per microsporangium. How many male gametophytes this anther can produce?

4. How do the pollen grains of Vallisneria protect themselves?

5. An anther with malfunctioning tapetum often fails to produce viable male gametophytes. Give any one reason.

6. How do seed bearing plants tide over dry and hot weather conditions?

7. Name the parts of the flower which the tassels of the corn-cob represent.

Short Answer Questions

8. How many haploid cells are present in mature female gametophyte of a flowering plant? Name them.

9. Why should a bisexual flower be emasculated and bagged prior to artificial pollination?

10. Draw a longitudinal section of a post pollinated pistil showing entry of pollen tube into a mature embryo sac. Label filiform apparatus, chalazal end, hilum, antipodals, male gametes and secondary nucleus.

11. (i) Write the characteristic features of anther, pollen and stigma of wind pollinated flowers.
(ii) How do flowers reward their insect pollinator? Explain.

12. Draw a diagram of a male gametophyte of an angiosperm. Label any four parts. Why is sporopollenin considered the most resistant organic material?

13. Differentiate between albuminous and non-albuminous seeds, giving one example of each.

14. Differentiate between geitonogamy and xenogamy in plants. Which one between the two will lead to inbreeding depression and why?

15. Differentiate between perisperm and endosperm giving one example of each.

16. L.S. of a maize grain is given below. Label the parts A, B, C and D in it.

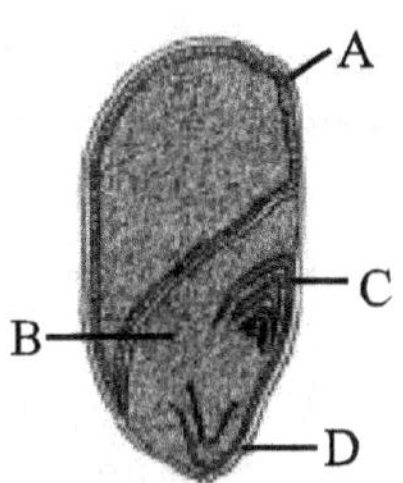

17. With the help of an example of each explain the following: Apomixis, parthenocarpy, polyembryony.

18. Where is sporopollenin present in plants? State its significance with reference to its chemical nature.

19. State one advantage and one disadvantage of cleistogamy.

20. In angiosperms, zygote is diploid while primary endosperm cell is triploid. Explain.

21. (i) Describe the endosperm development in coconut.
(ii) Why is tender coconut considered a healthy source of nutrition?
(iii) How are pea seeds different from castor seeds with respect to endosperm?

22. Name all the haploid cells present in an unfertilized mature embryo-sac of a flowering plant. Write the total number of cells in it.

23. Differentiate between the two cells enclosed in a mature male gametophyte of an angiosperm.

24. Geitonogamous flowering plants are genetically autogamous but functionally cross pollinated. Justify.

25. (i) How does cleistogamy ensure autogamy ?
(ii) State one advantage and one disadvantage of cleistogamy to the plant.

26. Explain the steps that ensure cross pollination in an autogamous flower.

27. Why are some seeds of citrus referred to as polyembryonic? How are they formed?

28. List the adaptive features of water pollinated flowers like *Vallisneria*.

29. State the similarity and differences between geitonogamy and xenogamy. Why do cleistogamous flowers assure seed sets?

30. Draw a labelled diagram of a male gametophyte of an angiosperm. Why does it posses two male gametes in fertilize one ovule?

31. How is parthenocarpy different from parthenogenesis?

Give an example of each.

32. How do plants produce seeds through apomixis? Explain with the help of an example

33. Write the mode of pollination in *Vallisneria* and water lily. Explain the mechanism of pollination in *Vallisneria*.

34. Make a list of any three outbreeding devices that flowering plants have developed and explain how they help to encourage cross-pollination.

35. Why are angiosperm anthers called dithecous? Describe the structure of its microsporangium.

36. Explain any three advantages that seeds offer to angiosperms.

37. Name the organic materials exine and intine of an angiosperm pollen grains are made up of. Explain the role of exine.

38. List the post-fertilisation events in angiosperms.

39. Why do moss plants produce very large number of male gametes ? Provide one reason. What are these gametes called?

40. Read the following statement and answer the questions that follow :

"A guava fruit has 200 viable seeds".

(a) What are viable seeds ?

(b) Write the total number of :
   (i) Pollen grains
   (ii) Gametes in producing 200 viable guava seeds.

(c) Prepare a flow-chart to depict the post-pollination events leading to viable-seed production in a flowering plant.

41. Differentiate between Parthenocarpy and Parthenogenesis. Give one example of each.

42. You are conducting artificial hybridisation on papaya and potato. Which one of them would require the step of emasculation and why? However for both you will use the process of bagging. Justify giving one reason.

43. Pollen banks are playing a very important role in promoting plant breeding programme the world over. How are pollens preserved in the pollen banks? Explain. How are such banks benefitting our farmers? Write any two ways.

44. For a layman, both apple and banana are fruits. But a biology student categorises fruits as true fruits, false fruits and parthenocarpic fruits. Justify.

45. Draw a schematic transverse section of a mature anther of an angiosperm. Label tis epidermis, middle layers, tapetum, endothecium, sporogenous tissue and the connective.

NCERT Exemplar

Multiple Choice Questions

1. Among the terms listed below, those that of are not technically correct names for a floral whorl are
    (i)   androecium   (ii) carpel
    (iii) corolla   (iv) sepal
    (a) (i) and (iv)   (b) (iii) and (iv)
    (c) (ii) and (iv)   (d) (i) and (ii)

2. Embryo sac is to ovule as .... is to an another.
    (a) stamen
    (b) filament
    (c) pollen grain
    (d) androecium

3. The outermost and innermost wall layers of microsporangium in an anther are respectively.
    (a) Endothecium and tapetum
    (b) Epidermis and endodermis
    (c) Epidermis and middle layer
    (d) Epidermis and tapetum

4. During microsporogenesis, meiosis occurs in
    (a) endothecium
    (b) microspore mother cells
    (c) microspore tetrads
    (d) pollen grains

5. From among the sets of terms given below, identify those that are associated with the gynoecium.
    (a) Stigma, ovule, embryo sac, placenta
    (b) Thalamus, pistil, style, ovule
    (c) Ovule, ovary, embryo sac, tapetum
    (d) Ovule, stamen, ovary, embryo sac

6. Autogamy can occur in a chasmogamous flower if:
    (a) pollen matures before maturity of ovule
    (b) ovules mature before maturity of pollen
    (c) both pollen and ovules mature simultaneously
    (d) both anther and stigma are of equal lengths

7. In a fertilised embryo sac, the haploid, diploid and triploid structure are:
    (a) synergid, zygote and primary endosperm nucleus
    (b) synergid, antipodal and polar nuclei
    (c) antipodal, synergid and primary endosperm nucleus
    (d) synergid, polar nuclei and zygote

Match the Following

8. Match the following Columns.

Column - I (Pollination technique)	Column - II (Pollinator)
A. Chiropterophily	I. Ant
B. Anemophily	II. Bat
C. Myrmecophily	III. Snail
D. Malacophily	IV. Wind

    (a) A – III; B – II; C – I; D – IV
    (b) A – II; B – IV; C – I; D – III
    (c) A – IV; B – III; C – II; D – I
    (d) A – I; B – III; C – II; D – IV

Assertion & Reason Questions

DIRECTIONS (Qs. 9-10) : *Each of these questions contains an assertion followed by reason. Read them carefully and answer the question on the basis of following options. You have to select the one that best describes the two statements.*

(a) If both Assertion and Reason are correct and the Reason is a correct explanation of the Assertion.

(b) If both Assertion and Reason are correct but Reason is not a correct explanation of the Assertion.

(c) If the Assertion is correct but Reason is incorrect.

(d) If both Assertion and Reason are incorrect.

9. **Assertion:** The mechanism of double-fertilisation was discovered by Nawaschin in *Lilium* and *Fritillaria* plants.
    Reason: In the mechanism of double fertilisation, three nuclei and two gametes are involved.

10. **Assertion:** Self-incompatibility is the phenomenon in which, pollen grains cannot germinate on the stigma of the same flower as the plants reject the pollen grains of self flower.
    Reason: Self-incompatiability is controlled by the environmental factors and physiological factors.

Very Short Answer Questions

11. Name the common function that cotyledons and nucellus perform.

Short Answer Questions

12. Why does the zygote begin to divide only after the division of primary endosperm cell?

13. The generative cell of a 2-celled pollen divides in the pollen tube but not in a 3-celled pollen. Give reasons.

Objective Practice Exercise

Multiple Choice Questions

1. Male gametophyte of angiosperms/monocots is
   (a) Microsporangium   (b) Nucellus
   (c) Microspore   (d) Stamen

2. One of the most resistant biological material is
   (a) lignin   (b) hemicellulose
   (c) lignocellulose   (d) sporopollenin

3. Which one produces androgenic haploids in anther cultures?
   (a) Anther wall
   (b) Tapetal layer of anther wall
   (c) Connective tissue
   (d) Young pollen grains

4. The male gametophyte (Microgametophyte) in case of monocots is
   (a) tetrad   (b) nucellus
   (c) megaspore   (d) microspore

5. Exine of pollen is formed by activity of
   (a) tapetum   (b) endothelium
   (c) middle layers   (d) endothecium

6. Seminiferous plant is
   (a) having only staminate flowers.
   (b) reproducing by seeds.
   (c) reproducing by vegetative propagation.
   (d) None of the above

7. Pollen grain (microspore) formation in *Cyperus* (Cypraceae) is
   (a) very common
   (b) artificially induced by removal of anthers
   (c) similar to megasporogenesis in majority of angiosperms
   (d) similar to the microsporogenesis commonly present within angiosperms

8. Male gametes or sperms are developed from generative cell by
   (a) meiotic division   (b) mitotic division
   (c) amitotic division   (d) None of these

9. Microsporogenesis occurs
   (a) on margins of leaves   (b) inside ovule
   (c) inside anther   (d) in essential floral organs

10. Wall of a pollen sac consists of
    (a) endothecium and tapetum
    (b) tapetum and middle layers
    (c) endothecium, middle layers and tapetum
    (d) epidermis, endothecium, middle layers and tapetum

11. Middle layers of the microsporangial wall
    (a) shrivel at maturity of anther
    (b) persist but remain thin-walled
    (c) degenerate before maturity
    (d) persist and become thickened

12. Tapetal cells are
    (a) glandular and amoeboid
    (b) glandular
    (c) invasive
    (d) ephemeral

13. Ubisch bodies are produced by
    (a) middle layers   (b) tapetal cells
    (c) pollen mother cells   (d) endothecium

14. In dicots, the most common pollen tetrad is
    (a) isobilateral   (b) tetrahedral
    (c) linear   (d) decussate

15. In monocots, the most common pollen tetrad is
    (a) isobilateral   (b) tetrahedral
    (c) linear   (d) T-shaped or decussate

16. The function of anther is
    (a) produce ubisch bodies
    (b) produce pollen grains
    (c) store and protect pollen grains
    (d) All the above

17. Intine of pollen grain is made of
    (a) callose   (b) pecto-cellulose
    (c) cellulose   (d) fat-like sporopollenin

18. Exine of pollen grain is formed of
    (a) callose   (b) pecto-cellulose
    (c) ligno-cellulose   (d) sporopollenin

19. Abundant occurrence of fossilised pollen grains is due to resistant
    (a) lignocellulose   (b) sporopollenin
    (c) pectocellulose   (d) pectolignin

20. Pollen grain is liberated in
    (a) one celled stage   (b) two celled stage
    (c) three celled stage   (d) two or three celled stage

21. Pollen tube is covered by
    (a) pectocellulose   (b) sporopollenin
    (c) cellulose   (d) lignocellulose

22. Which one forms the pollen tube?
    (a) Prothallial cell   (b) Vegetative cell
    (c) Generative cell   (d) Stalk cell

23. Number of prothallial cells present in the male gametophyte of angiosperms is
    (a) one   (b) two   (c) many   (d) zero

24. Growth of pollen tube is
    (a) apical (b) basal
    (c) intercalary (d) diffused
25. Number of nuclei present in the mature male gametophyte of angiosperms is
    (a) one (b) two (c) three (d) many
26. If an angiospermic male plant is diploid and female plant tetraploid, the ploidy level of endosperm will be
    (a) haploid (b) triploid
    (c) tetraploid (d) pentaploid
27. In some dicots, no distinct endosperm can be seen. Why?
    (a) The embryo has digested the endosperm.
    (b) The cotyledons have absorbed the endosperm.
    (c) The seeds never produced endosperm.
    (d) The endosperm has become the seed coat
28. Aleurone cells are present in endosperm of
    (a) cereals (b) legumes
    (c) Both 'a' and 'b' (d) None of these
29. Milky water of green coconut is
    (a) liquid chalaza
    (b) liquid nucellus
    (c) liquid endosperm
    (d) liquid female gametophyte
30. The endosperm found in angiospermic seed is different from that of gymnosperms in the sense that, in the former
    (a) it is formed before fertilization while in the latter it is formed after fertilization.
    (b) it is formed after fertilization.
    (c) it is cellular while in the latter it is nuclear.
    (d) it is nutritive while in the latter it is protective.
31. Multinucleate condition is present in
    (a) quiescent centre
    (b) maize
    (c) meristematic tissue
    (d) liquid endosperm of coconut
32. Fruit-eating bats tend to feed extremely rapidly on fruits and have relatively inefficient digestion (some times defecating seeds as early as an hour after feeding on them). Why are they good seed dispersal agents?
    (a) Seed survival in bat's guts is low.
    (b) Undigested seeds are deposited in a heap at the bat's root site.
    (c) Undigested seeds are deposited near the same plant that produced them.
    (d) Digested seeds are dispersed in bat waste products.
33. Dicot embryo consists of
    (a) radicle and plumule
    (b) radicle, plumule, cotyledons and sometimes endosperm
    (c) radicle, plumule, cotyledons and tegmen
    (d) radicle, plumule, cotyledons, tegmen and testa
34. Archesporium of ovule is
    (a) single celled derived from nucellar epidermis
    (b) single celled derived from nucellar hypodermis
    (c) multicellular derived from nucellar epidermis
    (d) multicellular derived from nucellar hypodermis
35. In dicot embryo, the radicle is formed by
    (a) epibasal tier of embryo
    (b) hypobasal tier of embryo
    (c) hypophysis of suspensor
    (d) terminal cell of suspensor
36. In monocot embryo, the radicle is produced by
    (a) terminal cell (b) middle cell
    (c) epiblast (d) suspensor
37. In the embryos of a typical dicot and a grass, true homologous structures are
    (a) coleorhiza and coleoptile
    (b) coleoptile and scutellum
    (c) cotyledons and scutellum
    (d) hypocotyl and radicle
38. Which condition is more advanced?
    (a) Bitegmic (b) Unitegmic
    (c) Tritegmic (d) Ategmic
39. Which condition is more advanced?
    (a) Bitegmic (b) Unitegmic
    (c) Tritegmic (d) Ategmic
40. Seeds are adaptively important because
    (a) they maintain dormancy.
    (b) they protect young plants during vulnerable stages.
    (c) they store food for young plants, and facilitate disperal.
    (d) All of the above
41. Nucellar polyembryony is reported in species of
    (a) *Brassica* (b) *Gossypium*
    (c) *Triticum* (d) Citrus
42. Seed coat is not thin, membranous in
    (a) coconut (b) groundnut
    (c) gram (d) maize
43. Which one of following is an example of parthenocarpic fruit.
    (a) Apple (b) Persimmon
    (c) Cashew (d) Latermelon
44. Aleurone layer participates in
    (a) protection of delicate embryo
    (b) transfer of food to cotyledons
    (c) enzyme synthesis
    (d) formation of scutellum
45. Which of the following floral parts forms pericarp after fertilization?
    (a) Nucellus (b) Outer integument
    (c) Ovary wall (d) Inner integument

46. Albuminous seeds store their reserve food mainly in

   (a) perisperm

   (b) endosperm

   (c) cotyledons

   (d) hypocotyl

47. The total number of nuclei involved in double fertilization in angiosperms are

   (a) two   (b) three

   (c) four   (d) five

48. Anther is typically

   (a) tetrasporangiate

   (b) bisporangiate

   (c) trisporangiate

   (d) monosporangiate

49. The functions of tapetum is to

   (a) dehiscence of anther

   (b) produce pollen grains.

   (c) provide nourishment to the developing pollen grains.

   (d) store and protect pollen grains.

50. Microsporogenesis occurs

   (a) on margins of leaves.

   (b) inside the ovule.

   (c) inside the anther.

   (d) in essential floral organs.

Match the following

51. Match the items in column I with those in column II and choose the correct answer.

	Column-I		Column-II
1.	Funicle	A.	Small opening of ovule
2.	Integuments	B.	Stalk of ovule
3.	Chalaza	C.	Protective envelopes of ovule
4.	Hilum	D.	Junction part of ovule and stalk
5.	Micropyle	E.	Basal part of the ovule

   (a) 1-B; 2-C; 3-E; 4-D; 5-A   (b) 1-A; 2-C; 3-B; 4-D; 5-E

   (c) 1-B; 2-C; 3-A; 4-D; 5-E   (d) 1-B; 2-D; 3-E; 4-A; 5-C

   (e) 1-C; 2-D; 3-E; 4-A; 5-B

52. Match the entries in Column I with those of Column II and choose the correct answer.

	Column I		Column II
A.	Cleistogamy	m.	Insect pollination
B.	Geitonogamy	n.	Bud pollination
C.	Entomophily	o.	Pollination between flowers in the same plant
D.	Xenogamy	p.	Wind pollination
		q.	Cross pollination

   (a) A-o, B-m, C-q, D-n   (b) A-m, B-q, C-n, D-o

   (c) A-n, B-o, C-m, D-q   (d) A-q, B-p, C-o, D-n

Chapter Test

Time : *30 Minutes*   **Max. Marks : *15***

Directions :

- Questions number **1-15** carry **1 mark** each.

1. There are ten flowers (each with 10 stamens) in one individual plant of Cratalaria. In each microsporangium of every stamen of all the flowers, there are 30 microspore mother cells. How many pollen grains are formed from the plant?
   (a) 4000   (b) 10000   (c) 24000   (d) 48000

2. Which of the following floral parts forms pericarp after fertilization?
   (a) Nucellus   (b) Outer integument
   (c) Ovary wall   (d) Inner integument

3. Fusion of one male gamete with egg and other of the same pollen tube with two polar nuclei is
   (a) triple fusion   (b) vegetative fertilization
   (c) double fertilization   (d) parthenogenesis.

4. After penetrating stigmatic and stylar tissue the pollen tube usually grows down towards the egg cell because
   (a) the egg cell attracts pollen tube
   (b) it grows under the influence of ovum
   (c) it has no other passage to follow
   (d) the filiform apparatus of synergids attract the pollen tubes

5. Match the items given in column-I with those given in column-II and choose the correct option given below.

Column-I		Column-II
A.	Parthenocarpy	I.	Inactive state
B.	Polyembryony	II.	Meiosis and syngamy are absent
C.	Apomixis	III.	Occurrence of more than one embryo
D.	Dormancy	IV.	Seedless fruit

   (a) A – I; B – II; C – III; D – IV
   (b) A – IV; B – III; C – II; D – I
   (c) A – IV; B – I; C – II; D – III
   (d) A – III; B – II; C – I; D – IV

DIRECTIONS (Qs. 6-7) : *Each of these questions contains an assertion followed by reason. Read them carefully and answer the question on the basis of following options. You have to select the one that best describes the two statements.*
   (a) If both Assertion and Reason are correct and the Reason is a correct explanation of the Assertion.
   (b) If both Assertion and Reason are correct but Reason is not a correct explanation of the Assertion.
   (c) If the Assertion is correct but Reason is incorrect.
   (d) If both Assertion and Reason are incorrect.

6. **Assertion:** Majority of plants use abiotic aganets for pollination, but only a small proportion of plant uses biotic agents.
   Reason: Pollination by water is more common amongst abiotic pollination.

7. **Assertion:** In some seeds such as black pepper and beet, remnants of nucellus are also persistant and this residual persistent nucellus is called perisperm.
   Reason: In angiosperm, the fruit is the final product of sexual reproduction.

Passage/Case Based Questions

DIRECTIONS (Qs. 8-12) : *Read the following passage and answer the question the follow.*

A biology student Ashu, read an article on apple being a false fruit. He asked his teacher about how fruit can be called false fruit and was explained about the development of fruits.

8. Fruit is a
   (a) post fertilisation product of pistel
   (b) product of flower
   (c) body having seeds
   (d) product of ovary

9. A true fruit is formed from
   (a) ovary   (b) ovary and thalamus
   (c) ovary and calyx   (d) ovary and receptacle

10. Parthenocarp is a fruit
    (a) formed from superior ovary
    (b) formed from inferior ovary
    (c) consisting of ripened ovary and thalamus
    (d) which does not possess seeds

11. Schizocarpic fruit splits up into
    (a) Achenial fruit   (b) Capsular
    (c) Schizocarpic   (d) Drupe

12. A fruit when is constricted in between the seeds is
    (a) Regma   (b) Samara
    (c) lomantium   (d) Frllicle

Very Short Answer Questions

13. What is the site of megasporogenesis?
14. What is intine?
15. How many megaspores give rise to embryo sac in monosporic type of development?

Solutions 

1.   **(c)** The tapetum is a layer of nutritive cells found within the sporangium, particularly within the anther, of flowering plants. Its main function is to provide nutrition to the developing microspore mother cells and pollen grains.

2.   **(c)** Egg apparatus consists of two synergids and one egg cell lying at the micropylar end. Synergids bear prominent structure called 'filiform' apparatus which are finger like projections. Synergids guide the path of pollen tube towards the egg, help in obtaining nourishment from the outer nucellar cells and also function as shock absorbers during the penetration of pollen tube into the embryo sac. Cytoplasm of egg is inactive, rich in ribosomes, and contains plastids.

3.   **(b)** In a fertilized ovule n, 2n and 3n conditions occur respectively in egg, nucellus and endosperm.

4.   **(b)**   5.   **(d)**

6.   **(a)** Tapetum is a layer of nutritive cells found within the sporangium, particularly within the anther, of flowering plants. Exine is the decay-resistant outer coating of a pollen grain or spore. It is made up of sporopollenin (most resistant organic material known). Pollenkit is a sticky covering found on the surface of pollen grains. It is especially common in plants that are pollinated by insects. Vegetative cells are involved in the formation of microspores. The vegetative cells are bigger, has abundant food reserves and a large irregular shaped nucleus. Sporogenous tissue is a group of compactly arranged homogenous cells. It is irregular in shape with abundant food reserves.

7.   **(b)** Both Assertion and Reason are true, but Reason is not correct explanation of Assertion.

In tapetum, cells are generally polyploid, multinucleate and possess dense cytoplasm. In tapetal cells, the nucleus divides but cytokinesis does not take place, so same cell contains two or more nuclei connective consist of vascular strand which is made up of vascular tissues.

8.   **(b)** Both Assertion and Reason are true, but Reason is not correct explanation of Assertion.

The tetrad is enclosed within a sac made up of callose. The sac is dissolved by the enzyme callase (secreted by tapetum) to release the microspore protoplast. Each microspore then begins to synthesize its own cell wall. In *Aristolochia elegans* all five types of tetrads have been reported. Mostly all four microspores are functional, but in some cases like in members of cyperaceal only one functional microspore is formed. The five type of microspore tetrads are tetrahedral, isobilateral, decussate, T-shaped and linear.

9.   **(b)** Both Assertion and Reason are true, but Reason is not correct explanation of Assertion.

The placenta is located inside the ovarian cavity. The development of ovule is the first stage in female gametogenesis.

10.   **(b)** Both Assertion and Reason are true, but Reason is not correct explanation of Assertion.

The MMC is a large cell containning dense cytoplasm and a prominent nucleus. MMC divides meiotically to form four haploid megaspore.

11.   Sepals.

12.   Sporopollenin.

13.   Four.

14.   Opuntia (prickly pear)

15.   Emasculation.

16.

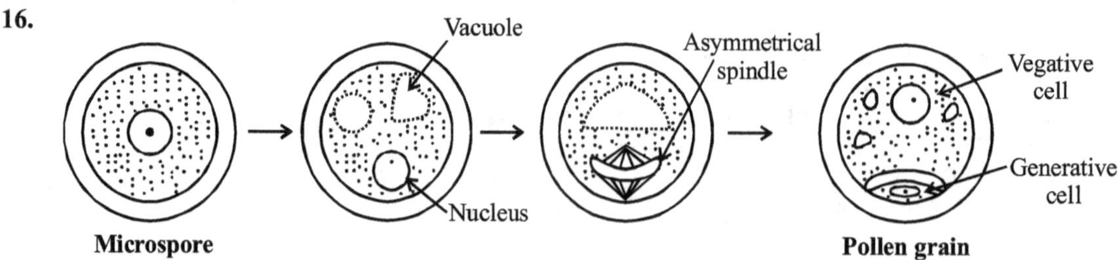

Fig. Stages of a microspore maturing into a pollen grain

17. The exine of pollen grains exhibit fascinating patterns and designs. These help classifing pollen grains to their respective families, genus or species.

18. The pistil has capability of recognizing compatible pollen grain. When a pollen grain comes in contact with the pistil there is a continuous dialogue between pistil and pollen. This dialogue is modified by chemical components of the pollen interacting with those of pistil. On the basis of this interaction the pistil accepts or rejects a pollen grain.

19. Pollen grains collected by bees are used for the variety of purposes like nature cure, cosmetics and as food supplements pollen grains are rich in nutrients (protein 7-26%, carbohydrates 24-48%, fats 0.9-14.5%). They are taken as tablets or syrups to enhance performance of athletes and race horces.

20. There are some insects which consume pollen from male organs and nectar from female flower without facilitaling pollination such insects are called as pollen or nector robbers.

Practice Exercise-2 

1. **(c)** Unisexuallity of flowers prevents autogamy but not geitonogamy because autogamy is the transfer of pollen grains from anther to stigma of same flower and geitonogamy is the fertilization of a flower by pollen from another flower on the same (or a genetically identical) plant. Therefore, geitonogamy occurs between bisexual flowers or unisexual flowers of the same plant.

2. **(d)** Cleistogamy is a self-fertilization that occurs within a permanently closed flower. In cleistogamous flower, the anther and stigma lies close to each other. When anther dehisces in the flower buds, pollen grains come in contact with the stigma to effect pollination. Thus, cleistogamous flowers are invariably autogamous as there is no chance of cross - pollen landing on the stigma. Cleistogamous flowers produce assured seed set even in the absence of pollinators.

3. **(a)** Emasculation is an outbreeding device to promote cross-pollination.

4. **(d)** Male reproductive organ is called androecium and their unit is called stamen. Stamen is also known as microsporophyll. A typical stamen differentiates into three parts- filament, anther and connective tissue. The anther is bilobed and the lobe encloses 4 pollen sacs or microsporangia. The integumented nucellus or megasporangium is called ovule.

5. **(a)**

6. **(d)** Both Assertion and Reason are false.
Pollination by water is quite rare in flowering plants and is limited to about 30 genera, mostly monocotyledons. Not all aquatic plants use water for pollination. In a majority of aquatic plants such as water hyacinth and water lily, the flower emerge above the level of water and are pollinated by insects or wind.

7. **(c)** Assertion is true but Reason is false,
Some flowers provide safe place for lying eggs. Such an example is that of the tallest flower of *Amorphaphallus*. The pollination by birds is called onithophily, while that by snails and slugs is called malacophily.

8. **(b)** Assertion and Reason are true, but Reason is not the correct explanation of Assertion.
Nectar and pollen grains are the usual floral rewards.

9. **(d)** Both Assertion and Reason are false.
Pollination guarantee the transfer of the right type of pollen. The pistil has the ability to recognise the pollen, whether it is of the right type or of the wrong type.

10. Pollination is the process of transfer of pollen grains from anther to stigma.
The two types of pollination found in flowering plants are:
(a) Self-pollination– than occurs within the same plant.
(b) Cross-pollination– that occurs between two flowers of two different plants but of the same kind.

11. Vallisnaria.

12. Ornithophily.

13. Pollination between different flowers of the same plant is called geitonogamy.

14. Pollination of flowers by bats is called chiropterophilly.

15. Bisexuality, homogamy and cleistogamy are the three adaptations that favours self-pollination.

16. Kigelia pinnata (Sausage tree)

17. Wind pollinated flowers (anemophilous flowers) are small and inconspicuous. Since they are pollinated with wind they are colourless, odourless, and nectarless. In these flowers, calyx and corolla are either reduced or absent so that reproductive parts become more exposed for pollination. Pollen grains are produced in large number & are light, small and dusty therefore can be blown to distances upto 1300 km. Stigma are hairy, feathery or branched for catching the wind blown pollen grains. E.g., Date palm, Maize, *Pinus*.

18. The main difference between autogamy and geitonogamy are as follows :-

	Autogamy		Geitonogamy
1.	When a perfect flower is pollinated by its own pollen, it is called autogamy.	1.	When pollen grains of one flower are transferred to stigma of another flower belonging to either the same plant or genetically similar plant, it is called geitonogamy.
2.	It occurs by three methods – homogomy, cleistogamy and bud pollination.	2.	In geitonogamy, the flower often show modification similar to one found in cross-pollination.

19. Self-pollination is the transference of the pollen grains from the anther of a flower to the stigma of either the same or genetically similar flower. It has many advantages which are as follows :

   a.   Maintains the purity of the race indefinitely.

   b.   No special devices required for attracting insect for pollination.

   c.   Eliminates certain bad recessive characters.

   d.   Large number of pollen grains are not required.

   e.   Used to maintain pure line for hybridization experiments.

This method has few disadvantages also which are as follows:

   a.   Introduction of useful characters is very rare.

   b.   Trait of disease resistance decreases.

   c.   Adaptability to changing environment decreases.

   d.   Vigour and vitality of the race decreases.

20. The main difference between entomophilous and hydrophilous flower are as follows :-

	Entomophilous flower	Hydrophilous flower
1.	The flowers are large or if small, they group to form a large mass.	The flowers are small and inconspicuous.
2.	Odour is commonly present and the flowers usually posses nectar or edible pollen.	Nectar and odour are absent.
3.	Pollen grains are heavy and surrounded by a yellow sticky substance called pollenkitt.	Pollen grains are light and unwettable due to mucliage cover.
4.	Stigmas are usually branched and sticky.	Stigmas are long, sticky but unwettable.
5.	*Rosa, Yucca, Amorphophallus* are few examples of entomophilous flower.	*Vallisneria, Zostera, Ceratophyllum* are few examples of hydrophilous flower.

21. Anemophilous species produces a large number of pollen grains which float in air and cause severe allergies and bronchial infections in some people. This often lead to chronic respiratory disorders like asthma, bronchitis, rhinitis etc. *Parthenium* or carrot grass is the major contributor of pollen allergy which entered India as contaminant with imported wheat but now spreaded in all parts of the country.

22. Pollination is the mechanism of the transfer of pollen grains from the anther to the stigma of pistil. Whereas fertilization is the fusion of male & female gametes to produce zygote that finally develops into embryo.

23. The insects usually visit the flowers for nectar, edible pollen grains or for shelter therefore insect pollinated flowers are more showy or brightly coloured. Some flowers have special markings on the petals for guiding the insects to nectar glands. These flowers produce pleasant or foul odour for attracting insects. On the other hand, wind pollinated flowers are colourless, odourless and nectarless. The flowers are also small and inconspicuous. Thus, insects do not visit these flowers.

24. When pollination performed by bats, it is called chiropterophily.

Chiropterophilous flowers are dull-coloured with strong fermenting or fruity odour, abundant nectar and pollen grains. They secrete even more abundant nectar than the ornithophilous flowers. Pollen grains are also produced in more abundance. *Kigelia pinnata* (Sausage Tree), *Adansonia* (Baobab tree) are two examples of chiropterophilous plants (or bat pollinated plants).

25. Pollenkitt is the outermost oily, thick, sticky coating of pollen grains, mainly composed of lipids and carotenoids. It is secreted in case of entomophilous pollen grains.

Practice Exercise-3 

1.   **(d)**   In some, the thalamus also contributes to fruit formation & such fruits are called false fruits. for example:- apple, pear, strawberry and cashewnut.

2.   **(c)**   In a seed of maize, the scutellum is considered as cotyledon because it absorbs food materials and supplies them to the embryo.

3.   **(c)**   **4.**   **(a)**

5.   **(a)**   The seed coat develops from integuments originally surrounding the ovule. It is thick and hard in coconut which protects the embryo from mechanical injury and from drying out.

6.   **(c)**   Assertion is true but Reason is false.

The development of embryo takes place towards the micropylar end of the embryo sac as the zygote is located at this end.

7. **(b)** Both Assertion and Reason are true, but Reason is not correct explanation of Assertion.

Non-albuminous are present in pea, groundnut etc. where as albuminous seeds are found in wheat, maize, barley, castor, sunflower etc.

8. **(b)** Both Assertion and Reason are true, but Reason is not correct explanation of Assertion.

The polyembryony is found in gymnosperms, but also seen in few angiosperms like oranges, lemon, tobacco etc.

9. **(c)** Assertion is true but Reason is false.

The coconut water from tender coconut is free-nuclear endosperm and the surrounding white kernal is the cellular endospem.

10. A small opening at the apex of ovule is called micropyle.

11. Fusion of one male gamete with the egg to form zygote is called syngamy or fertilization.

12. Endosperm provides nourishment to the developing embryo.

13. Total 5 nuclei are taking part in double fertilization. 2 in syngamy and 3 in triple fusion.

14. Development of an embryo directly from an integument or nucellus is called adventive embryony.

15. Some plants are able to produce fruits without fertilization. Such fruits are called parthenocarpic fruits. Banana is one such example of parthenocarpic fruits. These fruits are either seedless or have non-viable seeds.

Grapes, oranges, apple, pear lemon are some examples of parthenocarpic fruits developed by horticulturists by using plant hormones.

16. The main difference between dicot and monocot seed are as follows :-

Dicot seed	Monocot seed
1. Embryos of dicot seed consists of two cotyledons.	1. Embryos of monocot seed posses only one cotyledon.
2. Radicle is called coleorrhiza (embryonic root) which is present between the two cotyledons.	2. Radicle found on the lower side of the embryo.
3. Plumule is called coleoptile (shoot tip) e.g. pulses, bean seeds.	3. Plumule also called shoot tip is present on the upper side (towards cotyledon) & is protected by leaf-like covering called coleoptile. e.g. maize & wheat.

17. (i) Microspore mother cell
Chromosome number = 16
Ploidy level = Diploid
(ii) Endosperm cell
Chromosome number = 24
Ploidy level = Triploid

18.

	Name of Part	Function
1.	Plumule	Gives rise to stem.
2.	Cotyledons	Provide nourishment to the embryo.
3.	Radicle	Gives rise to root.

19. Polyembryony is the phenomenon of development of more than one embryo in the same seed (1719) in *Citrus*. The reasons are
(i) Presence of more than one embryo in the same seed
(ii) Cleavage of one embryo into two or more embryos

20. Seeds are the basis of agriculture due to the dormancy and dehydration of seeds, they can be stored as food throughout the year and used to raise crop in the next season. The seeds of many plants remain viable for several years and they can germinate and flower after hundreds of years.

21. When the fruit develops from ovary it is called true fruit. And when the fruit develops from other parts except ovary it is called false fruit. In strawberry, cashew etc. thalmus develops into fruit.

22. Parthenocarpy helps in producing seedless fruits. It is of great advantage for us because we found seeds irritating during eating of fruits. Food processing industry also prefer seedless fruits because removal of seeds is a very difficult process.

Past year Exercise 

1. **(c)** The process of self-pollination is fully insured if the flower is cleistogamous. The clesitogamous flowers are the type of flower which does not open at all. In such flowers, the anther and stigma lie close to each other and when the anthers dehisce in the flower buds, and then the pollen grains come in contact with the stigma results in self-pollination.

2. The anther with malfunctioning tapetum cannot transport of nutrients to nourish the developing microspore mother cells and pollen grains. So, it fails to produce viable male gametophyte. Tapetum also secretes special proteins for pollen to recognise stigmatic compatibility.

3. A bilobed, dithecous anther is tetrasporangiate. The four microsporangia of an anther lie at its four corner.
   Total microsporangium = 4 × 100 = 400
   So, anther produces 400 male gametes.

4. In *Vallisneria*, pollen grains are coated by mucilage that protect them from wetting.

5. The pollen grains fail to develop into male gametophyte, due to the non-availability of nutrients because of malfunctioning tapetum.

6. The seed bearing plants tide over dry and hot weather conditions in the form of seeds while the rest of the plant perishes or in the form of some underground vegetative structure (rhizome, corm, sucker etc.) which perennates and form new plants on the approach of favourable conditions.

7. Style = ½, stigma = ½

8. I.n a majority of flowering plants, one of the megaspores is functional, while the other three degenerate. The functional megaspore develops into the female gametophyte (embryo sac). In mature female gametophyte, there are 6 haploid cells, 3 antipodals, 2 synergids and 1 female gamete.

9. Emasculation in a bisexual flower is required to prevent contamination of the stigma with the self pollen grains. Bagging is done to prevent contamination of the stigma of the emasculated flower with any other unwanted pollen grains.

10. L.S. of a post-pollinated pistil

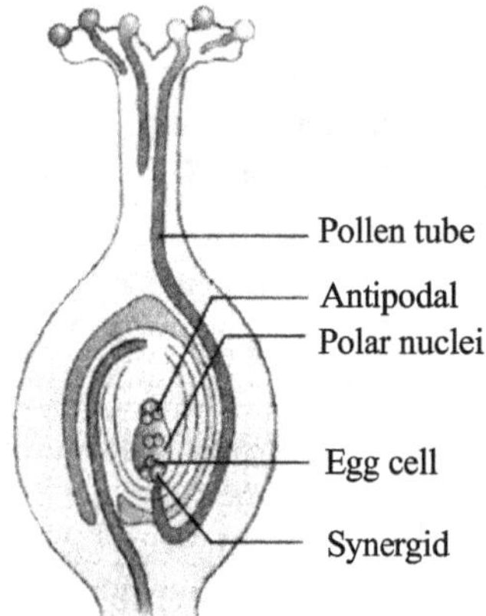

11. (i) (a) Anthers are well exposed for easy disperasal of pollen grains.
   (b) Pollen grains are light, small and dusty. They can be blowing to distances upto 1300 km.
   (c) Stigma is hairy, feathery or branched to catch the wind borne pollen grains.
   (ii) Flower rewards are
   (a) Nectar and edible pollen grains.
   (b) Safe place for insects to lay eggs for some flowers, e.g. *Amorphophallus* and *Yucca*.

12. (i) Male gametophyte of an angiosperm.

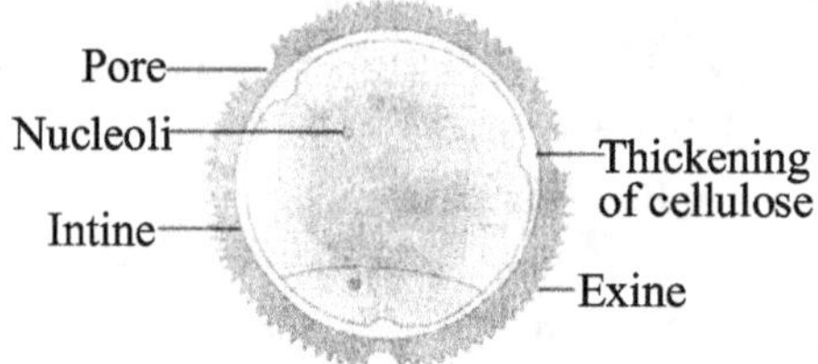

   Structure of a male gametophyte (pollen grain represents male magetophyte

   (ii) Sporopollenin is one of the hardest organic material known. It can withstand high temperatures, strong acids and alkali. No enzyme that degrades sporopollenin is so far known.

13. Differences between albuminous and non-albuminous seeds.

Albuminous Seeds	Non-albuminous Seeds
Seed contains some endosperm that acts as a food storage tissue. Examples, wheat, maize, barley, castor and sunflower.	Seeds that are devoid of endosperm. Examples, pea and groundnut.

14. Differences between geitonogamy and xenogamy.

Geitonogamy	Xenogamy
It is the transfer of pollen grains from the anther to the stigma of another flower of same plant.	It is the transfer of pollen grains from the anther to the stigma of a different plant.
The pollen grains are genetically similar to the plant.	The pollen grains are genetically different from the plant.

Geitonogamy will lead to inbreeding depression because the pollen grains are genetically similar resulting into inbreeding continuous inbreeding reduces fertility.

15. Differences between perisperm and endosperm are

Perisperm	Endosperm
It is remnants of persistent nucellus of ovule, present in the seeds of some plants.	It is a specialised nutritive tissue generally triploid structure.
It is a part that belongs to seed.	It contains reserve food materials.
It is usually dry.	It is usually in fluid form or soft.
Example Black pepper.	*Example* water of coconut, pea, beans.

16. A - Pericarp
    B- Scutellum (cotyledon)
    C - Coleoptile
    D - Coleorhiza

17. **Apomixis:** It is a form of asexual reproduction that mimics sexual reproduction, and seeds are produced without fertilisation is called apomixis or agamospermy, *e.g.*, Grasses.
Parthenocarpy: It is a commerical important process in which seedless fruit is formed without fertilisation, *e.g.*, Banana.
Polyembryony: The occurence of more than one embryo in a seed is known as polyembryony, *e.g.*, Orange.

18. Exine is composed of a highly resistant fatty substance called sporopollenin. It is not affected by high temperature, strong acids and alkali. It helps the pollen grains to be well preserved as fossils.

19. **Advantage -** Pollination and seed-set are assured even in the absence of pollinators.
Disadvantage - Cleistogamous flowers show pure autogamy. So, there is no chance of cross pollination.

20. In angiosperms embryo-sac (female gametophyte) is haploid (N) and develops from megaspore. The embryo-sac contains egg (N) a component of egg apparatus fuse with a male gamete (N) to form zygote (2N) which develops into embryo. Two polar nuclei (1N each) present in the central cell of embryo sac fuse with the second male gamete (N) to form primary endosperm nucleus (3N) which develops in to endosperm, a persistent or non persistent nutritive tissue.

21. (i) Endosperm development precedes embryo development. In coconut endosperm formation is **nuclear type**. Here, the primary endosperm nucleus divides repeatedly without wall formation forming a large number of nuclei which move to the periphery because of the formation of a large central vacuole. The multinucleate cytoplasm undergo cleavage to form multicellular endosperm in the outer part and free nucleate as well as vacuolar endosperm (coconut water) in the centre.
(ii) The tender coconut is considered a healthy source of nutrition is immature with soft and gentle solid white kernel (also called **coconut meat**) and the central watery fluid, free nuclear endosperm is called coconut milk or water which is highly nutritious, makes a refreshing drink because of the presence of proteins, oils, vitamins and minerals.
(iii) The seeds of pea are dicot, **non-endospermic/ex-albuminous** because the whole of endosperm is consumed in the development of embryo. The food is stored in massive cotyledons and there are no remnants of endosperm in the mature pea seeds.
However, in castor seeds, the whole of endosperm is not used completely during the development of embryo. The cotyledons are papery and the fleshy massive endosperm is present in the mature castor seeds. Seeds are dicot **endospermic albuminous.**

22. The unfertilized mature embryo-sac is 7-celled, 8-nucleate. The cells of embryo-sac are (i) 3-celled egg apparatus (2 synergids and an egg or oosphere) (ii) one central cell (binucleate) with 2 polar nuclei (iii) 3 antipodal cells.

23. The mature male gametophyte of angiosperm is 3-celled *i.e.* two male gametes and the tube cell/ vegetative cell.
The 2 male gametes are small, rounded, enclosed by little cytoplasm, present in the proximal part by pollen-tube whereas the tube cell/vegetative cell nucleus is irregular in out line present in the distal part of pollen tube. The male gametes are functional while the tube nucleus degenerate.

24. Geitonogamous flowering plants have open bisexual flowers in which pollen grains from the anther are transferred to the stigma of another flower of same plant (genetically similar to autogamy) involving different pollination agent like wind, water, insects, birds etc. Hence. The cross pollination (functionally similar to cross pollination) occurs in these plants.

25. (i) In cleistogamy, the flowers remain closed and never open. It involves autogamy i.e. the transfer of pollen from the anther to the stigma of same single bisexual flower, *e.g. Viola, Commelina.*
(ii) The main advantage of cleistogamy is assured pollination and hence assured seed set.
The disadvantage of cleistogamy is that genetic variations cannot be produced and it results in decreased yield and resistance to pathogens, poor tolerance to environmental stresses.

26. **Outbreeding Devices :** To avoid inbreeding depression and promote outbreeding, the plants have evolved certain devices/contrivances such as :
(i) **Dicliny** (unisexuality). Flowers unisexual *e.g.,* Papaya, Maize, Mulberry.
(ii) **Dichogamy**–Sex-organs mature at different times (a) **Protandry**–Anthers mature earlier, *e.g., Salvia,* Sunflower (b) **Protogyny**–Stigmas mature earlier, e.g., *Gloriosa, Plantago, Mirabilis,* etc.
(iii) **Prepotency**–Pollen grains of another flower germinate rapidly over the stigma than pollen of same flower, *e.g.,* Apple, grapes.
(iv) **Self-sterility/self-incompatibility**-Pollen-grains do not germinate on the stigma of same flower, a genetic mechanism to prevent inbreeding.
(v) **Heterostyly**-Anther and Stigma placed at different positions, 2 or 3 types of flowers with different lengths of stamens and heights of stigmas, *e.g., Primula,* jasmine.
(vi) **Herkogamy**-Mechanical device to prevent self pollination, e.g. formation of pollinia (translator) in *Calotropis,* in *Cyprepedium* the stigma lies on the route of insect entry while the anthers occur near the exit.

27. Occurrence of more than one embryo in a seed is called polyembryony. This phenomenon was first observed by Leeuwenhoek in *Citrus* seeds. Beside the presence of a normal embryo produced in *citrus* as a result of sexual reproduction, additional extra embryos are produced from the cells of nucellus or integuments by a process called **apomixis.**

28. **Pollination by water** or **hydrophilly,** the
    (i) Flowers are small inconspicuous
    (ii) Nectar and odour absent
    (iii) Pollen grains light, unwettable
    (iv) Perianth and other floral parts unwettable
    (v) Stigma long, sticky, unwettable.

    Female flowers reach the surface of water and male flowers are also released on to the surface of water, male flowers carried passively to the stigmas to effect pollination above water surface, e.g., *Vallisneria.*

29. The similarity between geitonogamy and xenogamy is that both types of pollinations are assisted by pollinating agencies, in transferring the pollens from anther of one flower, to the receptive stigma of another flower. The difference between the two is that in geitonogamy the pollen and stigma are genetically similar bacause they both belong to same plant but in xenogamy they are genetically different as they belong to different plants of same species. As cleistogamous flowers show homogamy remain closed causing self-pollinations and cleistogamy occurs late in the flowering season in some plants, e.g., *Commelina, Oxalis,* etc.

30. 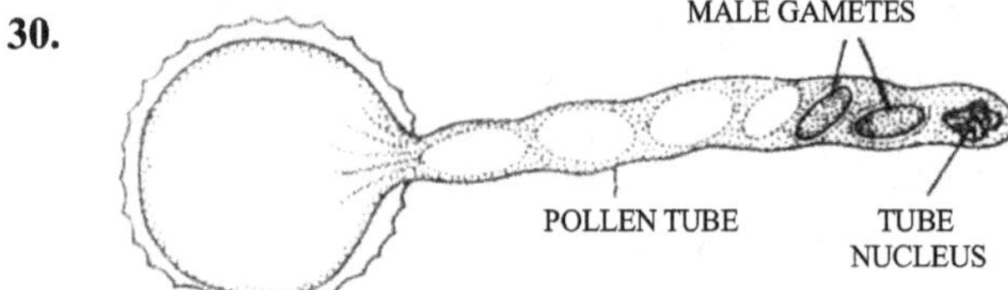

    Fig.: A male gametophyte

    The male gametophyte possesses two male gametes out of which one of the male gametes fuses with the egg resulting in the production of zygote (2N) while the second male gamete fuses with two polar nuclei or secondary diploid nucleus (2N) to form triploid primary endosperm nucleus (3N). This phenomenon involving two fusions, is called Double fertilisation.

31. **Parthenocarpy** is the phenomenon in flowering plants in which a fruit develops from an unfertilized ovary. The ovules remain immature *e.g.* Banana.

    Parthenogenesis is the phenomenon is which the egg (N) develops into a new organism without the act of fertilisation *e.g.* male honeybee, rotifers, *Ulothrix* (a green algae).

32. Apomixis or agamospermy modified form of reproduction that mimics sexual reproduction, in which the seeds are produced without fusion of gametes. Here only the ovule, take part in reproduction. The embryos may be produced from diploid egg, nucellar cells, integument cells – all diploid or from the cells of synergids (haploid embryos) *e.g., Citrus, Opunita.*

33. Mode of pollination in
    (i) *Vallisneria*-Epihydrophily
    (ii) Water lily - (emergent flowers) Entomophily (by insects).

    In *Vallisneria*, a dioecious plant male flowers abscise from the submerged spadix and rise to surface of water. The female plant produces long stalked solitary flowers having large sticky trifid stigmas. The male flowers come in contact with stigma of female flowers. The anther bursts and pollination is performed. After pollination, female flowers are pulled inside water by coiling of stalk.

34. **Dichogamy:** The condition in which the stamens and stigma of a bisexual flower mature at different times.

    Protandry: This is the condition where anthers mature earlier than the stigma and release pollens.

    Chasmogamous flowers : These are open flowers with exposed stamens and stigma which facilitate cross-pollination.

35. The anther consists of two sacs or lobes separated by a tissue called connective tissue.

    The anther is bilobed and each lobe or sac consists of two theca separated by a septum.

    Structure of Microsporangium

    (i) Epidermis : It is the outermost single layer of cell which is protective in nature.

    (ii) Endothecium : It is the second layer with thick cells, help in dehiscence and it protective in nature.

    (iii) Middle layer : It is the third layer composed of 1–3 layers of cells, help in dehiscence and is protective in nature.

    (iv) Tapetum : It is the fourth and innermost layer of cell with dense cytoplasm and multinuclei. It provides nourishment to the developing pollen grains.

36. (i) Reproductive process is not dependent on water.

    (ii) Seeds have sufficient food reserves to initiate embryo development and seedling development till the photosynthesis process is initiated.

    (iii) Seeds have better adaptive strategies for dispersal to new habitats and help the species to colonise in other areas.

37. The exine layer is made up of sporopollenin, which is one of the most resistant substances found in nature. The intine layer is made up of cellulose and pectin materials lying internal to exine.

Sporopollenin provides protection to the pollen/gamete/gametophyte from unfavourable conditions or chemicals (acids, enzymes and high temperature).

38. The events of endosperm and embryo development, maturation of ovule into seeds and ovary into fruit, are collectively termed as post-fertilization events.

The various post-fertilisation events occurring in angiosperms are:

(i) Endosperm is formed before the development of embryo. It accumulates food reserves and functions as the nutritive tissue for the developing embryo.

(ii) After fertilization the fertilized egg is called zygote which develops into an embryo. It undergoes successive divisions to form pro-embryo. It is followed by the formation of globular, heart-shaped and mature embryo.

(iii) A mature dicotyledonous embryo consists of two cotyledons, epicotyl and hypocotyl. On the other hand, a mature monocotyledonous embryo possesses only one cotyledon, a coleoptile and coleorrhiza.

(iv) Ripened ovules are known as seeds. Integuments of ovule form seed coat.

(v) A fruit is a seed containing part of a plant that develops from a fertilised ovary and often from other tissues that surround it.

39. Mosses are bryophytes and they need water for fertilisation. They lay their flagellated male gametes that swim across the water to reach the female gamete. During this process, many of the male gametes are destroyed or lost. Thus, moss plants produce very large number of male gametes so that even if some of the gametes get destroyed, the remaining can fertilise the female gamete.

These male gametes are called antherozoids.

40. (a) Those seeds that carry a living embryo and are capable of germinating into a seedling under appropriate conditions are termed as viable seeds.

(b) (i) Number of pollen grains required to form 200 seeds will be 200 only as each pollen grain carries to generative cells or male gametes and only one of the two are involved in zygote formation.

(ii) In total 400 gamete cells are required for production of 200 viable zygotes leading to formation of 200 guava seeds.

(c) Flow chart depicting the post pollination events:

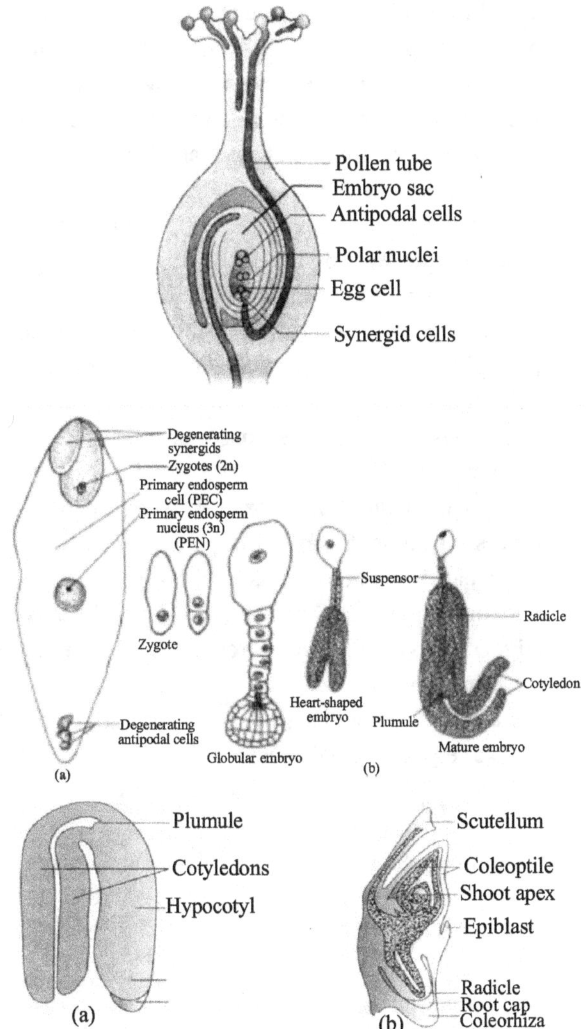

(a) The sequence of secretion of the given hormones in a pregnant woman is as follows:

(i) FSH (ii) LH (iii) hCG (iv) Relaxin

41. Parthenogenesis and parthenocarpy are two such processes that results in fruits and individuals from unfertilized ovules or eggs prior to fertilization.

In most plants, flowers need to be pollinated and fertilized to produce fruits. However, some plants can produce fruits before fertilization or without fertilization. Parthenocarpy is the process which produces fruits from unfertilized ovules in plants. Unfertilized ovules develop into fruits prior to fertilization. These fruits do not contain seeds.

Parthenogenesis is a type of reproduction commonly shown in organisms mainly by some invertebrates and lower plants. It can be described as a process in which unfertilized ovum develops into an individual (virgin birth) without fertilization. Therefore, it can be considered as a method of asexual reproduction.

The key difference between parthenogenesis and parthenocarpy is, parthenogenesis is shown by animals and plants while parthenocarpy is shown only by plants. Parthenogenesis is seen in organism like rotifers, honeybees and even some lizards and birds (turkey).

42. Artificial hybridisation is a technique to improve the plant breed by crossing two plants of desired characters. This process is achieved by emasculation and bagging.

Emasculation is the process of removing anthers from bisexual flowers without affecting the female reproductive part (pistil). It is not required in unisexual flowers during hybridisation.

Bagging is covering of the emasculated flower to prevent contamination by unwanted pollen grains.

- Potato plant bears bisexual flowers. Therefore the process of emasculation will be performed in potato and not in papaya that bears unisexual flowers.
- Bagging is used by both the plants because the stigma needs to be protected from getting pollinated with undesired pollen.

43. Pollen banks are used to store pollen grains for a short as well as very long period of time in viable conditions. These pollen grains can be used in various crop breeding programs, biochemical and physiochemical studies. The very important application of pollen bank is to preserve the biodiversity in the form of preservation of valuable of genetic resources.

The pollen grains can be stored by two methods:

(i) *Short term storage of pollen grains*, which includes storage under low temperature and low humidity; and storage in an organic solvent (simple method by which pollen grains are dried over silica and stored in organic solvents and maintained in refrigerator or deep freezer)

(ii) *Long term storage of pollen*: It includes storage of freeze or vacuum-dried pollen grains [in which pollen grains are stored at subzero temperature (–60 degrees C to –80 degrees C)] and cryopreservation (pollen grains are dried by using a 'Pollen Drier' containing air of 20 degrees C and 20–40 % humidity to bring their water content below a threshold level and stored in liquid nitrogen (–196 degrees C). This method is very effective for storage of pollen grains of a number of species, including cereals, even for over 10 years).

- The pollens preserved in pollen banks are benefitting farmers in the following two ways:

(i) By using these pollens the plants that are facing extinction can be reproduced.

(ii) Pollen grains can be later used in plant breeding programs.

(iii) By conserving agricultural biodiversity.]

44. Fruits that are matured ovaries of flowers are called true fruits and false fruits are develop only from the ovary. Fruits formed as a result of fertilization, while some species of fruits that are develop without fertilisation and such fruits are called parthenocarpic fruits. Banana is a parthenocarpy and seedless fruit.

45. Diagrammatic representation of mature anther:

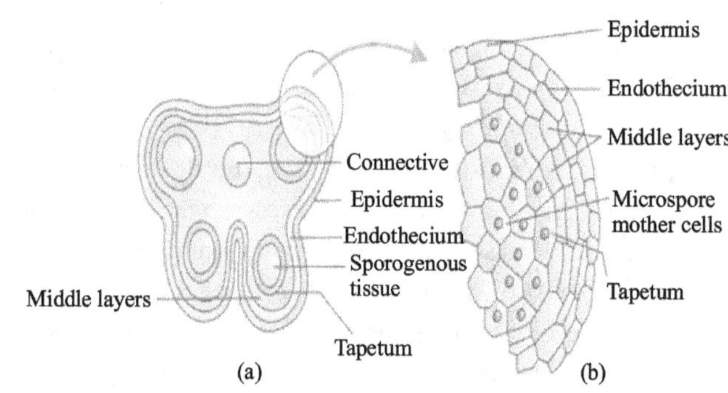

A typical angiosperm anther is bilobed with each lobe having two theca such as they are dithecous.

NCERT Exemplar

1. **(c)** Sepals collectively form a whorl, called as calyx while technically the carpel is known as gynoecium. The floral whorls formed by petals and stamens are called as corolla and androecium respectively.

2. **(c)** The pollen grains represent the male gametophytes. As, the anthers mature and dehydrate, the microspores dissociate from each other and develop into pollen grains. So, embryo sac is to ovule as pollen grains is to an anther.

3. **(d)** A typical microsporangium is generally surrounded by four-wall layers, *i.e.*, the epidermis (outermost protective layer), endothecium, middle fibrous layers and the tapetum (innermost nutritive layer).

4. **(b)** As the anther develops, the microspore mother cells of the sporogenous tissue undergoes meiotic divisions to form microspore tetrads. After dehydration, the microspore tetrad is separated into pollen grains.

5. **(a)** The gynoecium represents the female reproductive part of the flower that consists of pistil. Each pistil comprises three parts, *i.e.*, **stigma, style** and **ovary.** The **placenta** is located inside the ovarian cavity.

There are the megasporangia, arising from the placenta commonly called **ovules.** The functional megaspore undergoing the meiotic division develops into the female gametophyte of **embryo sac.**

In option 'b' thalamus is not a part of gynoecium. Thalamus forms the base of flower on which all the floral whorls rest upon, it is not associated with gynoecium. In option 'c' tapetum is not a part of gynoecuim.

Tapetum is the inner most nutritive layer of microsporangium and in option 'd' stamen is not a part of gynoecium. **Stamen** is male reproductive part (androecium) of plant. therefore, the other options are wrong.

6. **(c)** The method of self-pollination in which the stigma of a flower receive pollens from the anther of same flower is known as autogamy. For autogamy both sex organs of a chasmogamous flower should mature at the same time.

As chasmogamous flowers open at maturity, pollen release and for the process of autogamy stigma receptivity should be synchronised.

In such flowers, the length of anther and stigma plays secondary role in autogamy. *e.g.*, in case of protandry (pollens nature early) and protogyny (stigma matures early) leads to cross-pollination.

7. **(a)** (i) Synergid – haploid
   (ii) Polar nuclei – haploid
   (iii) Antipodal – haploid
   (iv) Zygote – diploid
   (v) Primary Endosperm Nucleus (PEN).
   Diploid secondary nucleus fertilises with a haploid male gamete to form a triploid PEN.

8. **(b)** Chiropterophily – Bat
   Anemophily – Wind
   Myrmecophily – Ant
   Malacophily – Snail

9. **(c)** Assertion is true but Reason is false.
   In the mechanism of double fertilisation, five nuclei and three gametes are involved.

10. **(c)** Assertion is true but Reason is false.
    Self incompatibility is controlled by the genes called self-sterile genes and these genes are within multiple alleles, eg s_1, s_2, s_3....... etc. self incompatibility is seen in tea and tobacco.

11. Nourishment.

12. The zygote needs nourishment during its development. As the mature, fertilised embryo sac offers very little nourishment to the zygote, the PEC divides and generates the endosperm tissue which nourishes the zygote. Hence, the zygote always divides after division of PEC.

13. In a 3-celled pollen, the generative cell has already divided and formed 2 male gametes. Hence, it will not divide again in the pollen tube. Since in a 2-celled pollen, the generative cell has not divided, it divides in the pollen tube.

1. **(c)** Microspore is haploid, uninucleate, minute spore produced in large number as a result of meiosis in microspore mother cell inside the microsporangia. These are the first cell of gametophytic generation in angiosperms.

2. **(d)** Each pollen has two layered wall. The outer layer is thick, tough, cuticularised called exine which is composed of a material called "sporopollenin". It is highly resistant to biological and physical decomposition, due to which pollens are preserved for a long time in fossils.

3. **(d)** Androgenic haploids are produced by young pollen grains because rest all are the diploid tissue.

4. **(d)** Microspore is the beginning of male-gametophyte.

5. **(a)** Ubisch bodies provided by tapetum help in thickening of exine.

6. **(b)** Seed producing plants are called seminiferous plants.

7. **(c)** In family cypraceae, only one nucleus (out of 4) remains functional after meiotic division of microspore mother cell (similar to megaspore formation).

8. **(b)** Generative cell is haploid and 2 male gametes are formed from it by mitotic division.

9. **(c)** 10. **(c)** 11. **(c)** 12. **(a)** 13. **(b)**
14. **(b)** 15. **(a)** 16. **(b)** 17. **(b)** 18. **(d)**
19. **(b)** 20. **(d)** 21. **(a)** 22. **(b)** 23. **(d)**
24. **(a)** 25. **(c)**

26. **(d)** The male gamete will be haploid (n). 2 polar nuclei will be diploid ($2n$). Endosperm formed by fusion of male gamete with two polar nuclei will be pentaploid.

$$\text{Male gamete} + 2 \text{ polar nuclei} \longrightarrow \text{Endosperm}$$
$$n \qquad (2n)+(2n) \qquad (5n)$$

27. **(b)**

28. **(a)** One or more specialized outer layers of endosperm of cereals are called aleurone layers.

29. **(c)** 30. **(b)** 31. **(d)** 32. **(c)** 33. **(b)**
34. **(b)** 35. **(c)** 36. **(b)** 37. **(c)** 38. **(b)**
39. **(b)** 40. **(d)**

41. **(d)** Polyembryony is the state of occurrence of more than one embryo in a seed. It was observed by Leeuwenhoek in citrus (orange) seeds. Polyembryony is commonly found in gymnosperms but it is also found in some of angiospermic plants such as orange, lemon and *Nicotiana*, etc.

42. **(a)** The seed coat develops from integuments originally surrounding the ovule. It is thick and hard in coconut which protects the embryo from mechanical injury and from drying out.

43. (a) 44. (c)

45. (c) Ovary wall forms pericarp after fertilization. Pericarp is the tissue that develops from the ovary wall of the flower and surrounds the seeds. The pericarp is typically made up of three distinct layers: the epicarp (outermost layer); the mesocarp (middle layer); and the endocarp (inner layer surrounding the ovary or the seeds). In a citrus fruit, the epicarp and mesocarp make up the peel.

46. (b) Endosperm is the nutritive tissue which provides nourishment to the embryo in seed plant. Albuminous seeds retain a part of endosperm as it is not completely used up during embryo development (*e.g.*, wheat, maize, barley, castor, sunflower).

47. (d) In the cytoplasm of the synergid, pollen tube releases the two male gametes. One of two male gametes fuses with egg to form diploid zygote (2n) while the other uses with two polar nucles of the central cell to produce triploid primary endosperm nucleus (3n).

48. (a) Typically, angiospermic anther is bilobed which is connected by connective and dithecous *i.e.*, each lobe has two theca. The bilobed structure of the anther is tetrasporangiate (four sporangia). In transverse section, it appears as four sided tetragonal structure consisting of two microsporangia in each lobe.

49. (c) The tapetum is a layer of nutritive cells found within the sporangium, particularly within the anther, of flowering plants. Its main function is to provide nutrition to the developing microspore mother cells and pollen grains.

50. (c) Microsporogenesis is the process of formation of microspores or pollen grains, from a pollen mother cell through meiosis, Each cell of sporogenous tissue serve as microspore mother cell (MMC). These MMCs undergo meiosis and form microspore tetrad and become haploid, microspores or pollen grains. As anthers mature microspores of the tetrad separate from each other and develops into pollen grains. Each microsporangium contains numerous pollen grains which are released after dehiscence of anther wall.

51. (a) 52. (c)

Chapter Test 

1. (d) *Crotalaria* is a member of Papilionaceae in which 10 stamens are present in flower. Each stamen has 4 microsporangia such as 10 x 4=40, in which microspore mother cells are found. Each microspore mother cells are found. Each microspore mother cell gives rise to a pollen tetrad such as 40 x 4= 160. So, one flower having 30 microsporangia it would be 160 x 30= 4800 pollen grains. So, in flowers there would be 4800 x10= 48000 pollen grains.

2. (c) Ovary wall forms pericarp after fertilization. Pericarp is the tissue that develops from the ovary wall of the flower and surrounds the seeds. The pericarp is typically made up of three distinct layers: the epicarp (outermost layer); the mesocarp (middle layer); and the endocarp (inner layer surrounding the ovary or the seeds). In a citrus fruit, the epicarp and mesocarp make up the peel.

3. (c) 4. (d)

5. (b) Parthenocarpy is the development of fruit without the formation of seeds due to lack of pollination, fertilization and embryo development. Polyembryony is the formation of more than one embryo from a single fertilized ovum or in a single seed. Apomixis is the development of an embryo without the occurrence of fertilization. Parthenogenesis is one form of apomixis. Dormancy is a state of temporary metabolic inactivity or minimal activity therefore helps an organism to conserve energy.

6. (d) Both Assertion and Reason are incorrect.
Majority of plants use biotic agents for pollination but only a small proportion of plant uses abiotic agents. Pollination by wind is more common amongst abiotic pollination.

7. (c) Assertion is true but Reason is incorrect.
In angiosperm, the seed is the final product of sexual reproduction and is often described as fertilised ovule.

8. (d) 9. (a) 10. (d) 11. (b) 12. (c)

13. Ovule.

14. The innermost layer of pollen grain is called intine.

15. One.

2

Human Reproduction

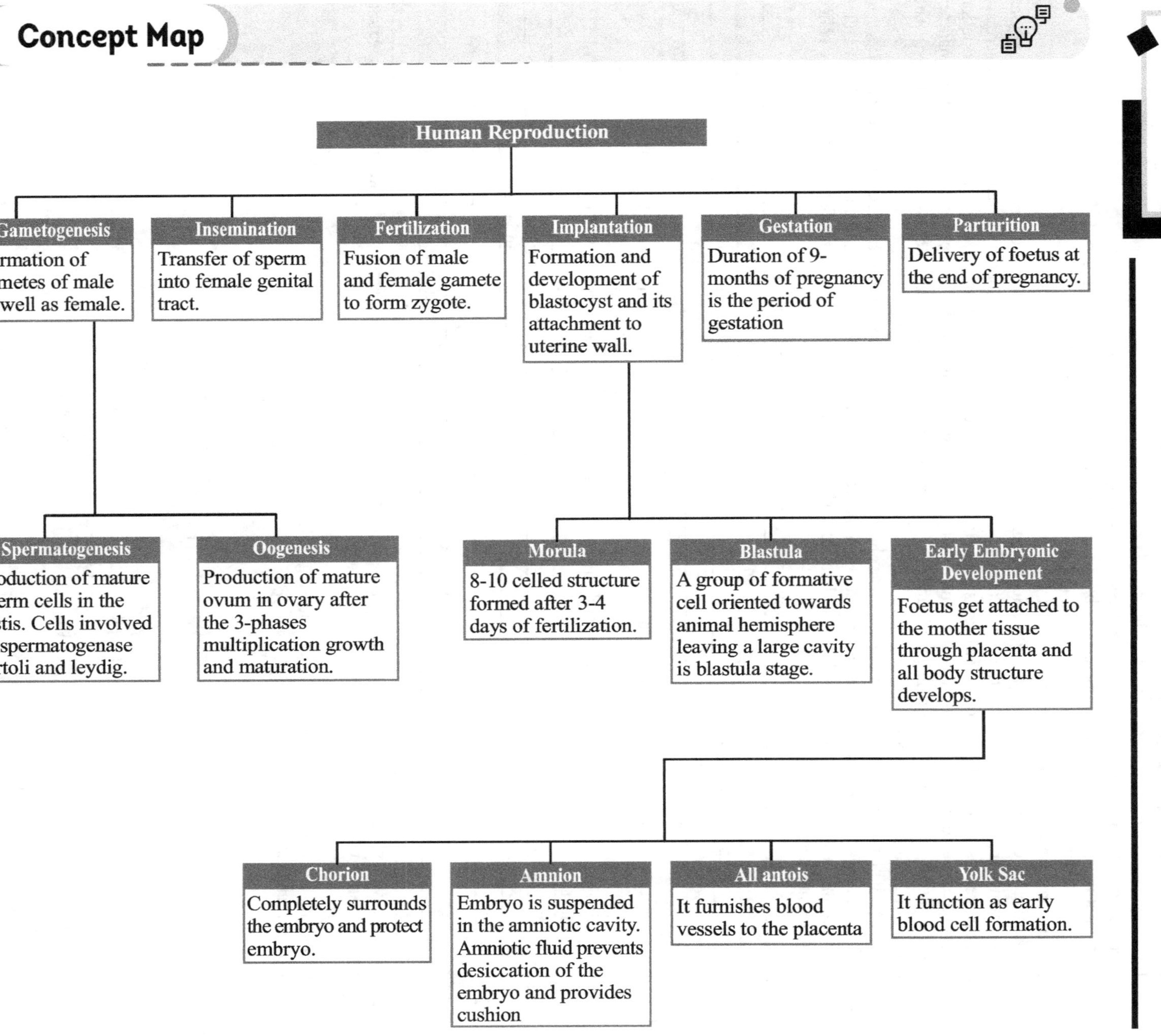

Topic 1   Male and female Reproductive Systems

Reproduction is the ability of living organisms to produce a new offspring similar to themselves. It is one of the fundamental characteristics of life. Reproduction are broadly classified as **asexual reproduction** and **sexual reproduction**. The organisms, thus, either reproduce asexually or sexually or through both these methods. Human are **unisexual** and **viviparous**.

The major reproductive events in human beings are

(1)   Gametogenesis – Formation of gametes.

(2)   Insemination – Transfer of sperms into female genital tract.

(3)   Fertilization – Fusion of male and female gametes leading to formation of zygote.

(4)   Implantation – Formation and development of blastocyst and its attachment to the uterine wall.

(5)   Gestation – Embryonic development; gestation is the time from conception to birth.

(6)   Parturition – Delivery of baby (the process of birth).

These reproductive events occur after puberty (period when reproductive organs starts functioning) and start secreting sex hormones which bring about development of secondary sex organs and appearance of secondary sexual characters. There are important differences between the reproductive events in the male and in the female, for example, in old age the sperm formation continuous in men, but formation of ovum stops in women. Testis are male gonads and produce male gametes (sperms) and male sex hormones (testosterone). Ovaries are female gonads and produce female gametes (ova) and female sex hormones (estrogen). The gonads are called **primary sex organs**.

The organs which neither produce gametes nor secretes sex hormones but perform important functions in reproduction are termed as secondary sex organs. The latter include the prostate, seminal vesicles, vasa deferentia and penis in male and fallopian tube, uterus, vagina and mammary glands in females. The characters which distinguish the male from the female externally are called **secondary sex characters**.

Table : Secondary sex characters in man and woman

	Character	Man	Woman
1.	General build up	More muscular	Less muscular
2.	Aggressiveness	More marked	Less marked
3.	Hair growth		
	(i) Facial	Beard, moustache present	Absent
	(ii) Axillary	Present	Present
	(iii) Pubic	Hair distribution more lateral and upwards towards	Upward growth not so marked and is
	(iv) Chest	Present	Absent
4.	Mammary glands	Undeveloped	Well developed
5.	Skin	More hairy and coarse	Less hairy and coarse
6.	Shoulder	Broad	Not broad
7.	Pelvis	Not broad	More broad
8.	Larynx	More apparent	Less apparent
9.	Voice	Low pitched	High pitched

Male reproductive system performs two major functions – spermatogenesis and transfer of sperm. It is located in the pelvis region. It consists of mainly three parts –

(i)   Primary sex organs *i.e.* a pair of testis.

(ii)   Secondary sex organ *i.e.* duct system & associated glands.

(iii) External genitalia.

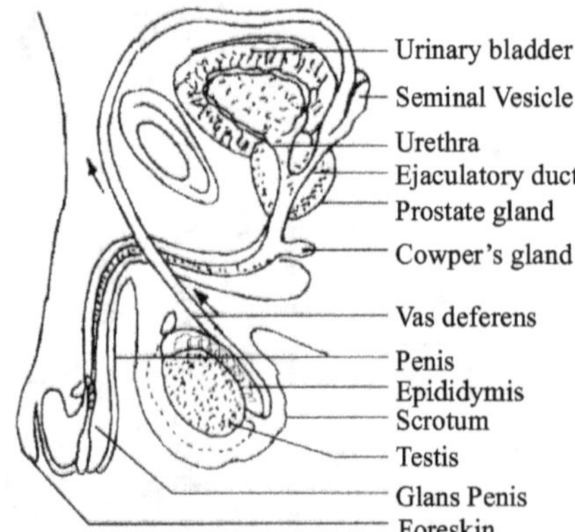

Fig. : Human male reproductive system

Testis

It is situated outside the abdominal cavity within a pouch called **scrotum**. Scrotum helps in providing optimal temperature ($2 - 2.5°C$ lower than normal body temperature) for sperm formation. Each testis is oval in shape. It is $4 - 5$ cm long & $2 - 3$ cm wide. Each testis is surrounded by a membranous covering of mesodermal origin called Tunica vaginalis. The inner coating of testis consists of white to brown connective tissue and is called Tunica fibrasa or T. albuginea it is protective in nature. Each testis has 250 compartment called testicular lobules. Each testicular lobules contain $1 - 3$ seminiferous tubules. Seminiferous tubule is the site of sperm formation by a process called spermatogenesis. In each seminiferous tubules two types of cells are present – male germ cells (spermatogonia) & sertoli cells. Spermatogonia undergo meiosis and form sperms while sertoli cells (also called subtentacular cells) provide nutrition to the germs cells. There is a space between seminiferous tubules, this space is called interstitial space & contain small blood vessel & interstitial cells or leydig cells. Leydig cells synthesise & secrete male sex hormones called androgens (testosterone).

Secondary Sex Organs

Male sex accessory ducts include rete testis, vasa efferentia, epididymis, a vas deferens, and an ejaculatory duct. The seminiferous tubules of the testis opens into the vasa efferentia through rete testis. **Vasa efferentia** leave the testis & open into epididymis located along the posterior surface of each testis. The **epididymis** leads to vas deferens that ascends to the abdomen & loops over the urinary bladder. It receives a duct from seminal vesicle & opens into urethra as the ejaculatory duct. These ducts store & transport the sperms from the testis to the outside through urethra. The **urethra** originates from the urinary bladder & extends through the penis to its external opening called urethral meatus.

External genitalia

The penis is the male external genitalia. It is a common pathway for passage of urine and semen. The penis contains three cylindrical masses of erectile tissue two dorsal corpora cavernous and one ventral corpus spongiosum. The corpus sponglosum, which contains the penile urethra is enlarged at the distal end of the penis to form glans penis. The glans (enlarged end of penis) covered by a loose fold of skin called **foreskin**. It is made up of special tissue that helps in erection of the penis to facilitate insemination.

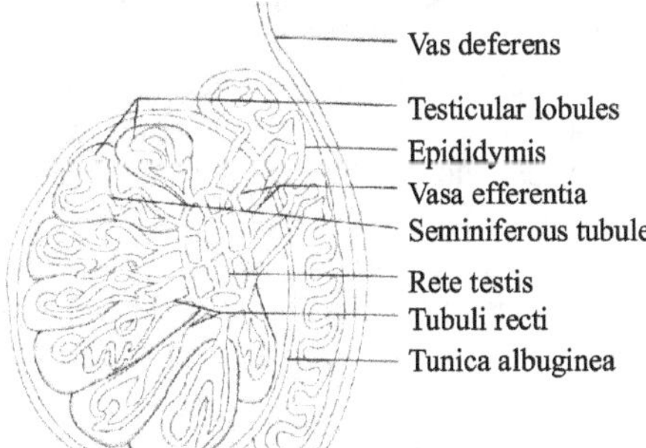

Fig. : Testis – internal structure

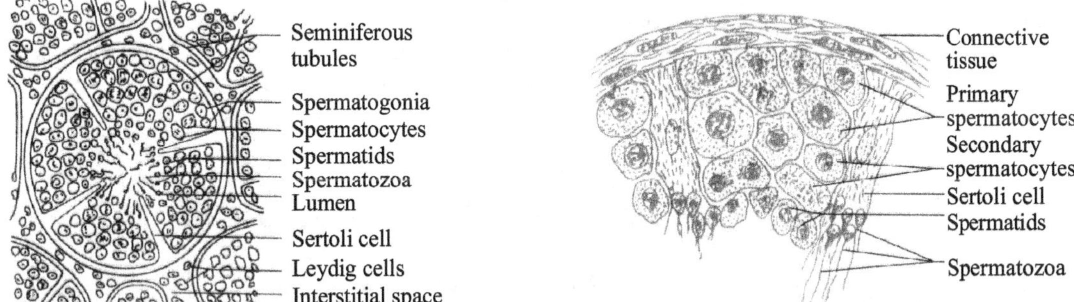

Fig. : T. S. of testis – a portion   **Fig. : T.S. of a seminiferous tubule (a portion enlarged)**

The male accessory glands include paired seminal vesicles a prostate and paired bulbourethral glands.

Seminal Vesicles

Seminal vesicles are 5 cm. long sac like glands lined by epithelium. Its walls contain muscles fibres and its excretory ducts open in ejaculatory duct. It contribute major portion of the seminal fluid. It provide, fructose, electrolytes and prostaglandins. It is remnant of mullerian duct and is also known as uterus masculina.

Prostate Glands

It lies at the base of the bladder & surrounds first part of the urethra. Secretion of the gland ejected during ejaculation. It contributes an alkaline component to the seminal fluid which adjusts vaginal pH and stimulates sperm motility.

Cowper's gland (bulbourethral gland) this gland is comparable to the bertholin's glands of females. It comprises 5% of the semen secretion. The semen or seminal plasma, mainly having fructose, calcium and certain enzymes is an alkaline fluid (pH - 7.4) and contain 100 million sperms per ml. About 3-5 ml semen is produced per ejaculation.

FEMALE REPRODUCTIVE SYSTEM

The female reproductive system includes the ovaries, fallopian tube, uterus, vagina, accession glands and external genital organ. It is located in the abdomen & pelvis region. Different parts of female reproductive system can be categorise as:

It consists of mainly three parts –

(i)   Primary sex organs i.e., a pair of ovaries.

(ii)   Secondary sex organs i.e., oviducts, uterus, vagina & associated glands.

(iii)   External genitalia.

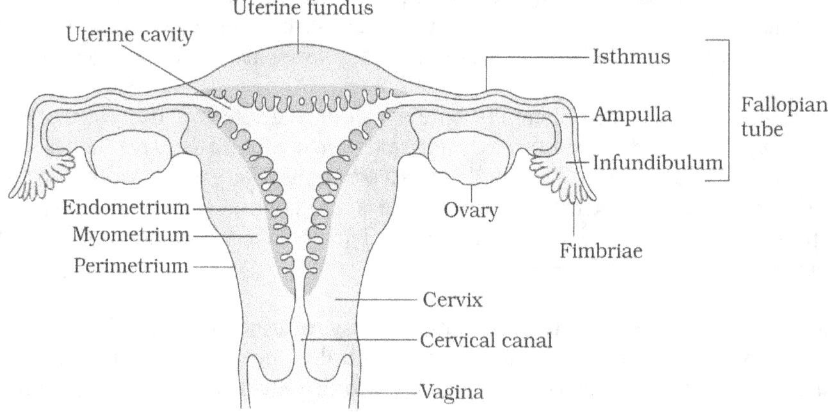

Fig. : Female reproductive system

Ovary

Ovaries, the primary sex organs in human female responsible for producing female sex hormones (estrogen, progesterone etc.) and gamete (ova). The ovaries are attached to the abdominal wall by an ovarian ligament called mesovarium. The region of attachment is called hilis. Ovary is located one on each side of the lower abdomen. The ovaries are attached to the abdominal wall by an ovarian ligaments. Each ovary is covered by a thin epithelium which encloses the ovarian stroma. The stroma is divided into two zones – a peripheral **cortex** & an inner **medulla**. Scattered throughout the cortex are many rounded or oval bodies, called ovarian or Graafian follicles at various stages of development. The medulla is a loose connective tissue with abundant blood vessels, lymphatic vessels & nerve fibres. Each follicle contains a large ovum surrounded by many layers of follicle cells. The follicle cells of a maturing follicle secrete estrogens into the blood. Every month the most mature ovum from one ovary is released. At birth female's ovaries contain 2 million follicles, each with an ovum that has begun meiosis but which is arrested in prophase of the first meiotic division. At this stage the ova are called primary oocyte. Mature follicle has three distinct layer – outer theca externa (fibrous) middle theca interna (cellular) and inner membrana granulosa. A female child at birth possess 800000 follicles in ovaries, but about 400 mature and discharge their ova, the rest undergo degeneration. In the cortex both young & mature follicles along with a mass of yellow cells called **corpus luteum** is also present. Corpus luteum contain a yellow pigment lutein & secrete the hormone progesterone during pregnancy & hormone relaxin toward the end of pregnancy. The ovarian cortex may have a white body or **corpus albicans** which represents a degenerating corpus luteum.

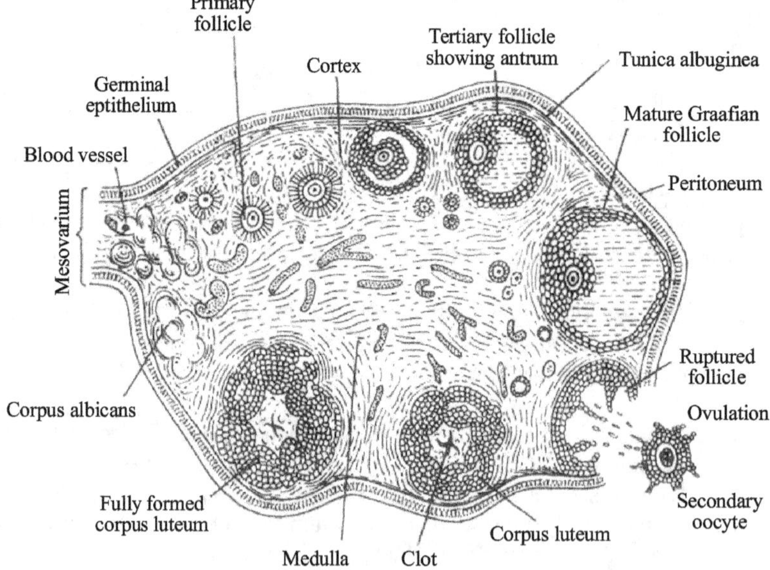

Fig. : A section of a mammalian ovary

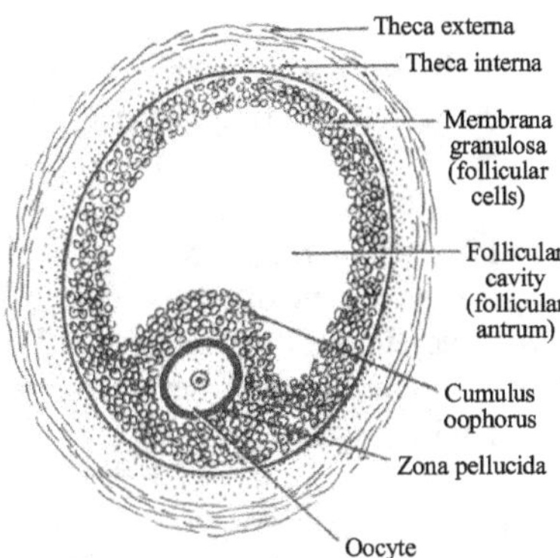

Fig. : Mature Graafian follicle

Secondary Sex Organs

Oviducts (Fallopian Tubes)

Each oviducts extends from the periphery of each ovary to uterus. Each tube is 100 mm long. The oviducts is divided into four regions infundibulum, ampulla, isthmus and uterine part.

(i)   **Infundibulum :** It is the broad, funnel shaped proximal part. Its margin bears motile, finger like processes called **fimbriae**. Fimbriae helps in collection of the ovum after ovulation. It leads to a wider part of the oviduct called ampulla.

(ii)   **Ampulla :** It is long, wide & major part of the fallopian tube next to the infundibulum. It is the site of fertilization.

(iii)   **Isthmus:** It is the very short, narrow thick walled straight part that follows the ampulla.

(iv)   **Uterine part :** It is narrow duct that passes through the uterine wall and communicates with the uterine cavity.

Uterus (Womb)

It is located between the urinary bladder and the rectum. It is attached to the body wall by a double fold of peritoneum, the mesometrium. Its shape is like an inverted pear.

The wall of uterus has three layers of tissue –

(i)   The external thin membranous **perimetrium**.

(ii)   Middle thick layer of smooth muscle **myometrium**.

(iii)   Inner glandular layer called **endometrium**.

The endometrium undergoes cyclical changes during menstrual cycle. The myometrium exhibits strong contraction during delivery of the baby. The uterus receives embryo & provide optimal conditions for its survival & growth. The uterus expels the young one at its birth. The uterus opens into vagina through a narrow **cervix**. The cavity of the cervix is called **cervical canal** which alongwith vagina forms the **birth canal**.

Vagina

Vagina is a fibromuscular tube stretching from the uterus to the vestibule. It is meant to receive male's penis during copulation & also allow menstrual flow. The opening of vagina is often covered partially by a membrane called hymen and its presence or absence is not a reliable indicator of virginity or sexual experience. Beside that it is also a part of birth canal.

External Genitalia (Vulva)

Vulva include mons pubis, labia majora, labia minora, hymen & clitoris. Mons pubis is a cushion of fatty tissue covered by skin & pubic hair. The **labia majora** are fleshy folds of tissue, which extend down from the mons pubis and surround the vaginal opening. The **labia minora** are paired folds of tissue under the labia majora. In the upper most angle of the vulva, in front of urethral opening is located a small erectile clitoris which is highly sensitive as it contains numerous sensory nerve endings for touch and pressure. The **clitoris** is a female homologue of the male penis.

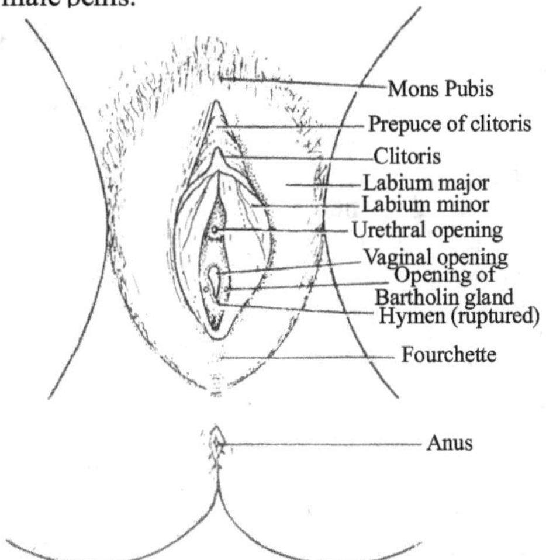

Fig. : The external genitalia in the female

Bartholin's Glands

It is also known as **vestibular glands**. A pair of Bartholin's glands occur on each side of the vaginal orifice. These glands correspond to the Cowper's glands of the male & are round in shape. It secrete a clear, viscid fluid under sexual excitement. This fluid serves as a lubricant during copulation.

Mammary Glands

A functional mammary gland is characteristic of all female mammals. Mammary glands (breasts) are paired structures that contain glandular tissue & variable amount of fat. The glandular tissue of each breast is divided into 15-20 mammary lobes containing clusters of cells called alveoli. The cells of alveoli secrete milk which is stored in the cavities of alveoli. The alveoli open into mammary tubules. The mammary tubules join to form a mammary duct. Several mammary duct join to form a wider mammary ampulla which is connected to lactiferous duct through which milk is sucked out.

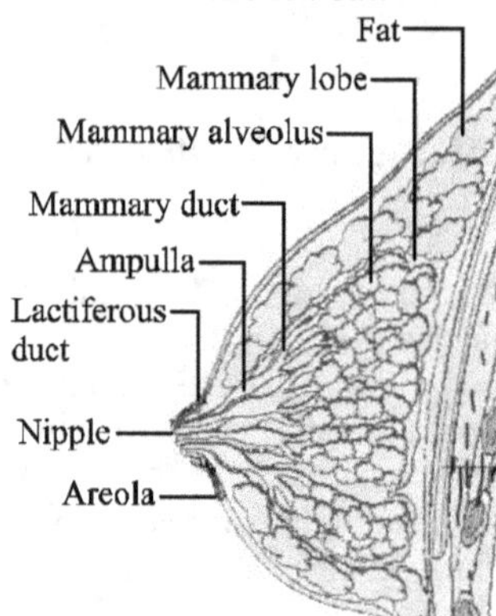

Fig. : Mammary glands

Practice Exercise-1

Multiple Choice Questions

1. If proximal centriole of mature sperm is destroyed. Which of the following is going to be affected?
   (a) Motility (b) Fertilization
   (c) Cleavage (d) None of these

2. Which of the following is a transporting tube leading from the bladder to which brings urine outside the body *via* penis?
   (a) Urethra (b) Epididymis
   (c) Ejaculatory duct (d) Urethra meatus

3. Read the following statement and answer the question.
   "The urethra originates from a structure (called 'X') and extends through the male external genitalia (called 'Y' which helps in introducing semen into the vagina) to its external opening called urethral meatus."
   Identify X and Y.
   (a) X - Urinary bladder ; Y - Penis
   (b) X - Vas efferentia ; Y - Penis
   (c) X - Ejaculatory duct ; Y - Ureter
   (d) X - Bulbourethral gland ; Y - Ureter

4. A sac shaped like an upside down pear with a thick lining and muscles in the pelvic area where a fertilized egg or zygote comes to grow into a baby is called ________.
   (a) oviduct (b) uterus
   (c) vagina (d) vulva

5. Bartholin's glands are situated
   (a) on the either side of vagina in humans
   (b) on either side of vas deferens in humans
   (c) on either side of penis in humans
   (d) on either side of Fallopian tube in humans.

6. Which of the following is not a uterine function?
   (a) Waste removal for the developing embryo.
   (b) Nutritional support of the growing embryo.
   (c) Place of fusion of male and female gametes.
   (d) Mechanical protection of the developing embryo.

Match the following

7. In the given columns, column-I contain structures of female reproductive system and column-II contain its feature. Select the correct match from the option given below.

Column-I (Structures of female reproductive system)		Column-II (Features)
A.	Ampulla	I. It undergoes cyclical changes during menstrual cycle.
B.	Labia majora	II. It helps in collection of ovum after ovulation.
C.	Oviduct	III. Wider part of fallopian tube where fusion of male and female gametes takes place.
D.	Fimbriae	IV. Larger hairy folds which extend down from the mons pubis and surrounds the vaginal opening.
E.	Endometrium	V. Also called fallopian tubes, which extend from the periphery of each ovary to the womb.

(a) A – I; B – II; C – III; D – V; E – IV
(b) A – III; B – I; C – II; D – V; E – IV
(c) A – III; B – IV; C – V; D – II; E – I
(d) A – II; B – IV; C – III; D – V; E – I

8. In the given columns, column I contain structures of male reproductive system and column II contains its feature. Select the correct match from the options given below.

Column I (Structure of Male Reproductive System)		Column II (Features)
A.	Seminiferous tubule	I. Network of seminiferous tubule
B.	Rete testis	II. Secondary sexual characters
C.	Leydig cells	III. Meiosis and sperm formation occurs
D.	Prepuce	IV. Place of implantation
		V. Terminal skin of penis

(a) A – I; B – II; C – III; D – V
(b) A – III; B – I; C – II; D – V
(c) A – III; B – I; C – IV; D – II
(d) A – II; B – IV; C – III; D – V

Assertion & Reason Questions

DIRECTIONS (Qs. 9-12) : *Each of these questions contains an assertion followed by reason. Read them carefully and answer the question on the basis of following options. You have to select the one that best describes the two statements.*

(a) If both Assertion and Reason are correct and the Reason is a correct explanation of the Assertion.
(b) If both Assertion and Reason are correct but Reason is not a correct explanation of the Assertion.
(c) If the Assertion is correct but Reason is incorrect.
(d) If both Assertion and Reason are incorrect.

9. **Assertion:** The male reproductive system is located in the pelwious region and it includes a pair of testes along with accessory dutcts, glands and external genitalia.
   Reason: The testes of human males are situated inside the abdominal cavity within a pouch called rectum.

10. **Assertion:** The ovaries are located one on each side of the lower abdomen and each ovary is about 2-4 cm in length and is connected to the pelvic wall and uterus by ligaments.
    Reason: Each ovary is covered by a thick epithelium which encloses the ovarian stroma and the stroma is divided into two zones viz peripheral medulla and an inner cortex.

11. **Assertion:** Male urethra is also called urinogenital duct.
    Reason: The male urethra carries both urine and sperms.

12. **Assertion:** The female reproductive system consist of a pair of ovaries along with a pair of oviducts, uterus, cervix, vagina and the external genitalia located in pelvic.
    Reason: The female reproductive parts along with a pair of the mammary glands are integrated structurally and functionally to support the processes of ovulation, fertilisation, pregnancy, birth and child care.

Passage/Case Based Questions

DIRECTIONS (Qs. 13-15) : *Read the following passage and answer the questions that follow.*

Refer the diagram given below of human sperm and answer the questions that follows-

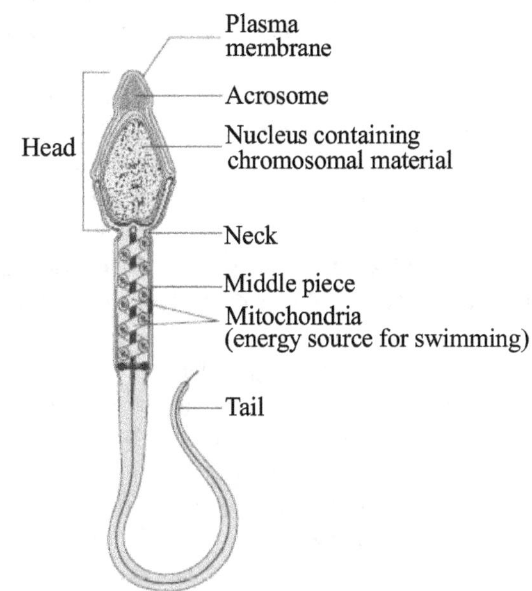

13. State the significance of cap like structure called acrosome on the human sperm.
14. What are the roles of proximal centriole in the neck region of sperm?
15. What do you understand by semen?

Very Short Answer Question

16. Sperms have a tail, whereas egg do not. Why so?

Short Answer Questions

17. Define puberty ?
18. What is reproduction ?
19. What is sexual reproduction ?
20. What is the benefit of sexual reproduction ?
21. What does employ human reproduction ?
22. What is the position of testes in the body ?
23. Give a detailed account of male sex hormones.
24. Why do testes of mammals descend in the scrotum ?
25. Where is female reproductive system situated in the body?
26. What is ovarian cycle ?
27. What is the internal structure of uterus ?
28. What name will identify the external female genitals ?
29. Write the function of seminal vesicles.
30. Mention the function of scrotum?
31. Differentiate secondary sexual characters in male and female?

Topic 2 Gametogenesis, Mensuration, Human Development

GAMETOGENESIS

It is the process of production of gametes in the primary sex organs. The production of sperm called spermatozoons and the production of ova (female gametes) from ovary is called ogenesis.

Spermatogenesis

Production of mature sperm cell in the testis is known as spermatogenesis. It starts at the age of puberty. It occurs in seminiferous tubules. Cells involved in spermatogenesis are – sertoli cells & Leydig cells.

Spermatogonia (2N) divide mitotically into primary spermatocytes (2N), which divide by meiosis-I into secondary spermatocytes (1N). Secondary spermatocytes (1N), divides by meiosis -II into spermatids (1N) which are transformed into spermatozoa (1N) by **spermiogenesis**. After spermiogenesis, sperm heads become embedded in the **Sertoli cells**, and are finally released from the seminiferous tubules by the process called **spermiation**. Each spermatozoan or sperm is a long, flagellated, motile cell.

Structive of Sperm : Sperm is a microscopic structure consisting of four parts head, neck middle piece and tail. Head consists of large posterior haploid nucleus and a small anterior cap-like acrosome. Acrosome contains proteolytic and lysosomal enzymes, popularly called sperm lysis, e.g, hyaluronidase, corona penetrating enzyme, crosin and zona lysine. Neck is present between the head and middle piece. Neck region contains centriole, middle piece is a long cylindrical part of sperm which lies between the neck and tail. Axoneme or axial filament of mitochondrial runs through it. The same is covered by a mitochondrial spiral of 10-14 turns Mitochondial activity helps in providing energy. The distal ends bears a ring centriole or annulus of uncertain role. Tail is very long slender and tapering and is formed of cytoplasm.

Significance of spermatogenesis

(i)   One spermatogonium produces four sperms.

(ii) Sperms have half number of chromosomes.

(iii) After fertilization the diploid chromosomes number is restored in zygote. It maintains the chromosome numbers.

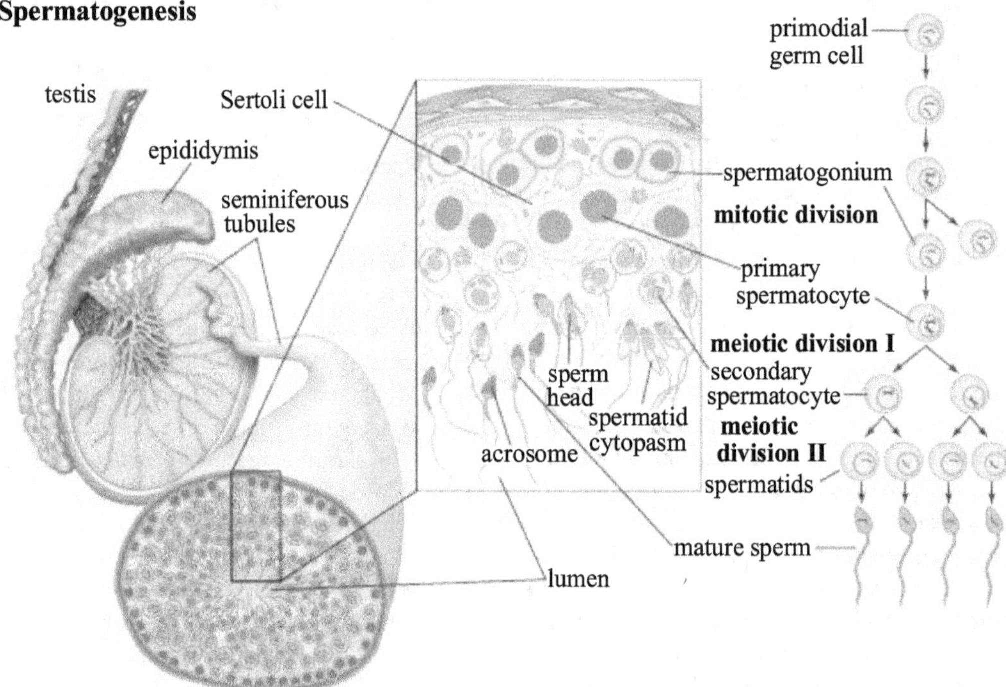

Fig. : Spermatogenesis

Hormonal control of Spermatogenesis :
Spermatogenesis starts at the age of puberty due to significant increase in the secretion of gonadotropin releasing hormone (GNRH). The increased levels of GnRH then acts at the anterior pituitary gland and stimulate secretion of two gonadotropins – luteinising hormone (LH) and follicle stimulating hormone (FSH).
LH acts at the Leydig cells and stimulates synthesis and secretion of androgens. Androgens, in turn, stimulate the process of spermatogenesis. FSH acts on the Sertoli cells and stimulates secretion of some factors which help in the process of spermiogenesis.

$$\text{Hypothalamus} \xrightarrow{\text{GnRH}} \text{Anterior pituitary} \rightarrow \begin{cases} \text{FSH} \rightarrow \text{Sertoli cell} \xrightarrow{\text{Factor}} \text{Spermiogenesis} \\ \text{LH} \rightarrow \text{Interstitial cell} \\ \qquad\qquad\quad \downarrow \\ \text{Androgen} \rightarrow \text{Spermatogenesis} \end{cases}$$

The human male ejaculates about 200 to 300 million sperms during a coitus of which, for normal fertility, at least 60 per cent sperms must have normal shape and size and at least 40 per cent of them must show vigorous motility. Sperms released from the seminiferous tubules, are transported by the accessory ducts. Secretions of epididymis, vas deferens, seminal vesicle and plasma along with the sperms constitute the **semen**. The functions of male sex accessory ducts and glands are maintained by the testicular hormones (androgens).

Oogenesis
It occurs in ovary and is also completed in three phases.
1.   Multiplication phase   2.   Growth phase   3.   Maturation phase
As in testis, in ovaries also, the primordial germ cells are extra-gonadal in origin. In human these cells originate from embryonic mesoderm and via yolk sac migrate to the ovary. In many other vertebrates, these germ cells are endodermal in origin. In Oogenesis, the phase, comparable to **spermiogenesis** is absent and the ootid can be directly named as ovum.

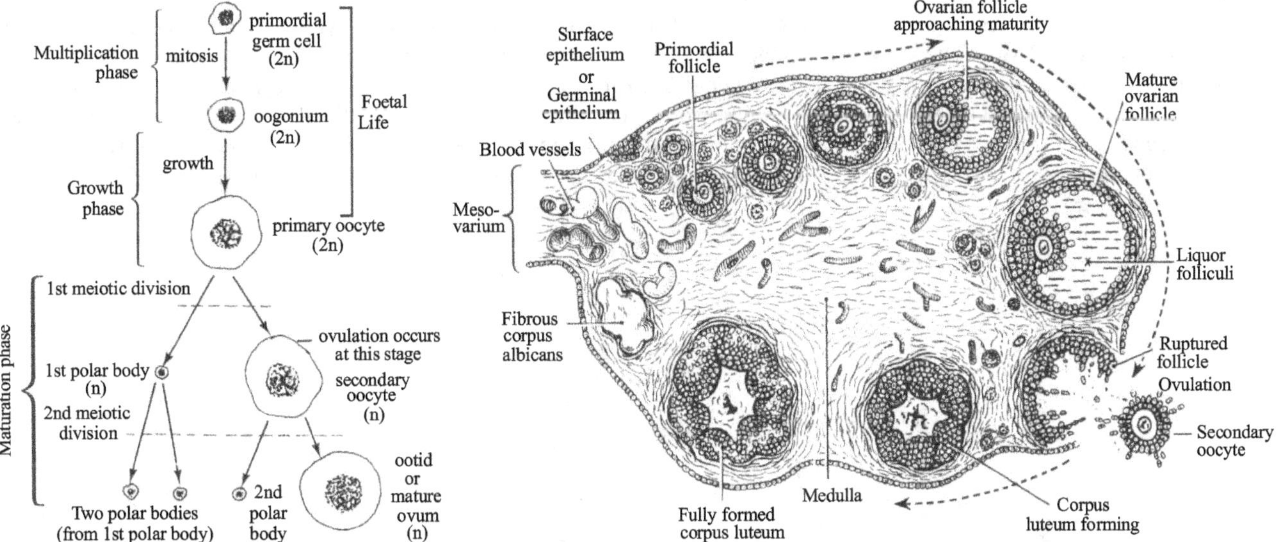

Fig. : Diagrammatic representation of oogensis   **Fig. : C. S. of ovary showing oogenesis and formation of corpus luteum**

1.   **Multiplication phase -**
      This phase, from beginning to the end, is completed before birth (in foetus). First the primordial germ cells divide by mitotic division and form a large number of Oogonia. These Oogonia get surrounded by follicular cells, derived from germinal epithelium (better called surface epithelium), of ovary. The follicle cells keep on multiplying inside ovary and the size of ovarian follicle increases. The mature follicles in the ovary of mammals are called **Graafian follicles**. A large number of these follicles degenerate during the phase from birth to puberty, only 60,000-80,000 primary follicles are left in each ovary.

2.   **Growth phase -**
      In this phase, which also begins during foetal life, the Oogonia increase in size and are now known as primary oocytes. The number of primary Oocyte at birth ranges from 3-4 lakhs. Growth phase continues upto puberty and the number of follicles left at this stage is only ~2 lakhs. The rest of the follicles start degenerating (**Follicular atresia**). Such ovarian follicles are disposed off by phagocytosis. Some group of cells in connective tissue of ovary (stroma), around follicles become active. Such cells are called interstitial cells, and secrete a small amount of androgen.
      The follicle cells multiply by mitotic divisions to form several layers. The development of 'antrum' cavity amongst the follicle cells, differentiates inner follicular layer (cumulus / cumulus oophoricus) from outer follicular layer. The fluid secreted in the antrum by follicles cells is called liquor folliculi. The two follicular layers remain connected through a stalk/pedicel of follicle cells. The outer follicular layer is called stratum granulosum (later, theca interna). It is the layer whose cells (granulosa cells) secrete estrogen during follicular phase of menstrual cycle.

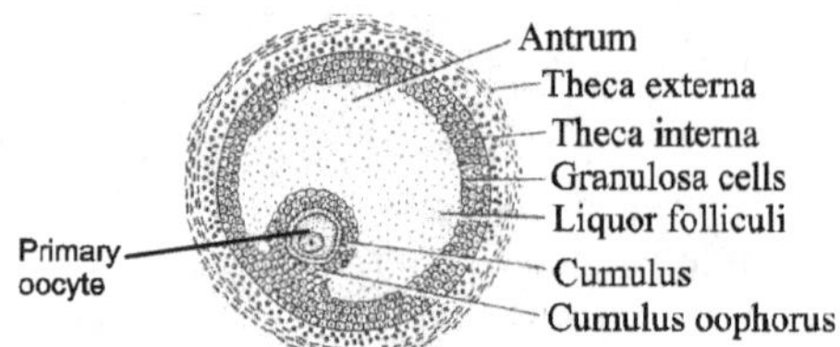

Fig. : A mature graafian follicle

Outside plasma membrane, the **vitelline membrane** is secreted between primary Oocyte and the inner follicular layer. In mammals the thick vitelline membrane is known as **zona pellucida**. It is transparent and non-cellular, and is composed of glycoproteins. The space between plasma membrane and vitelline membrane is called **perivitelline space**.

Size of nucleus (amount of nuclear sap) and the amount of cytoplasm increases. The nucleus during growth phase is so big that it is named as germinal vesicle. The preparations for meiosis begin during growth phase. The chromosomes for the longest duration remain in diplotene stage. Due to uncoiling of DNA the transverse loops develop, and the chromosome are now called as **'Lamp brush chromosome'**. The RNA transcription at uncoiled loops of DNA is faster, and a large amount of RNAs is synthesized. As the amount of rRNA increases, the number of nucleoli also increases (In frogs' Oocyte the number of nucleoli is > 600). The synthesis of yolk (vitellogenesis) in vertebrates also occurs during this phase. In most of the vertebrates the yolk is synthesized in liver and reaches primary Oocyte through blood and follicle cells.

3. **Maturation phase -**

    During this stage the germinal vesicle loses nuclear sap and all RNAs to become smaller and compact. This diploid nucleus now moves toward periphery and 1st part of the meiosis (reduction division) begins. This division is very much unequal. The outer smaller cell, released into perivitelline space is called **1st polar body** (polocyte), whereas the inner and larger cell (having all reserve food material) is called secondary Oocyte.

    Both the secondary oocyte and polar body are haploid structures. It is this secondary Oocyte (with one polar body) which is released during **ovulation**. The second part of the mieosis is an equational division which takes place only after the contact of sperm. The nucleus of secondary oocyte divides again to form another *i.e.*, 2nd polar body. The secondary Oocyte now becomes **Ootid**. As there is no metamorphosis in Ootid, the same may be called as ovum. Meanwhile the 1st polar body may also divide (as it usually does) into two polar bodies. The maximum number of polar bodies present with the ovum can be three.

    Human ovum, besides having 2 or 3 polar bodies, also has a covering of zona pellucida and **corona radiata**, the latter is the inner most layer of cumulus.

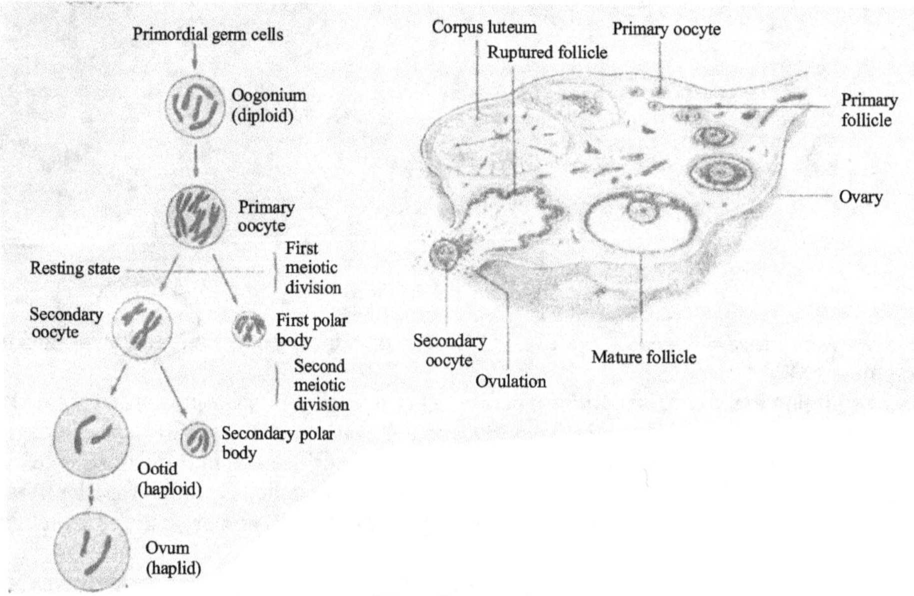

Fig. : Oogenesis

MENSTRUAL CYCLE

It involves cyclic changes in female's reproductive tract culminating in menstruation that is flow of cast off uterine and fallopian tube lining along with blood and tissue fluid through the vagina.

In non-primate mammals there is **estrous cycle**. During breeding season, in estrous cycle, the level of estrogen rises in blood and it causes sex urge. This period is also known as **heat period**. The number of breeding seasons may be different in different animals. The suspension of estrous cycle is called **anestrum**.

Menstrual cycle consists of **Menstrual phase**, **proliferative phase** (follicular phase) and **secretory phase** (Luteal phase).

In follicular phace there is development of follicles in ovary this phase is also called as proliferative phase as there is proliferation of endometrium in uterus.

1. **Follicular phase** – In follicular please there is development of follicles in ovary This phase is also called as proliferative phase as there is proliferation of endometrium in uterus. It last for about 14 days. Lining of the uterus and fallopian tubes proliferates. A graafian follicle grows, matures and secretes oestrogen. It ruptures to release its egg (secondary oocyte) after about 14 days. The secretion of gonadotropins (LH and FSH) increases gradually during the follicular phase, and stimulates follicular development as well as secretion of estrogens by the growing follicles.

   Both LH and FSH attain a peak level in the middle of cycle (about 14th day). Rapid secretion of LH leading to its maximum level during the mid-cycle called LH surge induces rupture of Graafian follicle and thereby the release of ovum (**ovulation**). The follicular phase ends with ovulation.

2. **Luetal phase** – It lasts for about 10 days. The empty graafian follicle forms corpus luteum which secretes progesterone. The lining of uterus and fallopian tubes undergoes further hypertrophy which is necessary for implantation of the fertilised ovum and other events of pregnancy.

   The rising level of progesterone, by feed back mechanism, inhibits the secretion of LH and gonadotropin releasing hormone. When the progesterone level drops, the corpus luteum begins to degenerate and transforms from yellow to a white body, called corpus albicans. The persistence of corpus luteum for about 12-14 days (if fertilization does not occur) is called luteal phase. When corpus luteum degenerates fully the endometrium begins to break down. The blood vessels and mucus glands rupture. The blood, mucus and endometrium cells, all pass out from the uterus to outside as menstrual flow. This takes 3-5 days, and after this the maturation of Graafian follicle under FSH restarts. Menstrual (Bleeding) phase – It lasts for about 4 days. If fertilization does not occur, the corpus luteum degenerate, and the lining of uterus and fallopian tubes breakdown, resulting in menstrual flow. Menstruation only occurs if the released ovum is not fertilised. Lack of menstruation may be indicative of pregnancy. However, it may also be caused due to some other underlying causes like stress, poor health etc. This occurs after 25 days and continues 3 to 5 days. The basal part of endometrial lining remain intact during menstruation and produces new uterine lining.

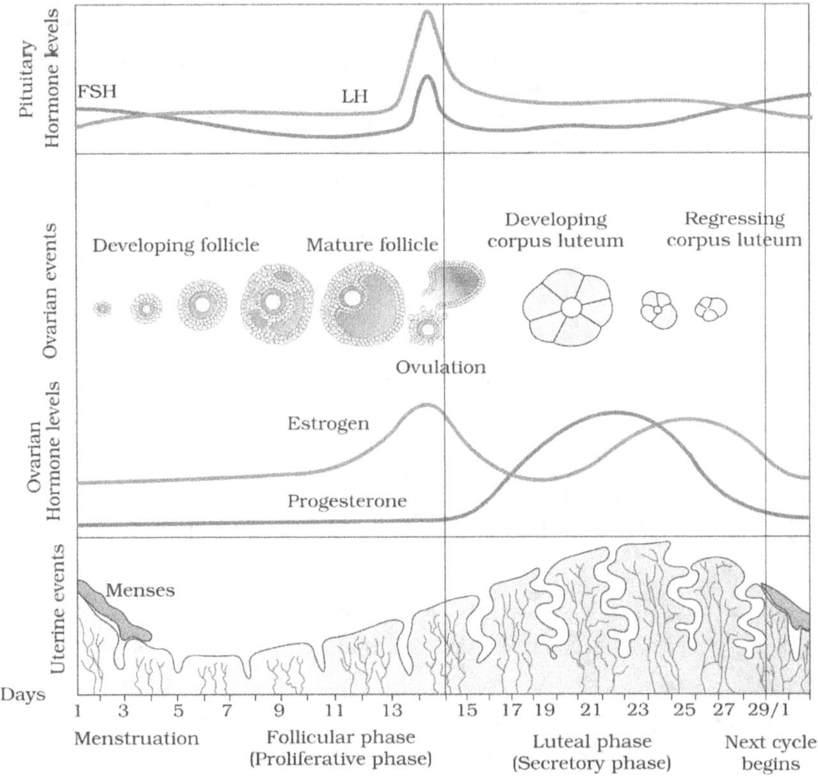

Fig. : Diagrammatic presentation of various events during menstrual cycle

HUMAN DEVELOPMENT

1. Egg :

The egg in human is microlecithal, homolecithal/ isolecithal and Regulative type. Its size is less than 0.1 mm. The plasma membrane of it is surrounded by a non- cellular, transparent and secretory coating, called **zona Pellucida** (in non- mammals this coating is called Vitelline membrane). The zona pellucida is surrounded by a cellular layer (consisting of follicle cells), called **corona radiata.**

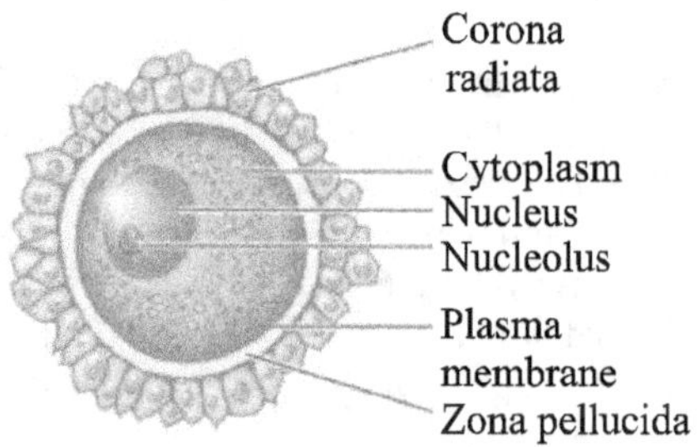

Fig. : Unfertilized egg

2. Fertilization

During copulation, the semen is transferred into the vagina of female body, the process called insemination The motile sperms move through the cervix, enter the uterus and reach the ampullary-isthmic junction of the fallopian tube. The ovum released from the ovary also reaches the ampullary-isthmic junction, where fertilization takes place. Both, the sperms and the eggs have short fertility and survival periods. If one of the 2- gametes is delayed in reaching the site, the fertilization will not be successful. The secretions of the female genital tract remove coating substances deposited on the surface of the sperms particularly those on the acrosome. Thus the receptor site on the acrosome are exposed and sperm become active to penetrate the egg. This phenomenon of sperm activation in mammals is known as capacitation.

In contact with the surface of egg covering, the acrosome releases its contained hydrolytic enzymes also called sperm lysin. It is known as acrosomal reaction. Important sperm lysin are hyaluronidase, corona penetrating enzymes and zona lysin or acrosin. Hyaluronidase dissolves the cementing substances of corona cells resulting in their seperation. Corona penetating enzymes bring about degeneration of obstructing corona cells. As the sperm head reaches zona pellucida compatibility reaction occer which results in emptying of acrosome and degeneration of zona pellucida by acrosn or zona lysin. Compatibility reaction is determined by special protein present over zona pellucida and sperm surface. They are collectively called fertilizin, in case of egg and antifertilizin in case of sperm.

Binding of the sperm to the egg induces depolarization of the egg plasma memberane. Immediate after the fusion of sperm and egg plasma memberane, the egg shows a cortical reaction to further check the entry of more sperms. The egg extends around the entering sperm finger-like processes, called micro-villi which constitute a fertilization cone. The latter takes the entire sperm into the egg. The sperm entry stimulates the egg (secondary oocyte) to haploid mature ovum and a second poler body. Mixing up of the chromosomes of a spermatozoan and an ovum is called kanyogamy. This complete the act of fertilization. The ovum in now a diploid cell having 23 pairs of chromosomes and is termed zygote.

3. Cleavages :

The cleavage in human zygote is equal Holoblastic and the fate of the cleaving cells is not predetermined (Indeterminate type). The pattern of cleavages in human egg is Radial.

1st Cleavage is normal meridional and two equal sized cells are formed. It occurs about 15 hours after fertilization. (As the fertilization occurs in Ampullary-Isthmic junction of fallopian tube or uterine duct, the cleavage also begins from this region and its process is completed when the egg reaches uterus.)

In 2nd cleavage one cell divides meridionally and other equatorially . This type of cleavage is called Rotational cleavage. The subsequent cleavages are asynchronous i.e. all the blastomere do not divide at the same time and odd number of cells may occur.

After 8-celled stage the blastomere huddle together to form a compact mass of cells (compaction). A 8-16 celled structure, formed after 3-4 days of fertilization, is called morula. It is a solid ball-like structure resembling mulberry fruit. By the time embryo reaches morula stage the cells of corona radiata start eroding.

4. Blastula

During morula stage, the peripheral cells are separated from inner cells of the embryo. The peripheral layer forms trophoblast. The inner cell mass (group of formative cells) is oriented towards animal hemisphere leaving a large cavity, called blastocoel. This is called blastula stage and is about 5-days old. The number of cells in blastula ranges from 32 to 64. The blastula stage in mammals is known as Blastocyst.

[The formative cells (inner cell mass) form the embryo/foetus whereas the trophoblast layer forms extra embryonic membrane – chorion (a part of placenta). The inner cell mass also contains stem cells that have the potency to give rise to all the tissues and organs of the body]

After blastula stage the Zona pellucida also erodes (blastocyst hatches out of Zona-pellucida) and the trophoblast is exposed. Blastula reaches uterus and gets attached to the endometrium uterine wall; the attachment is called implantation. This attachment occurs when the embryo is 6 to 8 days old (after fertilization).

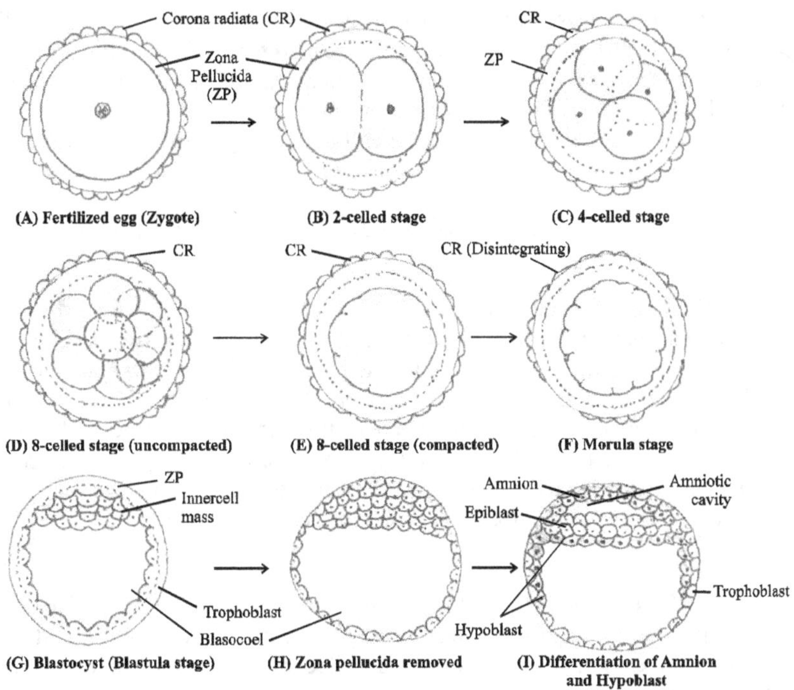

Fig. : Development stages of growing embryo

The trophoblast (future chorion) becomes syncytial to form synctiotrophoblast and digests endometrium lining of the uterus so that the embryo is completely embedded into the uterine wall.

The uterine tissue, below and above of the embryo, is now differentiated into **decidua basilaris** and **decidua capsularis**. The embryo now increases in size. The lining of uterus opposite to the site of implantation is called **decidua parietalis**.

5. Early Embryonic Development :

The outer cells of inner cell mass, close to trophoblast, differentiate into **Amnion**. The amnion secretes amniotic fluid which later acts as a shock absorber and prevents the embryo from mechanical injury and dehydration. The trophoblast now differentiates into **Chorion** (another extra embryonic membrane, after amnion). The chorion develops chorionic villi which penetrate into uterine tissue and later branch to almost fuse with maternal tissue. The structure formed jointly by foetal tissue and maternal tissue is called **Placenta**.

Later, during embryonic development, the Allantois (another extra embryonic membrane) arises as an outgrowth from the posterior part of gut, and its membrane gets fused with the chorionic membrane to form the *allantochorion* membrane. Due to the participation of allantois with chorion, the placenta in human is called **Allantochorion** placenta. The chorionic villi penetrate deep into blood vessel of uterus and since, they come in direct contact of blood, the placenta in human is also known as Haemochorial placenta.

After differentiation of ectoderm from outer part of inner cell mass and endoderm from inner part of inner cell mass, and the mesoderm, between the two layers; the structure becomes triploblastic (3- layered). All body structures develop from these three germ layers.

6. Later Embryonic/ Foetal Development :

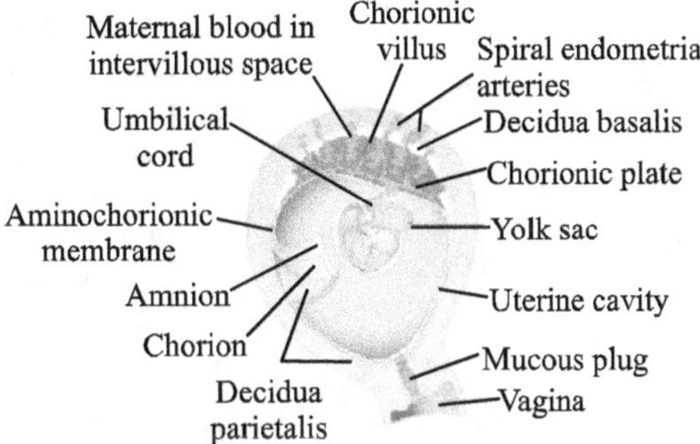

Fig. : Embryonic foetal development

The duration of about 9 months (266-days or 38 weeks) of pregnancy (Gestation period) can be divided into 3- trimesters. In I-Trimester (1st, 2nd & 3rd months or 12 weeks) the pharyngeal arches, endocrine glands like thyroid, parathyroid and thymus are well differentiated; the limbs with digits are well formed; external genitalia are formed; heart also develops after 1- month of pregnancy and starts beating. The crown to rump length (CR-length) of 2- months old embryo is ~ 2.5 cm.

In II-Trimester (4th, 5th & 6th months or 24 weeks) the movements in the body of foetus begin during 5th month. Though Head-hair also appear in 5th month but the body hair and eye-lashes develop by the end of II- trimester. The eye-lids also separate during this period.

In III- Trimester (7th, 8th and 9th months or 36/38 weeks) there starts fast growth in the preformed body organs.

7.   Parturition :

The expulsion or delivery of foetus at the end of pregnancy is called parturition or child birth. Before parturition there are vigorous contractions in uterus (labour pains) which are induced by a complex neuro endocrine mechanism. The signals for parturition originate from fully developed foetus & placenta and induce mild uterine contractions called foetal ejection reflex, which in turn triggers the release of oxytocin hormone from post. Lobe of pituitary of the mother. The oxytocin makes the contraction of uterine muscles stronger, which stimulates the further secretion of oxytocin. The stimulatory reflex between uterine contraction and oxytocin secretion continues resulting in expulsion of child, through birth canal. Now the umbilical cord is cut. The remaining part of umbilical cord and the placenta are expelled from the uterus little later, and is called after birth. To induce child expulsion the doctors inject oxytocin hormone.

LACTATION

Production of milk in the females breasts following the birth of a young one in mammals is called lactation. During pregnancy, the breast enlarges due to growth of mammary glands secretion of storage of milk beings after birth of the young one, usually within 24 hours, under the influence of protaine. the actual release of milk, called milk let down, requires the presence of oxytocin which brings about contraction of the smooth nuscles of the ducts within the mammary glands.

After birth, the breast first release is not milk but colostrum for 2 or 3 days. This is this, yellowish, fluid often called foremilk, It contains cells from the avleoili and is rich in protein antibodies, but logo in fat. Breast feeding during the initial fat. Breast feeding during the initial period of infant growth in recommender by doctors for bringing up a healthy body.

Practice Exercise-2

Multiple Choice Questions

1. In the process of spermatogenesis, first maturation division is called _______.
(a) mitotic division
(b) reduction division
(c) amitotic division
(d) None of the these

2. Level of which hormones are at their highest during the luteal phase (second half of the cycle) of the menstrual cycle?
(a) Estrogen
(b) Progesterone
(c) Luteinizing hormone
(d) Follicular stimulating hormone

3. What is the stage of oocyte at the time of ovulation?
(a) Propase stage of I-meiotic division
(b) Prophase stage of II-meiotic division
(c) Metaphase of I-meiotic division
(d) Metaphase of II-meiotic division

4. Primary germ layers are
(a) ectoderm and inner cell mass only.
(b) trophoblast, ectoderm and mesoderm.
(c) endoderm and mesoderm only.
(d) ectoderm, endoderm and mesoderm.

Match the following

5. In the given columns, column-I contain features of developing child and column-II contain the time of their occurrence. Select the correct match.

Column-I (Features of developing child)		Column-II (Time of there occurrence)
A.	Heart sound	I. By the end of the second month of pregnancy
B.	Foetus develops limbs and digit	II. During the fifth month
C.	Formation of major organ system	III. First sign of growing foetus
D.	First movement of foetus and appearance of hair on head	IV. By the end of 12 weeks
E.	Body covered with hair, eyelid separate, eyelashes are formed	V. By the end of 24 weeks

(a) A – I; B – II; C – III; D – IV; E – V
(b) A – III; B – I; C – IV; D – II; E – V
(c) A – II; B – I; C – III; D – V; E – IV
(d) A – III; B – IV; C – II; D – V; E – I

6. Match the column-I with column-II and select the correct option.

	Column-I		Column-II
A.	Fertilization	I.	Mitotic division
B.	Implantation	II.	Embryo with 8 to 16 blastomeres
C.	Cleavage	III.	Ampullary-isthmic junction
D.	Morula	IV.	Structure formed by the continuous division of 8 to 16 blastomeres
E.	Blastocysts	V.	Embedding of blastocysts in the endometrium

   (a)   A – I; B – II; C – IV; D – V; E – III
   (b)   A – III; B – I; C – IV; D – II; E – V
   (c)   A – III; B – V; C – I; D – IV; E – II
   (d)   A – III; B – V; C – I; D – II; E – IV

Assertion & Reason Questions

DIRECTIONS (Qs. 7-10) : *Each of these questions contains an assertion followed by reason. Read them carefully and answer the question on the basis of following options. You have to select the one that best describes the two statements.*

(a) If both Assertion and Reason are correct and the Reason is a correct explanation of the Assertion.

(b) If both Assertion and Reason are correct but Reason is not a correct explanation of the Assertion.

(c) If the Assertion is correct but Reason is incorrect.

(d) If both Assertion and Reason are incorrect.

7. **Assertion:** The reproductive cycle in the female primates (eg- monkey, apes and human being) is called menstrual cycle.
Reason: The first menstruation begin at puberty (12-13 years in girls) and is called menopause.

8. **Assetion:** Implantation occurs on 7th day after the fertilisation.
Reason: Fertilisation guarantees the establishment of pregnancy.

9. **Assertion:** Spermatogenesis requires 72-74 days to get completed.
Reason: Sperms reach the epididymis and stay there for 2-3 days for maturation i.e., to become motile.

10. **Assertion:** The oogonia are continuously formed and added after birth.
Reason: These cells start division and enter into prophase of the mitotic division and get temporarily arrested at that stage called primary oocyte.

Very Short Answer Questions

11. Which method can cause increased egg production ?
12. What is the function of fertilization ?
13. What leads to fertilization ?
14. Three primary cell layers formed in which stage?
15. What is placenta ?
16. How many stages are there in between fertilization to birth?
17. In which organ is corpus luteum is formed ?
18. Which cord is dipped and cut, after delivery ?
19. What the mammals possess for ensuring effectiveness of reproduction ?
20. Which hormone is detected in the urine of pregnant females?
21. What is termed the development of new organs?
22. What is the meaning of gametogenesis ?
23. Fish, Frog and reptile — Which animal has developed organs for internal fertilization ?
24. What is called the bag-like fluid structure surrounding the human embryo ?
25. Maintenance of pregnancy is under the control of which hormone ?
26. Which hormone is also called a feminine hormone?
27. Which hormones control the proliferation of endometrium of uterus.
28. Sertoli cells are regulated by which pituitary harmones.
29. Bartholin's gland of female correspond to which glendo in male ?

Short Answer Questions

30. After how many days menstrual cycle takes place?
31. Which hormone stimulates the development of the endometrium ?
32. How is polyspermy prevented ?
33. What are the prevention for fertilization ?
34. What is gestation period ?
35. What is colostrum ?
36. What are the different types of fertilization ?

Important Tips & Formulae

- Secretions of seminal vesicles, prostate gland and paired bulbourethral glands constitute the seminal plasma which is rich in fructose, calcium and certain enzymes.
- In testis, the immature male germ cells (spermatogonia) produce sperms by spermatogenesis that begins at puberty.
- The spermatogonia (sing. spermatogonium) present on the inside wall of seminiferous tubules multiply by mitotic division and increase in numbers.
- Primary spermatocytes periodically undergo meiosis. A primary spermatocyte completes the first meiotic division (reduction division) leading to formation of two equal, haploid cells called secondary spermatocytes, which have only 23 chromosomes each.
- The secondary spermatocytes undergo the second meiotic division to produce four equal, haploid spermatids.
- The spermatids are transformed into spermatozoa (sperms) by the process called **spermiogenesis**. After spermiogenesis, sperm heads become embedded in the Sertoli cells, and are finally released from the seminiferous tubules by the process called **spermiation**.
- Spermatogenesis starts at the age of puberty due to significant increase in the secretion of gonadotropin releasing hormone (GnRH).
- LH (luteinising hormone) acts at the Leydig cells and stimulates synthesis and secretion of androgens. Androgen stimulates the process of spermatogenesis.
- FSH (follicle stimulating hormone) acts on the Sertoli cells and stimulates secretion of some factors which help in the process of spermiogenesis.
- The process of formation of a mature female gamete is called **oogenesis** and is initiated during the embryonic development stage when a couple of million gamete mother cells (oogonia) are formed within each fetal ovary no more oogonia are formed and added after birth.
- The cells start division and enter into prophase-I of the meiotic division and get temporarily arrested at that stage, called **primary oocytes**.
- Each primary oocyte then gets surrounded by a layer of **granulosa cells** and then called the **primary follicle**.
- The primary follicles get surrounded by more layers of granulosa cells and a new theca and called **secondary follicles**.
- The secondary follicle soon transforms into a tertiary follicle which is characterised by a fluid filled cavity called **antrum.**
- It is an unequal division resulting in the formation of a large haploid secondary oocyte and a tiny first polar body.
- The secondary oocyte retains bulk of the nutrient rich cytoplasm of the primary oocyte.
- The tertiary follicle further changes into the mature follicle or Graafian follicle. The secondary oocyte forms a new membrane called zona pellucida surrounding it. The Graafian follicle now ruptures to release the secondary oocyte (ovum) from the ovary by the process called **ovulation**.
- The ovum released by the ovary is also transported to the ampullary-isthmic junction where fertilisation takes place.
- Fertilisation can only occur if the ovum and sperms are transported simultaneously to the ampullary-isthmic junction.
- The process of fusion of a sperm with an ovum is called **fertilisation**. During fertilisation, a sperm comes in contact with the zona pellucida layer of the ovum and induces changes in the membrane that block the entry of additional sperms.
- The secretions of the acrosome help the sperm enter into the cytoplasm of the ovum through the zona pellucida and the plasma membrane. This induces the completion of the meiotic division of the secondary oocyte. The second meiotic division is also unequal and results in the formation of a second polar body and a haploid ovum (ootid).
- The haploid nucleus of the sperms and that of the ovum fuse together to form a diploid zygote.
- The structure of sperm is composed of head, neck, a middle piece and a tail.
- The sperm head contains an elongated haploid nucleus, the anterior portion of which is covered by a cap-like structure, acrosome.
- The acrosome is filled with enzymes (hyaluronidase) that help fertilisation of the ovum.
- The middle piece possesses numerous mitochondria, which produce energy for the movement of tail that facilitate sperm motility essential for fertilisation.
- The seminal plasma along with the sperms constitutes the semen.
- The edges of the infundibulum possess finger-like projections called **fimbriae**, which help in collection of the ovum after ovulation.
- The infundibulum leads to a wider of the oviduct called **ampulla**. The last part of the oviduct, isthmus has a narrow lumen and it joins the uterus.
- The endometrium undergoes cyclical changes during menstrual cycle while the myometrium exhibits strong contraction during delivery of the baby.
- The middle layer of the uterus is called **myometrium** which is composed of thick layer of smooth muscle.
- Menopause is a phase in women when ovulation and menstruation ceases. It occurs between the age of 45-55 years and marks the end of the fertility.
- The placenta is connected to the embryo through umbilical cord that helps in the transport of substances to and forms the embryo.
- The placenta facilitates the supply of oxygen and nutrients to the embryo and also removal of carbon dioxide and excretory/waste materials produced by the embryo.
- Placenta also acts as an endocrine tissue and produces several hormones like human chorionic gonadotropin (hCG), human placental lactogen (hPL), estrogens, progestogens, etc.

- A hormone called **relaxin** is also secreted by the ovary in the later phase of pregnancy.
- The inner cell mass contains certain cells called **stem cells** which have the potency to give rise to all the tissues and organs.
- Foetal ejection reflex triggers release of oxytocin from the maternal pituitary and oxytocin hormone acts on the uterine muscles that causes stronger uterine contraction.
- The mitotic division starts as the zygote moves through the isthmus of the oviduct called cleavage towards the uterus and forms 2, 4, 8, 16 daughter cells called **blastomeres**.
- The embryo with 8 to 16 blastomeres is called a **morula**. The morula continues to divide and transforms into blastocyst as it moves further into the uterus.
- The blastomeres in the blastocyst are arranged into an outer layer called trophoblast and an inner group of cells attached to trophoblast called the **inner cell mass**.

- The trophoblast layer then gets attached to the endometrium and the inner cell mass gets differentiated as the embryo.
- After attachment, the uterine cells divide rapidly and cover the blastocyst. As a result, the blastocyst becomes embedded in the endometrium of the uterus. This is called implantation and it leads to pregnancy.
- After implantation, the inner cell mass (embryo) differentiates into an outer layer called ectoderm and an inner layer called endoderm.
- A mesoderm soon appears between the ectoderm and the endoderm. These three layers give rise to all tissues (organs) in adults.
- That the inner cell mass contains certain cells called stem cells which have the potency to give rise to all the tissues and organs.

NCERT Questions

1. Fill in the blanks:

(a) Humans reproduce _______ (asexually/sexually).

(b) Humans are _____ (oviparous, viviparous, ovoviviparous).

(c) Fertilization is _______ in humans (external/internal).

(d) Male and female gametes are _______ (diploid/haploid).

(e) Zygote is _______ (diploid/haploid).

(f) The process of release of ovum from a mature follicle is called _______.

(g) Ovulation is induced by a hormone called _______.

(h) The fusion of male and female gametes is called _______.

(i) Fertilization takes place in _______.

(j) Zygote divides to form _______ which is implanted in uterus.

(k) The structure which provides vascular connection between foetus and uterus is called _______.

Sol.

(a) sexually

(b) viviparous

(c) Internal

(d) haploid

(e) Diploid

(f) ovulation

(g) LH (Luteinizing hormone)

(h) fertilization

(i) ampullary-isthmic junction

(j) blastula

(k) placenta (Umbilical cord)

2. Draw a labelled diagram of male reproductive system.

Sol.

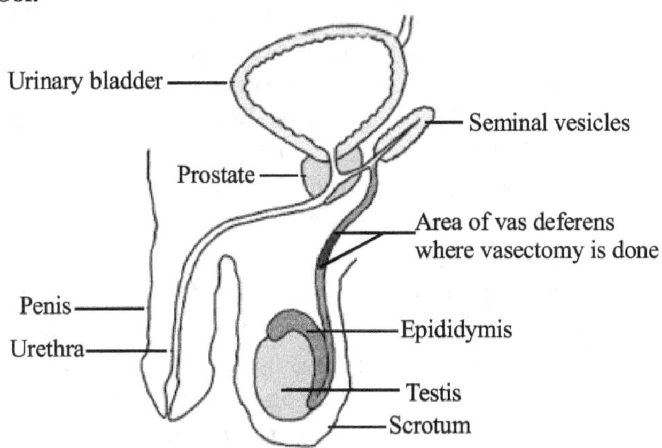

Fig. : Male reproductive system

3. Draw a labelled diagram of female reproductive system.

Sol.

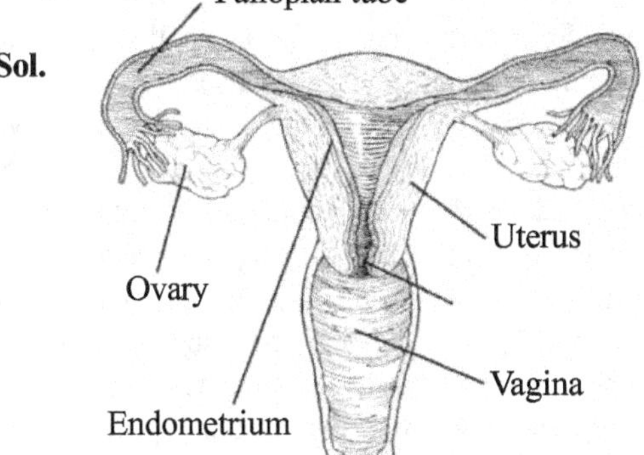

Fig. : Female reproductive system

4. **Write two major functions each of testis and ovary.**

Sol. **Testes** – Testes are the primary sexual organs in male. Two major functions of testes are –

(i) Testosterone production from leydig cells.

(ii) Production of sperm cells in seminiferous tubules.

Ovary – Ovaries are the primary female sex organs. Two main functions of ovaries are –

(i) Productions of female germ cells called eggs or oocytes.

(ii) Production of hormones – estrogens & progesterone which affect many of the female secondary sexual character & reproductive functions.

5. **Describe the structure of a seminiferous tubule.**

Sol. The seminiferous tubule is a structural unit in the adult testis. The seminiferous tubule are situated in testicular lobules.

Both ends of the tubule are connected to central region of the teatis and ferma network of small duct ules called rete testis. It is lined by germinal epithellium. It is a specific location of meiosis.

Seminiferous tubule consists of two types of cells – *Sertoli* or *supporting cells & spermatogenic cells. Sertoli cells,* are elongated and pyramidal & partially envelop the spermatogenic cells. The cells provide nourishment to the developing spermatogenic cells. Spermatogenic cells are stacked in 4-8 layers. These cells divide several times & differentiate to produce spermatozoa. Between seminiferous tubules lie the interstitial cells or leydig cells which produces testosterone hormone.

6. **What is spermatogenesis? Briefly describe the process of spermatogenesis.**

Sol. Spermatogenesis is the process of producing sperms with half the number of chromosomes (haploid) as somatic cells. It occurs in seminiferous tubules. Sperm production begins at puberty continues throughout life with several hundred million sperms being produced each day. Once sperm are formed they move into the epididymis, where they mature and are stored.

During spermatogenesis one spermatogonium produces 4 sperms. Spermatogenesis completes through the following phases – multiplicative phase, growth phase, maturation phase & spermiogenesis. In multiplicative phase the sperm mother cells divide by mitosis & produce spermatogonia. The spermatogonia grow in size to form large primary spermatocytes by getting nourishment from sertoli cells in growth phase. Maturation phase involves meiosis I in which primary spermatocytes divide to produce secondary spermatocyte and meiosis II which produces spermatids. Thus each primary spermatocyte gives rise to four haploid spermatids. Spermiogenesis or spermateliosis is process of formation of flagellated spermatozoa from spermatids. Spermiogenesis begins in the seminiferous tubules but usually completed in epididymis.

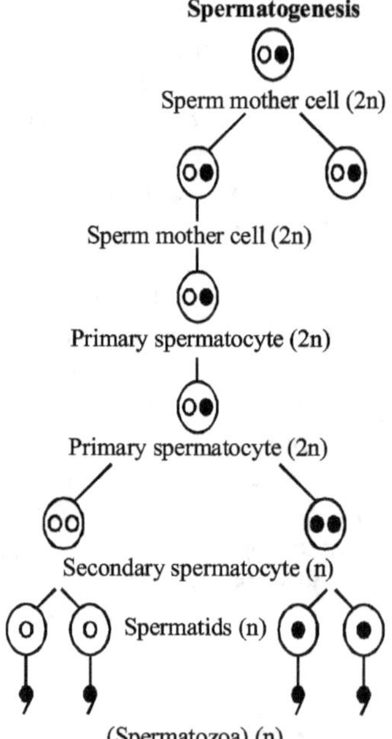

7. **Name the hormones involved in regulation of spermatogenesis.**

Sol. After sexual maturity, spermatogenesis starts due to the secretion of gonadotropin releasing hormone (GnRH) from the hypothalamus of brain. GnRH acts on pituitary gland stimulates secretion of luteinizing hormone (LH) and follicle stimulating hormone (FSH). LH induce the Leydig's cells of the testis to produce male sex hormones called androgens. High level of androgens stimulate the process of spermatogenesis.

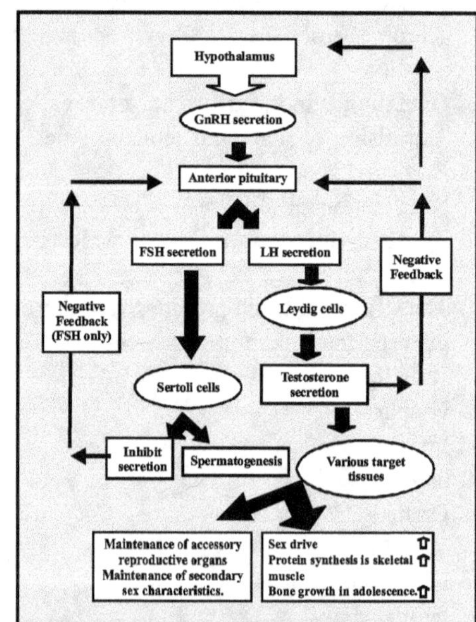

8. **Define spermiogenesis and spermiation.**

Sol. Spermiogenesis is the process of transformation of nonmtile haploid spermatids into mature flagellated spermatozoa. It is a fyinal stage of spermatogives.

Spermiation is the process of release of mature spermatozoa. In this spermatozoa are shed into the lumen of seminiferous tubule for transport.

9.   Draw a labelled diagram of sperm.

Sol.

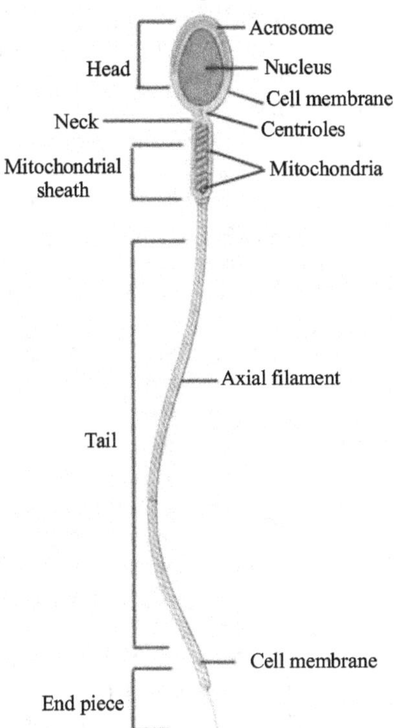

10.   What are the major components of seminal plasma?

Sol.   Seminal plasma is the fluid in which sperm is ejaculated. Major components of seminal plasma are secretions from seminal vesicles, prostrate and bulbourethral gland and sperms from testis. It is rich in fructose and contains enzymes, citric acid, hormones like prostaglandins, calcium and clotting proteins.

11.   What are the major functions of male accessory ducts and glands?

Sol.   Major functions of male accessory ducts are :
- •   Aid in sperm transport.
- •   Temporary storage of spermatozoa.

Male accessory glands secretions constitute the seminal plasma. These secretions are rich in fructose, ascorbic acid, citrate, calcium, certain enzymes and prostaglandins. These secretions nourish and activate the spermatozoa to swim.

12.   What is oogenesis? Give a brief account of oogenesis.

Sol.   The process of formation of mature female gamete (ovum) is called oogenesis. It occurs in the ovaries of female reproductive system. Oogenesis is a discontinuous process it begins before birth, stops in midprocess & only resumes after menarch. It occurs in three phases : **Multiplicative phase** (formation of oogonia mitotically from the primary germ cells), **growth phase** (growth of oogonia into primary oocyte) & **Maturation phase** (formation of mature ova from primary oocyte through meiosis). Maturation phase produces two haploid cells – Larger one called secondary oocyte & the smaller one called polar bodies (1st polar body). Meiosis II of secondary oocyte results in the formation of functional egg or ovum and a second polar body. The first polar body may also divide to form two polar bodies of equal sizes which do not take part in reproduction & ultimately degenerates. Formation of polar bodies maintains the half number of chromosomes in the ovum. First maturation division may be completed in the ovaries just prior to ovulation but second one (Final) is completed outside the ovary after fertilization. Secondary oocyte is female gamete in which the 1st meiotic division is completed & second meiotic division (Metaphase stage) has begin. The egg is released at secondary oocyte stage under the effect of LH.

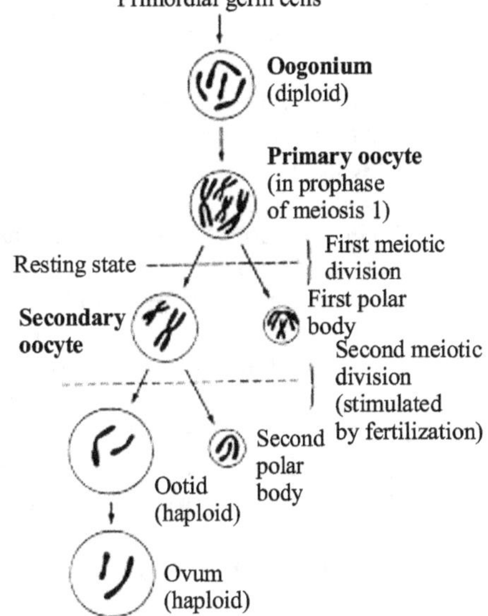

13.   Draw a labelled diagram of a section through ovary.

Sol.

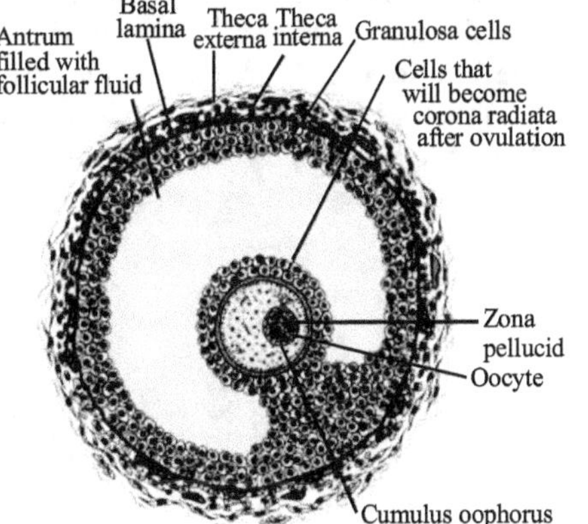

14.   Draw a labelled diagram of a Graafian follicle?

Sol.

Fig. : Graafian follicle

15. **Name the functions of the following:**
    (a) Corpus luteum   (b) Endometrium
    (c) Acrosome   (d) Sperm tail
    (e) Fimbriae

Sol. (a) **Corpus luteum :** The corpus luteum secretes large amounts of progesterone which is essential for maintenance of the endometrium.

    (b) **Endometrium** is necessary for implantation of the fertilized ovum and other events of pregnancy.

    (c) The **acrosome** is filled with Lytic enzymes that help during fertilization of the ovum. It is formed from golgi complex

    (d) **Sperm tail :** Tail facilitates sperm motility which is essential for fertilization.

    (e) **Fimbriae :** Fimbriae help in collection of the ovum after ovulation.

16. **Identify True/False statements. Correct each false statement to make it true.**
    (a) Androgens are produced by sertoli cells.
                       (True/False)
    (b) Spermatozoa get nutrition from sertoli cells.
                       (True/False)
    (c) Leydig cells are found in ovary.   **(True/False)**
    (d) Leydig cells synthesize androgens.   **(True/False)**
    (e) Oogenesis takes place in corpus luteum.
                       (True/False)
    (f) Menstrual cycle ceases during pregnancy.
                       (True/False)
    (g) Presence or absence of hymen is not a reliable indicator of virginity or sexual experience.   **(True/False)**

Sol. (a) False, Androgens or male sex hormones are secreted by Leydig cells.
    (b) True.
    (c) False, Leydig cells are found in testis.
    (d) True.
    (e) False, Oogenesis takes place in ovary.
    (f) True.
    (g) True.

17. **What is menstrual cycle? Which hormones regulate menstrual cycle?**

Sol. Menstrual cycle is the cyclic change in the reproductive tract of primate female. This period is marked by a characteristic event repeated almost every month (28 days with minor variation) in the form of a menstrual flow (i.e. shedding of the endometrium of the uterus with bleeding. It may be temporarily stopped only in pregnancy. Hormones involved in the regulation of menstural cycle are pitintary or ovarian hormones. These are LH, FSH, estrogen and progesterance.

18. **What is parturition? Which hormones are involved in induction of parturition?**

Sol. The average duration of human pregnancy is about 9 months which is called gestation period. Parturiton (or labour) means child birth. Parturition is the sequence of actions by which a body and the after birth (placenta) are expelled from the uterus at child birth. The process usuallly starts spontaneously about 280 days after conception, but it may be stonted by arti ficial means.

The process of part urition is induced by a complex neurorendocrine mechanism involving cortical, estrogen adoxytocin..

19. **In our society the women are often blamed for giving birth to daughters. Can you explain why this is not correct?**

Sol. Blaming women for giving birth to daughters is not correct because Y chromosome is transferred only by male. One X-chromosome is already there so, if there is Y chromosome then male child will be borne otherwise on addition of another X-chromosome, daughter will be born.

20. **How many eggs are released by a human ovary in a month? How many eggs do you think would have been released if the mother gave birth to identical twins? Would your answer change if the twins born were fraternal?**

Sol. One egg is released by human ovary in a month.
Identical twins : Identical twins are formed when a single fertilized egg splits into two genetically identical parts. The twins share the same DNA set, thus they may share many similar attributes. However, since physical appearance is influenced by environmental factors and not just genetics, identical twins can actually look very different.
Fraternal twins : These twins are formed when two fertilized eggs are formed. The twins share the different DNA set, thus they may share different attributes (dizygotic embryo).

21. **How many eggs do you think were released by the ovary of a female dog which gave birth to 6 puppies?**

Sol. Since dogs have multiple births, several eggs mative and are released at the same time. If fertilized, the egg will implanctem the uterine wall. Dogs bear their litters roughly I weeks after fertilizations although the length of gerstation cam very from 56 to 72 days. An average litter consists of about six puppies, though this number may vary widely based on the breed god, on this basis 6 eggs were released by the ovary of a female dog which gave birth to 6 puptions.

Past year Exercise

Very Short Answer Questions

1. List the changes the primary oocyte undergoes in the tertiary follicular stage in human embryo.

2. Mention the function of trophoblast in human embryo.

3. Name the embryonic stage that gets implanted in the uterine wall of a human female.

4. What stimulates pituitary to release the hormone responsible for parturition? Name the hormone.

5. Mention the difference between spermiogenesis and spermiation.

6. Write the location and function of Sertoli cells in humans.

7. When do the oogenesis and the spermatogenesis initiate in human females and males respectively?

8. Where is acrosome present in humans? Write its function.

9. How is the entry of only one sperm and not many ensured into an ovum during fertilisation in humans?

10. Write the physiological reason, why a woman generally cannot conceive a child after 50 years of age?

11. Name the cells that nourish the germ cells in the testes. Where are these cells located in the testes?

12. Name the stage of cell division where segregation of an independent pair of chromosomes occurs.

Short Answer Questions

13. Study the sectional view of human testis showing seminiferous tubules given below.

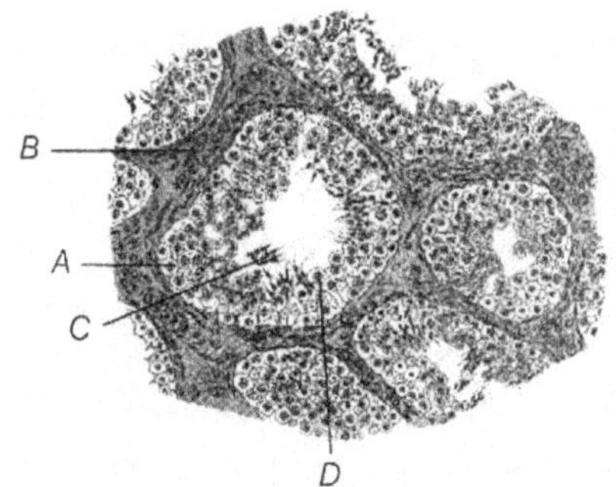

   (i) Identify A, B and C
   (ii) Write the function of A and D.

14. How and at what stage of menstrual cycle is corpus luteum formed in human females? When does it regress?

15. Draw a labelled sectional view of seminiferous tubule of a human male.

16. Placenta acts as an endocrine tissue. Justify.

17. Differentiate between menarche and menopause.

18. Differentiate between major structural changes in the human ovary during the follicular and luteal phase of the menstural cycle.

19. Mention the fate of corpus luteum and its effect on the uterus in absence of fertilisation of the ovum in human female.

20. Explain the role of Sertoli cells in the development of sperms.

21. (i) When does oogenesis begin?
   (ii) Differentiate between the location and function of Sertoli cells and Leydig cells.

22. Draw a labelled diagram of the reproductive system in human female.

23. Draw a labelled diagram of the microscopic structure of a human sperm.

24. Describe how the changing levels of FSH, LH and progesterone during menstrual cycle induce changes in the ovary and the uterus in human female?

25. Name the hormones produced only during pregnancy in human female. Mention their source organ.

26. (i) Where do the signals for parturition originate in humans?
   (ii) Why is it important to feed the newborn babies on colostrum?

27. Write the function of each one of the following
   (i) Fimbriae (oviducal)
   (ii) Coleoptile
   (iii) Oxytocin

28. Write the function of each one of the following
   (i) Middle piece in human sperm
   (ii) Tapetum in anthers
   (iii) Luteinising hormone in human males.

29. Write the function of each of the following
   (i) Seminal vesicle
   (ii) Scutellum
   (iii) Acrosome of human sperm

30. Give reasons for the following
   (i) The human testes are located outside the abdominal cavity.
   (ii) Some organisms like honeybees are called parthenogenetic animals.

31. Explain the steps in the formation of an ovum from an oogonium in humans.

32. When and where do chorionic villi appear in humans ? State their function.

33. Draw a diagram of the microscopic structure of human sperm. Label the following parts in it and write their functions.

(a) Acrosome

(b) Nucleus

(c) Middle piece

34. (a) Draw a diagram of the structure of a human ovum surrounded by corona radiata. Label the following parts:

(i) Ovum

(ii) Plasma membrane

(iii) Zona pellucida

(b) State the function of Zona Pellucida.

35. Name the stage of the human embryo that gets implanted in the uterus and draw its labelled diagram.

36. Why is ZIFT a boon to childless couples? Explain procedure.

37. Why are the human testes located outside the abdominal cavity? Name the pouch in which they are present.

38. Write the location and functions of the following in human testes :

(a) Sertoli cells   (b) Leydig cells

39. Write the effect of the high concentration of LH on a mature Graafian follicle.

40. Name and explain the role of the inner and middle walls of the human uterus.

41. Draw a labelled diagram of the sectional view of a human seminiferous tubule (six parts to be labelled).

42. (a) Arrange the following hormones in sequence of their secretion in a pregnant woman.

(b) Mention their source and the function they perform: hCG, LH, FSH, Relaxin.

43. Draw a diagram of a mature human sperm. Label any three parts and write their functions.

44. Draw a labelled diagram to show interrelationship of four accessory ducts in a human male reproductive system.

45. List the four different human male accessory ducts.

NCERT Exemplar

Multiple Choice Questions

1. Spot the odd one out from the following structures with reference to the male reproductive system
(a) Rete testis
(b) Epididymis
(c) Vasa efferentia
(d) Isthmus

2. Acrosomal reaction of the sperm occurs due to
(a) its contact with zona pellucida of the ova
(b) reactions within the uterine environment of the female
(c) reactions within the epididymal environment of the male
(d) androgens produced in the uterus

3. Which one of the following is not a male accessory gland?
(a) Seminal vesicle
(b) Ampulla
(c) Prostate
(d) Bulbourethral gland

4. Urethral meatus refers to the:
(a) urinogenital duct
(b) opening of vas deferens into urethra
(c) external opening of the urinogenital duct
(d) muscles surrounding the urinogenital duct

5. Morula is a developmental stage
(a) between the zygote and blastocyst
(b) between the blastocyst and gastrula
(c) after the implanation
(d) between implanation and parturition

Match the following

6. Match the following and choose the correct options.

	Column I		Column II
A.	Trophoblast	1.	Embedding of blastocyst in the endometrium
B.	Cleavage	2.	Group of cells that would differentiate as embryo
C.	Inner cell mass	3.	Outer layer of blastocyst attached to the endometrium
D.	Implantation	4.	Mitotic division of zygote

Codes

	A	B	C	D
(a)	2	1	3	4
(b)	3	4	2	1
(c)	3	1	2	4
(d)	2	4	3	1

7. Match between the following representing parts of the sperm and their functions and choose the correct option.

	Column I		Column II
A.	Head	1.	Enzymes
B.	Middle piece	2.	Sperm motility
C.	Acrosome	3.	Energy
D.	Tail	4.	Genetic material

Codes

	A	B	C	D		A	B	C	D
(a)	2	4	1	3	(b)	4	3	1	2
(c)	4	1	2	3	(d)	2	1	3	4

Assertion & Reason Questions

DIRECTIONS (Qs. 8-9) : *Each of these questions contains an assertion followed by reason. Read them carefully and answer the question on the basis of following options. You have to select the one that best describes the two statements.*
(a) If both Assertion and Reason are correct and the Reason is a correct explanation of the Assertion.
(b) If both Assertion and Reason are correct but Reason is not a correct explanation of the Assertion.
(c) If the Assertion is correct but Reason is incorrect.
(d) If both Assertion and Reason are incorrect.

8. **Assertion:** The sperm head contains an elongated haploid nucleus, the anterior portion of which is covered by a cap-like structure, acrosome.
Reason: The acrosome is formed by the Golgi complex of the spermatid.

9. **Assertion:** Spermatogenesis starts at the age of puberty due to significant increase in the secretion of gonadotropin releasing hormone (GnRH).
Reason: The increased levels of GnRH then acts at the anterior pituitary gland and stimulate secretion of two gonadotropins –LH and FSH.

Very Short Answer Questions

10. What is the role of cervix of the human female system in reproduction?

Short Answer Questions

11. Corpus luteum in pregnancy has a long life. However, if fertilisation does not take place it remains active only for 10-12 days . Why?

12. Placenta has endocrine function. Does it have other functions? Explain.

Objective Practice Exercise

Multiple Choice Questions

1. The tightly convoluted tubule that lies along the posterior surface of the testis is
(a) the seminiferous tubule
(b) the rete testis
(c) the epididymis
(d) the ductus deferens

2. The major part of the semen is the secretion of
(a) Cowper's gland
(b) Perennial gland
(c) Prostate gland
(d) Seminal vesicle

3. The head of epididymis is called
(a) caput epididymis
(b) cauda epididymis
(c) gubernaculum
(d) vas deferens

4. Sugar fructose is present in the secretion of
(a) Bartholin's gland
(b) Cowper's gland
(c) Perineal glands
(d) Prostate gland

5. Cowper's glands are found in
(a) Female amphibians
(b) Male mammals
(c) Female mammals
(d) Male amphibians

6. Which one is a primary sex organ?
(a) Testis
(b) Scrotum
(c) Prostate
(d) Penis

7. Seminal plasma in human males is rich in
(a) fructose and calcium
(b) glucose and calcium
(c) DNA and testosterone
(d) ribose and potassium

8. Which accessory genital gland occurs only in mammalian male?
(a) Prostate gland
(b) Perineal gland
(c) Cowper's gland
(d) Bartholin gland

9. The duct which carries sperms from testis and epididymis to the penis is
(a) Vasa efferentia
(b) Vasa deferentia
(c) Ureter
(d) Seminiferous tubules

10. Seminal fluid has sperms and secretions of
(a) Follicles, ureters and prostate gland
(b) Prostate, cowper's and bartholin's gland
(c) Seminal vesicle, prostate and cowper's glands
(d) Seminal vesicle, ureters and prostate gland

11. Scrotal sacs of man and rabbit are connected with the abdominal cavity by
(a) Inguinal canal
(b) Haversian canal
(c) Vagina cavity
(d) Spermatic canal

12. Which accessory genital gland occurs only in male mammal?
(a) Cowper's gland
(b) Bartholin gland
(c) Prostate gland
(d) Perineal gland

13. The enlarged end of penis is covered by a loose fold of skin called
(a) glans penis
(b) foreskin
(c) hymen
(d) urethral meatus

14. Which of the following is a transporting tube leading from the bladder which brings urine outside the body *via* penis?
(a) Ureter
(b) Epididymis
(c) Ejaculatory duct
(d) Urethra meatus

15. Which gland releases a small amount of fluid just prior to ejaculation to decrease acidity in the urethra caused by urine?
(a) Prostate
(b) Glans penis
(c) Seminal vesicle
(d) Bulbourethral gland

16. A sperm cell moving from the lumen of the seminiferous tubule to the exterior of the body passes through all of the following structures except the
(a) seminal vesicle
(b) epididymis
(c) ductus deferens
(d) urethra

17. The function of the seminal vesicle is to
(a) produce a solution of fructose to provide energy for the mitochondria of the sperm.
(b) secrete alkaline fluids that neutralize the acidity of the female's reproductive tract.
(c) initiate the muscular contractions leading to emission.
(d) produce prostaglandins that stimulate contractions of the male reproductive organs.

18. Which of the following is not part of the female external genitalia?
(a) Clitoris
(b) Vagina
(c) Labia majora
(d) Labia minora

19. Which of the following organs is devoid of glands?
(a) Uterus
(b) Vagina
(c) Vulva
(d) Oviduct

20. Which of the following is a finger like structure and lies at the upper junction of the two labia minora above the urethral opening?
(a) Clitoris
(b) Oviduct
(c) Ampulla
(d) Chorionic villi

21. 10 oogonia yield 10 primary oocytes, then how many ova are produced on completion of oogenesis
(a) 5
(b) 10
(c) 20
(d) 40

22. In mammals, meiosis to produce the female egg cell is initiated in the
    (a) ovary (b) uterus
    (c) vagina (d) cervix

23. At the time of fertilization, sperm head enters in the egg from
    (a) Anywhere (b) Animal pole
    (c) Vegetal pole (d) Lateral side of egg

24. Which one of the following is the precise site of embryo implantation in a normal pregnancy?
    (a) Endometrium (b) Vagina
    (c) Oviduct (d) Cervix

25. Fertilization occur in
    (a) Uterus (b) Ureter
    (c) Vagina (d) Fallopian tube

26. The fertilization in human occurs at the junction of
    (a) Infundibulum and ampulla
    (b) Isthmus and fundus
    (c) Ampulla and isthmus
    (d) Cervix and fundus

27. Into which structure is a human oocyte released upon ovulation?
    (a) Fallopian tube (b) Ovary
    (c) Abdominal cavity (d) Uterus

28. Follicular atresia is
    (a) Formation of corpus luteum
    (b) Degeneration of follicles till puberty
    (c) Formation of Graffian follicle
    (d) Increase in number of follicles

29. The follicular cells surrounding the human egg constitute
    (a) Zona pellucida (b) Vitelline membrane
    (c) Corona radiata (d) Zona radiata

30. Antrum is the cavity of
    (a) Ovary (b) Blastula
    (c) Gastrula (d) Graafian follicle

31. Immediate membrane covering the mammalian egg is
    (a) Corona radiata (b) Zona pellucida
    (c) Vitelline membrane (d) Chorion

32. Which of the following hormones is produced in women only during pregnancy?
    (a) Relaxin (b) Estrogen
    (c) Oxytocin (d) Progesterone

33. In human female, menopause is a stage in which
    (a) oogenesis starts at puberty.
    (b) menstruation starts at puberty.
    (c) corpus luteum starts secreting progesterone for maintaining pregnancy.
    (d) menstruation stops at the age of 50 years and reproductive capacity is arrested.

34. Which of the following is the first change that occurs to the zygote after fertilization?
    (a) It divides to form a hollow ball of cells, called the blastocyst.
    (b) It begins to secrete the hormones.
    (c) It contacts the endometrial wall of the uterus and becomes buried inside it.
    (d) It initiates the formation of a placenta.

35. Which of the following does not occur in the time during and immediately following fertilization?
    (a) Fusion of the sperm and ovum nuclei
    (b) Division of the oocyte cell by meiosis
    (c) Implantation of the ovum in the uterus
    (d) Digestion of cell layers around the oocyte by sperm

36. What is true for cleavage?
    (a) Size of embryo increases
    (b) Size of cells decrease
    (c) Size of cells increase
    (d) Size of embryo decreases

37. Semen is a constituent of seminal plasma with _______.
    (a) ovum (b) sperm (c) zygote (d) follicle

38. Which of the following is not a paired structure in male?
    (a) Urethra (b) Vas deferens
    (c) Epididymis (d) Ejaculatory duct

39. If proximal centriole of mature sperm is destroyed. Which of the following is going to be affected?
    (a) Motility (b) Fertilization
    (c) Cleavage (d) None of these

40. The functional maturation of sperms in males, occurs in
    (a) Rete testis (b) Epididymis
    (c) Lobules of testis (d) Fallopian tube

41. Identify the structure on the basis of the given statement which surrounds the primary sex organ of male reproductive system. "It is responsible for maintaining the low temperature by about 2 - 2.5° C from normal body temperature to mature sperm."
    (a) Penis (b) Scrotum
    (c) Ureter (d) Urethra

42. Which of the following is a finger like structure and lies at the upper junction of the two labia minora above the urethral opening?
    (a) Clitoris (b) Oviduct
    (c) Ampulla (d) Chorionic villi

43. Which of the following produces sperms in spermatogenesis?
    (a) Sertoli cells.
    (b) Interstitial cells.
    (c) Primary spermatocytes.
    (d) Immature male germ cells.

44. Which of the following contains a fluid filled cavity called antrum?
    (a) Primary spermatocyte.
    (b) Primary follicle of ovary.
    (c) Tertiary follicle of ovary.
    (d) Secondary spermatocyte.

45. Menstruation is triggered by a sudden decline in the amount of hormone secreted by corpus luteum. Identify the hormone.
    (a) Luteinizing hormone
    (b) Follicle stimulating hormone
    (c) Progesterone
    (d) Estrogen

46. Level of which hormones are at their highest during the luteal phase (second half of the cycle) of the menstrual cycle?
    (a) Estrogen
    (b) Progesterone
    (c) Luteinizing hormone
    (d) Follicular stimulating hormone

47. Which phase of menstrual cycle is also called proliferative phase?
    (a) Luteal   (b) Ovulatory
    (c) Follicular   (d) Menstruation

48. Which phase of menstrual cycle is also called secretory phase?
    (a) Luteal   (b) Ovulatory
    (c) Follicular   (d) Menstruation

49. Which of the following indicates pregnancy?
    (a) Lack of menstruation.
    (b) Occurrence of menstrual flow.
    (c) When released ovum is not fertilized.
    (d) When Graafian follicle matures and endometrium regenerates through proliferation.

50. When semen is released by the penis into the vagina during copulation, then it is called _____.
    (a) ovulation
    (b) insemination
    (c) menstruation
    (d) gametogenesis

51. The given table shows differences between spermatogenesis and spermiogenesis. Select the incorrect option.

	Spermatogenesis	Spermiogenesis
(a)	Process of formation of spermatozoa.	Process of differentiatin of spermatozoon form a spermatid.
(b)	It changes a haploid stucture into another haploid structure.	It involves conversion of a diploid structure into haploid structure.
(c)	Growth and divisions occur.	Divisions and growth are absent.
(d)	A spermatogonium forms four spermatozoa.	A spermatid forms a single spermatozoon.

52. Match column I with column II and select the correct option from the codes given below.

	Column I		Column II
A.	Acrosome	(i)	Rudimentary erectile tissue
B.	Endometrium	(ii)	Uterus
C.	Polar body	(iii)	Oogenesis
D.	Clitoris	(iv)	Spermatozoon

    (a) A-(ii), B-(i), C-(iv), D-(iii)
    (b) A-(iv), B-(ii), C-(iii), D-(i)
    (c) A-(iv), B-(iii), C-(ii), D-(i)
    (d) A-(iv), B-(iii), C-(i), D-(ii)

Chapter Test 

Time : *30 Minutes* **Max. Marks : *15***

Directions :

- Questions number **1-15** carry **1 mark** each.

1. At the time of fertilization, chromosome number
   - (a) is halved
   - (b) remains haploid
   - (c) becomes diploid
   - (d) does not change

2. Which layer of blastocysts gets attached to the endometrium?
   - (a) Trophoblast
   - (b) Inner cell mass
   - (c) Umbilical cord
   - (d) Both (a) and (c)

3. Primary germ layers are
   - (a) ectoderm and inner cell mass only.
   - (b) trophoblast, ectoderm and mesoderm.
   - (c) endoderm and mesoderm only.
   - (d) ectoderm, endoderm and mesoderm.

4. If for some reason, the vasa efferentia in the human reproductive system get blocked, the gametes will not be transported from
   - (a) testes to epididymis
   - (b) epididymis to vas deferens
   - (c) ovary to uterus
   - (d) vagina to uterus

5. Match the column-I with column-II and select the correct option. Match from the options given below

Column-I		Column-II
A.	Primary oocyte	I.	It is formed when oogonia starts division and temporarily arrested at rophase of meiosis I.
B.	Secondary oocyte	II.	A large haploid cell which retains bulk of nutrient rich cytoplasm of the primary oocyte.
C.	Primary follicle	III.	A large number of these degenerate during the phase from puberty to birth.
D.	Oogonia	IV.	Gamete mother cell.
E.	Secondary follicle	V.	Surrounded by more layers of granulosa cells and a new theca.
F.	Graafian follicle	VI.	Rupture to release ovum from the ovary.

   - (a) A – I; B – II; C – III; D – IV; E – V; F – VI
   - (b) A – III; B – I; C – IV; D – II; E – V; F – VI
   - (c) A – VI; B – IV; C – V; D – II; E – I; F – III
   - (d) A – II; B – IV; C – III; D – V; E – I; F – VI

DIRECTIONS (Qs. 6-7) : *Each of these questions contains an assertion followed by reason. Read them carefully and answer the question on the basis of following options. You have to select the one that best describes the two statements.*

   - (a) If both Assertion and Reason are correct and the Reason is a correct explanation of the Assertion.
   - (b) If both Assertion and Reason are correct but Reason is not a correct explanation of the Assertion.
   - (c) If the Assertion is correct but Reason is incorrect.
   - (d) If both Assertion and Reason are incorrect.

6. **Assertion:** After 50 years of age, the human males may suffer from ADPM.
   Reason: In ADAM, there is low production of testosterone, dihydrotesterone, androgen binding proteins, sperm production and libido.

7. **Assertion:** The first movements of the foetus and appearance of hair on the head are usually observed during the fifth month.
   Reason: By the end of 24th week (second trimester), the body is covered with fine hair, eye-lids separate and eyelashes are formed.

Passage/Case Based Questions

DIRECTIONS (Qs. 8-12) : *Read the following passage and answer the questions that follow.*

Spermatogenesis is the production of sperms from male germ cells (spermatogonia) inside the testes (semniferous tubule). This process begin at puberty.

Observe the following flow diagram and answer the questions that follows-

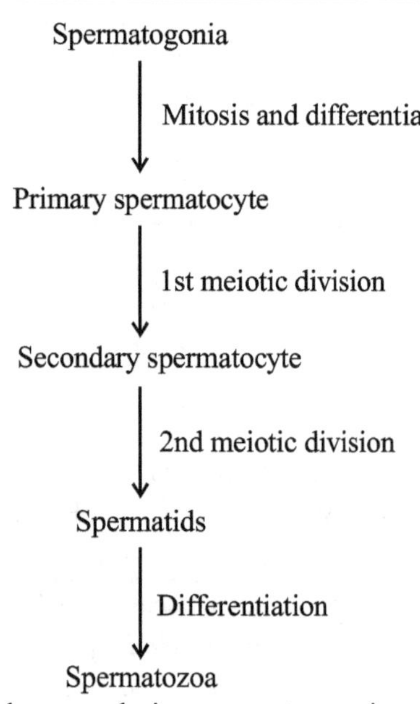

8. This happens during spermatogenesis
   - (a) Meiosis
   - (b) Mitosis
   - (c) Meiosis and mitosis
   - (d) None of these
9. The process of spermatogenesis is induced by
   - (a) TSH
   - (b) FSH
   - (c) MSH
   - (d) ACTH

10. The number of spermatozoa, a single primary spermatocyte finally produced in spermatogenesis is
    - (a) 2
    - (d) 4
    - (c) 6
    - (d) 8
11. In spermatogenesis, the phasis of maturation involve
    - (a) formation of spermatids from primary spermatocyte through meiosis
    - (b) growth of spermatogonia into primary spermatocytes
    - (c) formation of spermatogonia from gonocytes through mitosis
    - (d) formation of oogonia from spermatocyte through meiosis
12. The correct sequence of cell stage in spermatogenesis is
    - (a) spermatocyte $\rightarrow$ spermatids $\rightarrow$ spermatogonia $\rightarrow$ spermatozoa
    - (b) spermatogonia $\rightarrow$ spermatids $\rightarrow$ spermatocyte $\rightarrow$ spermatozoa
    - (c) spermatocytes $\rightarrow$ spermatogonia $\rightarrow$ spermatid $\rightarrow$ spermatozoa
    - (d) spermatogonia $\rightarrow$ spermatocytes $\rightarrow$ spermatids $\rightarrow$ spermatozoa

Very Short Answer Questions

13. What happens in ovulation?
14. When does the antrum develop?
15. What consists of follicle?

Solutions 

Practice Exercise-1 

1. **(c)** With the proximal centriole the sperm adds a division centre in the egg, as the centriole of the ovum ceases to function.

2. **(a)** The urethra originates from the urinary bladder and extends through the penis to its external opening called urethral meatus.

3. **(a)** The urethra originates from a structure [called urinary bladder (X)] and extends through the male external genitalia [called penis (Y) which helps in introducing semen into the vagina] to its external opening called urethral meatus.

4. **(b)** The uterus is a female reproductive organ located between the bladder and the rectum, in the pelvic area. The main purpose of the uterus is to nourish a foetus prior to birth. In menstruating females, the ovaries release eggs which travel *via* the fallopian tubes to the uterus.

5. **(a)** Bartholin's glands are a pair of small glands situated on each side of the vaginal opening in human females. They secrete a thick, viscid secretion for lubrication during copulation.

6. **(c)** Male and female gametes are fused in ampullary-isthmic junction of fallopian tube. Fusion of gametes is not the function of uterine wall.

7. **(d)** The menstrual cycle is the series of changes a woman's body goes through to prepare for a pregnancy. About once a month, the uterus grows a new lining (endometrium) to get ready for a fertilized egg. When there is no fertilized egg to start a pregnancy, the uterus sheds its lining. This is the monthly menstrual bleeding (also called menstrual period).

8. **(b)** Seminiferous tubules are located in the testes, which are the specific location of meiosis, and the subsequent formation of sperms. Rete testis is a network of small tubules found in the part of the testicle that carries sperm. Leydig cells or interstitial cells of Leydig produce the hormone called testosterone which contributes to male secondary sexual characters. Prepuce is the foreskin, skin surrounding and protecting the head of the penis as well as clitoris.

9. **(c)** Assertion is true but Reason is false.
The testes of human males are situated outside the abdominal cavity within a pouch called scrotum. It is connected to the abdomen via inguinal canal.

10. **(c)** Assertion is true but Reason is false.
Each ovary is covered by a thin epithelium which encloses the ovarian stroma and the stroma is divided into two zones, viz a peripheral cortex and an inner medulla.

11. **(a)** Both Assertion and Reason are true, Reason is the correct explanation of Assertion.
The male urethra is lined by pseudostratified epithelium.

12. **(b)** Both Assertion and Reason are true but Reason is not the correct explanation of Assertion.
Ovaries are the primary female sex organs that produce the female gamete (ovum) and several steroid hormones.

13. In human male sperm, the acrosome is a vesicle present at its tip. It contain soluble proteolytic enzymes. When the sperm comes in contact with the ovum there is aerosome reaction. This reaction enables the sperm to break through the protective coat of the egg. Which is zone pellucids. Hence the sperms enters the ovum and followed by nuclear fusion resulting in fertilisation.

14. The proximal centrolie serves as the microtubule-organizing center after fertilisation. They accumulate centrosomal components from the oocyte to form sperm aster, zygote aster and mitotic apparatus after fertilisation.

15. Semen is a greyish white bodily fluid that is secreted by the gonads of male of male animals. It carries sperm or the spermatozoa and fructose and other enzyme that help sperm to survive and facilitate successful fertilisation.

16. Eggs are stationary. Sperms released have to travel up to the eggs with the help of tail.

17. Puberty is onset of reproductive phase of human i.e. period when reproductive organ becomes functional. Boys attain puberty at 14-15 years of age while girls at 12-15 years.

18. The ability to reproduce is one of the unifying characteristics of all living things. Sexual reproduction produces offsprings that are genetically different from their parents.

19. In sexual reproduction, new individuals are produced by the fusion of haploid gametes to form diploid zygote. Sperms are male gametes, Ova (ovum, singular) are female gametes.

20. Sexual reproduction offers the benefit of generating genetic variation among offspring, which enhances the chances of the population's survival.

21. Human reproduction employs internal fertilization, and depends on the integrated action of **hormones**, the **nervous system**, and the reproductive system. **Gonads** are sex organs that produce gametes.

22. Testes are suspended outside the abdominal cavity by the **scrotum**, a pouch of skin that keeps the testes far from the body at an optimal temperature for sperm development. **Seminiferous tubules** are inside each testis, and where sperm are produced by meiosis.

23. Male sex hormones are androgens secreted from the Leydig cells. Testosterone is the most abundant-androgen released by Leydig cells. Testosterone is responsible for the growth & development of male secondary sex organs & male secondary characteristics.

24. Because human sperm cells cannot develop at body temperature. The temperature of scrotum is congenial for sperm production, as it is lower by 2°C than the normal body temperature (37°C).

25. The female gonads, ovaries, are located within the lower abdominal cavity. The ovary contains many **follicles** composed of a developing egg surrounded by an outer layer of follicle cells.

26. After puberty, the ovary cycles between a follicular phase (maturing follicles) and **luteal** phase (presence of the **corpus luteum**) and menstruation phase. These cyclic phases are interrupted only by pregnancy and continue until menopause, when reproductive capability ends.

27. The uterus has an inner layer, the **endometrium**, in which a fertilized egg implants. At the lower end of the uterus, the **cervix** connects the uterus to the vagina.

28. The female external genitals are collectively known as the **vulva**. The sides of the vulva have two small fleshy folds, the labia minora (lesser lips) which are hidden by larger hairy folds the labia majora (greater lips). In the upper most angle of the vulva, in front of the urethrel opening is located a small erectile clitoris which is highly sensitive.

29. Seminal vesicles secrete spermatozoa activating substances, such as fructose, citrate, prostaglandins & several proteins. Prostaglandins in the semen may stimulate contractions of the female uterus, which help move sperm up the female reproductive tract.

30. Scrotum is the sac of skin, situated out side the body cavity and allows sperms to develop at the optimum temperature (2-2.5°C lower than the normal body temperature.)

31.

	Secondary sex characters in male	Secondary sex characters in female
1.	Body is more muscular and stronger	Body is less muscular and weaker.
2.	Beard, moustaches and chest hair are present	Beard, moustaches and chest hair are absent.
3.	Mammary glands are poorly developed	Mammary glands (breasts) are very well developed.
4.	Pelvis is narrow	pelvis is broad.
5.	Larynx is more apparent	Larynx is less apparent

Practice Exercise-2

1. (b) The immature male germ cells or primary spermatocyte duplicates its DNA and subsequently undergoes meiosis I which is a reductional division to produce two haploid secondary spermatocytes.

2. (b) The ovulation (ovulatory phase) is followed by the luteal phase (latter phase of the menstrual cycle) during which the remaining parts of the Graafian follicle transform as the corpus luteum, which produces progesterone. So progesterone is highest at luteal phase.

3. (d)

4. (d) Primary germ layers are ectoderm, endoderm & mesoderm. Many animals are primarily triploblastic, as endoderm (inner) and ectoderm (outer) interact to produce a third germ layer, called mesoderm (middle). Together, the three germ layers will give rise to every organ in the body, from skin and hair to the digestive tract.

5. (b)

6. (d) Fertilization is the fusion of male and female gametes which takes place in the ampullary isthmic junction of fallopian tube. Implantation is the attachment of the blastocysts in the endometrium. Cleavage is the mitotic cell division which takes place on fertilized egg. Morula is the solid mass of 32 cells formed from the zygote after successive mitotic division. Blastocysts is the developmental stage which embedded in the uterine endometrium by a process called implantation and leads to pregnancy. The blastocyst is a structure formed in the early development of mammals.

7. (c) Assertion is true but Reason is false.
The first mestruation begins at puberty (12-13 years in girls) and is called menarche. Mestruation occurs in every 28 or 29 days in human females. Mestrual cycle stops in women around 50 years of age. This is known as menopause.

8. (c) Assertion is true but Reason is false.
Fertilisation does not guarantee the establishment of pregnancy. But pregnancy is guaranteed by implantation.

9. (c) Assertion is true but Reason is false.
Sperms reach the epididymis and stay there for 8-17 days for maturation.

10. (d) Assertion and Reason are false.
No more oogonia are formed and added after birth. These cells start division and enter into prophase II of the meiotic division and get temporarily arrested at that stage, called primary oocytes.

11. Hormone therapy.

12. Transmission of genes from both parents to offspring.

13. Contact between sperm and egg.

14. Gastrulation.

15. The nourishing connection between the mother's and embryo's systems.

16. 3 trimesters. **17.** Ovary. **18.** Umbilical cord.

19. Placenta, yolk sac, and reduced number of eggs.

20. HCG (Human Chorionic Gonadotropin).

21. Morphogenesis.

22. Production of gametes (Sperm or Ova).

23. Reptile.
Note : Fishes and frogs lay their eggs in water. The sperms are also shed in water and fertilization is external. These animals do not develop any organs for sperm transfer. But, the reptiles, being terrestrial animals, have adaptations for internal fertilization.

24. Amnion. **25.** Progesterone.

26. Oestrogen. **27.** Oestrogen

28. Follicle stimulating harmone (FSH)

29. Cowper's glands

30. Menstrual cycles vary from between 15 and 31 days. The first day of the cycle is the first day of blood flow (day 0) known as menstruation.

31. Estrogen and progesterone stimulate the development of the endometrium and preparation of the uterine inner lining for implantation of a zygote.

32. An egg reacts rapidly to the entry of the sperms. First, the egg becomes activated and undergoes depolarization of its membrane. Second the egg exhibit cortical reaction & shows zona reactions. The plasma membrane is altered immediately to make the egg impervious to any other sperm.

33. Fertilization is the fusion of egg & sperm. Vasectomy, oral contraceptives, condom and diaphragm prevents fertilization.

34. Gestation period refers to the period of pregnancy. From the day of the fertilization, the embryo starts growing and reaches a final stage period.

35. Colostrum is a first secretion from the breast, occurring shortly after childbirth. It is a thick yellowish in colour and very rich in proteins and salts. It contains large granular cells called colostrum corpuscles.

36. The phenomenon of fusion of the male and female germ cells or gametes is called fertilization. If the fusion takes place outside the body of the parents, as in fishes and amphibians, it is called external fertilization, on the other hand, if the fusion takes place within the body of the mother, as in reptiles, birds and mammals, it is called internal fertilization. Fertilization ensures restoration of the original diploid nature of the parent. It causes new combinations of characters.

Past year Exercise 

1. In human embryo, the primary oocyte grows in size and undergoes meiosis-I and forms a larger cell, the secondary oocyte and a smaller cell, the first polar body.

2. In human embryo, trophoblast forms the foetal part of placenta and does not form any part of the embryo proper.

3. Blastocyst.

4. Foetal ejection reflex causes quick release of oxytocin from the maternal posterior lobe of pituitary gland which is responsible for parturition.

5. Difference between spermiogenesis and spermiation is

Spermiogenesis	Spermiation
It is the process of transforming spermatids into matured spermatozoa or sperms.	Sperms get attached to Sertoli cells to draw nourishment and finally released from seminiferous tubules by the process called spermiation.

6. Location of Sertoli cells-within lining of seminiferous tubule of testis.
   Function : They provide nutrition to the developing sperm cells.

7. Oogenesis initiate in foetal stage of females while Spermatogenesis in males, starts at puberty.

8. Acrosome is present in head region of the mature sperm.
   Function : Enzymes present in acrosome help in fertilization of the ovum.

9. During fertilization, a sperm comes in contact with the zona pellucida layer of the ovum and induces changes in the membrane that prevents the entry of additional sperms. This ensures that only one sperm can fertile an ovum.

10. At the age of 50, the woman undergo menopause *i.e.*, stop menstruation and thus, cannot conceive.

11. Sertoli cells nourish the germ cells in the testes. The bases of the sertoli cells adhere to the basal lamina and their apical ends frequently extend into the lumen of the seminiferous tubules.

12. During Anaphase-I of meiotic cell-division where segregation of an independent pair of chromosome occurs.

13. (i) A – Spermatogonia   B – Interstitial cells
       C – Spermatozoa.
    (ii) A – Spermatogonia produce the spermatozoa (sperms)
    C – Sertoli cells provide nutrition to the germ cells.

14. After ovulatory phase (ovulation), the luteal phase starts. The remaining parts of ruptured Graafian follicle transform as corpus luteum in this phase. The corpus luteum secretes large amount of progesterone which is essential for the maintenance of endometrium.
    In the absence of fertilization, the corpus luteum degenerates causing disintegration of endometrium leading to menstruation.

15. Sectional view of seminiferous tubule in human male.

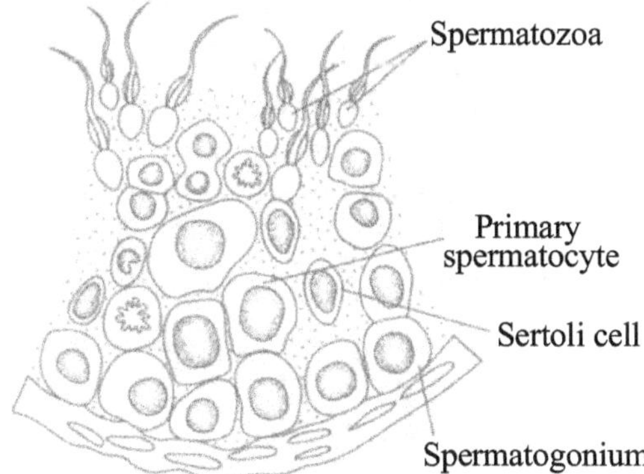

Fig.: Diagrammatic sectional view of a seminiferous tubule (enalarged)

16. Placenta acts as an endocrine tissue and secrets hormones like hCG (human Chorionic Gonadotropin), hPL (human Placental Lactogen), Oestrogens, Progesterone. During pregnancy the levels of hormones like estrogens, progestrogens, cortisol, prolactin, thyroxine, etc. are increased several-folds in the maternal blood. All these hormones support foetal growth and metabolic changes in mother and maintenance of pregnancy.

17. Differences between menarche and menopause.

Menarche	Menopause
1. It refers to the beginning of menstrual cycle in human female at puberty.	It refers to the stoppage of menstrual cycle at the age of about 45-50 in human female.
2. It indicates the start of reproductive phase.	It indicates the end of reproductive phase.

18. Differences between follicular and luteal phase.

Follicular Phase	Luteal Phase
1. Primary follicles in the ovary grow to be come mature follicle (Graafian follicle).	The ruptured Graafian follicle transforms into corpus luteum.
2. Changes in follicular phase are due to high level of FSH, LH and oestrogen.	It secretes large amount of progesterone.

19. The corpus luteum degenerates in case of fertilization does not occur. The endometrium layer of uterus disintegrates, leading to menstrual flow.

20. Sertoli cells are located on the inside lining of seminiferous tuble. They provide nutrition to the developing sperm cells.

21. (i) Oogenesis begins during the embryonic development stage when a couple of million gamete mother cells (oogonia) are formed within each foetal ovary.

    (ii) (a) Sertoli cells are located on the inside lining of seminiferous tubule. These cells provide nutrition to the germ cells.

        (b) Leydig cells or interstitial cells are located in the regions outside the seminiferous tubule called interstitial spaces. These cells synthesise and secrete testicular hormone called androgens.

22. Reproductive system of human female.

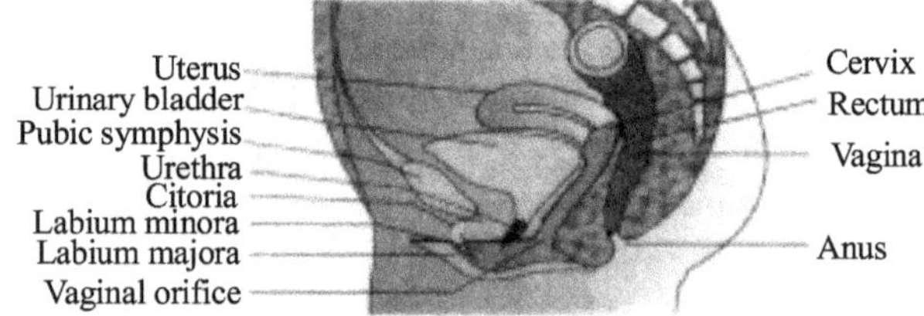

Fig.: Lateral view of female reproductive system

23. Structure of human sperm.

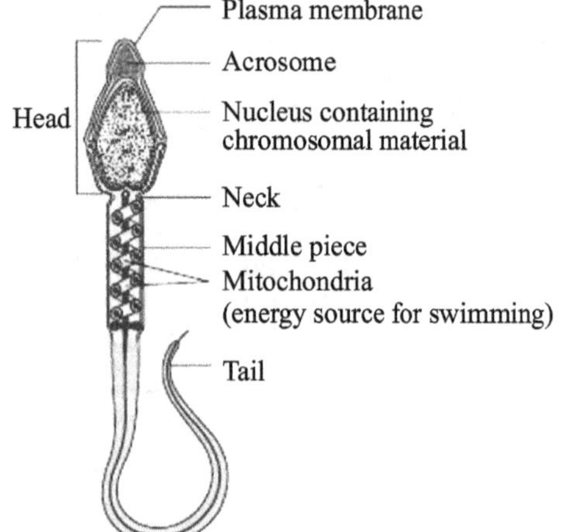

24. Menstrual cycle in human female is under hormonal control in the following ways

    (i) Follicular or proliferative phase is under the influence of FSH from the anterior pituitary.

    (ii) The follicular cells of mature follicle secrete estrogens, which control the growth and maintenance of the secondary sex organs like uterus, fallopian tube, etc.

25. The hormones produced only during pregnancy in human female are human Chorionic Gonadotropin (hCG), human Placental Lactogen (hPL) and relaxin.

hCG and hPL - are secreated by placenta while Relaxin is secreted by the ovary.

26. (i) The signals for parturition originate from fully developed foetus and placenta and induce mild uterine contractions called foetal ejection reflex which in turn triggers the release of oxytocin hormone.

    (ii) Colostrum is the yellow milk produced during the initial few days of lactation. It contains several antibodies (IgA) essential to develop resistance for the newborn babies.

27. (i) **Fimbriae** are the feathery finger-like projections present at the end of Fallopian tubes and it collects the ovum after its release from the ovary into the Fallopian tube.

    (ii) **Coleoptile** is a conical sheath present in the monocot seeds, its function is to protect the developing plumule.

    (iii) **Oxytocin** is a hormone secreted by the posterior pituitary and it stimulates the contraction of uterine muscles during child birth (parturition).

28. (i) **Middle piece in human sperm** contains several mitochondria which produces energy for the motility of the sperm.

    (ii) **Tapetum in anthers** It is the innermost layer of the anther. The main function of tapetum is to provide nourishment to the developing pollen grains.

    (iii) **Luteinizing hormones** in human male stimulates the Leydig cells to produce testosterone.

29. (i) Secretions of **seminal vesicle** glands constitute the seminal plasma which is rich in fructose, calcium and certain enzymes and hormones. The fructose is a source of energy for sperms. Alkaline nature of seminal fluid neutralises the acidic nature of female reproductive tract.

    (ii) **Scutellum** is a tissue present in seed to absorb food from the adjacent endosperm and develop into growing embryo.

    (iii) **Acrosome** is the cap-like covering or structure that is present at the tip of the sperm (male gamete). It contains enzymes, that help the sperm enter in to the cytoplasm of the ovum through the zona pellucida and plasma membrane.

30. (i) Testes are located outside the abdominal cavity within a pouch called scrotum. Scrotum keeps the testes at a temperature 2-2.5°C lower than the internal body temperature, which is necessary for the synthesis of sperms.

(ii) In honeybees, worker bees are all females. Sometimes, they may develop functional ovaries and lay unfertilized eggs, which normally result into drone bees. Hence, worker bees are capable of producing diploid eggs parthenogenetically and replaces the queen bee if she dies.

31. Oogenesis starts during embryonal stages where millions of gamete mother cells -oogonia are formed in foetal ovary. Oogonia start meiotic division and enter **prophase-I** and get temporarily arrested at this stage to form **primary oocytes.** Each primary oocyte gets surrounded by a layer of granulosa cells forming **primary follicle.**

Primary follicles form **secondary follicles**, surrounded by more layers of granulosa cells.

Secondary follicle transforms into **tertiary follicle** with a fluid filled cavity-**antrum** having **theca externa** and **theca interna**. Primary oocyte completes Ist meiotic division (grows in size) forming large haploid **secondary oocyte** and a tiny **first polar body.**

Tertiary follicle transforms into mature **Graafian follicle** which bursts to release ovum/secondary oocyte **(ovulation).**

The second meiotic division in secondary oocyte is completed after the penetration of sperm, to form **haploid ovum (ootid) and secondary polar body.**

32. After implantation, the finger-like projections called chorionic villi develop from the trophoblast, and get surrounded and interdigitated with the uterine tissue jointly, to form a structural and functional unit between the developing embryo (foetus) and maternal body (called placenta).

The placenta facilitate the supply of O_2 and nutrients to the embryo and removal of CO_2 and excretory waste material from the embryo.

33.

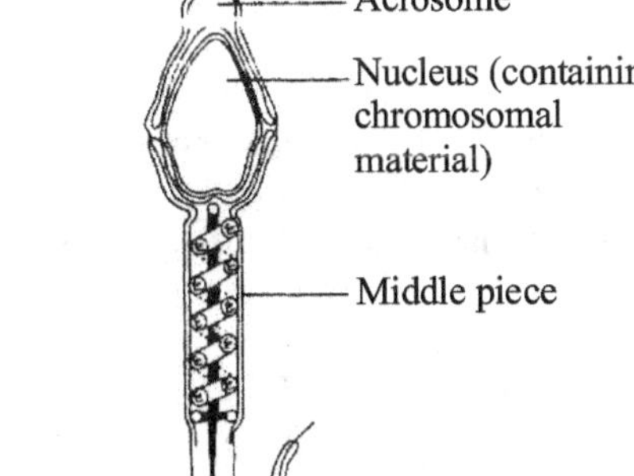

Fig : Structure of a sperm

Functions

(a) Acrosome : It contains hydrolytic enzymes which are used to contact and penetrate the egg (ovum) at the time of fertilization.

(b) Nucleus : The nucleus contains DNA as the hereditary genetic material and fuses with the female nucleus in the ovum at the time of fertilization for the inheritance of characters to the offspring.

(c) Middle piece : It contains mitochondria and provides energy for the movement of sperm.

34. (a)

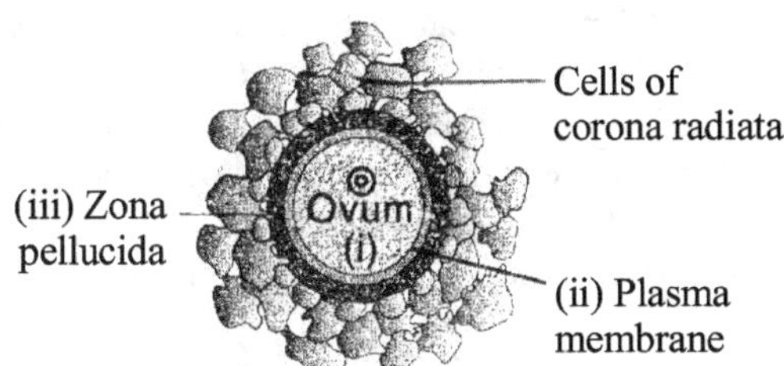

(b) Zona pellucida is layer of glycoprotein that surrounds the plasma membrane of mammalian egg cell.

Just after the fusion of sperm and plasma membrane of secondary oocyte, cortical granules present below the plasma membrane, release enzymes, which harden the zona pellucida to prevent entry of additional sperms.

35. Name of stage = Blastocyst

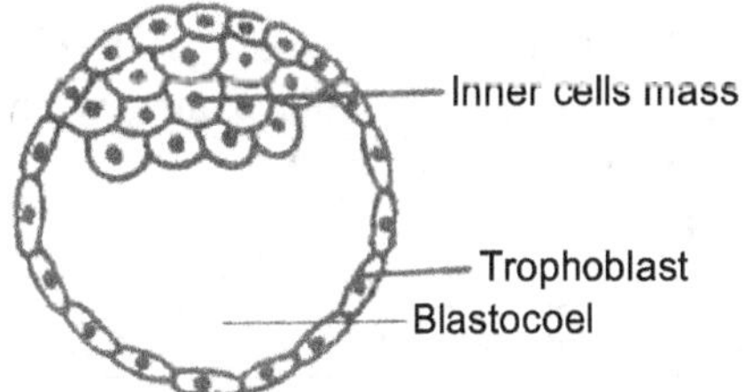

Fig. A blastocyst

36. ZIFT (zygote intra-fallopian transfer) is a part of test-tube baby programme performed specially where the male partner is infertile. The egg is extracted from female and is *in-vitro* fertilized by the sperms of husband/donor. The zygote. is made to develop into embryo. When the embryos are at 8-celled blastomere stage, are transferred into fallopian tube.

37. A pair of testes is situated outside the abdominal cavity within a pouch called **scrotum.** The scrotum helps in maintaining the low temperature of the testes ($2 - 2.5°C$ lower than the normal internal body temperature) necessary for spermatogenesis.

38. (a) Sertoli cells are found in seminiferous tubule membranes and provide nutrition to the germ cells.

(b) The regions outside the seminiferous tubules contain masses of cells called interstitial cells or leydig cells. These cells synthesize and secrete the male hormones called androgens (testosterone) which maintain male sex characteristics.

39. LH secretion increases during mid of menstrual cycle and it is responsible for rupturing of Graafian follicle to release female gamete, *i.e.* secondary oocyte. This process is called **ovulation** and as mentioned above, occurs on 14th day of the cycle in a normal case.

40. Uterus is a pear shaped structure whose wall is composed of three layers, outer-perimetrium, middle-myometrium and inner-endometrium.

The inner glandular wall of the uterus is known as endometrium.

Role - During the menstrual cycle, the endometrium wall grows into a thick, blood vessel-rich, glandular layer. This condition of the endometrium favours the implantation of the foetus. If fertilization does not occur, the endometrium is shed during the haemorrhagic phase of the menstrual cycle. The middle wall of the uterus is known as myometrium.

Role- It consists of smooth muscles. It brings about contraction while delivery of the baby.

41.

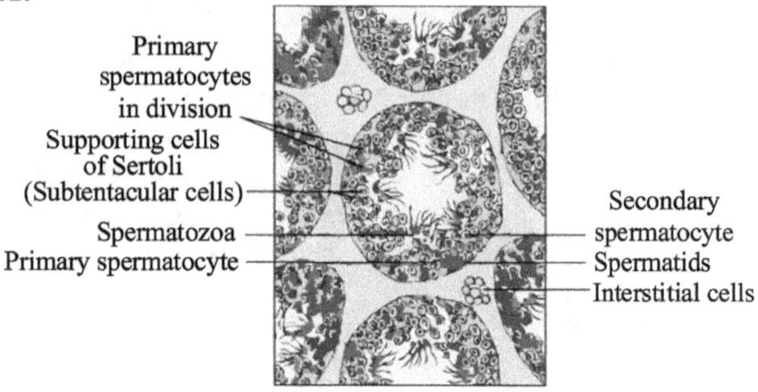

Fig: Sectional view of a human seminiferous tubule

42. (a) The sequence of secretion of the given hormones in a pregnant woman is as follows:

   (i) FSH   (ii) LH

   (iii) hCG   (iv) Relaxin

Hormone	Source	Functions
FSH	Anterior pituitary lobe	Stimulates the growth of ovarian follicles and maturation of primary oocytes
LH	Anterior pituitary lobe	Induces ovulation and maintains corpus luteum
hCG	Chorionic cells of placenta	Maintains the corpus luteum and stimulates it to secrete progesterone
Relaxin	Ovary	Helps during child birth by relaxing the pelvic muscles as well as muscles of the cervix.

43.

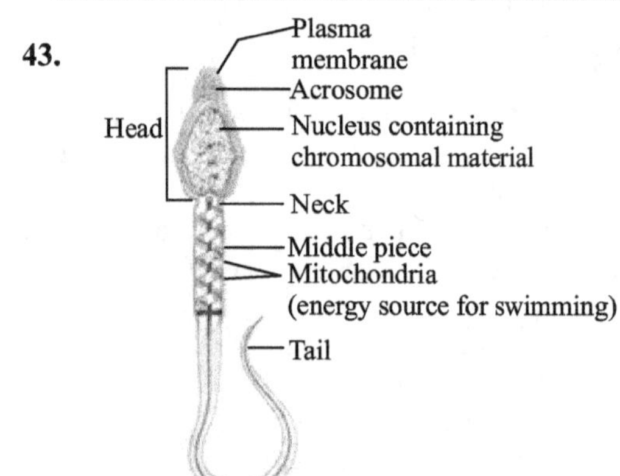

(1) **Acrosome :** It is a cap like structure, filled with hydrolytic enzymes that help fertilisation of the ovum.

(2) **Middle piece :** Possesses numerous mitochondria, which produces energy for the movement of tail.

(3) Facilitate sperm motility essential for fertilization.

44. The internal organs of the male reproductive system are called accessory organs. They include the vas deferens, seminal vesicles, prostate gland, and bulbourethral glands. Labelled diagram showing interrelationship of four accessory ducts in a human male reproductive system is given below:

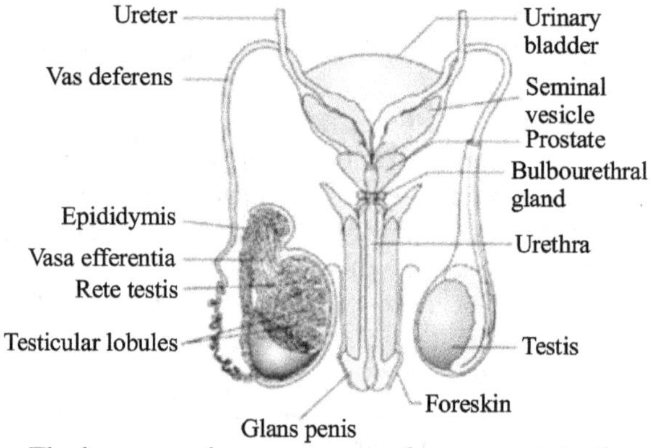

45. The human male sex accessory ducts are rete testis, vasa efferentia, vas deferens and epididymis.

Rete testis: The seminiferous tubules of the testis open into the vasa efferentia through rete testis.

Vasa efferentia: It leaves the testis and opens into the epididymis which is located along the posterior surface of each testis.

Epididymis: This leads to vas deferns which ascends to the abdomen and loops over the urinary bladder. The epididymis receives a duct from seminal vesicle that opens into urethra as the ejaculatory duct.

NCERT Exemplar

1. **(d)** Isthmus is the part of female reproductive system. The fallopian tube (oviduct) in female reproductive system consists four regions, *i.e.*, Infundibulum, ampulla, isthmus and uterine part. Isthmus has a narrow lumen and it joins the uterus. It is the line that separates the body of the uterus from the cervix.

2. **(a)** One of the three glycoproteins (ZP3) that functions as a sperm receptor, binds to a complementary molecule on the surface of the sperm head. This binding of the sperm head to the receptor molecule ZP3 induces the acrosome of the sperm to release its hydrolytic enzymes (sperm lysins).

3. **(b)** Ampulla is one of the four region of Fallopian tubes. The oviducts (Fallopian tubes), uterus and vagina constitute the female accessory ducts.

4. **(c)** From the urinary bladder the urethra originates and extends through the penis to its external opening called urethral meatus. Opening of vas deferens along with a duct of seminal vesicle open into urethra as the ejaculatory duct.

5. **(a)** The sperms and ovum fuses together to form a diploid zygote. As the zygote moves through the isthmus of the oviduct towards the uterus, the mitotic division (cleavage) starts and forms 2, 4, 8, 16 daughter cells called blastomeres. The embryo containig 8-16 blastomeres is called a morula. The morula further divides and transforms into blastocyst, further gets embedded in the endometrium of the uterus. This is called implantation.

6. **(b)**

	Column I	Column II
A.	Trophoblast	Outer layer of blastocyst attached to the endometrium
B.	Cleavage	Mitotic division of zygote
C.	Inner cell mass	Group of cells that would differentiate as embryo
D.	Implantation	Embedding of blastocyst in the endometrium

7. **(b)**

	Column I	Column II
A.	Head	Genetic material
B.	Middle piece	Energy
C.	Acrosome	Enzymes
D.	Tail	Sperm motility

8. **(b)** Assertion and Reason are true, but Reason is not the correct explanation of Assertion.
The acrosome is filled with enzymes that help in fertilisation of the ovum.

9. **(b)** Assertion and Reason are true, but Reason is not the correct explanation of Assertion.
Gonadotropin releasing hormone (GnRH) is a hypothlamic hormone.

10. Cervix helps in regulating the passage of sperms into the uterus and forms the birth canal to facilitate parturition.

11. This is because of a neural signal given by the maternal endometrium to its hypothalamus in presence of a zygote to sustain the gonadotropin (LH) secretion, so as to maintain the corpus luteum as long as the embryo remains there. In the absence of a zygote, therefore, the corpus luteum can not be maintained longer.

12. Placenta facilitates the supply of oxygen and nutrients to the embryo. It also removes CO_2 excretory wastes produced by embryo.

Objective Practice Exercise

1. **(c)** The epididymis is comma-shaped mass of thread-like tubules attached to the posterior border of a testis.

2. **(d)**   3. **(a)**   4. **(d)**   5. **(b)**   6. **(a)**

7. **(a)** Seminal plasma in human males are rich in fructose, calcium and certain enzymes. They provide a medium for transport of sperms, nourishes and activates sperms.

8. **(c)** A bulbourethral gland (or Cowper's gland) is one of two small exocrine glands present in the reproductive system of human males. They are homologous to Bartholin's glands in females.

9. **(a)**   10. **(c)**   11. **(a)**   12. **(c)**

13. **(b)** Foreskin is a double-layered fold of smooth muscle tissue, blood vessels, neurons, skin, and mucous membrane that covers and protects the glans penis and the urinary meatus when the penis is not erect. The foreskin is mobile, fairly stretchable, and acts as a natural lubricant.

14. **(d)** The urethra originates from the urinary bladder and extends through the penis to its external opening called urethral meatus.

15. **(d)** Bulbourethral gland, also called as Cowper's gland, is one of two small exocrine glands in the male reproductive system. This gland releases a small amount of fluid just prior to ejaculation to decrease the acidity in the urethra. Bulbourethral gland are homologous to Bartholin's glands present in females.

16. **(a)** The structures through which a sperm passes from the testis to the exterior include the epididymis, ductus deferens, ejaculatory duct, prostatic urethra, membranous urethra, and penile urethra. The secretions of the prostate gland empty into the prostatic urethra; the secretions of the seminal vesicles empty into the ejaculatory duct; and the secretions of the bulbourethral glands empty into the penile urethra.

17. **(a)** The seminal vesicles are involved in producing the seminal fluid. One of the components of the seminal fluid is an energy source for the sperm in the form of fructose.

18. **(b)** The vagina is an internal reproductive organ and is not considered as part of the vulva.

19. **(b)**

20. **(a)** Clitoris is a small, sensitive, erectile part of the female genitals at the anterior end of the vulva. It is homologous with the penis.

21. **(b)**

22. **(a)** Oogenesis begins with primordial germ cells in the ovary.

23. **(b)**

24. **(a)** This is the capillary-rich inner wall of the uterus, where implantation is accomplished for the developing human embryo.

25. **(d)**   26. **(c)**

27. **(c)** The female reproductive system is not completely closed, and the egg is released into the abdominal cavity near the opening of the oviduct.

28. **(b)**   29. **(c)**   30. **(d)**   31. **(b)**   32. **(a)**

33. **(d)** In human beings, menstrual cycle ceases around 50 years of age; that is termed as menopause.

34. **(a)** The zygote divides mitotically to form 8, 16 daughter cells called blastomeres. This stage is called morula which continues to divide and transforms into blastocyst.

35. **(c)** Implantation is not the immediate process. It takes 5 days to occur after fertilization.

36. **(b)**

37. **(b)** Semen, or seminal fluid, is an alkaline fluid that contains spermatozoa embedded in seminal plasma. Semen is ejaculated by male reproductive system during orgasm.

38. **(a)** Urethra is not a paired structure in male. The urethra is a tube that connects the urinary bladder to the urinary meatus for the removal of fluids from the body. In male, the urethra travels through the penis, and carries semen as well as urine and in female, the urethra is shorter and emerges at the female external urethral orifice above the vaginal opening.

39. **(c)** With the proximal centriole the sperm adds a division centre in the egg, as the centriole of the ovum ceases to function.

40. (b)

41. (b) Scrotum is a part of the external male genitalia located behind and underneath the penis. It is the small muscular sac that contains and protects the testicles, blood vessels, and part of the spermatic cord. The scrotum protects the testicles (or testes, the primary male sex organ) from temperature changes. In order to insure normal sperm production, the scrotum keeps the testes at a temperature slightly cooler than the rest of the body by contracting or expanding.

42. (a) Clitoris is a small, sensitive, erectile part of the female genitals at the anterior end of the vulva. It is homologous with the penis.

43. (d) Immature male germ cells (also called as spermatogonia) produce sperms in the process of spermatogenesis. Spermatogonia proliferate continuously by mitotic divisions around the outer edge of the seminiferous tubules, next to the basal lamina. Some of these cells stop proliferation and differentiate into primary spermatocytes. After they proceed through the first meiotic division, two secondary spermatocytes are produced. The two secondary spermatocytes undergo the second meiotic division to form four haploid spermatids. These spermatids differentiate morphologically into sperm by nuclear condensation, ejection of the cytoplasm and formation of the acrosome and flagellum.

44. (c) In biology, antrum is a general term for a cavity or chamber, which may have specific meaning in reference to certain organs or sites in the body. Tertiary follicle of ovary contains a fluid filled cavity called antrum and a secondary oocyte ready for ovulation.

45. (c) The corpus luteum secretes large amounts of progesterone which is essential for maintenance of the endometrium and the pregnancy but its decrease in secretion triggers the menstrual cycle.

46. (b) The ovulation (ovulatory phase) is followed by the luteal phase (latter phase of the menstrual cycle) during which the remaining parts of the Graafian follicle transform as the corpus luteum, which produces progesterone. So progesterone is highest at luteal phase.

47. (c) The menstrual phase is followed by the follicular phase. During this phase, the primary follicles in the ovary grow to become a fully mature Graafian follicle and simultaneously the endometrium of uterus regenerates through proliferation.

48. (a) Luteal phase is also called as the secretory phase of menstruation cycle. The luteal phase begins with the formation of the corpus luteum and ends in either pregnancy or luteolysis. The main hormone associated with this stage is progesterone, which is significantly higher during the luteal phase than other phases of the cycle.

49. (a) During pregnancy, all events of the menstrual cycle stop and there is no menstruation.

50. (b) The process of insemination is the release of semen containing male gametes, the sperms, into the female reproductive tract during coitus.

1. (b) Spermatogenesis involves conversion of a diploid structure (spermatogonia) into haploid structures (spermatozoa). Spermiogenesis changes a haploid structure (spermatid) into another haploid structure (spermatozoon).

2. (b)

Chapter Test 

1. (c) Fertilization through the process of the fusion of haploid male and female gametes, ensures the restoration of the diploidy of the human foetus.

2. (a) The outer wall of the blastocyst *i.e.,* the trophoblast gets attached to the endometrium of the uterus during implantation.

3. (d) Primary germ layers are ectoderm, endoderm & mesoderm. Many animals are primarily triploblastic, as endoderm (inner) and ectoderm (outer) interact to produce a third germ layer, called mesoderm (middle). Together, the three germ layers will give rise to every organ in the body, from skin and hair to the digestive tract.

4. (a) Vasa efferentia are fine ciliated ductules that arise from the seminiferous tubules of testis (where sperms are formed) and Open into apididymis which in a man of long narrow closely coiled tubule lying along the inner side of testis. Epididymis stores the sperms. Then, if vasa efferentia get blocked, sperms will not be from perted from tenter to epididymis.

5. (b)

6. (a) Assertion and Reason are true and Reason is the correct explanation of Assertion
ADAM is called andropause in males.

7. (b) Assertion and Reason are true, but Reason is not the correct explanation of Assertion.
By the end of nine months or 40 weeks (third trimester) of pregnancy, the foetus is fully developed and is ready for delivery.

8. (c)   **9.** (b)   **10.** (b)   **11.** (a)

12. (d)

13. During ovulation, the mature follicle (Graafian follicle) bursts and ovum is released.

14. Due to accumulation of fluid, the follicular cavity increases in size and a fluid-filled eccentric cavity, the antrum develops.

15. A follicle consists of an oocyte surrounded by one or more layers of follicular cells, the granulosa cells which are derived from the germinal epithelium. The mature follicle, the Graafian follicle, is about 2.5 cm in diameter.

3 — Reproductive Health

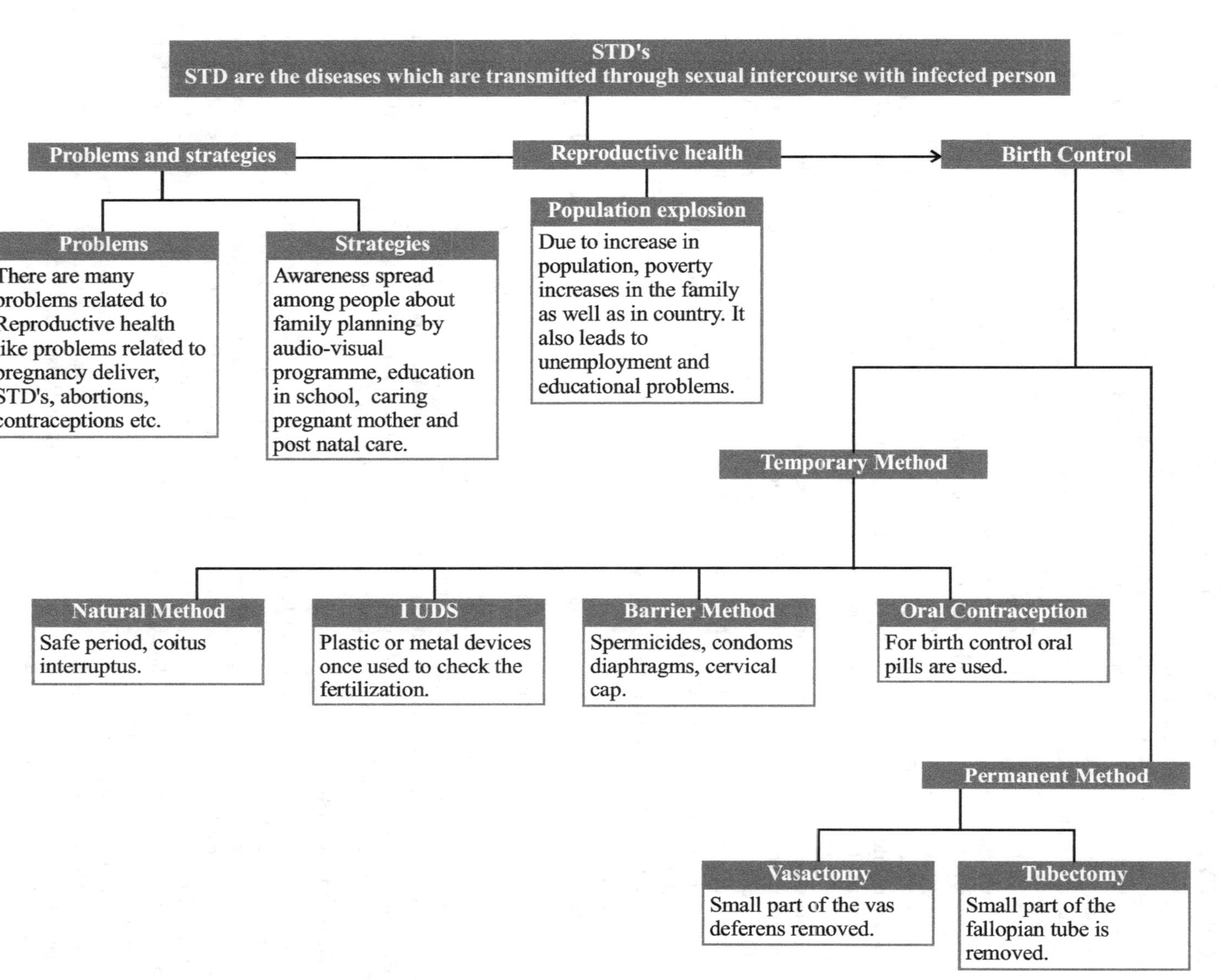

Topic 1 — Reproductive Health, Population Explosion and Birth Control 

According to the World Health Organization (WHO), the reproductive health means a total well-being in all aspect of reproduction, i.e., physical, emotional social and behavioural. Good reproductive health implies that people are able to have a satisfying & safe sex life, the capability to reproduce and the freedom to decide when and how often to do so. Health is affected by _________.

(i)   Genetic disorders and deficiencies with which an individual is born.

(ii)   Infections.

(iii)   Life style that includes - food and water, rest, exercise and habits.

REPRODUCTIVE HEALTH - PROBLEMS AND STRATEGIES

India was the first in the world to initiate various action plans/programmes at national level to attain total reproductive health as a social goal. To achieve total reproductive health, some plans and programmes were started. Family planning programme was initiated in 1951 and was periodically assessed. These programmes were popularly named as **Reproductive and Child Health Care (RCH) programmes**. The main aim of such programmes is

(i)   To create awareness among people about reproductive organs, accessory organs of reproduction, secondary sexual characters, adolescence and associated changes, safe and hygienic sexual practices.

(ii)   With the help of audio-visual and print-media governmental and non-governmental agencies have taken various steps to create awareness among the people about reproduction related aspects. Parents, other close relatives, teachers and friends, also have a major role in the dissemination of the above information.

(iii)   For successful action plan to attain reproductive health requires good infrastructural facilities, professional expert knowledge and material support. These are necessary to provide medical help and care for reproduction related problems like menstrual problems, infertility, pregnancy, delivery, contraception, abortions, sexually transmitted diseases (STDs), etc.
        Implementation of better techniques and new strategies are also required to provide better care and to help people for reproductive health.

(iv)   **Amniocentesis** is a foetal sex determination and disorder test based on the chromosomal pattern in the amniotic fluid surrounding the developing embryo. It is being used to kill the normal female foetus. It is legally banned in our country because to avoid female foeticide.

(v)   To prevent & control sexually transmitted diseases by providing proper information about reproductive organs, adolescence.

(vi)   Knowledge about available birth control methods, care of pregnant mothers, post natal care of the mother and the child, importance of breast-feeding, equality of sex etc. among fertile couples and those in marriageable age group and other goals of RCH programmes.

Maternity and Child Health and Family Planning

This programme of health centres

(i)   Gives necessary information, guidance and help to the mothers before and after delivery, so that they may properly look after themselves and the infants.

(ii)   It also ensures safe delivery of infant and post-natal care.

(iii)   It provides for immunization of infants and prophylaxis against anaemia and vitamin deficiency.

(iv)   Trained midwives are necessary for such types of programmes.

(v)   It ensure to educate the newly wedded couples about the advantages of small family.

To implement various action plans/programmes successfully for building up a reproductively healthy society, we must have strong infrastructural facilities, professional expertise and material support. It is necessary to provide medical assistance and care to people during pregnancy, delivery, STDs, abortions, contraception, menstrual problems, infertility etc.

POPULATION EXPLOSION

The total number of individuals of a species living in an area form as population. The rapid increase in human population size over a relatively short period is called human population explosion. Scientific study of human population is called **demography**.

Increased health facilities and improvement in technology leading to better living conditions, have an explosive impact on the growth of population. The world population was about two billions in 1900 A.D. and it is 6 billions in just 100 years. A similar trend was observed in India too. Our population which was approximately 350 million at the time of our independence reached close to the billion by 2000 and crossed 1 billion in May 2000. This means that every sixth person in the world is an Indian. The probable reasons of human population explosion are :

(i)   decline in death and increase in longevity.

(ii)   decline in **maternal mortality rate (MMR)**.

(iii)   decline in **infant mortality rate (IMR)**.

(iv)   increase in the number of people in the reproductive age.

(v)   lack of education.

(vi)   increased food production.

(vii)   eradication of fatal epidemic diseases.

(viii) Better sanitation.

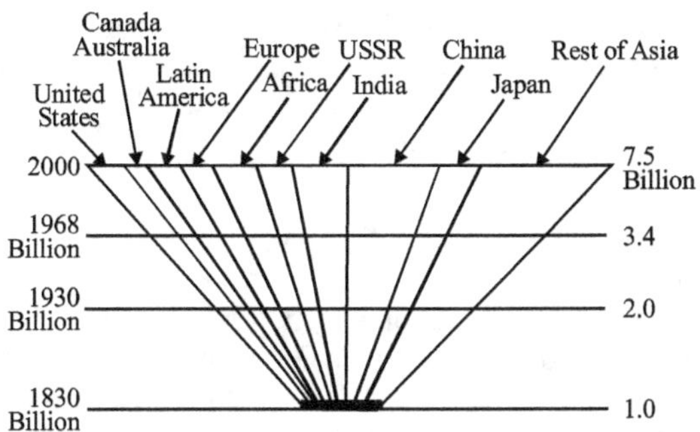

Fig. Estimated population of different nations by the year 2000

Effects of population Explosion
(i)   Socioeconomic problems due to shortage of space, food, unemloyment, poverty, educational and medical facilities.
(ii) Rapid ecodegradation due to deforestation and pollution etc.
(iii) Energy crisis due to greater demands of fuelwood, oil, gas, coal electricity.

Measures to control population Explosion
(i)   Presently, human population is doubling every 35 years. If this continues, soon earth will be over crowded with human beings.
(ii) People, particularly those in the reproductive age group, should be educated about the advantage of small family.
(iii) Raising the age of marriage is more effective means to control the population (now marriageable age of female is 18 years and that of male is 21 years).
(iv) Man has started realising his fate and has initiated plans to check this rate of increase by adopting following measures:
    (a) Planned control of population   (b) Education
    (c) Increasing marriageable age   (d) Family planning

BIRTH CONTROL

The process used to prevent conception or pregnancy without interfering with reproductive health of individual its called **Birth control**. The methods or devices used to limit the number of offsprings are called birth control methods or contraceptive. The various method are–

(i) Natural Methods

(safe period, coitus interruptus, abstinence, lactational amenorrhea).
Safe Period : A weak before & a week after the menses is considered as the safe period (rhythm method) for sexual intercourse. This idea is based on the following facts–
(a) Ovulation occur on the 14th day of menstruation.
(b) Ovum survives for about 2 days.
(c) Sperm remains alive for about 3 days.

Coitus Interruptus involves the withdrawal of the penis by the male before the ejaculation so that semen is not deposited in the vagina & there is no fertilization.
These methods avoid meeting of sperm and ovum and include periodic abstinence, coitus interruptus and lactational amenorrhea.
Periodic abstinence is one such method in which the couples avoid or abstains from coitus from day 10 to 17 of the menstrual cycle when ovulation could be expected. As chances of fertilization are very high during this period, it is called the **fertile period**. Therefore by obtaining from coitus during this period, conception could be prevented.
Lactational amenorrhea (absence of menstruation) method is based on the fact that ovulation & therefore the cycle do not occur during the period of intense lactation following parturition.

(ii) Barrier Method

(spermicides, condoms, diaphragms, cervical cap). Barrier methods prevent coming closer of ovum & sperm. Spermicidal creams, jellies & foams; if introduced into the vagina before intercourse they adhere to the mucous membrane & immobilise and kill sperms by inhibiting oxygen uptake.
Condom (Nirodh); is a rubber sheath to cover the erect penis. It checks pregnancy by preventing deposition of semen in the vagina. It is also a safeguard against AIDS & other sexual diseases. Both the male and the female condoms are disposable (not reusable), can be self-inserted and thereby give privacy to the user.
Diaphragms & cervical cap; are rubber plastic covers that are fitted on the cervix & check the entry of sperms into the uterus.

(iii) Intra Uterine Devices (IUDs)

Intrauterine devices are plastic or metal devices placed in the uterus. They contain either copper or a common synthetic hormone used in oral contraceptives. These include loop, copper-T, spiral etc. They prevent fertilization of the egg or implantation of egg. These IUDs are available in three forms–
(a) **Non-medicated** (e.g, Lippes loop).

(b) **Copper-T** releases Cu^{2+} which prevents implantation of fertilized egg. Copper seems to enhance the cellular response in endometrium by altering the biochemical composition of cervical mucus. Copper ions may affect the sperm motility, capacitation & survival.

(c) **Hormone releasing** (e.g, Progestasert, LNG-20). The hormone releasing IUD's in addition, make the uterus unsuitable for implantation and the cervix rostile to the sperms.

(iv) Oral Contraceptives

Birth control pills (oral contraceptive) chuk ovulation by inhibiting the secretion of **follicle stimulating (FSH)** and **luteinizing hormone (LH)** that are necessary for ovulation.

Such contraceptives are small oral doses of either progestogens or progestogen-estrogen combinations and are used by the females. They are used in the form of tablets and hence are popularly called the **pills**. The common pills are taken daily for a period of 21 days starting preferably within the first five days of menstrual cycle. After a gap of 7 days (during which menstruation occurs) it has to be repeated in the same pattern till the female desires to prevent conception. The pills inhibit ovulation and implantation as well as alter the quality of cervical mucus to prevent / retard entry of sperms. Pills are very effective with lesser side effects and are well accepted by the females.

Saheli– The new oral contraceptive for the females contains a non-steroidal preparation. It was developed by scientists at Central Drug Research Institute (CDRI) Lucknow, India. It is a 'once a week' pill with very few side effects and high contraceptive value. Morning Pills, i Pills and 72 hrs pills are also available for emergency use to avoid possible pregnancy due to rape or casual unprotected coitus or intercourse.

Permanent Methods

Permanent methods includes vasectomy in male and tubectomy in female. The surgical operation are minor and are usually performed under local anaesthesia. Permanent method is also called **surgical method** or **sterilization method**.

Vasectomy in male involves a cut in the scrotal sac, cutting or burning of the vas deferens (tubes that carry sperm) & blocking both the cut ends. Vasectomy prevents the passage of sperm into seminal fluid by blocking the vas deferens.

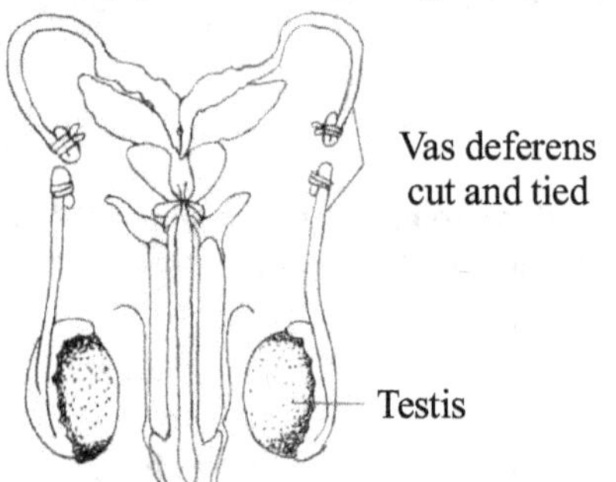

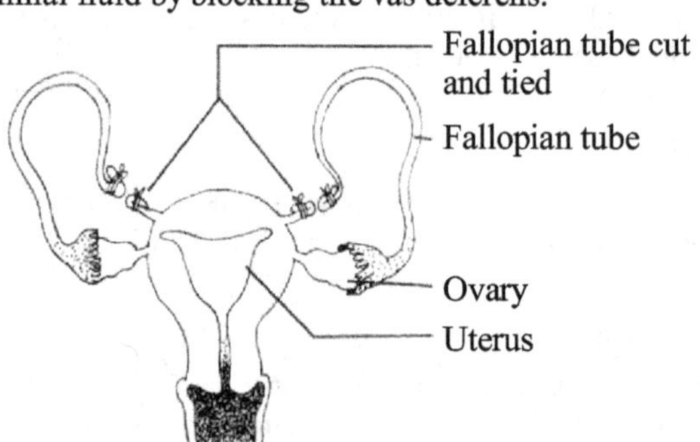

Fig. Vasectomy   **Fig. Tubectomy**

Female sterilization (called **tubectomy**) prevents fertilization by interrupting the passage through fallopian tube. Eggs continues to be produced but they fail to pass into the uterus. In tubectomy, a small part of the fallopian tube is removed or tied up through a small incision in the abdomen or through vagina.

Practice Exercise-1

Multiple Choice Questions

1. RCH stands for
   (a) Routine Check-up of Health
   (b) Reproduction *cum* Hygiene
   (c) Reversible Contraceptive Hazards
   (d) Reproductive and Child Health Care

2. Progestogens in the contraceptive pill
   (a) prevents ovulation
   (b) inhibits estrogen
   (c) checks attachment of zygote endometrium
   (d) All of the above

3. Contraceptive oral pills help in birth control by
   (a) Killing the sperms in uterus
   (b) Forming barriers between sperms and ova
   (c) Preventing ovulation
   (d) Killing the ova.

4. Copper-T acts by
   (a) Suppression of fertilization by forming a membrane
   (b) Disturbing the site of implantation of blastocyst
   (c) Acting as a barrier
   (d) None of these

Match the following

5. Given below are four methods (A-D) of contraceptive in column-I and their modes of action in achieving contraception in column-II. Match the columns and select the correct option :

	Column -I (Method)		Column -II (Mode of Action)
A.	The contraceptive pill	I.	Prevents sperms reaching cervix
B.	Condom	II.	Prevents implantation
C.	Vasectomy	III.	Prevents ovulation
D.	Copper T	IV.	Semen contains no sperms

(a) A–II; B–III; C–I; D–IV
(b) A–III; B–I; C–IV; D–II
(c) A–IV; B–I; C–II; D–III
(d) A–III; B–IV; C–I; D–II

Assertion & Reason Questions

DIRECTIONS (Qs. 1-9) : *Each of these questions contains an assertion followed by reason. Read them carefully and answer the question on the basis of following options. You have to select the one that best describes the two statements.*

(a) If both Assertion and Reason are correct and the Reason is a correct explanation of the Assertion.
(b) If both Assertion and Reason are correct but Reason is not a correct explanation of the Assertion.
(c) If the Assertion is correct but Reason is incorrect.
(d) If both Assertion and Reason are incorrect.

6. **Assertion:** India was amongst the first countries in the world to initiate action plants and programmes at a national level to attain total reproductive health as a social goal.
Reason: The family planing programmes were initiated in 1991.

7. **Assertion:** Statutary raising of marriageable age of the female to 21 years and that of males to 18 years and insentives given to couples with small families are two of the other measures taken to tackle this problem.
Reason: India's population growth rate is about 1.4 percent a year and china's 2 percent a year.

8. **Assertion:** Saheli is a new oral contraceptive for the females contains a non-steroidal preparation.
Reason: Saheli is a daily pill with many side effects and low contraceptive value.

9. **Assertion:** Surgical intervention blocks gamete transport and thereby prevent conception.
Reason: Surgical methods are generally advised for the male/female partner as a terminal method to prevent any more pregnancies.

Passage/Case Based Questions

DIRECTIONS (Qs. 10-11) : *Read the passage carefully and answer the questions that follows.*

Reproductive and Child Health (RCH) programmes are currently in operation. One of the major tasks of these programmes is to create awareness amongst people about the wide range of reproduction related aspects. As this is important and essential for building a reproductively healthy society.

10. 'Providing sex education in schools is one of the way to meet this goal' Give four points in support of your opinion regarding this statement.

11. List any two 'indicators' that indicate a reproductively healthy society.

Very Short Answer Questions

12. What is reproductive health?
13. Effective periods of pills are longer, true or false?
14. How surgical intervention prevents conception?
15. Which is the most important step to overcome population problem ?
16. What are the characteristics of ideal contraceptive ?
17. Name one effective and popular method of barrier.
18. What is the surgical method to prevent pregnancy?
19. Sex education should be encouraged in school, yes or no.?
20. Which part of fallopian tube is closest to ovary?

Short Answer Questions

21. What has increased population growth ?
22. Why should sex education be introduced in schools ?
23. What is 'Saheli' ?
24. What is required to provide assistance to people?
25. What are the reasons for increased population ?
26. What is the fertile period ?
27. What is lactational amenorrhea ?
28. What are the female barrier methods ?
29. What are IUDs ?
30. What are the important aspects of reproductive health ?
31. Discus the function of cu ions of IUDS.

Topic 2   Medical Termination of Pregnancy (MTPs), STD and Infertility 

Medical termination of pregnancy or abortion is the intentional or voluntary termination of pregnancy before the foetus become viable. Certain pills act as abortants. They function by inducing menstruation which check the implantation of the Zygote or detaches the implanted egg. Induced abortion is one of the most widely used methods of fertility control in the world. Government of India legalised MTP under "Medical Termination of Pregnancy act, 1971" with some strict conditions to avoid its misuse. Such restrictions are all they more important to check indiscriminate and illegal female foeticides which are reported to be high in India. MTP are essential in certain cases where continuation of the pregnancy could be harmful but also it is misused to abort female foetus.

SEXUALLY TRANSMITTED DISEASES (STDs)

Sexually transmitted diseases (STDs) or **Veneral Disease** or **Reproductive Tract Infections** are the diseases or infections which are transmitted through sexual intercourse with infected persons. Common STDs includes AIDS, gonorrhoea, syphilis, genital herpes, hepatitis-B etc.

The following table provides a list of the sexually transmitted diseases and their causative agents.

	Disease	Causative Agent
(i)	Syphilis	*Treponema pallidum*
(ii)	Gonorrhoea	*Neisseria gonorrhoeae*
(iii)	Chlamydiasis	*Chlamydia trachomatis*
(iv)	Trichomoniasis	*Trichomonas vaginalis*
(v)	AIDS	Human Immuno-deficiency Virus (HIV)
(vi)	Hepatitis-B	Hepatitis virus
(vii)	Genital Herpes	Herpes simplex virus, Human papilloma virus

(i)   **Gonorrhoea :** is caused by diplococcus bacterium, *Neisseria gonorrhoeae*. The bacterium passes into genital tubes, form pus containing discharge, pain over genitalia and burning during unination.

(ii)   **Trichomoniasis :** is due to tetraflagellate protozoan called *Trichomonas vaginalis*. In females it causes foul smelling vaginitis with yellowish discharge, vulvar erythema and burring dysuria. In males, the pathogen produces urethritis, epididymitis, prostatitis and burning dysuria.

(iii)   **Genital worts :** is caused by *Human papilloma Virus* (HPV). It produces warts over the skin, external genitalia and perianal area.

(iv)   **Genital herpes :** is caused by *Herpes simplex virus*. There are vesicular pustular lessions and then clusters of reddish ulcers over external genitalia and perianal areas, swelling of inguinal and lymph nodes, itching pain, vaginal and urethral discharge, dysuria and headache.

(v)   **Syphilis :** is caused by spirochaete *Treponema palladium*. An infectious but painless primary ulcers heals up. Skin lession, rashes, swollen joints and flu-like illness, and hair loss occur in secondary stage. In tertiary stage chronic ulcers develops on nose laver legs and potato. Damage to internal organs also occurs.

(vi)   **AIDS :** is caused by Human immuno deficiency virus (HIV). The symptoms of AIDS, include fever lethargy, pharyngitis, weight loss, nausea, headache, rashes etc. As HIV attacks helper T lymphocytes, the patients gets immune deficiency and he/she in unable to protect himself/herself against infections.

(vii) **Hepatitis B :** is caused by hepatitis B virus (BHV). Its symptoms include fatigue, jaundice (yellowing skin), persistent low grade fever, rash and abdominal pain. It can cause cirrhosis..

INFERTILITY

It refers to the facture to achieve a clinical pregnancy even after 12 months or more of regular unprotected sexual intercourse. A large number of couples are infertile, i.e., they are unable to produce children inspite of unprotected intercourse. There are many reasons of infertility in males and females. There reason may be physical, immunological or even psycological. In India often the female is blamed for the couple being childless but more often the problem lies in male partner. The most common male infertility factors includes lack or few sperm cells production. The most common female infertility factor is an ovulation disorder and other reason include blocked fallopian tube. Infertility disorders are diagnosed in infertility clinics and some of these can be cured through corrective treatment. In cases where in corrective treatment of infertility is not possible, couples are assisted to have children through special programmes called **Assisted Reproduction Technologies (ART)**.

Some Important techniques that fall under ART are as follows-

(i)   **Artificial Insemination Technique (AIT)** Infertility in male is either due to inability of male partner to achieve an erection of penis to inseminate the female or due to very low sperm count in the semen. Thus can be corrected by artificial insemination technique (AIT). In Artificial insemination the semen collected either from the husband or a healthy donar is artificially introduced either into the vagina or into the uterus of the female.

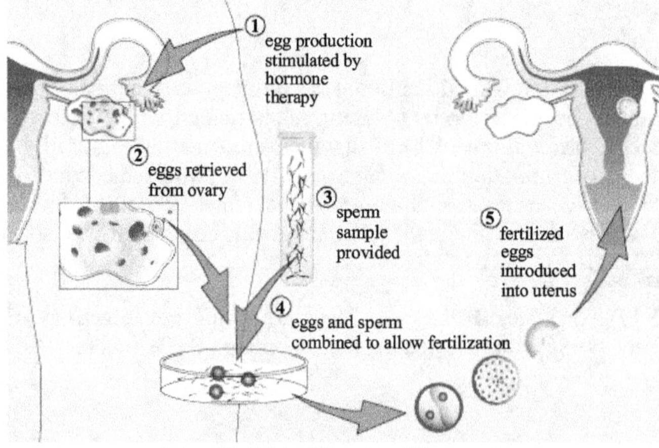

Fig. : IVF (In Vitro Fertilization)

(ii) Gamete intra fallopian transfer (GIFT)

This method involves the transfer of an ovum collected from a donor female into another female, who cannot produce ova, but can provide suitable conditions for fertilization and further development of the foetus upto parturition.

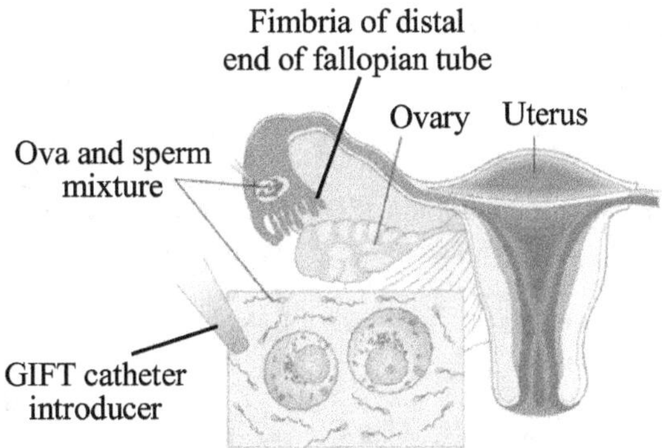

Fig. : Gamete intrafallopian transfer (GIFT). Multiple ova and washed sperm are injected into the fallopian tube, where fertilization may occur.

(iii) Zygote Intra Fallopian Transfer

This method involves pre-embryos (zygote upto 8 cells) rather than gametes are transferred into the oviducts. The advantage of ZIFT over IVF is that embryo enters the uterus after 24 hrs in ZIFT. So it spends less time in laboratory.

(iv) Intra cytoplasmic sperm injection (ICSI)

In this method, the sperm is directly injected into the ovum to form an embryo in the laboratory and then embryo transfer is carried out.

(v) Artificial insemination

In this method, the semen collected from the husband or a healthy donor, is artificially introduced into the vagina or into the uterus (intra-uterine insemination).

Test tube baby programme

In this method, ova from the wife or a donor female and the sperms from the husband or a donor are allowed to fuse under simulated conditions (as that of the body) *in vitro* fertilization. The zygote or early embryo is transferred into the uterus or fallopian tube; it is called Embryo Transfer (ET). The first test tube baby Louise Joy Brown, was born to Lesley and Gibert Brown on July 25, 1978, in Oldham, Lancashire, England with the help of Dr. Patrick Steptoe and Dr. Robert Edwards.

IVF is the most effective ART. It is often used when a woman's fallopian tubes are blocked or when a man produces too few sperm. Doctors treat the woman with a drug that causes the ovaries to produce multiple eggs. Once mature, the eggs are removed from the woman. They are put in dish in the laboratory along with the man's sperm for fertilization. After 3 to 5 days, healthy embryos are implanted in the woman's uterus.

Amniocentesis

Amniocentesis is a prenatal diagnostic technique in which a sample of amniotic fluid from the womb of a pregnant woman is taken during the early stages of foetal development and the cells are cultured and analysed. By this method the chromosomal abnormalities, the sex of the foetus and development disorders could be detected. It is misused for female foeticides. Determination of sex by amniocentesis has been banned.

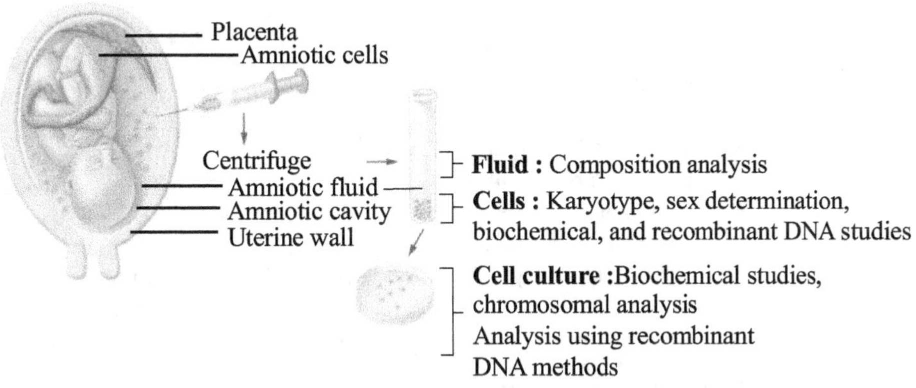

Fig. : Amniocentesis

Practice Exercise-2

Multiple Choice Questions

1. MTPs are considered relatively safe during the ______ weeks of pregnancy.
   (a) 12　　(b) 15　　(c) 18　　(d) 20

2. It is a disease which mainly affects mucous membrane of urinogenital tract, In males burning feeling on passing urine after a yellow discharge occurs that is accompanied by fever headache and feeling of illness its name is
   (a) Phenylketonuria　　(b) Gonorrhoea
   (c) AIDS　　　　　　　(d) None of these

3. Which of the following methods can be used for women who cannot produce ovum but can provide suitable environment?
   (a) IUD　　(b) GIFT　　(c) IUI　　(d) ICSI

4. Artificial insemination mean
   (a) transfer of sperms of husband to a test tube containing ova.
   (b) artificial introduction of sperms of a healthy donor into the vagina.
   (c) introduction of sperms of a healthy donor directly into the ovary.
   (d) transfer of sperms of a healthy donor to a test tube containing ova.

Match the following

5. Select the correct match of the techniques given in column I with its feature given in column II.

	Column I		Column II
A.	ICSI	I.	Artificially introduction of semen into the vagina or uterus.
B.	IUI	II.	Transfer of ovum collected from a donor into the fallopian tube where fertilisation occurs
C.	IUT	III.	Formation of an embryo by directly injecting sperm into the ovum
D.	GIFT	IV.	Transfer of the zygote or early embryo (with up to 8 blastomeres) into the fallopian tube.
E.	ZIFT	V.	Transfer of embryo with more than 8 blastomeres into the uterus

   (a) A – V; B – IV; C – I; D – III; E – IV
   (b) A – I; B – II; C – III; D – IV; E – V
   (c) A – III; B – V; C – II; D – IV; E – I
   (d) A – III; B – I; C – V; D – II; E – IV

Assertion & Reason Questions

DIRECTIONS (Qs. 6-9) : *Each of these questions contains an assertion followed by reason. Read them carefully and answer the question on the basis of following options. You have to select the one that best describes the two statements.*
   (a) If both Assertion and Reason are correct and the Reason is a correct explanation of the Assertion.
   (b) If both Assertion and Reason are correct but Reason is not a correct explanation of the Assertion.
   (c) If the Assertion is correct but Reason is incorrect.
   (d) If both Assertion and Reason are incorrect.

6. **Assertion:** MTPs are also essential in certain cases where continuation of the pregnancy could be harmful or even fatal either to the mother or to the foetus or both.
   Reason: MTPs are considered safe during the first 25 weeks of pregnancy.

7. **Assertion:** HIV can also be transmitted by sharing of injection needles, surgical instruments etc. with infected persons, transfusion of blood or form an infected mother to the foetus too.
   Reason: Hepatitis B, genital herpes and HIV infections are caused by bacterial infection.

8. **Assertion:** In very rare cases, a surrogate mother may have to be used to bring up in vitro fertilised ovum to maturity.
   Reason: Success rate of test tube baby is more than 90%.

9. **Assertion:** Transfer of an ovum collected from a donor into the fallopian tube of another female who cannot produce an ovum is called GIFT.
   Reason: Transfer of early embryo with up to 8 blastomeres into the fallopian tube of the female, is called ZIFT.

Very Short Answer Questions

10. What is intentional or voluntary termination of pregnancy before full term ?
11. Name two prevention to avoid STD.
12. Expand IVF and GIFT.
13. Amniocentesis increases one evil, what is that ?

Short Answer Questions

14. Name some sexually transmitted diseases.
15. Which STDs are non-curable completely ?
16. What is ICSI ?
17. Why ICSI are very limited to general people ?
18. What are the complications of STDs ?
19. Mention one methods of easy parenthood for childless couples.
20. Name two methods of embryo transfer used in test tube baby programme.

Important Tips & Formulae

- IUDs are ideal contraceptives for the females for who want to delay pregnancy and/or space children.
- IUDs is one of most widely accepted methods of contraception in India.
- These devices are inserted by doctors or expert nurses in the uterus through vagina.
- IUDs are of three types such as:
  (i)   Non-mediated IUDs such as Lippes loop,
  (ii) Copper releasing IUDs such as CuT, Cu7, Multiload 375
  (iii) Hormone releasing IUDs such as Progestasert, LNG-20
- IUDs increase phagocytosis of sperms within the uterus and the Cu ions released suppress sperm motility and the fertilising capacity of sperms.
- The hormone releasing IUDs, in addition, make the uterus unsuitable for implantation and the cervix hostile to the sperms.
- Oral administration of small doses of either progestogens or progestogen-estrogen combinations is another contraceptive method used by the females. They are used in the form of tablets and hence are popularly called the pills.
- Pills have to be taken daily for a period of 21 days starting preferably within the first five days of menstrual cycle.
- After a gap of 7 days (during which menstruation occurs) it has to be repeated in the same pattern till the female desires to prevent conception.
- They inhibit ovulation and implantation as well as alter the quality of cervical mucus to prevent/ retard entry of sperms.
- Saheli -the new oral contraceptive for the females contains a non-steroidal preparation. It is a 'once a week' pill with very few side effects and high contraceptive value.
- Progestogens alone or in combination with estrogens can also be used by females as injections or implants under the skin such as Levonorgestrel Norplant and hormone injections such as Depo-Provera.
- Embryo transfer (ET) is one of such methods of In Vitro fertilisation and this method is popularly known as **test tube baby** programme. In which ova from the wife/donor (female) and sperms from the husband/donor (male) are collected and are induced to form zygote under simulated conditions in the laboratory.
- The zygote or early embryos (with upto 8 blastomeres) could then be transferred into the fallopian tube (ZIFT-zygote intra fallopian transfer) and embryos with more than 8 blastomeres, into the uterus (IUT - intra uterine transfer), to complete its further development.
- Embryos formed by in-vivo fertilisation (fusion of gametes within the female) also could be used for such transfer to assist those females who cannot conceive.
- Transfer of an ovum collected from a donor into the fallopian tube (GIFT - gamete intra fallopian transfer) of another female who cannot produce one, but can provide suitable environment for fertilisation and further development is another method attempted.
- Intra cytoplasmic sperm injection (ICSI) is another specialised procedure to form an embryo in the laboratory in which a sperm is directly injected into the ovum.
- Infertility is caused either due to inability of the male partner to inseminate the female or due to very low sperm counts in the ejaculates, could be corrected by artificial insemination (AI) technique.
- In artificial insemination technique, the semen collected either from the husband or a healthy donor is artificially introduced either into the vagina or into the uterus (IUI - intra-uterine insemination) of the female.

NCERT Questions

1. **What do you think is the significance of reproductive health in a society?**

Sol. Sexuality & sexual health affects almost every one's lives. Reproductive health in a society forms a crucial part of general health. In India it is realised that a significant number of adolescents could not be reached through educational institutions, since many children drop out of school because they marry in their very young age & becomes pregnant particularly in rural areas. Due to lack of education & without any knowledge of sexuality or contraception, many young people enter marriage. Creating awareness, among people about various reproduction related aspects & providing facilities & support for building up a reproductively healthy society are the major tasks.

2. **Suggest the aspects of reproductive health which need to be given special attention in the present scenario.**

Sol. Providing medical facilities and care to the problems like menstrual irregularities, pregnancy related aspects, delivery, medical termination of pregnancy, STDs, birth control, infertility, post natal child maternal management is another important aspect of the reproductive and child health care programme.

3. **Is sex education necessary in schools? Why?**

Sol. Yes, sex education is necessary in school. Because introduction of sex education in school encourage to provide the right or correct information to the young generation so as to discourage children from believing in myths & having misconceptions about sex related aspects. Proper information about reproductive organs, safe & hygenic sexual practices, STD's etc. would help people, those in the adolescent age group to lead a healthy reproductive life. In many countries, sexual education raises much contentious debate. Chief among the controversial points is whether covering **child sexuality** is valuable or detrimental; the use of birth control such as **condoms** and **hormonal contraception**, and the impact of such use on pregnancy, outside marriage, teenage pregnancy, and the transmission of STDs. Increasing support for abstinence – only sex education by conservative groups has been one of the primary causes of the controversies.

4. **Do you think that reproductive health in our country has improved in the past 50 years? If yes, mention some such areas of improvement.**

Sol. Bringing sexual and reproductive health services to the millions of people living in countries which still suffer from short life expectancies, high levels of child and maternal mortality, child labour and illiteracy and poor overall health remains a major challenge for governments and non government organizations. Massive child immunization programme lead to decrease in infant mortality rate, family planning use of contraceptives reduced the rate of sexually transmitted disease, etc. It is estimated that the 80% of world's population now lives in developing countries or do 90% of the world's young people. The total world population will rise from six to nine billion people in the next 50 years.

5. **What are the suggested reasons for population explosion?**

Sol. In the past, human populations have rarely been subject to explosion. Increased health facilities along with better living conditions had an explosive impact on the growth of population. The powerful long-term momentum that is built into the human age structure means that the effects of fertility changes become apparent only in the future. For these reasons, it is now conventional practice to use the technology of population projection or a means of better understanding the implications of trends.

6. **Is the use of contraceptives justified? Give reasons.**

Sol. Yes, the use of contraceptives is justified. To overcome the population growth rate, contraceptive method are used. It will help in bringing birth rate down & subsequently curb population growth. With the rapid spread of HIV/AIDS in the country, there is now a growing realization about the need to know about contraceptions & condoms.

7. **Removal of gonads cannot be considered as a contraceptive option. Why?**

Sol. Removal of gonads or its parts is a surgical method of sterilization. Vasectomy and tubectomy are carried out in males and females respectively. It will lead to infertility & both male and female will be dependent on hormones in their remaining life to regulate functioning of reproductive organs. These are very effective but their irreversibility is very poor, so they are not good options for contraception.

8. **Amniocentesis for sex determination is banned in our country. Is this ban necessary? Comment.**

Sol. Sex determination is banned in our country. Most people in obstetrics and medical genetics do not support prenatal testing for gender while some other cultures do agree with that. There is speculation that this striking gender imbalance is largely the result of abortion of foetuses discovered to be female after a sex determination ultrasound or aminocentesis procedure. The solution to the problem is not passing more laws, such as banning sex determination ultrasounds but raising the social & economic status of women.

9. **Suggest some methods to assist infertile couples to have children.**

Sol. ART (Assisted Reproductive Technologies) is a term that describes several different methods used to help infertile couples. ART involves removing eggs from a woman's body, mixing them with sperm in the laboratory and putting the embryos bath into a woman's body.

Success rates vary depending on many factors. Something that affects the success rate of ART includes:

- age of the partners,
- reason for infertility,
- clinic,
- type of ART,
- if the egg is fresh or frozen, and
- if the embryo is fresh or frozen.

Various methods are now available to help such couples are — invitro fertilization, gamete intra fallopian transfer, intracytoplasmic sperm injection & artificial insemination.

  (i) Invitro fertilization – Patient's egg & her partner's sperm are collected & mixed together in a laboratory to achieve fertilization outside the body. The embryo produced may then be transferred into the female patient. It is commonly known as test tube baby programme.

  (ii) Gamete Intra Fallopian Transfer (GIFT) – A procedure in which eggs are retrieved from a woman, mixed with sperm & immediately replaced in one or other of the women's fallopian tubes so that they fertilize inside the body (*invivo*).

  (iii) Intra Cytoplasmic Sperm Injection (ICSI)– In this method, sperm & eggs are retrieved from both the parents. A single sperm is injected directly into an egg, then the fertilized egg is implanted into the woman's uterus.

  (iv) Artificial insemination – In this technique, the semen is collected either from husband or a healthy donor & is artificially introduced either into the vagina or into the uterus of the female (IUI-Intra uterine insemination).

10. **What are the measures one has to take to prevent from contracting STDs?**

Sol. (i) Avoid sex with unknown partners/multiple partners.

  (ii) Always use condoms during intercourse.

  (iii) In case of doubt, go for medical professional for early detection and get complete treatment if diagnosed with disease.

  (iv) Education & counselling of persons at risk on ways to adopt safer sexual behaviour.

11. **State True/False with explanation**

  (a) Abortions could happen spontaneously too. (True/False)

  (b) Infertility is defined as the inability to produce a viable offspring and is always due to abnormalities/defects in the female partner. (True/False)

  (c) Complete lactation could help as a natural method of contraception. (True/False)

  (d) Creating awareness about sex related aspects is an effective method to improve reproductive health of the people. (True/False)

Sol. (a) True.

  (b) False. It is due to abnormalities/defects in either male or female or both the partners.

  (c) True, but it is limited to period up to six months after parturition.

  (d) True.

12. **Correct the following statements :**

  (a) Surgical methods of contraception prevent gamete formation.

  (b) All sexually transmitted diseases are completely curable.

  (c) Oral pills are very popular contraceptives among the rural women.

  (d) In E. T. techniques, embryos are always transferred into the uterus.

Sol. (a) Surgical methods of contraception prevent gamete transport & thereby prevent conception.

  (b) Except for hepatitis-B, genital herpes and HIV infections, other STD diseases are completely curable if detected early and treated properly.

  (c) Oral pill are very popular contraceptives among the educated urban women.

  (d) In ET technique, embryos with 8 blastomeres are transferred into fallopian tube and more than 8 blastomeres are transferred into the uterus.

Past year Exercise

Very Short Answer Questions

1. Mention one positive and one negative application of amniocentesis.
2. Why is tubectomy considered a contraceptive method?
3. Our government has intentionally imposed strict conditions for M.T.P. in our country. Justify giving a reason.

Short Answer Questions

4. Explain the Zygote Intra Fallopian Transfer Technique (ZIFT). How is Intra Uterine Transfer Technique (IUT) different from it?
5. (i) Give any two reasons for infertility among young couple.
   (ii) Test-tube baby programme is a boon to such couples. Explain the steps followed in the procedures.
6. A pregnant human female was advised to undergo MTP. It was diagnosed by her doctor that the foetus she is carrying has developed from a zygote formed by an XX-egg fertilised by Y-carrying sperm. Why was she advised to undergo MTP?
7. Suggest and explain any three Assisted Reproducive Technologies (ART) to an infertile couple.

8. Draw the following diagrams related to human reproduction and label them.
   (a) The zygote after the first cleavage division
   (b) Morula stage
   (c) Blastocyst stage (sectional view)
9. A woman has certain queries as listed below, before starting with contraceptive pills. Answer them.
   (a) What do contraceptive pills contain and how do they act as contraceptives ?
   (b) What schedule should be followed for taking these pills ?
10. (a) Name any two copper releasing IUDs.
    (b) Explain how do they act as effective contraceptives in human females.
11. Your school has been selected by the Department of Education to organize and host an interschool seminar on "Reproductive Health-Problems and Practices". However, many parents are reluctant to permit their wards to attend it. Their argument is that the topic is "too embarrassing." Put forth four arguments with appropriate reasons and explanation to justify the topic to be very essential and timely.
12. Why is breast-feeding recommended during the initial period of an infant's growth? Give reasons.

NCERT Exemplar

Multiple Choice Questions

1. The method of directly injecting a sperm into ovum is assisted by reproductive technology is called
   - (a) GIFT
   - (b) ZIFT
   - (c) ICSI
   - (d) ET

2. Increased IMR and decreased MMR in a population will
   - (a) cause rapid increase in growth rate
   - (b) result in decline in growth rate
   - (c) not cause significant change in growth rate
   - (d) result in an explosive population/exp

3. Intensely lactating mothers do not generally conceive due to the
   - (a) suppression of gonadotropins
   - (b) hypersecretion of gonadotropins
   - (c) suppression of gametic transport
   - (d) suppression of fertilisation

4. Emergency contraceptives are effective if used within 72 hrs of
   - (a) coitus
   - (b) ovulation
   - (c) menstruation
   - (d) implantation

5. From the sexually transmitted diseases mentioned below, identify the one which does not specifically affect the sex organs.
   - (a) Syphillis
   - (b) AIDS
   - (c) Gonorrhoea
   - (d) Genital warts

Assertion & Reason Questions

DIRECTIONS (Qs. 6-7) : *Each of these questions contains an assertion followed by reason. Read them carefully and answer the question on the basis of following options. You have to select the one that best describes the two statements.*

- (a) If both Assertion and Reason are correct and the Reason is a correct explanation of the Assertion.
- (b) If both Assertion and Reason are correct but Reason is not a correct explanation of the Assertion.
- (c) If the Assertion is correct but Reason is incorrect.
- (d) If both Assertion and Reason are incorrect.

6. **Assertion:** Amniocentesis is a foetal sex determination test based on the chromosomal pattern in the amniotic fluid surrounding the developing embryo.
   Reason: Amniocentesis is presently completely banned in India.

7. **Assertion:** Pill Mala D is taken daily and the pill saheli taken weekly.
   Reason: Oral contraceptives have pregnancy rates less than 1 percent.

Very Short Answer Question

8. Comment on the RCH programme of the government to improve the reproductive health of the people.

Short Answer Questions

9. All reproductive tract infections (RTIs) are STDs, but all STDs are not RTIs- Justify with example.

10. Enumerate and describe any five reasons for introducing sex-education to school-going children.

Objective Practice Exercise 

Multiple Choice Questions

1. The most important component of the oral contraceptive pills is
   - (a) Progesterone
   - (b) Growth hormone
   - (c) Thyroxin
   - (d) Luteinizing hormone

2. Amniocentesis is the withdraw of amniotic fluid in
   - (a) Menopause
   - (b) Lactation
   - (c) Gestation
   - (d) Pregnancy

3. Action of vaginal diaphragm is
   - (a) Prevent the ova to come in the uterus
   - (b) Prevent the sperm to come in contact with ova
   - (c) Spermicidal
   - (d) Anti-implantational

4. Surgical removal or cutting and ligation of the ends of oviduct is known as
   - (a) Tubectomy
   - (b) Oviductomy
   - (c) Vasectomy
   - (d) Ovarioctomy

5. Surgical removal of testes is known as
   - (a) Testectomy
   - (b) Gonadectomy
   - (c) Castration
   - (d) None of these

6. Removal of a segment surgically and ligation of cut ends of vas deferens is known as
   - (a) Tubectomy
   - (b) Vasectomy
   - (c) Gonadectomy
   - (d) Castration

7. The chemical method of contraception includes
   - (a) Jellies only
   - (b) Creams and foams only
   - (c) Oral contraceptives only
   - (d) All of the above

8. Which one of the following is tested by the technique of amniocentesis?
   - (a) Biochemical abnormalities in the foetus
   - (b) Errors of metabolism in the foetus
   - (c) Chromosomal abnormalities in the foetus
   - (d) All of the above

9. Which of the following is a method for birth control?
   - (a) IUDs
   - (b) GIFT
   - (c) HTF
   - (d) IVE-ET

10. Which of the following is not *true* about the birth control pill?
    - (a) The pill works by preventing ovulation.
    - (b) The pill works by preventing implantation.
    - (c) The ovarian cycle is suspended by the birth control pill.
    - (d) The birth control pill contains low doses of estrogen and progesterone.

11. Which of the following birth control measures can be considered as the safest?
    - (a) The rhythm method
    - (b) The use of physical barriers
    - (c) Temination of unwanted pregnancy
    - (d) Sterilization techniques

12. The most important component of the oral contraceptive pills is
    - (a) progesterone
    - (b) growth hormone
    - (c) thyroxine
    - (d) luteinizing hormone

13. Condoms are barriers that cover
    - (a) Penis in male and ovary in female.
    - (b) Penis in male and cervix and vagina in female.
    - (c) Scrotum in male and cervix and vagina in female.
    - (d) Cervix in male and vagina in female.

14. Using which contraceptive also provides protection from contracting STDs and AIDS?
    - (a) Diaphragms
    - (b) Spermicidal foams
    - (c) Condoms
    - (d) Lactational amenorrhoea

15. Copper-T is a device that prevents
    - (a) implantation of blastocyst
    - (b) ovulation
    - (c) fertilization
    - (d) egg maturation

16. One of the legal methods of birth control is
    - (a) by abstaining from coitus from day 10 to 17 of the menstrual cycle
    - (b) by having coitus at the time of day break
    - (c) by a premature ejaculation during coitus
    - (d) abortion by taking an appropriate medicine

17. Tubectomy
    - (a) Prevents implantation
    - (b) Prevents foetal development
    - (c) Prevents fertilization
    - (d) All above

18. Contraceptive oral pills help in birth control by
    - (a) Killing the sperms in uterus
    - (b) Forming barriers between sperms and ova
    - (c) Preventing ovulation
    - (d) Killing the ova.

19. According to which of the following organization "reproductive health means a total well-being in all aspects of reproduction"?
    - (a) WHL
    - (b) UNESCO
    - (c) WHO
    - (d) WWW

20. RCH stands for
    - (a) Routine Check-up of Health
    - (b) Reproduction Cum Hygiene
    - (c) Reversible Contraceptive Hazards
    - (d) Reproductive and Child Health Care

21. 'Saheli' a new oral contraceptive developed by
    (a) All Indian Institute of Medical Science
    (b) Central Drug Research Institute
    (c) Health Care Pvt. Ltd.
    (d) Bharat Immunologicals & Biologicals corp. Ltd.

22. Which of the following is traditional method of contraception?
    (a) Implantation (b) Lactational amenorrhoea
    (c) Condoms (d) Sterilization

23. Tying up or removing a small part of fallopian duct is called
    (a) vasectomy (b) ductus arteriosus
    (c) archidectomy (d) tubectomy

24. Amniocentesis is
    (a) Digestion of amino acid
    (b) Conversion of glucose to amino acids
    (c) Taking out the cells of the foetus
    (d) Killing of child before birth

25. Which of the following birth control measures can be considered as the safest?
    (a) The rhythm method
    (b) The use of physical barriers
    (c) Temination of unwanted pregnancy
    (d) Sterilization techniques

26. Test-tube baby means a baby born when
    (a) It develops from a non-fertilized egg
    (b) It developed in a test-tube
    (c) It is developed through tissue culture method
    (d) The ovum is fertilised externally and thereafter implanted in the uterus

27. Using which contraceptive also provides protection from contracting STDs and AIDS ?
    (a) Diaphragms (b) Spermicidal foams
    (c) Condoms (d) Lactational amenorrhoea

28. STD/VD/UTI are
    (a) devices which are used to delay the pregnancy.
    (b) infections which are caused by food contamination.
    (c) diseases which are transmitted through sexual intercourse.
    (d) action plans and programmes to create awareness about various reproductive related health and problems.

29. Assisted reproductive technologies (ART)
    (a) include social awareness programmes to educate people about reproductive health and diseases.
    (b) include research organization working on to produce new and more effective contraceptives for birth control.
    (c) include a number of special techniques which assist infertile couples to have children.
    (d) both (b) and (c)

30. Which of the following disease is completely curable if detected early and treated properly?
    (a) Syphilis (b) Hepatitis B
    (c) Genital herpes (d) HIV infection

31. Non-gonococcal urethritis is caused by
    (a) *Neisseria gonorrhoeae*
    (b) *Chlamydia trachomatis*
    (c) *Treponema pallidum*
    (d) *Trichomonas vaginalis*

32. Profuse, yellowish, greenish frothy smelling discharge from vagina is due to infection of
    (a) *Treponema pallidum*
    (b) *Chlamydia*
    (c) *Trichomonas vaginallis*
    (d) *Neisseria*

33. In which year, MTP was legalised in India?
    (a) 1971 (b) 1951
    (c) 1981 (d) 1923

34. Intensely lactating mothers do not generally conceive due to the
    (a) suppression of gonadotropins.
    (b) hypersecretion of gonadotropins.
    (c) supression of gametic transport.
    (d) supression of fertilization.

35. Identify the correct reasons of infertility.
    1. Drugs 2. Diseases
    3. Congenital 4. Use of Contraceptives
    5. Immunological or psychological
    6. Assisted reproductive technology
    (a) 1, 2, 3 (b) 3, 4, 6
    (c) 1, 2, 3, 5 (d) All of these

36. Which of the following assisted reproductive technology has been used for the longest time period?
    (a) *In vitro* fertilization
    (b) Artificial insemination
    (c) Intracytoplasmic sperm injection
    (d) Gamete intra fallopian transfer

37. Which of the following STDs are not completely curable?
    (a) Chlamydiasis, gonorrhoea, trichomoniasis
    (b) Chancroid, syphilis, genital warts
    (c) AIDS, syphilis, hepatitis B
    (d) AIDS, genital herpes, hepatitis B

38. It is a disease which mainly affects mucous membrane of urinogenital tract, In males burning feeling on passing urine after a yellow discharge occurs that is accompanied by fever headache and feeling of illness its name is
    (a) Phenylketonuria (b) Gonorrhoea
    (c) AIDS (d) None of these

39. Given below are some examples of sexually transmitted diseases. Identify the one or more which specifically affect the sex organs.
    1. AIDS 2. Syphilis
    3. Gonorrhea 4. Genital warts
    (a) 1 only (b) 1, 2 only
    (c) 2, 3, 4 only (d) All of these.

40. Which of the following infections can also be transmitted by sharing of injection needles, surgical instruments, etc., with infected persons, transfusion of blood, or from an infected mother to the foetus too?
(a) Hepatitis B and HIV
(b) Genital herpes and HIV
(c) Syphilis and Hepatitis B
(d) Chlamydiasis and Trichomoniasis

41. Which of the following is the correct sequence of events in development of test tube baby?
(a) Removal of unfertilized ovum → invitro fusion of sperm and ovum → development of zygote upto 32 cell stage → Embryo transfer into the uterus of mother
(b) Fusion of sperm and ovum invitro → Removal of unfertilized ovum and transfer into the uterus of mother → formation and development of zygote upto 32 cell stage
(c) Embryo transfer into the uterus of mother → formation and development of zygote upto 32 cell stage → fusion of sperm and ovum invitro → removal of unfertilized ovum
(d) Formation and development of zygote upto 32 cell stage → fusion of sperm and ovum invitro → removal of unfertilized ovum → embryo transfer into the uterus.

42. Withdrawal method of natural contraception involves
(a) withdrawal of penis before ejaculation.
(b) withdrawal of penis after ejaculation.
(c) avoiding intercourse during ovulation.
(d) using natural herbbs to prevent pregnancy.

43. A national level approach to build up a reproductively healthy society was taken up in our country in
(a) 1950s   (b) 1960s
(c) 1980s   (d) 1990s

44. What is the marriageable age for the females and males respectively in India?
(a) 18, 18   (b) 18, 25
(c) 21, 18   (d) 18, 21

45. Condoms are one of the most popular contraceptives because of the following reasons
(a) these are effective barriers for insemination
(b) they do not interfere with coital act
(c) these help in reducing the risk of STDs
(d) All of the above

46. The correct surgical procedure as a contraceptive method is
(a) ovariectomy   (b) hysterectomy
(c) vasectomy   (d) castration

47. The technique which makes use of amniotic fluid for the detection of prenatal disorder is called as
(a) leproscopy   (b) amniocentesis
(c) endoscopy   (d) ultrasound

48. Contraceptive oral pills help in birth control by
(a) Killing the sperms in uterus
(b) Forming barriers between sperms and ova
(c) Preventing ovulation
(d) Killing the ova.

49. Which of the following groups of contraceptives are included under barrier methods?
(a) Condom, Vaults, IUDs, Cervical caps
(b) IUDs, Diaphragm, Abstinence, Injections
(c) Condom, Diaphragm, Cervical caps, Vaults
(d) Surgical methods, Oral contraceptives, Cervical caps, vaults

50. Progestasert and LNG-20 are
(a) implants   (b) copper releasing IUDs
(c) non-medicated IUDs   (d) hormone releasing IUDs

Match the following

51. Given below are four methods (A-D) and their modes of action (i-iv) in achieving contraception. Select their correct matching from the four options that follow.

Method		Mode of Action
A. Oral pill	(i)	Prevents sperms reaching cerbix
B. Condom	(ii)	Suppresses sperm motility
C. Vasectomy	(iii)	Prevents ovulation
D. Copper T	(iv)	Semen contains on sperms

(a) A-(ii), B-(iv), C-(i), D-(ii)
(b) A-(ii), B-(iii), C-(i), D-(iv)
(c) A-(iii), B-(i), C-(iv), D-(ii)
(d) A-(iv), B-(i), C-(ii), D-(iii)

2. Match the contraceptive methods given under column I with their examples given under column II and select the correct option form the given codes.

Column I		Column II
A. Chemical	(i)	Tubectomy and vasectomy
B. IUDs	(ii)	Copper T and loop
C. Barriers	(iii)	Condom and cervical cap
D. Sterilisation	(iv)	Spermicidal jelly and foam
	(v)	Coitus interruptus and calendar method

(a) A-(iv), B-(ii), C-(iii), D-(i)
(b) A-(iv), B-(v), C-(ii), D-(iii)
(c) A-(i), B-(iii), C-(ii), D-(v)
(d) A-(iv), B-(ii), C-(v), D-(i)

Chapter Test

Time : *30 Minutes*   **Max. Marks : 15**

- Questions number **1-15** carry **1 mark** each.

1. The diaphragm, cervical cap and vaults are
(a) disposable contraceptive devices
(b) Reusable contraceptives
(c) Non-medicated IUDs
(d) Cu-releasing IUDs

2. It is a disease which mainly affects mucous membrane of urinogenital tract, In males burning feeling on passing urine after a yellow discharge occurs that is accompanied by fever headache and feeling of illness its name is
(a) Phenylketonuria   (b) Gonorrhoea
(c) AIDS   (d) None of these

3. The first case of IVF-ET technique success, was reported by:
(a) Bayliss and Starling Taylor
(b) Robert Steptoe and Gilbert Brown
(c) Louis Joy Brown and Banting Best
(d) Patrick Steptoe and Robert Edwards

4. The technique called gamete intra fallopian transfer (GIFT) is recommended for those females
(a) who cannot produce an ovum.
(b) who cannot retain the foetus inside uterus.
(c) whose cervical canal is too narrow to allow passage for the sperms.
(d) who cannot provide suitable environment for fertilization.

5. Match the column I with column II:-

	Column I		Column II
(A)	Gonorrhoea	(i)	Human Immunodeficiency virus
(B)	Hepatitis	(ii)	Treponema pallidum
(C)	AIDS	(iii)	Balillus anthralis
(D)	Syphilis	(iv)	Entamoeba histolytica
		(v)	HPV (Hepatitis B Virus)
		(vi)	Neisseria gonorrhoeae

(a) A– (v), B - (iv), C - (i), D - (ii)
(b) A– (iii), B - (iv), C - (ii), D - (vi)
(c) A– (vi), B - (v), C - (i), D - (ii)
(d) A– (iv), B - (v), C - (ii), D - (vi)

DIRECTIONS (Qs. 6-7) : *Each of these questions contains an assertion followed by reason. Read them carefully and answer the question on the basis of following options. You have to select the one that best describes the two statements.*
(a) If both Assertion and Reason are correct and the Reason is a correct explanation of the Assertion.
(b) If both Assertion and Reason are correct but Reason is not a correct explanation of the Assertion.
(c) If the Assertion is correct but Reason is incorrect.
(d) If both Assertion and Reason are incorrect.

6. **Assertion:** Natural method of contraception work on the principle of avoiding chances of ovum and sperm mating.
Reason: Periodic abstinance is one such method in which the couples avoid or obtain from coitus from day 1 to 7 of the menstrual cycle when ovulation could be expected.

7. **Assertion:** Condom should be used regularly and put on before starting coital activity, otherwise sperm containing lubricating fluid may be left in the vagina.
Reason: Condom should be reused again after two hours.

Passage/Case Based Questions

DIRECTIONS (Qs. 8-12) : *Read the following passage and answer the questions that follows.*

A newly married couple was afraid of using contraceptive and IUDs. So they opted for natural method of contraception. During a random councelling session, the couple found that natural contraception is not reliable, instead they can use barrier contraceptive.

8. Natural method of birth control include
(a) Abstinence
(b) Lactational amenorrhoea
(c) Coitus interrupts
(d) All of these

9. Which one of the following is the most widely accepted method of contraception in India, as at present?
(a) IUD   (b) Cervical cap
(c) Tubectomy   (d) Diaphragms

10. The action of contraceptive is
    (a) prevention of ovulation and fertilisation
    (b) prevent ovulation only
    (c) prevent rapid passing of eggs in the oviduct
    (d) prevention of ovulation, implantation and fertilization only.

11. Which is the hormonal method of birth control?
    (a) Pill
    (b) Vasectomy
    (c) Copper IUD
    (d) Femidom

12. What is the function of copper T?
    (a) stop oblituation of the blastocoel
    (b) checks mutation
    (c) stops fertilisation
    (d) stop zygote formation

Very Short Answer Questions

13. Where does oogenesis occur in female body?
14. Which hormone controls spermatogenesis ?
15. List any two factors which make contraceptive as an ideal contraceptive.

Solutions 

1. **(d)** Reproduction-related areas are currently in operation in India come under the popular name 'Reproductive and Child Health Care (RCH) programmes.

2. **(a)** Birth control pills (oral contraceptives) check ovulation in female by inhibiting the secretion of follicle stimulating hormone and luteinizing hormone that are important for ovulation.

3. **(c)**   4. **(b)**

5. **(b)** A contraceptive pill prevents ovulation, condom prevents sperms to reach the cervix, vasectomy allows the semen to flow but the latter contains no sperms. Copper-T prevents implantation in females.

6. **(c)** Assertion is true but Reason is false.
    Family planning was initiated in India in 1951. It creased awareness regarding prevention of unwanted pregnancies by adopting safe methods.

7. **(d)** Both Assertion and Reason are incorrect.
    Statutary raising of marriageable age of the female is 18 years and that of males is 21 years and insentives given to couples with small families are two of the other measures taken to tackle this process. India's population growth rate is about 2% a year and china's 1.4%.

8. **(c)** Assertion is true but Reason is incorrect.
    Saheli is a non-steroidal contraceptive pill that is taken once a week. It has high contraceptive value and is well accepted as it has very few side effects.

9. **(b)** Both Assertion and Reason are true, but Reason is not the correct explanation of Assertion.
    Surgical methods are also called sterilisation. It is a procedure that renders an individual incapable of further reproduction, hence is a permanent method of birth control.

10. Providing sex education is one of the best ways to create a reproductively healthy society. Sex education helps in achieving this goal by:
    (a) Providing proper knowledge to curious adolescents and preventing them from being misguided and preventing them from believing myths about sex-related aspects.
    (b) Creating awareness about sexually transmitted diseases and ways to prevent them.
    (c) Providing proper information about reproductive organs and various adolescents and related changes.
    (d) Proper information about safe and hygienic sexual practices.

11. Two indicators of a reproductively healthy society are as follows-

    (a) In a reproductively healthy society, there is no emphasis on the selection of a particular sex. Hence, the ratio of male and female individuals is maintained.
    (b) The members of the society have physically and functionally normal reproductive organs and normal emotional and behavioural interactions among them in all sex related aspects.

12. The term simply refers to healthy reproductive organs with normal functions.

13. False.

14. By blocking gamete transport.

15. To educate people about the benefits of small families.

16. User-friendly, easily available, effective with no or least side-effects.

17. Intra Uterine Devices (IUDs)

18. Sterilization.

19. Yes.

20. Infundibulum

21. Improved health facilities and better living conditions promoted an explosive growth of population.

22. It should also be encouraged to provide right information about the reproduction and sex related aspects to the young so as to discourage children from believing in myth.

23. Saheli is a new oral contraceptive for the females. It contains a non-steroidal preparation. It is a once a week pill with high contraceptive value and very few side effects. It was developed by scientists at Central Drug Research Institute (CDRI) in Lucknow.

24. Implementation of better techniques and new strategies from time to time.

25. A rapid decline in death rate, **maternal mortality rate (MMR)** and **infant mortality rate** (IMR).

26. 10 to 17th day of of the menstrual cycle when ovulation could be expected. As chances of fertilization are very high during this period.

27. Lactational amenorrhea (absence of menstruation) method is based on the fact that ovulation and therefore the cycle do not occur during the period of intense lactation following parturition.

28. Diaphragms, cervical caps and valves are barriers made of rubber that are inserted into the female reproductive tract.

29. Intra Uterine Devices (IUDs) are small devices made of metal or plastic that contain either copper or a common synthetic hormone used in oral contraceptives. These are available as the non-medicated IUDs (e.g., Lippes loop), Copper releasing IUDs (Cu T, Cu 7, Multiload 375) and the hormone releasing IUDs (Progesterones), LNG-20.

30. Providing medical facilities and care to the problems like menstrual irregularities, pregnancy related aspects, delivery, medical termination of pregnancy, STDs, birth control, infertility, post natal child maternal management is another important aspect of the reproductive and child health care programme.

31. It present the fertilization of the egg or implantation of the embryo. IUD's increases phagocytesis of sperm and also cuions supresses sperm motoility.

Practice Exercise-2 

1. **(a)** MTP is the intentional or voluntary termination of pregnancy before term. MTPs are considered relatively safe during the first trimester, *i.e.,* up to 12 weeks of pregnancy.

2. **(b)**

3. **(b)** Gamete Intrafallopian Transfer technique is used for such females who cannot produce ovum.
This method involves the transfer of ovum collected from a donor into the fallopian tube of another who cannot produce egg but provide a suitable enviroment for fertilisation.

4. **(b)** In artificial insemination (AI) technique, the semen collected either from the husband or a healthy donor is artificially introduced either into the vagina or into the uterus (IUI – intrauterine insemination) of the female.

5. **(d)** ICSI (Intracytoplasmic sperm injection) - Formation of embryo by directly injecting sperm into the ovum
IUI (intrauterine insemination) - Artificial introduction of semen into the vagina or uterus
IUT (Intra uterine transfer) - Transfer of an embryo with more than 8 blastomeres into the uterus
GIFT (Gamete intrafallopian transfer) - Transfer of ovum collected from a donor into the fallopian tube where fertilisation occurs
ZIFT (Zygote intrafallopian transfer) - Transfer of the zygote or early embryo (with up to 8 blastomeres) into the fallopian tube

6. **(c)** Assertion is true but Reason is false.
MTPs are considered relatively safe during the first trimester i.e., upto 12 weeks of pregnancy. Second trimester abortions are much more risky.

7. **(c)** Assertion is true but Reason is false.
Hepatitis B, genital herpes and HIV infections caused by Hepatitis B virus, Herpes simplex type 2 virus and Human Immuno deficiency virus respectively. These diseases are difficult to cure.

8. **(c)** Assertion is true but Reason is false.
Success rate of test tube baby is less than 20%.

9. **(b)** Both Assertion and Reason are true, but Reason is not the correct explaination of Assertion.

In GIFT the gametes (each egg and sperm) are then injected into the fallopian tube using a surgical operation known as laparoscope. The doctor will use usual anesthesis. While in ZIFT fertile eggs are implanted inside the uterus and become fetus via the same process.

10. Medical termination of pregnancy (MTP).

11. (i) Avoid sex with unknown partners/multiple partners.
(ii) Safe and hygienic sexual practices.

12. IVF – *in vitro* fertilization.
GIFT – Gamete intrafallopian transfer.

13. Female foeticide.

14. Gonorrhoea, syphilis, genital herpes, chlamydiasis, genital warts, trichomoniasis, hepatitis-B, HIV leading to AIDS are some of the STDs.

15. Except for hepatitis-B, genital herpes and HIV infections, other diseases are completely curable if detected early and treated properly.

16. Intra cytoplasmic sperm injection (ICSI) is a procedure to form an embryo in laboratory in which a sperm is directly injected into the ovum.

17. ICSI need specialized professionals and expensive instrumentations.

18. Pelvic inflammatory diseases (PIDs), still birth, ectopic pregnancies, infertility are some of the complications of STD's.

19. Adoption of orphan and destituted children who require care taking to survive in the world is an alternate and easy option for parenthood for childless couples. Our laws also help in legal adoption of such children.

20. (i) Zygote intra-fallopian transfer (ZIFT)
(ii) Intra-uterine transfer (IUT)

Past year Exercise 

1. Amniocentesis
(i) **Positive application** It can be used to diagnose any genetic disorder in foetus.
(ii) **Negative application** It can be used as female foeticide.

2. In tubectomy, a small part of fallopian tubes or oviducts is tied up to block the transport of ova. So, it is considered as contraceptive method.

3. Our government has imposed strict conditions for M.T.P. to avoid its misuse. Such restrictions are very important to prevent sex determination before birth of a child and illegal female foeticides in our country.

4. (i) **ZIFT** (Zygote Infra Fallopian Transfer Technique) In this technique zygote or early embryo with up to 8 blastomeres is transferred into the fallopian tube.
(ii) **IUT** Embryo with more than 8 blastomeres is transferred into the uterus.

5. (i) The reasons of infertility in young people are physical, congenital disease, use of drugs, immunological reactions of even psychological.

6. In this case, zygote will be XXY and develop into a male with Klinefelter's syndrome. These individuals show feminine characters, gynaecomastia and are sterile. Due to these disorders, the woman was prescribed MTP.

   (ii) In test-tube programme

      (a) Ova from the wife or a donor female and the sperms from the husband or a donor allowed to fuse under simulated conditions in the laboratory. It is called *in vitro* fertilisation.

      (b) Embryo is transferred into the uterus or fallopian tube for further development. The process of embryo transfer is done in following ways :

   • Zygote or embryo up to 8 blastomeres is transferred into Fallopian tube.

   • Embryo with more than 8 blastomeres is transferred into uterus.

7. **Assisted Reproductive Technologies (ART) :**

   (i) Test-tube baby : The programme includes **in-vitro fertilization** of egg (IVF) followed by **embroy transfer** (ET) is one of such method.

      (a) Embryo transfer at 8-celled blastomere stage in **fallopian** of female is called **zygote intra-fallopian transfer** (ZIFT) or

      (b) embryos with 16, or 32 blastomere stage are transferred into the uterus to complete further development and termed as **intrauterine transfer** (IUT).

   (ii) In vivo fertilization (fusion of gametes within the female) involves the transfer of embryo from a female to another female who cannot conceive.

   (iii) Gamete intra-fallopian transfer (GIFT) : It includes the transfer of an ovum from a donor into the fallopian tube of another female who cannot ovulate due to one or other reason.

8. (a)

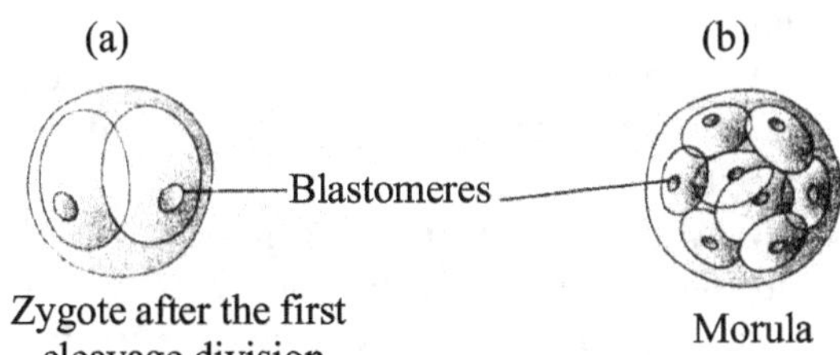

Zygote after the first cleavage division

Morula

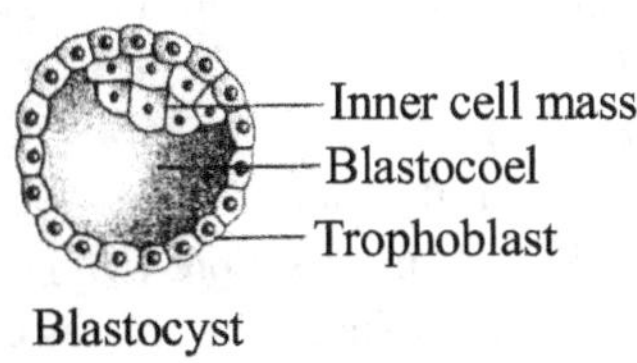

Blastocyst

(c)

9. (a) Contraceptives pills are small oral doses of either progesterone or progestrogen-ertrogen combinations. The pills inhibit ovulation and implantation as well as after the quality of cervical mucus to prevent/retard the entry of sperms. Thus, inhibit the pregnancy conditions.

   (b) The pills are taken daily for a period of 21 days starting preferably within the first five days of menstrual cycle. After a gap of 7 days (during which menstruation occurs) it has to be repeated in the same pattern till the female desires to prevent conception.

10. (a) Cu-T and Cu7 are copper releasing IUDs.

    (b) IUDs work as contraceptive in following ways :

       (i) Increases phangocytosis of sperms.

       (ii) Making uterus less suitable for implantation.

       (iii) making cervix hostile to sperms.

       (iv) Suppressing sperm motility and fertilising ability by releasing copper ions.

11. Reproductive health is the total well-being in all aspects of reproduction. It includes the physical, emotional, behavioural and social well-being of an individual. Therefore, there is an urgent need to educate and discuss topics related to the reproductive health.

    Following are the topics about reproductive health that should be discussed with the students:

    Sexually transmitted diseases, such as AIDS and Gonorrhoea, are transferred from one individual to another through sexual contact. Therefore, making the students aware about these diseases will help to prevent their spread.

    Lack of knowledge about the reproductive status may lead to unwanted pregnancies. Hence, it is necessary to create awareness among people, especially the youth.

    Learning about one's sexuality at a proper age may help the students to know about the different changes happening in their body; thereby, leading to a better mental and physical state of health.

    Counselling and creating awareness about reproductive health also help to curb the problems of infertility, birth control, mortality, etc.

12. Breastfeeding is recommended in the initial period of an infant's growth because of the following reasons:

    1. It provides passive immunity to the baby through colostrum.

    2. It provides balanced nutrition to the bab

NCERT Exemplar

1. (c) **ICSI** (India Cytoplasmic Sperm Injection) is a specialised method to form an embryo in the laboratory in which a sperm is directly injected into the ovum placed in a nutrient broth.

   GIFT (Gamete Intra Fallopian Transfer) is a procedure in which eggs are removed from woman's ovary with man sperm and transferred to one of the fallopian tube.

ZIFT (Zygote Intra Fallopian Transter) is a procedure (similar to in vitro fertilisation and embryo transfer in which the zygote (early embryo) up to 8 blastomeres is transferred directly intoi the Fallopian tube.

ET (Embryo Transfer) is a method in which the fertilisation occurs in vitro and the zygote formed is transferred into the uterus of the female who cannot conceive.

2. **(c)** **IMR** (Infant Mortality Rate) and **MMR** (Maternal Mortality Rate) both are responsible for affecting the growth rate inversely. It means decline in IMR as well as MMR will result in high population growth and vice-versa. Here, increased IMR will result in decline in growth rate. while, decreased MMR will cause rapid increase in growth rate.

   Therefore, IMR increased and MMR has been decreased in a population, it will not cause any significant change in growth rate.

3. **(a)** Breast feeding is one of the natural contraceptive methods. It reduces fertility by affecting the production of certain reproductive hormones. It is suppresses the production of Gonadotropin-Releasing Hormone (GRH) and Follicle Stimulating Hormone (FSH).

   The release of these hormones triggers ovulation. Breast feeding also leads to increased level of prolactin, that inhibits ovulation.

4. **(a)** Intake of higher dosed progestogens or progestogen-estrogen combinations within 72 hrs of coitus have been found to be very effective as emergency contraceptives. These could be used to avoid possible pregnancy due to rape or casual unprotected intercourse. These drugs disrupt the ovulation and fertilization.

5. **(b)** Syphills, gonorrhoea and genital wants as STD caused by *pallicum*, *Neissenia gonorrhoeae* and *human papilloma virus*. These pathogens directly infect and damage sex organs causing ichting fluid discharge, sight path and swelling of genitallia.

   AIDS (Acquired Immuno Deficiency Syndrome) is a caused by HIV virus in humans. It is transmitted through sexual contacts from infected to healthy person. The HIV virus does not directly affect sex organs as such but produce other set of symptoms in the body of infected person.

6. **(c)** Assertion is true but Reason is false.
   Amniocentesis can be used to detect the chromosomal abnormalities in the developing embryo. Hence in India, it has statutary ban.

7. **(b)** Assertion and Reason are true, but Reason is not the correct explanation of Assertion.
   A combined pill is the most commonly used birth control pill. It contains synthetic progestrone and oestrogen in doses high enough to check ovulation.

8. Creating public awareness regarding reproduction related aspects and providing facilities to build up a healthy society with added emphasis on the health of mother and child are the basic aims of the RCH programmes.

9. Among the common STs-gonorrhea, syphilis, genital herpes, chlamydiasis, hepatitis-B, AIDS etc., hepatitis-B, and AIDS are not infections of the reproductive organs though their mode of transmission could be through sexual contact also. All other diseases are transmitted through sexual contact and are also infections of the reproductive tract.

10. Proper information about reproductive organs-physiology and its functioning; discourage myths and misconceptions about sex-related aspects; knowledge about safe and hygienic sexual practices; adolescence and related changes, prevention of STDs, AIDs etc.

Objective Practice Exercise 

1. **(a)**

2. **(d)** Amniotic fluid is secreted by amnion of foetus during pregnancy.

3. **(b)**   4. **(a)**

5. **(c)** Permanent method of birth control in which testes are surgically removed, is called castration.

6. **(b)**   7. **(d)**   8. **(c)**

9. **(a)** Intra utrine device (Copper-T) inhibit fertilization and help in birth control.

10. **(b)** The birth control pill interferes with the maturation of the follicles and the ova, inhibiting release of an egg.

11. **(d)** Sterilization techniques can be considered as the safest birth control measures. It provides a permanent and sure birth control. It is called vasectomy in male and tubectomy in female.

12. **(a)**

13. **(b)** Condoms are barriers made of thin rubber/latex sheath that are used to cover the penis in the male or vagina and cervix in the female, just before coitus so that the ejaculated semen would not enter into the female reproductive tract. This can prevent conception.

14. **(c)**

15. **(a)** Copper 'T' is an intrauterine device which prevents the fertilized egg becoming implanted in the wall of the womb.

16. **(d)** Medical termination of pregnancy (MTP) or induced abortion become legal in India from 1971 with some strict conditions to avoid its misuse. Such restrictions are important to check indiscriminate and illegal female foeticides which are reported to be high in India. All the other options are of natural methods of contraception.

17. **(c)**   18. **(c)**

19. **(c)** The World Health Organization (WHO) is a specialized agency of the United Nations (UN) that is concerned with international public health. It was established on 7 April 1948, headquartered in Geneva, Switzerland.

20. **(d)** Reproduction-related areas are currently in operation in India come under the popular name 'Reproductive and Child Health Care (RCH) programmes.

21. **(b)** 'Saheli'–an oral contraceptive for the females was developed at Central Drug Research Institute (CDRI) in Lucknow, India.

22. **(b)** Lactational amenorrhoea is the absence of menstruation. It is the breast sucking of mother by her child for a long time which is considered to contribute a gap for pregnancy. It is based on the fact that ovulation and the menses do not occur during the period of intense lactation following parturition.

23. **(d)** Female sterilization (called **tubectomy**) prevents fertilization by interrupting the passage throug fallopian tube. Eggs continues to be produced but they fail to pass into the uterus. In tubectomy, a small part of the fallopian tube is removed or tied up through a small incision in the abdomen or through vagina.

24. **(c)**

25. **(d)** Sterilization techniques can be considered as the safest birth control measures. It provides a permanent and sure birth control. It is called vasectomy in male and tubectomy in female.

26. **(d)**   27. **(c)**

28. **(c)** Sexually transmitted diseases (STDs) are caused by infections that are passed from one person to another during sexual contact. Most STDs initially do not cause symptoms. Symptoms and signs of disease may include: vaginal discharge, penile discharge, ulcers on or around the genitals and pelvic pain.

29. **(c)** Assisted reproductive technologies (ART) include a number of special techniques which assist infertile couples to have children. *In-vitro* fertilization is one such technique.

30. **(a)** Syphilis is a chronic bacterial disease that is contracted chiefly by infection during sexual intercourse, but also congenitally by infection of a developing foetus. Syphilis is completely curable if detected early and treated properly.

31. **(b)**   32. **(c)**

33. **(a)** Medical Termination of Pregnancy (MTP) was legalised in 1971 by Government of India with some strict conditions to avoid its misuse.

34. **(a)**

35. **(a)** Infertility is defined as not being able to get pregnant despite having frequent, unprotected sex for at least a year for most people and six months in certain circumstances. Reasons for infertility include drugs, diseases, and congenital problems, immunological or psychological problems.
Contraception is the deliberate use of artificial methods or other techniques to prevent pregnancy as a consequence of sexual intercourse. Assisted reproductive technology (ART) is the technology used to achieve pregnancy in procedures such as fertility medication, artificial insemination, in vitro fertilization and surrogacy. It is reproductive technology used primarily for infertility treatments, and is also known as fertility treatment.

36. **(b)** Artificial insemination is the assisted reproductive technology that has been used for the longest time period. It can help treat certain kinds of infertility in both men and women. In this procedure, sperms are inserted directly into a woman's cervix, fallopian tubes, or uterus. This makes the trip shorter for the sperm and by passes any possible obstructions. Intra uterine insemination (IUI), in which the sperm is placed in the uterus, is the most common form of artificial insemination.

37. **(d)** AIDS, genital herpes and hepatitis B are sexually transmitted diseases which are not completely curable.

38. **(b)**

39. **(c)** Syphilis, gonorrhea and genital warts are sexually transmitted disease which specifically affects the sex organs. Syphilis is caused by the spirochete bacterium *Treponema pallidum*. Gonorrhea is caused by *Neisseria gonorrhoeae*, a bacterium that can grow and multiply easily in mucus membranes of the body. Genital warts, which are also called condylomata acuminata or venereal warts, are growths in the genital area caused by a sexually transmitted papilloma virus.
The AIDS (Acquired immunodeficiency syndrome) is a severe immunological disorder caused by the retrovirus HIV. The illness alters the immune system, making people much more vulnerable to infections and diseases.

40. **(a)** Hepatitis B is an infectious disease caused by the hepatitis B virus (HBV) which affects the liver. HIV (human immunodeficiency virus) is a virus that attacks the immune system, the body's natural defense system. Without a strong immune system, the body has trouble fighting off disease. Both the diseases can also be transmitted by sharing of injection needles, surgical instruments, etc., with infected persons, transfusion of blood, or from an infected mother to the foetus too.

41. **(a)**

42. **(a)** Withdrawal of penis before ejaculation.

43. **(a)** India was the first amongst countries in the world to initiate action plans and programmes at a national level to attain total reproductive health as a social goal. The programmes called 'family planning' were initiated in 1951 and were periodically assessed over the past decades.
To create awareness among people about various reproduction related aspects, providing facilities and support for building up a reproductively healthy society are the major tasks of these programmes.

44. **(d)** Marriageable age is the age at which a person is allowed by law to marry. In India this age has been set as 18 for woman and 21 for man (without parents' consent).

45. **(d)** Condoms are used as barriers made of thin rubber/latex sheath used to cover the penis in the male or vagina and cervix in females. It prevents the deposition of ejaculated semen into the vagina of the female. It should be discarded after a single use. It is also a safe guard against transmission of AIDS and other Sexually Transmitted Diseases (STDs).

46. **(c)** Surgical methods, are terminal and permanent methods, which block the transport of gametes, thereby preventing conception. In males, this is called vasectomy, while in females, this is called tubectomy.

47. **(b)** Amniocentesis or amniotic fluid test or AFT is a medical procedure which is used in prenatal diagnosis of chromosomal abnormalities and foetal infections. This is the same procedure used for sex determination.

48. **(c)**

49. **(c)** Condom, diaphragm, cervical caps, and vaults are included under barrier methods of contraception. Barrier methods of birth control are physical or chemical barriers that prevent sperm from passing through the woman's cervix into the uterus and fallopian tubes to fertilize an egg. Some methods also protect against sexually transmitted disease (STDs).

50. **(d)** The hormone releasing Intra Uterine Devices (IUDs) such as Progestasert and LNG-20 increase phagocytosis of sperms within the uterus and makes the uterus unsuitable for implantation & the cervix hostile to the sperms. Progestasert is a hormone releasing T-shaped. IUDS which is made of ethylene and vinylacete. Copolymer that contains titanium oxide.

51. **(c)**   **52.** **(a)**

Chapter Test

1. **(b)** Diaphragms, cervical caps and vaults are reusable barrier contraceptives made of rubber that are inserted into the female reproductive tract to cover the cervix during coitus. They prevent conception by blocking the entry of sperms through the cervix.

2. **(b)**   **3.** **(d)**

4. **(a)** Gamete Intra fallopian Transfer (GIFT) is recommended for those females who cannot produce an ovum. In this process, the eggs of the donor woman are removed and in a form of mixture with sperm transferred into fallopian tube of another woman who cannot produce ovum, but can provide suitable environment for fertilization. Thus in GIFT, site of fertilization is fallopian tube, not laboratory.

5. **(c)** Gonorrhoea, hepatitis, AIDS and syphilis all are sexually transmitted disease that are cause because of the infection by *Neisseria gonorrhoeae*, Hepatitis B Virus, Human Immunodeficiency Virus (HIV) *Ireponema pallidum.*

6. **(c)** Assertion is true but Reason is false.
Periodic abstinence is one such method in which the couples avoid or abstain from coitus from day 10 to 17 of the menstrual cycle when ovulation could be expected. As chances of fertilisation are very high during this period, it is called the fertile period.

7. **(c)** Assertion is true but Reason is false.
Condom should be discarded after a single use. It is also a safeguard against infection of AIDS and sexual diseases.

8. **(d)**   **9.** **(a)**   **10.** **(a)**   **11.** **(a)**

12. **(c)**

13. Oogenesis takes place in the ovaries.

14. Interstitial cells or leyding cells that lie between seminiferous tubules secrete testosterone hormone, which is essential for making sperm (spermatogenesis).

15. (i) User friendly & easily available
(ii) Effective & reversible with no or at least side effects.

4 Principles of Inheritance and Variation

Chromosomal Theory of Inheritance

Principles of Inheritance and Variation
- Study of Inheritance and variation is known as Genetics.
- Mendel was the father of genetics.
- Inheritance is the process by which characters are passed from parent to offspring.
- Variation is the difference by which progeny differs.

Linkage and Recombination
- Exception of Mendels 3rd law.
- Ex-Morgan studied eye colour in drosophilla.

Corren

Incomplete Dominance
- Where dominant allele do not completely expresses itself.
- It is not a blending inheritance. Ex-In Mirabilis falapa and Antirrhinum majus. RR and rr colour of flowers forms pink flower in F1 generation. In F2 Red, Pink, White.

According to Mendel
- Genes were factors which are transmitted from one generation to other.
- Theory was formuled by re-discovery of Mendel by 3-scientist devries, Correns and Teashermark in 1900.
- Mendels laws of segregation & independent assortment is on chromosomal theory.

Mendel

Laws

Law of Dominance
- Pair of alles present in F_1 hybrid in which only one expresses itself. (Ex-Tt - F1)
- Shown in Monohybrid cross.

Law of segregation
- Law of purity of gametes i.e. Each gamete is pure itself eg. Monohybrid cross.

Law of independent assortment
- It is not univeral and based on dihybrid cross.
- Ex-F2 progeny lethal genes 2 : 1.

Mutation
(Gene mutation)

(Chromosomal mutation) Deletion Duplication Inversion Translocation

(Due to change in number)

- Polyploidy
- Aneuploidy

Crosses

Monohybrid
Mendel taken one pair of contrasting trait T and 't' of pea-Homozigously formed TT and 'tt' in F1 progeny. **Ex.** Self pollination of F1 plant produced 'Tt' 3 : 1 3 Tall, 1 Dwarf obtained F2 progeny.

Dihybrid
Mendel taken two pairs of contrastic characters simultaneously. **Ex.** In cross of yellow round and green wrinkled seeds we have phenotypic expression YyRr and produces 2:1:2 as geno type the colour of seeds and shape of seeds have segregated independently and each gamete has one factor.

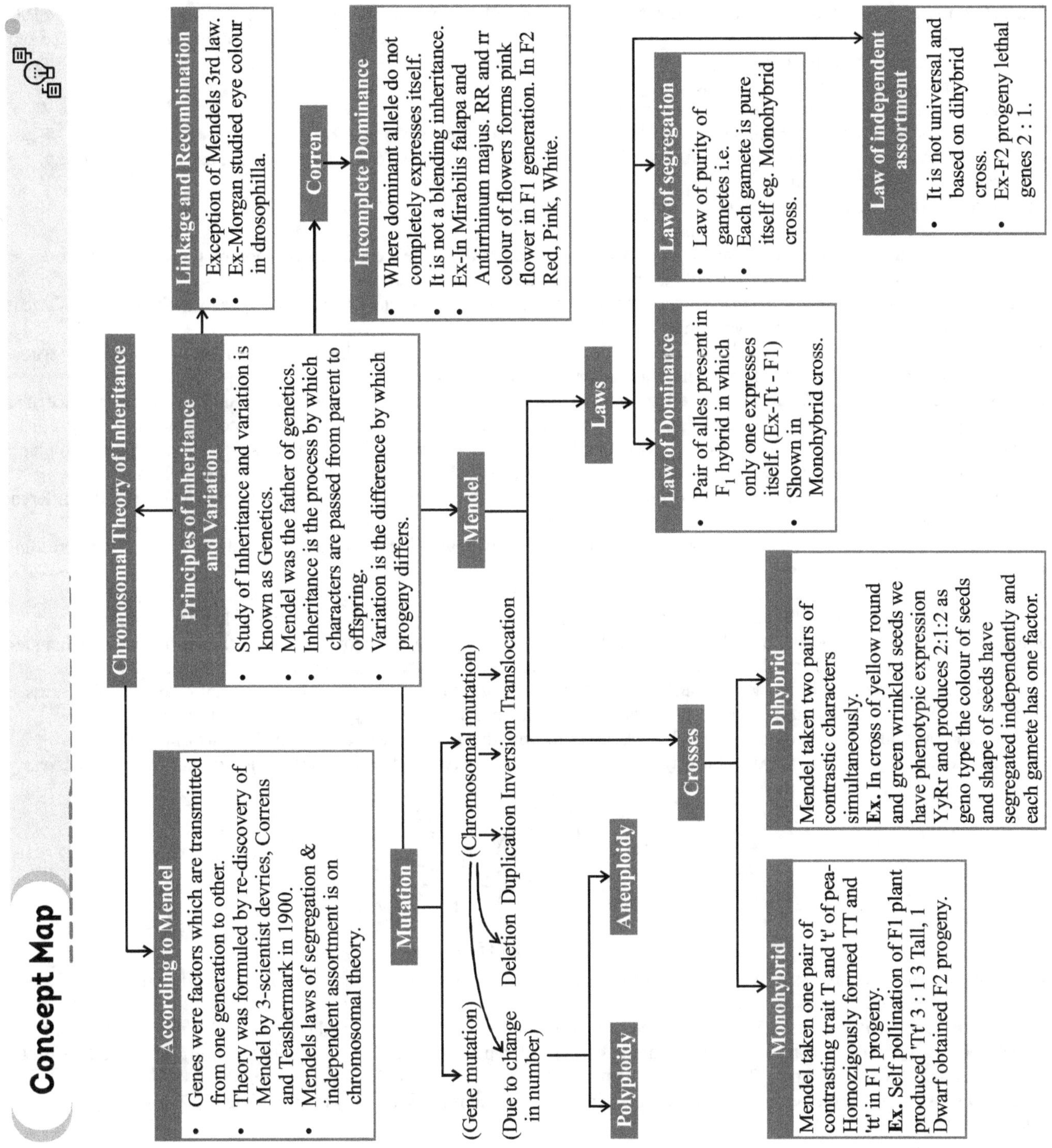

Topic 1   Mendalism & Likage and Recombination 

Genetics is the study of inheritance and variation. Heredity or inheritance is the process by which characters are passed on from parent to progeny. Variation is the characteristic difference by which progeny differs from their parents. The characteristic differences exhibited by the individuals of the same species, race and family is called variation.

TERMINOLOGIES OF MENDELIAN EXPERIMENT

Genes or mendelian factor : Units of inheritance. They contain information required to express a particular trait.

Homozygous : Both alleles are same/similar for a character. E.g., TT = Tall, tt = Dwarf.

Heterozygous : Alleles are dissimilar for a character. E.g., Tt = Tall.

Punnett square : It is a graphical representation to calculate the probability of all genotypes of offspring in a genetic cross. R.C. Punnett introduced punnett square (in 1927) to figure out the probable result of genetic cross. The following points must be kept in mind when constructing the punnet square –

(i)   A letter represent a contrasting character, e.g. T.

(ii)   A capital letter, e.g. T represents a dominant character or allele.

(iii)   A small or lower case letter, e.g. t represent the recessive character or trait.

(iv)   The male gametes are placed to the left of the female gametes. The gametes of both the sexes are usually encircled, e.g. T .

(v)   Paired letter represents the genotype.

Phenotype : External appearance or trait of an individual.

Genotype : Genetic constitution of an organism.

Alleles or allelomorphs : The two Mendelian factors which occur on the same locus in the two homologous chromosomes of an individual and control the expression of a character are called **alleles** or **allelomorphs.**

Gene locus : A particular portion or region of the chromosome representing a single gene is called gene locus. The alleles of a gene occupy the same gene locus on the two homologous chromosomes.

Dominant factor or allele : It is one of the pairs of alleles which can express itself whether present in homozygous or heterozygous state., eg., the factor for tallness in hybrid and homogenous states or Tt and TT.

Recessive factor or allele : The factor of an allelic or allelomorphic pair which is unable to express its effect in the presence of its contrasting factor in a heterozygous is called recessive factor or allele. A recessive allele is represented by small letter. e.g. t in Tt. The effect of recessive factor becomes known only when it is present in the pure or homozygous state, e.g. tt in dwarf pea plant.

Hybrid : The heterozygous organism produced after crossing to genetically different individuals is called hybrid.

F_1 Generation : F_1 or first filial generation is the generation of hybrids produced from a cross between the genetically different individuals called parents.

F_2 Generation : F_2 or second filial generation is the generation of individuals which arises as a result of inbreeding or interbreeding amongst individuals of F_1 generation.

Genome : It is a complete set of chromosomes where every gene and chromosome is represented singly as in a gamete.

Gene pool : The aggregate of all the genes and their alleles present in an interbreeding population is known as gene pool.

Back cross : It is cross which is performed between hybrid and one of its parents. It is employed in certain crop improvement techniques. Back cross are used by animal and plant breeders to rapidly improve a breed/variety by making a useful gene (trait) homozygous.

Test cross : It is a cross to know whether an individual is homozygous or heterozygous for dominant character. Test cross is crossing of offspring with unknown dominant phenotype with the individual homozygous recessive for the trait.

(i)   If unknown offspring is homozygous (TT), then crossing with dwarf recessive (tt) gives all Tall offspring i.e., Tt

(ii)   If unknown offspring is heterozygous Tall (Tt), then crossing with dwarf recessive (tt) results in 50% tall (Tt) and 50% dwarf (tt) progeny.

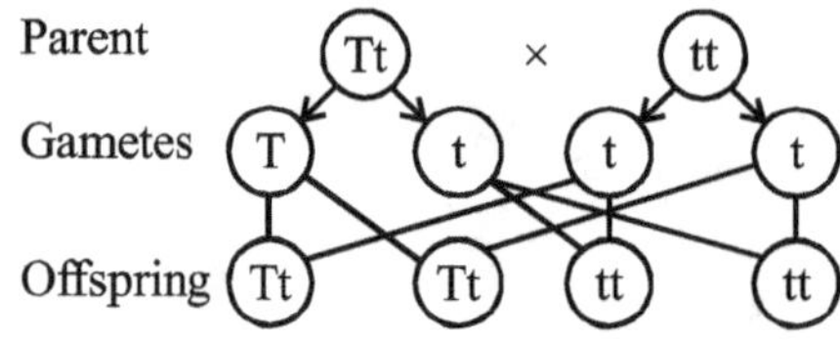

50% tall : 50% dwarf

Monohybrid cross : It is a cross between two organisms of a species which is made to study the inheritance of a single pair of alleles or factors of a character.

Monohybrid ratio : It is a ratio which is obtained in F_2 generation when a monohybrid cross is made and the offspring of F_1 generation are selfbred. Monohybrid ratio is usually 3 : 1 (phenotypic ratio) or 1 : 2 : 1 (genotype ratio) in which 25% of the individuals carry the recessive trait, 25% pure dominant and 50% have hybrid dominant trait.

Dihybrid cross : It is a cross between two organisms of a species which is made to study the inheritance of two pairs of factors or alleles of two genes.

Dihybrid ratio : It is a ratio which is obtained in the F_2 generation when a dihybrid cross is made and the offspring of F_1 generation are self-bred. Dihybrid ratio is $9 : 3 : 3 : 1$ (phenotypic ratio) where 9/16 first recessive and second dominant and 1/16 carry both the recessive traits.
True breeding line : A true breeding line is the one that has undergone continuous self pollination, shows stable trait inheritance and expression for several generations.
Genotype : It is the gene complement of an individual. It is remains the same throughout the life of an individual.
Phenotype : It is the external manifestation of gene products brought to expression. It may change with time & environment.
Emasculation : Removal of male sex organs (anthers) is called emasculation. In plant breeding emasculation is the technique of removal of stamens of a bisexual flowers to prevent self breeding.

MENDELS LAW OF INHERITANCE

The first scientific study leading to formulation of laws of inheritance was carried out by Gregor Johann Mendel. Mendel conducted cross hybridization experiments on Garden Pea plant (*Pisum sativum*) and studied transmission of characters that had 2 opposing traits. e.g., character is height and traits are tall (T) and dwarf (t). Mendel selected garden pea (Pisum sativum) as experimental material because
(i)   Plant had traits with two contrasting forms of each other.
(ii)   Flower was cleistogamous (male and female parts enclosed in same flower). Therefore naturally self pollinated, this helped to avoid the bagging procedure in breeding experiments.
(iii)   The plant had a short (seasonal) life cycle so that transmission of traits from one generation to next could be studied in short period of time.
(iv)   Pea plant had several true breeding lines.
(v)   It is easy to cultivate.
Because garden pea is self fertilizing, the anthers held to be removed before maturity. The process of removal of anthers is called emasculation. Mendel selected seven pair of contrasting characters (given in table) & luckily all were related as dominant & recessive. There was no blending or incomplete inheritance.

Table : Contrasting traits studied by Mendel in Pea

S.No.	Character	Dominant trait	Recessive trait
1	Height	Tall	Dwarf
2	Flower colour	Violet (Purple)	White
3	Flower position	Axial	Terminal
4	Seed shape	Round	Wrinkled
5	Seed colour	Yellow	Green
6	Pod colour	Green	Yellow
7	Pod shape	Inflated	Constricted

Hybridization/cross pollination of plant takes place after emasculation and dusting the stigma of female parent with pollen of desired male parents, e.g., cross pollinating tall and dwarf variety of plant. Such a cross where transmission of one character is studied is called monohybrid cross. Collection of seed obtained as a result of cross fertilization and grow them to obtain F_1 hybrid/first filial (F_1) generation. Self-pollination of F_1 plants produces second filial F_2 generation. After that self-pollination of F_2 plants takes place.

Observation of Mendel's experiment :
(i)   All F_1 progenies were tall for height. He called these hybrids. F_1 always resembled either of parent. The traits that appeared in the F_1 generation was called dominant and the other which did not appear in the F_1 population was called recessive. The results of reciprocal cross were the same.
(ii) F_2 generation showed reappearance of character which is not shown in F_1 generation. 1/4th of F_2 plants were dwarf and 3/4th were tall. None of the character showed blending i.e., no plant was of intermediate height. Either they were tall or dwarf. Identification of $3 : 1$ ratio as hidden $1 : 2 : 1$ of pure and hybrid forms.

Inference of Mendel's experiment :
    (i)   Only one parental trait expresses in F_1 generation. That trait is called **dominant**.
    (ii)   Both traits expressed in F_2 in proportion of $3 : 1$.

Result of Mendel's experiment :
    (i)   He stated that some factors are being stably passed from parent to offspring through gametes, over successive generation.
    (ii)   Observed or expressed monohybrid Mendelian ratio is $3 : 1$ of dominant to recessive form of trait.

Significance of Mendel's experiment :
    (i)   This was first statistical analysis and mathematical logic applied to problems in Biology.
    (ii)   His experiment had large sampling size of about 6000 plants which gave greater credibility to data that he collected.
    (iii)   His inferences were confirmed flow experiments or successive generations e.g. his test plants, that proved his results are general rule of inheritance and not case specific.
    (iv)   On the basis of these experiments he formulated **2 laws of inheritance**. Law of dominance and law of segregation.

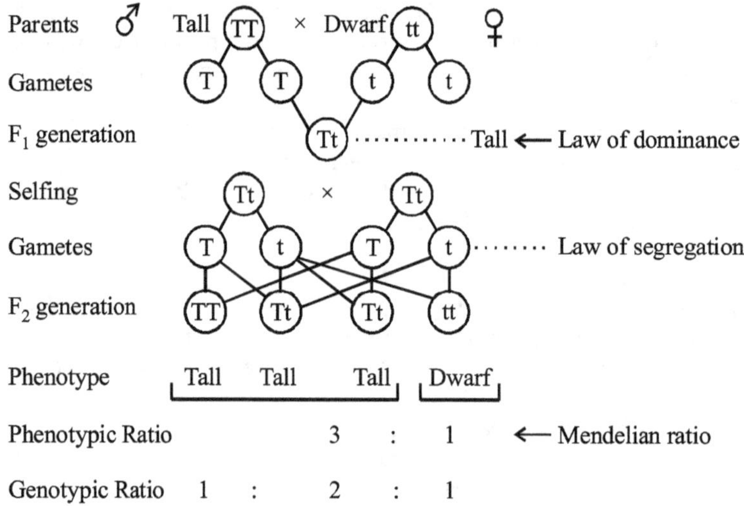

Fig. : Diagrammatic representation of Mendelian laws of Inheritance

LAW OF DOMINANCE

Law of dominance states that only one factor expresses itself in F_1 generation. Characters are controlled by discrete genetic units called factor. A character is represented in an organism (diploid) by at least two factors. The two factors lie on the two homotogous chromosomes at the same locus.

In a dissimilar pair of factor, one member of pair dominates (occur more frequently) than other. This is used to explain appearance of one parental trait in F_1 generation in monohybrid cross and expression of both factors expresses in F_2 generation in the proportion of 3 : 1 ratio. In a hybrid where both the conrasting alleles are present, only one factor/allele called dominant is able to express its effect while the other factor/allele called recessive remains suppressed in F_1 generation. This the called law of dominance.

LAW OF SEGREGATION

Parents contain 2 factors for a character which might be similar or dissimilar and segregate/separate from each other during gamete formation so that gamete gets one factor only from parent. This law established the fact that alleles do not blend and both the traits are recovered as such in F_2 generation. This law is also known as '**Law of purity of gametes**' because each 'gamete is pure in itself i.e. having either T (i.e. gene for tallness) or t (i.e. gene for dwarfness). Mendel formulated this law with the help of monohybrid cross.

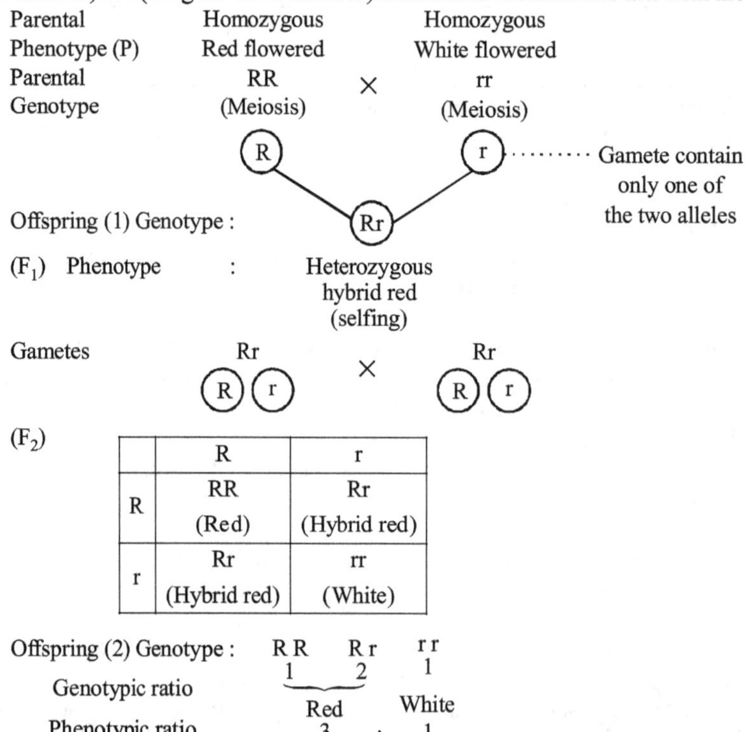

(F₂)

	R	r
R	RR (Red)	Rr (Hybrid red)
r	Rr (Hybrid red)	rr (White)

Fig. : A monohybrid cross in Pea showing that factors of a character segregate at the time of formation of gametes

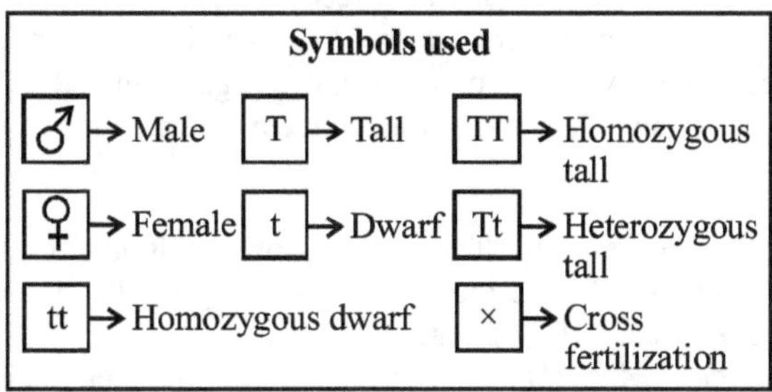

LAW OF INDEPENDENT ASSORTMENT

This law states that genes of different characters located in different pairs of chromosomes are independent of one another in their segregation during gamete formation. This law was proposed by Mendel based on the results of dihybrid crosses, where inheritance of two traits were considered simultaneously. Independent assortment is not applicable for the genes located on the same chromosomes i.e. linked genes. The following cross between a pure-breeding plant with yellow, round seeds and another pure breeding plant with green, wrinkled seeds, can be taken as an example to explain this law.

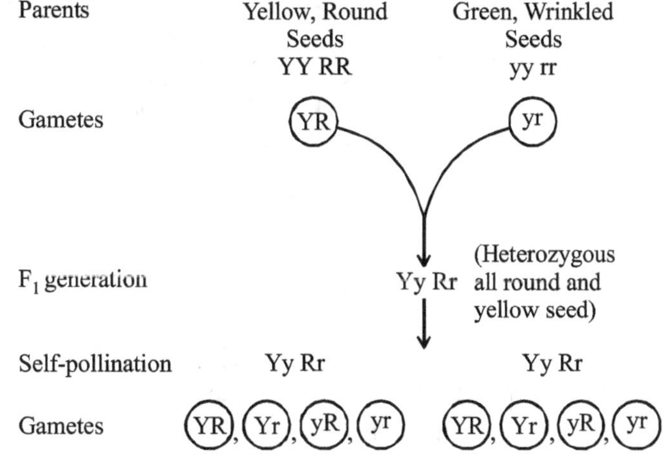

F_2 generation

	YR	Yr	yR	yr
YR	YY RR (yellow, round)	YY Rr (yellow, round)	Yy RR (yellow, round)	Yy Rr (yellow, round)
Yr	YY Rr (yellow, round)	YY rr (yellow, wrinkled)	Yy Rr (yellow, round)	Yy rr (yellow, wrinkled)
yR	Yy RR (yellow, round)	Yy Rr (yellow, round)	yy RR (green, round)	yy Rr (green, round)
yr	Yy Rr (yellow, round)	Yy rr (yellow, wrinkled)	yy Rr (green, round)	yy rr (green, wrinkled)

The Phenotypic ratio is :

Yellow round	:	Yellow wrinkled	:	Green round	:	Green wrinkled
9	:	3	:	3	:	1

Wrinkled yellow and round green are recombinants.
Round yellow and wrinkled green are parental combinations.
The genotypic ratio is :

YYRR	:	YYRr	:	YyRR	:	YyRr	:	YYrr
1	:	2	:	2	:	4	:	1

Yyrr	:	yy RR	:	yy Rr	:	yy rr
2	:	1	:	2	:	1

In this cross, the factors for colour of seeds and those for shape of seeds have segregated independently and each gamete has one factor for each of these two traits. Mendel might not have discovered the law of independent assortment of traits if the pea plant had a smaller number of chromosomes per cell, since in that event, more than one gene studied could have occurred on each chromosome bringing in phenomenon of linkage in contradiction to law of independent assortment.

INCOMPLETE DOMINANCE

Incomplete dominance was discovered by Correns in inheritance of flower colour in dog-flower (Snapdragon or *Antirrhinum majus*). It is the phenomenon where dominant allele do not completely express itself. Incomplete dominance is not blending inheritance because parental characters reappear in F_2 generation.

Example, In *Mirabili's jalapa* (four O' clock) & *Antirrhinum majus* (Snapdragon or dog flower), there are two types of flower colour in pure state-red & white. When the two types of plants are crossed the hybrid or plants of F_1 generation have pink flowers. If the letter are selfed, the plants of F_2 generation are of three types-red, pink & white flowered in the ratio of 1 : 2 : 1. i.e., pure dominant : hybride : pure recessive.

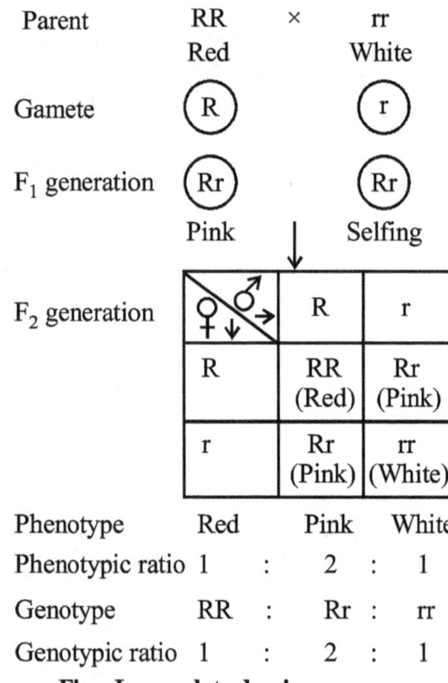

Fig. : Incomplete dominance

Findings of Incomplete Dominance

(i) F_1 had a phenotype that did not resemble either of 2 parents and was in between the two.

(ii) Genotype and phenotype ratio is same unlike monohybrid cross of complete dominance.

(iii) Incomplete dominance shows that dominant gene is not coding for fully functional enzyme.

CODOMINANCE

In codominance, both the alleles of a gene are equally dominant i.e. the dominant character is not able to suppress the recessive character & thus both the characters appear side by side in F_1 hybrids. F_1 generation resembles both the parents. ABO blood group – controlled by gene I, sickle cell anaemia. ABO blood group system in human beings is an example of both codominant and multiple alleles. Human beings have six genotypes and four blood groups or blood groups or blood group phenotypes – A, B, AB and O. The blood groups are determined by two types of anti gens present in the surface coating of red blood cells – A and B. The antigens occur on oligosaccharide rich head region of a glycophorin. Blood group A person having antigen B, AB have both antigen while blood group O person do not carry any antigen in the coating of their erythrocytes. In human population, 3 different alleles for ABO blood group system are found I^A, I^B and I^0 or i. I^A and I^B are mutant allele and are dominant over I^0 or i, which is wild allele. I^A and I^B are responsible for A and B antigen (glycoproteins) while I^0 or i does not produce any of these A or B antigens. A person is having only two of these three alleles and blood type can be determined by their antigen type. Six genotype combinations are possible with these three alleles.

Blood type	Genotype	Antigen	Anti bodies
A	$I^A I^A$ or $I^A i$	A	b
B	$I^B I^B$ or $I^B i$	B	a
AB	$I^A I^B$	Both A and B	Neither a nor b
O	ii	Neither A nor B	Both a and b

MULTIPLE ALLELES

Multiple alleles can be defined as a set of three, four, or more allelomorphic genes or alleles, which have arisen as a result of mutation of the normal gene & which occupy the same locus in the homologous chromosomes. There is absence of crossing over in multiple alleles & the mode of inheritance in case of multiple alleles is called **multiple allelism.**

The well known example of multiple allele in human is blood group, which also shows codominance. ABO blood group system is discovered by **Landsteiner.** Four human Blood groups are A, B, AB and O – 4 phenotypes.

Letters **A** and **B** refers to 2 type of antigens coating red blood cells of person having either A/B type blood.

AB	→ contains formation of antigen.
O	→ contains neither antigen.
Allele I^A	→ determines formation of antigen A
I^B	→ determines formation of antigen B.
I	→ do not produce any antigen.
I^A and I^B	→ are completely dominant over O.
I^A and I^B	→ are codominant when present together.
I^A and I^B	→ multiple alleles of same character.

Sperm →		O	A		B		AB	
Egg ↓		i	i	I^A	i	I^B	I^A	I^B
O	i	ii / O	ii / O	$I^A i$ / A	ii / O	$I^B i$ / B	$I^A i$ / A	$I^B i$ / B
A	i	ii / O	ii / O	$I^A i$ / A	ii / O	$I^B i$ / B	$I^A i$ / A	$I^B i$ / B
A	I^A	$I^A i$ / A	$I^A i$ / A	$I^A I^A$ / A	$I^A i$ / A	$I^A I^B$ / AB	$I^A I^A$ / A	$I^A I^B$ / AB
B	i	ii / O	ii / O	$I^A i$ / A	ii / O	$I^B i$ / B	$I^A i$ / A	$I^B i$ / B
B	I^B	$I^B i$ / B	$I^B i$ / B	$I^A I^B$ / AB	$I^B i$ / B	$I^B I^B$ / B	$I^A I^B$ / AB	$I^B I^B$ / B
AB	I^A	$I^A i$ / A	$I^A i$ / A	$I^A I^A$ / A	$I^A i$ / A	$I^A I^B$ / AB	$I^A I^A$ / A	$I^A I^B$ / AB
AB	I^B	$I^B i$ / B	$I^B i$ / B	$I^A I^B$ / AB	$I^B i$ / B	$I^B I^B$ / B	$I^A I^B$ / AB	$I^B I^B$ / B

Fig. : Chart showing inheritance of blood groups by children of various parentage

There are six different genotypic combination according to 4 phenotype on basis of 3 alleles.

Table : Phenotype ratio of F_2 generation in dihybrid crosses

(i)	Complementary gene	9 : 7
(ii)	Supplementary gene	9 : 3 : 4
(iii)	Dominant epistasis	12 : 3 : 1
(iv)	Recessive epistasis	9 : 3 : 4
(v)	Duplicate genes	15 : 1
(vi)	Lethal genes (in homozygous conditions) (monohybrid cross)	2 : 1

CHROMOSOMAL THEORY OF INHERITANCE

Mendel held that the traits were transmitted from one generation to the next by stable particular units called **factors,** which are now called as **genes.** Chromosome theory was formulated after rediscovery of Mendel's work by three scientists (de Vries, Correns and Tschermak) in 1900. In fact it was correns who summarised Mendel's conclusions in the familiar term of two principles & coined the term factor. It was an American William Sutton, who noticed the striking similarity between the behaviour of chromosomes during gamete formation & fertilization, and the transmission of Mendel's hereditary factor.

Table : Similarities between behaviour of chromosomes with Mendel's factors/genes.

	Behaviour of chromosomes & genes during meiosis & Fertilization	Behaviour of Mendel's Factor
1.	Chromosomes occurs in pairs in a diploid cell & in organisms. Paired chromosomes are called as homologous chromosomes.	Mendel's factor occurs in pairs as each traits is controlled by a pair of factors.
2.	Homologous chromosomes separate out or segregate during meiosis at the time of gamete formation.	A pair of factors separate or segregate during gamete formation.
3.	One chromosomes of a homologous pair passes into a gamete.	Only one factor is present in a gamete.
4.	During fertilization, gametes unite restoring the chromosomes number. Each homologous pair has one paternal & one maternal chromosomes.	During fertilization, gametes unite. Each organisms contains two factors, one from each parent.
5.	Chromosomes retain their individuality during segregation. Each pair segregates independently of every other pair.	Factors remains unchanged from generation to generation. Each factor segregate independently of every other factor.

Since Mendel's factor or genes, the unit of heredity are present on the chromosomes Mendel's law of segregation & independent assortment can be explained better by the chromosome theory as it is the chromosomes that separate (segregate) & assort independently in meiosis. These similarities led **Walter Sutton & Theordore Boveri** (1902) to postulate the chromosomes theory of inheritance. Three postulates of chromosomal theory of inheritance are –

(i)   Both chromosomes and genes were found in pairs in diploid cell
(ii) 2 alleles of a gene pair are also located on homologous sites on homologous chromosomes. Homologous chromosomes separate and gene pairs (allele), segregate during meiosis.
(iii) Paired condition of both chromosome and genes were restored during fertilization.

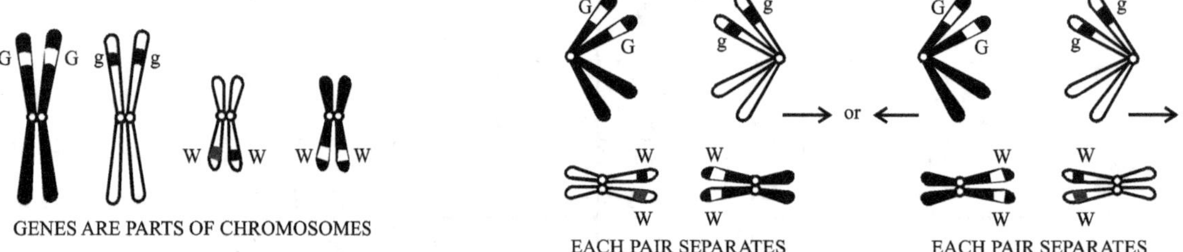

GENES ARE PARTS OF CHROMOSOMES

EACH PAIR SEPARATES   EACH PAIR SEPARATES

Fig. : Replication of chromosomes and factors   **Fig. : Segregation of chromosomes as well as factors during gametogenesis**

This theory states that : Mendelian genes (factors) are located on chromosome and it is the chromosome that segregate and independently assort. The latter happens during meiotic cell division.

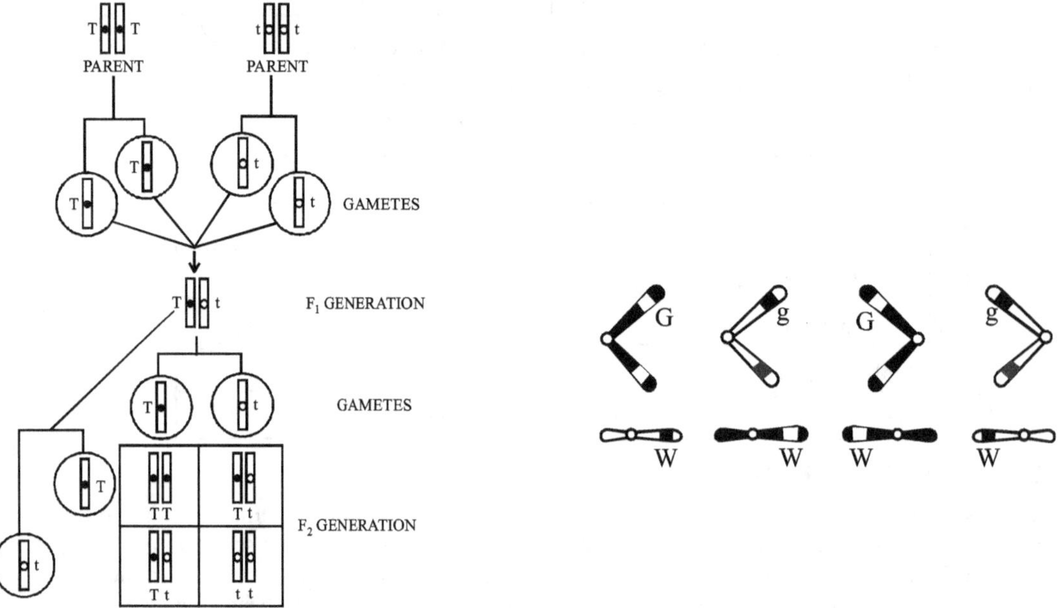

Fig. : Law of segregation interpreted on the basis of genes or factors (solid and hollow) situated on two different chromosomes   **Fig. : Independent assortment during gametogenesis resulting in the formation of parent as well as recombinant gametes**

The term gene (for Mendelians factor) and allele (for any one of the contrasting trait of Mendelian factor) was discovered by **Johannsen** and **Bateson** respectively.

LINKAGE AND RECOMBINATION

Experimental verification of the chromosomal theory of inheritance by Thomas Hunt Morgan & his colleagues led to discovering the 'basis of variation that sexual reproduction produced. T. H. Morgan is popularly called as father of experimental genetics. Morgan worked with tiny fruit flies – *Drosophila melanogaster* and postulated chromosome theory of Linkage which states that

(i) Linked genes are genes which stay together during transmission from generation to generation.
(ii) Linked genes occur on the same chromosome.
(iii) Genes are arranged in a linear fashion on the chromosome.
(iv) Each gene occupies a specific place on the chromosome.
(v) Genes tend to maintain original parental combination of the allele with the exception of an occasional crossing over.
(vi) Crossing over occurs due to weakening of linkage between two genes.
(vii) Strength of the linkage between two genes is inversely proportional to the distance between the two, i.e., two linked genes show higher frequency of crossing over if the distance between them is higher and lower frequency if the distance is small.

Morgan carried out several dihybrid crosses in Drosophila to study sex-linked genes. Normal eye colour in flies is red and mutant is white eyed.

Cross 1: Yellow-bodied, white-eyed females X Brown-bodied, red-eyed males (wild type)

Cross 2: White-eyed, miniature winged X Red eyed, large winged (wild type)

Their F_1 progenies were obtained which were inter-crossed. Then he obtained F_2 progeny and F_2 ratio was observed

He found that, the two genes did not segregate independently of each other and the F_2 ratio deviated from the 9:3:3:1 ratio, (expected when the two genes are independent).

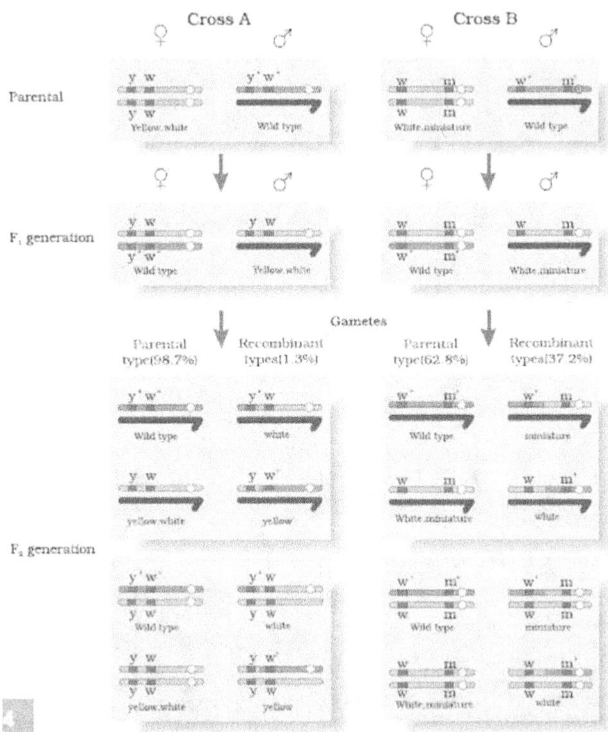

Fig. : Linkage – Results of two dihybrid crosses conducted by Morgan, Cross A shows crossing between gene y and W : Cross B shows crossing between genes w and m. Here dominant wild type alleles are represented with (+) sign in superscript.

Note : The strength of linkage between y and w is higher than w and m.

Explanation of deviation from Mendelian ratio:

Genes involved are located on the X chromosome. When two genes are located on the same chromosome, the proportion of parental gene combinations was much higher than the non-parental type. Morgan attributed this due to the physical association or linkage of the two genes and coined the term linkage. Morgan found that even when genes were grouped on the same chromosome, some genes were very tightly linked while others were loosely linked. Tightly linked genes show low recombination. Loosely linked genes show high recombination. Genes white and yellow were very tightly linked and showed only 1.3% recombination while white and miniature wing showed 37.2% recombination, hence loosely linked. Alfred Sturtevant used the recombination frequency between gene pairs as a measure of physical distance between genes and 'mapped' their position on the chromosome. In this way, genetic maps were prepared, which are used today for genome sequencing projects as in Human Genome Project.

Phenotype : Red eyed female : Red eyed male : White eyed male

         50   :   25   :   25

This criss cross pattern of inheritance is of sex linked (X-linked genes) genes. **Linkage** is the phenomenon of certain genes staying together during inheritance through generations without any change or separation due to their being present on the same chromosomes. Linkage in the genes can be identified by test cross. Linked genes refers to genes on the same chromosomes and assorted together or show very low recombination. Sex linkage is the phenotypic expression of an allele that is related to the gender of the individual & is directly tied to the sex chromosomes. Genes that are present on the X & Y chromosomes are called sex linked genes. The rearrangements of linked genes due to crossing over is known as **recombination**. Recombination also occurs due to chance separation of chromosomes during gametogenesis & their random coming together during fertilization. Alfred Sturtevant used the frequency of recombination between gene pairs on the same chromosomes as a measure of the distance between genes & mapped their position on the chromosomes. Today genetic maps are extensively used as a starting point in the sequencing of whole genome. It has very much used in Human Genome Sequencing.

Importance of linkage :

(i)   The possibility of variation in gametes is reduced by linkage (unless crossing over occurs).

(ii)   Linear arrangement of genes on chromosomes.

        Recombinant types are new allelic combinations different from those of parents due to crossing over in their linkage groups.

(iii)   Frequency of recombination is given as.

$$= \frac{\text{Total no. of recombination in test cross}}{\text{Total progeny in the test cross}} \times 100$$

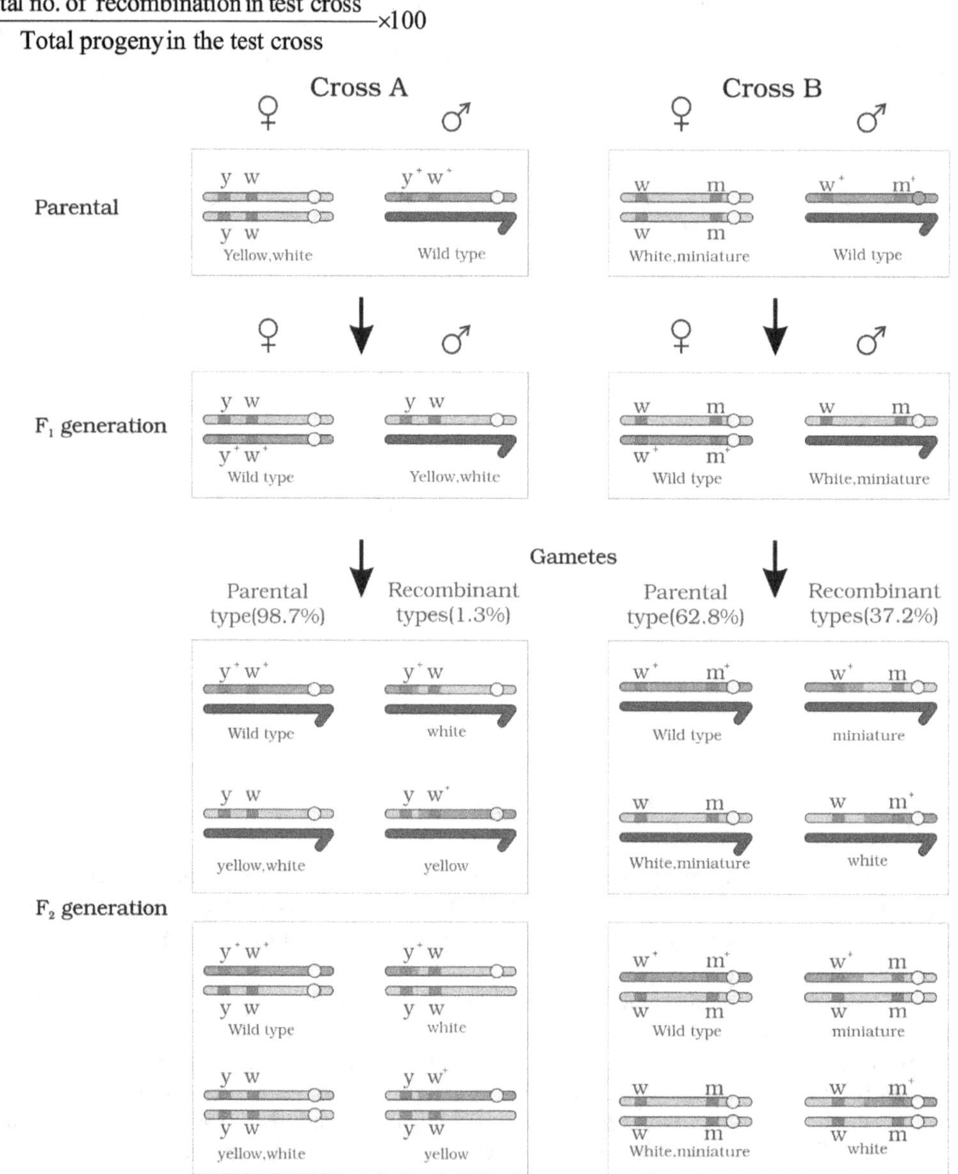

Fig. : Linkage – Results of two dihybrid crosses conducted by Morgan, showing crossing between gene y and w. Here dominant wild type alleles are represented with (+) sign in superscript

Practice Exercise-1

Multiple Choice Questions

1. Mendel selected pea as material for his experiments because
   (a) it is an annual plant with comparatively short life cycle.
   (b) the flowers are self-pollinated.
   (c) the number of seeds produced is quite large.
   (d) all of the above.

2. In fruit fly the maleness is determined by
   (a) Chromosomal ploidy
   (b) Ratio of X chromosome to Y chromosome
   (c) Presence of Y chromosome
   (d) None of these

3. Human blood grouping is ABO instead of ABC because O in it refers to
   (a) no antigen A or B on RBCs.
   (b) other antigens besides A and B.
   (c) overdominance of its gene over A and B.
   (d) one antibody only either anti-A or anti-B.

4. The monohybrid genotypic ratio 1 : 2 : 1 in F_2 generation indicates
   (a) segregation
   (b) independent assortment
   (c) dominance
   (d) incomplete dominance

5. Which of the following crosses will give tall and dwarf pea plants in same proportions?
   (a) TT × tt
   (b) Tt × tt
   (c) TT × Tt
   (d) tt × tt

6. What proportion of the offsprings obtaied from cross AABBCC × AaBbCc will be completely heterozygous for all genes segregated indpendently?
   (a) 1/8   (b) 1/4   (c) 1/2   (d) 1/16

7. The **Mirabilis jalapa** when two F1 pink flowered plants were crossed with each other, the F2 generation produced 40 red, 80 pink and 40 white flowering plants. This is a case of
   (a) duplicate genes   (b) lethal genes
   (c) incomplete dominance   (d) epistasis

Match the following

8. Match the terms in Column-I with their description in Column-II and choose the correct option

	Column-I		Column-II
A.	Dominance	I.	Many genes govern a single character
B.	Codominance	II.	In a heterozygous organism, only one allele expresses itself
C.	Pleiotropy	III.	In a heterozygous organism, both alleles express themselves fully
D.	Polygenic	IV.	A single gene inheritance influences many characters

(a) A – II, B – I, C – IV, D – III
(b) A – II, B – III, C – IV, D – I
(c) A – IV, B – I, C – II, D – III
(d) A – IV, B – III, C – I, D – II

Assertion & Reason Questions

DIRECTIONS (Qs. 9-12) : *Each of these questions contains an assertion followed by reason. Read them carefully and answer the question on the basis of following options. You have to select the one that best describes the two statements.*

(a) If both Assertion and Reason are correct and the Reason is a correct explanation of the Assertion.
(b) If both Assertion and Reason are correct but Reason is not a correct explanation of the Assertion.
(c) If the Assertion is correct but Reason is incorrect.
(d) If both Assertion and Reason are incorrect.

9. **Assertion:** Mendel was born on 22nd july, 1822 to a farmers family in the Austria.
   Reason: Mendel died due to heart attack in the year 1901.

10. **Assertion:** The Mendalian factors are also called unit factor which are known as genes.
    Reason: Chemically, a gene is a linear segment of DNA called cistron.

11. **Assertion:** The flower colour of sweet pea shows the inheritance of complementary genes.
    Reason: The ratio obtained for complementary genes is 9:1.

12. **Assertion:** Pleiotropy should not be confused with polygenic traits.
    Reason: In polygenic traits, multiple genes result in a single phenotype.

Very Short Answer Questions

13. What is monohybrid cross ?
14. What is dihybrid cross ?
15. What is significance of Mendelian study ?
16. Define punnett square.
17. What is variation ?
18. What is test cross ?
19. What is utility of test cross ?
20. Who formed linkage map first ?
21. Who found chromosomal theory of inheritance?

Short Answer Questions

22. Name 4 characters chosen for Mendelian study.
23. What is law of purity of gametes ?
24. Differentiate between test cross and backcross.
25. What is incomplete dominance ?
26. What is codominance ?
27. What is multiple allelism ? Explain.
28. What is dihybrid cross ?
29. Write 3 postulates of chromosomal theory of inheritance?
30. Significance of chromosomal theory of inheritance.
31. Differentiate between linkage and recombination.

Topic 2 — Sex Determination, Genetic Disorders and Pedigree Analysis 

Henking discovered X body in spermatogenesis of few insect and it was given name of X chromosome. Due to involvment of X and Y chromosomes in determination of sex, they were called **sex chromosome.** Rest of the chromosomes which determine other metabolic character of the body are called **autosomes.**

Chromosomal determination of sex varies in different organisms. MC Clung (1901) reported similar condition of chromosomes in grasshopper and discovered that X-body of Henking was a chromosome and hence named X-chromosome. Wilson and Stevens separately (1905) reported in Drosophila (fruitfly) that one-set (pair) of chromosomes had similar chromosomes in females, but different chromosomes in males. The odd chromosomes in male was named as Y-chromosome. They also reported that X-chromosome was paired in females.

Methods of Sex Determination

1. **On the basis of Sex-Chromosomes -**

   (i) **XY♂ and XX♀ system** – eg. Most of the fishes, Amphibians, Reptiles and Mammals.

   In such cases the Y-chromosome is male determining, and the absence of Y-chromosome determines the femaleness. Moreover, the male sex is **heterogametic** (producing two types of sperms – X-containing and Y-containing) while female is **homogametic** (producing one type of eggs/ova – all X-containing). The X-containing sperm and Y-containing sperms can also be called as Gynosperm and Androsperm respectively. In human also, it is the genetic make -up of sperms that determines the sex of the child and it is very unfortunate that women are blamed for producing female children (daughters) and even ill-treated for this false notion.

   (ii) **XO ♂ and XX ♀ system** – eg. Bugs, Grasshoppers and Locusts.

   In such sex mechanism also, the male is heterogametic sex, producing two types of sperms (i.e., with or without X-chromosome) and female is homogametic sex, producing only one type of eggs (all X-containing).

   (iii) **Sex mechanism in *Drosophila* –**

   The diploid complement in *Drosophila* is 8 (6 + 2), with 3-pairs of autosomes and 1-pair of sex chromosomes. The sex mechanism in this case is XY♂ and XX♀, but the maleness is not decided by the presence of Y-Chromosome, as it is genetically inactive or inert.

   According to **'Genic balance theory'** of C.B. Bridges, the sex in *Drosophila* is determined by the ratio of the number of X-chromosomes to the number of ploidy/autosomal sets, in the individual. The ploidy number in haploid, diploid and triploid will be respectively 1, 2 and 3.

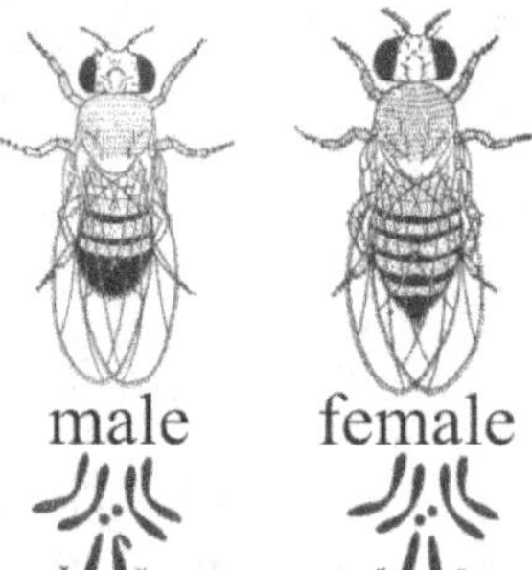

Fig. : *Drosophila* (fruit fly) – Male and female with their Karyotype

   (iv) **ZZ♂ and ZW ♀ system** – eg. Birds, (Chick or Fowl) few Butterflies and Moths.

   In such cases male is homogametic producing similar type of sperms and female is heterogametic producing two different types of Ova/eggs. As the Sex mechanism in this case is just opposite to that of reptiles or mammals; to avoid confusion, the X-chromosome is represented by Z and Y is represented by W-Chromosomes. The actual sex mechanism is XX-male and XY-female. Unlike mammals, the sex in birds is decided by the Ova/eggs of the female and not by the sperms of the male (Other butterflies and moths have ZZ♂ and ZO ♀ system)

2. **On the basis of Ploidy-** *eg.* Honey bees, wasps and ants.

   In above insects, the sex chromosomes are not differentiated and the sex is determined on the basis of ploidy of the individual. In honey bees the males and drones are haploid and develop from unfertilized eggs, of females (mother). They do not have father and cannot have sons; but have grandfather (mother's father) and grandsons (daughter's sons). The females are diploid and are derived from fertilized eggs. In males the chromosome number is 16 and in females it is 32. During sperm production there occurs equational division (not meiosis), as the males are already haploid.

Both queen and the workers are females, the latter being sterile. This differentiation develops due to the different type of food given to the developing embryos. If the embryos are fed on Royal jelly (salivary secretion of worker bees) throughout the developmental period, they become queens, and if fed on Bee bread (honey plus partly digested pollens) they develop into workers. The fertile members in the Bee colony are Drones (haploid males) and Queen (diploid female).

3. **On the Basis of Environmental Factors-** *eg. Bonellia* (an echiuroid worm), Crocodile, Turtle.

In certain cases, where, neither the sex chromosomes are differentiated nor there is difference in the ploidy of the individuals, the sex determining mechanism is different. In *Bonellia viridis,* the male (~ 3-4 mm) lives symbiotically inside the uterus of female individual (~ 100 mm). The fertilized eggs, when released from the body, can form male or female individual depending on the micro environment in which they develop. If a fertilized egg comes in contact of a substratum like rock or vegetation it becomes a female individual, and if the egg comes in contact of proboscis of a developing female individual, it becomes a male individual. In case of the eggs of Alligator or crocodile, if the surrounding temperature is 30°C or below, the hatched individuals are females and if the surrounding temperature is around 34°C, the males are produced. Thus, here temperature decides the sex of the individuals. The sex determination in turtle is also affected by surrounding temperature. (In turtles, the temprature below 28°C produces males and above 31°C females. In snails even the adults can change the sex. The sex determination can also be categorized on the basis of fertilization as:

(i)   **Progamic** i.e. sex determination before fertilization ex. males of Honeybee
(ii) **Syngamic** i.e sex determination during fertilization ex - Human
(iiii) **Epigamic** i.e., sex determination after fertilization ex - *Bonellia*

MUTATION

Phenomenon that results in alteration of DNA sequence and consequently results in change in genotype and phenotype of an organism is called **mutation**. **Mutagens** are various chemical and physical factors that induce mutations, e.g., UV radiations, carcinogenic chemicals like Nicotine, Nitric oxide (NO).

Mutation

Gene Mutation
(point mutation)

It involves change in single nucleotide. It is a process in which new alleles of a gene are produced.

Two types – *Induced mutation* (produced in response to specific external factors & chemicals) and *spontaneous mutation* (occur randomly, naturally or automatically due to internal reasons). **Muller (1927)** was the first to produced induced mutation in *Drosophila* by exposing them to X-rays.

Chromosomal Mutation

due to structural change

due to change in number

Change in number of sets of chromosomes – **Polyploidy**

Change in number of pair of chromosome – **Aneuploidy**

Deletion or deficiency
A chromosome fragment is lost

Duplication
Addition of a part of chromosomes.

Inversion
Part of chromosomes segment is inverted by 180°

Translocation
Exchange of part of chromosome between 2 non-homologous chromosome

Flow Chart : Types of Mutation

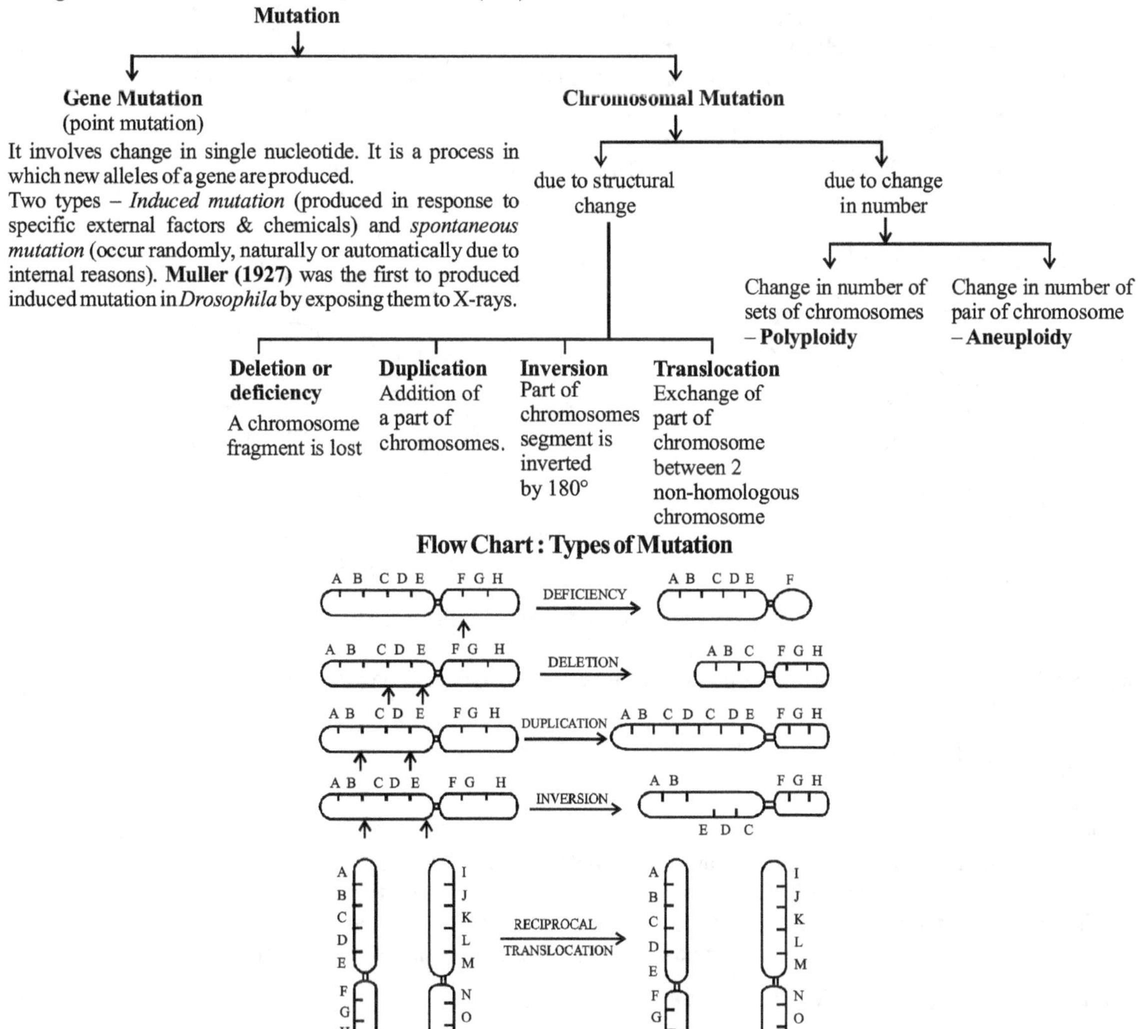

Fig : Types of chromosome aberrations

Mutagens

Mutagens are of 2 types :

(1) **Physical mutagens or radiations,** *e.g.*, X-rays, α-rays, γ-rays, UV-rays, etc.

Radiations are of 2 types :

(a) **Ionizing radiations,** *e.g.*, X-rays, α-rays, γ-rays. These have high penetrating power.

(b) **Non-ionizing radiations,** *e.g.,* UV-rays (first used by Altenburg, 1930). They have low penetrating power.

(2) **Chemical mutagens :** Use of chemicals for inducing mutations was first made by **C. Auerbach** during World war II. She used mustard gas (having delayed effect after 2, 3 generation), ethyl urethane, formaldehyde, phenol, etc. Other chemicals, which are being used as mutagens nowadays are maleic hydrazide, hydroxylamine, hydrazine, nitrous acid, methyl methane sulphonate (MMS) and ethyl methane sulphonate (EMS), etc. Different varieties of crop plants have been produced by mutation like Sharbati Sonora variety of wheat. It has been developed by γ-rays mutation on sonora-64 variety (Mexican dwarf wheat variety).

It was developed by **M. S. Swaminathan** and used in Green Revolution of India.

GENETIC DISORDER

A genetic disorder is a disease that is caused by an abnormality in an individual's DNA. Genetic disorder may be grouped into two categories – **Mendelian disorders** & **chromosomal disorders**.

Mendelian disorders

Mendelian disorders are chiefly determined by alteration or mutation in the single gene. It can be studied by pedigree analysis. Their pattern of inheritance down the family line can be traced. out They can be dominant or recessive–diluted either by autosomes or sex chromosomes.

Examples of Mendelian disorders are —

1. **Haemophilia :** Haemophilia is also known as bleeders diseases (John Otta, 1803)

(i) It is a popular example of sex linked inheritance in human beings.

(ii) A protein involved in clotting of blood is affected in an affected individual; if person gets a cut, will result in non stop bleeding.

(iii) It occurs due to deficiency of plasma thromboplastin or antihaemophilia globulin during which the exposed blood does not clot.

(iv) Females are heterozygous and carriers of haemophilia.

(v) Male are hemizygous for gene and affected since other chromosome is Y.

(vi) It is in family pedigree of Queen Victoria of England since she is a carrier of disease.

(vii) If female is carrier   If female normal and male affected

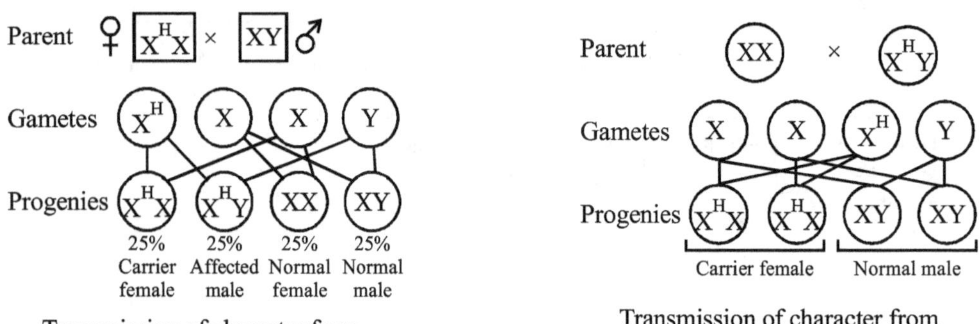

Fig. : Criss cross pattern of inheritance

(viii) The possibility of female being haemophilic is rare since for this genetic constitution of parents should be ♀  and

♂ 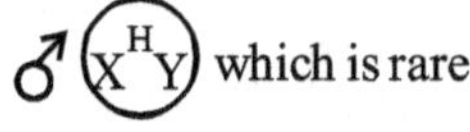 which is rare.

2. **Sickle cell anaemia**

(i) Sickle cell anaemia is an autosomal recessive trait.

(ii) It is transmitted when both the patients are carrier/heterozygous for gene.

(iii) It is a blood disease where the RBCs becomes sickle shaped as compared to normal one.

(iv) It is due to inheritance of defective allele coding for β-globin. It results in the transformation of Hb^A into Hb^{-S} in which glutamic acid is replaced by valine at 6th position in each of two β-chains of haemoglobin.

(v) 2 alleles $\underline{Hb}^A$, $\underline{Hb}^S$ → Sickle cell anaemia.

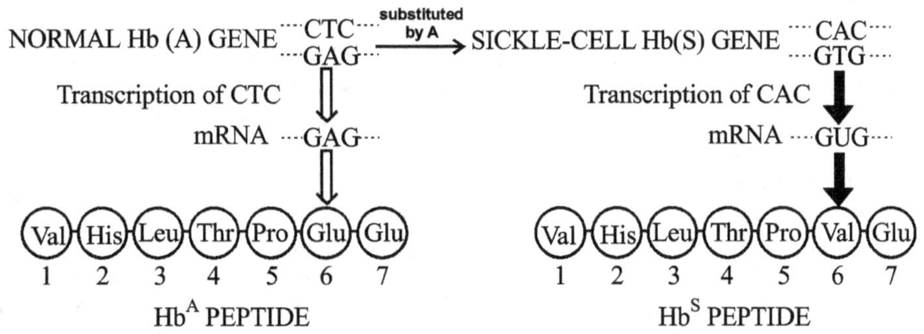

Fig. : β -chain peptide in Hb^A and Hb^S

(vi)   The sickle cell are rigid & exhibit a higher viscosity to flow causing them to lodge in capillaries.

(vii)   The major characteristics of this disease are anaemia & a tendency of RBC to change shape (from biconvex to sickle shaple) at low oxygen concentration.

(viii) It is an excellent example of single mutation.

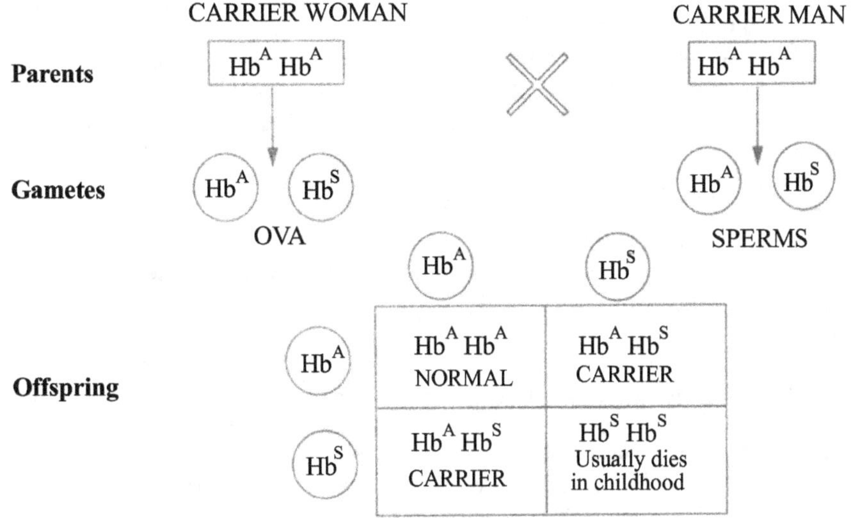

1 Normal : 2 Carrier

3 genotypes are –   Hb^{A}Hb^S → Carrier

Hb^{A}Hb^A → Normal

Hb^{S}Hb^S → Diseased

Fig. : A cross between two sickle cell carriers in human beings to show that the gene is lethal in the homozygous state.

3.   Phenylketonuria

(i)   Phenylketonuria is an inborn error of metabolism.

(ii)   It is an autosomal recessive trait.

(iii)   Affected individual lacks enzyme phenylalanine hydroxylase that converts amino acid phenylalanine to tyrosine.

(iv)   Phenylalanine accumulates and converts to phenylpyruvic acid and it accumulates in brain resulting in mental dementia.

(v)   Excreted out through urine due to poor absorption in kidney.

(vi)   It is characterized by severe mental retardation, hypopigmentation of skin & hair, eczema, etc.

Chromosomal Disorders

Genetic disorder or chromosomal disorder are caused due to absence or excess or abnormal arrangement of one or emore chromosome. All genetic disorders (called genomatic mutations) can be broadly classified into two categories:

I.   Chromosomal disorders   II.   Mendelian disorders

The chromosomal disorders (aberrations) can be structural or numerical. The numerical variations can be – 1. Euploidy variations 2. Aneuploidy variations

Euploidy variations - In such variations the chromosome number is a multiple of the haploid set, other than diploid. This condition arises due to failure of cytokinesis after telophase. The individual can be triploid (3n), tetraploid (4n) or pentaploid (5n) etc. Such individual are also known as *polyploid* individuals. Polyploidy is comon in plants but does not survive in human beings, however it does survives in insects like *Drosophila* and honey bees.

Aneuploidy variations - In such variations the diploid chromosome number changes by addition or subtraction of 1, 2 or a few chromosomes. The addition of one or more chromosomes to the normal Diploid complement is called **Hyperploidy**, whereas the loss of one or more chromosomes is called **Hypoploidy**. Aneuploidy cases can be of monosomy $(2n - 1) = 45$ chromosomes, trisomy $(2n + 1) = 47$ chromosome, tetrasomy $(2n + 2) = 48$ chromosomes or nullisomy $(2n - 2) = 44$ chromosomes. Aneuploidy develops due to non-disjunction (non-separation) of chromosomes, generally during meiosis- I.

1.   **Aneuploidy of Sex Chromosomes –**

    (i)   **Turner's syndrome- (XO) :** It is monosomy $(2n - 1)$ of sex chromosomes. The total chromosome number is 45 (44 A + X). The individuals are females because of the absence of Y-chromosome.   The prominent symptoms of this syndrome are 'webbed neck', 'broad shoulders', 'low-set pinna' and short statured reproductive organs and secondary sexual characters are under developed and the individual are sterile. The ovaries are also rudimentary. Such individuals do not menstruate or ovulate. The frequency of occurrence of such syndrome is 1/2500 of normal births.

    (ii)   **Klinefelter's syndrome- (XXY or XXXY) :** It develops mainly due to trisomy of sex chromosomes (2n + 1). The total chromosome number is generally 47 (44 A + XXY). The conditions like XXXY or XXXXY are also of Klinefelter's syndrome (nX + XY). The number of chromosome in all cases is > 46. More the number of X chromosomes, more is the mental retardation in such syndromes. The individuals are males because of the presence of Y chromosome. Male reproductive organs and secondary sexual characters are poorly developed. There can be, sometimes, breast development (Gynaecomastia) in such syndromes. Such individuals are tall statured and sterile. The frequency of occurrence of such syndrome is 1/700, of live births.

    (iii)   **Meta female (Super female) – (XXX or XXXX) :** This conditions develops mainly due to trisomy of sex chromosomes. The sex mechanism can be represented by nX + XX, where n is ≥ 1.

        The chromosome number is generally 47 (44 A + XXX) in case of mata female. Here also, Mental retardation increases with the increase in the number of X chromosomes, and such individual are females and can be sterile or fertile.

    (iv)   **Meta male (Super male) or Criminal syndrome (Jacob's syndrome) – (XYY) :** Such syndrome develops generally due to trisomy of sex chromosomes (44 A + XYY), and has more than one Y-chromosome. The chromosome number is generally 47. The sex mechanism can be represented as nY + XY.

        Such individuals are male with robust body and have criminal bent of mind. The crime may be non-violent and petty. They can be fertile or sterile.

2.   **Aneuploidy of Autosomes**

    (i)   **Down's syndrome or Mongollid Idiocy - (21-21-21)**

        It was first described by **Langdon Down (1866)** It is most common congenital disorder with a frequency of 1/700 live births. It is a case of trisomy of 21st chromosome (G-group - chromosome). The diploid number of chromosomes in this case is 47. (45A + XX/XY) It can be male or female, since the syndrome is autosomal. The frequency of occurrence of this syndrome is higher in the mother of older age because of the weakening of spindle fibres of 21st pair of chromosomes in the Oocytes, already formed during foetal life. The frequency does not change with the age of the father as spermatogenesis takes very short time (~65 days) in completion. The life span of such syndromes is generally short (around 18 years).

        Upper eye-lid is folded (Epicanthus condition) as in Mongolian race. Mental and psychomotor development retarded. IQ is less than 25 (Idiotic). Short statured, face rounded and flat, mouth open, tongue furrowed and saliva keeps dribbing. Simian crease is prominent in the middle of the palm. Many loops on finger tips

        The above case of Down's Syndrome is not expected to run in the families. However, in some cases where there is translocation of a major portion of 21st Chromosome to 14th chromosome, such Down's syndrome can run in the families. The individuals with such aberration have normal number of 46 chromosomes but exhibit Down's syndrome. Such Down's syndrome is known as **'Familial Down's syndrome'**.

    (ii)   **Edward's syndrome - (18-18-18)**

        It is due to trisomy of 18th chromosome (of E- group) The diploid number of chromosomes is 47. The individual is Male or female with kidney, heart and finger deformity Life span very short (around 6 months).

    (iii)   **Patau's syndrome - (13-13-13)**

        It is trisomy of 13th Chromosome (of D-group) The diploid number of chromosomes is 47. The individual is Male or female. Life span of the individuals is very short (around 3 months). Malformations include hare-lip, cleft palate, cardiovascular disorders, Smaller head (Microcephalus-condition), eye defect (blind), deaf, and brain disorder. Polydactyli (extra digits) is also conspicuous in such syndromes.

PEDIGREE ANALYSIS

Pedigree analysis is the diagrammatic illustration depicting the passage of a certain traits through successive generations in a family linkage. A record of the occurrence of a trait in several generation of a human family is called pedigree analysis.

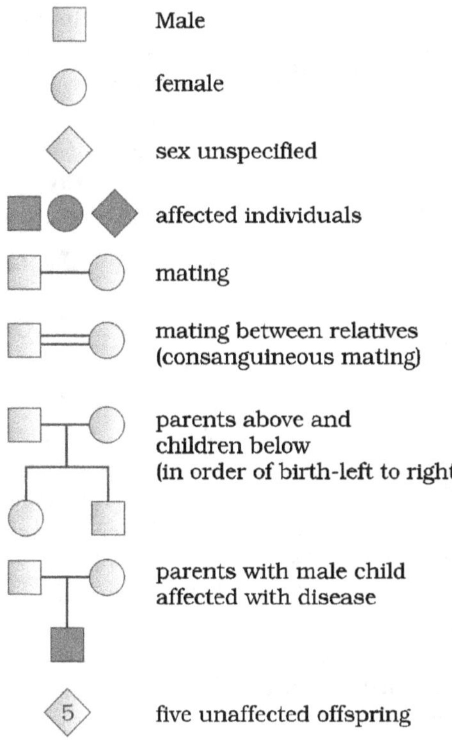

Fig. : Symbols used in the human pedigree

Pedigree analysis is useful in many ways like –

(1) It helps to fill up the possible genotypes by knowing the phenotypes only.
(2) Helps to study the pattern of inheritance of a dominant or recessive trait.
(3) It helps genetic counsellors to advice couples about the possibility of having genetic defective childrens.
(4) Helps to identify the possible origin of the defective gene in the family in a population.
(5) It provides a strong tool which is utilised to trace the inheritance of a specific trait.

Practice Exercise-2 

Multiple Choice Questions

1. Sex is determined in human beings
  (a) by ovum.
  (b) at time of fertilization.
  (c) 40 days after fertilization.
  (d) seventh to eight week when genitals differentiate in foetus.

2. The 'X' body of Henking was observed in
  (a) all sperms during spermatogenesis.
  (b) all eggs during oogenesis.
  (c) half of the sperms during spermatogenesis.
  (d) half of the eggs during oogenesis.

3. Which of the following is incorrect regarding ZW-ZZ type of sex determination?
  (a) It occcurs in birds and some reptiles
  (b) Females are homogametic and males are heterogametic
  (c) 1 : 1 sex ratio is produced in the offsprings
  (d) All of these

4. In sickle-cell anaemia, shape of RBCs under oxygen tension becomes
  (a) biconcave disc like
  (b) elongated and curved
  (c) circular
  (d) spherical

5. Inheritance of which of the following traits is shown in the given cross?
  (a) X-linked dominant trait
  (b) X-linked recessive trait
  (c) Autosomal recessive trait
  (d) Autosomal dominant trait

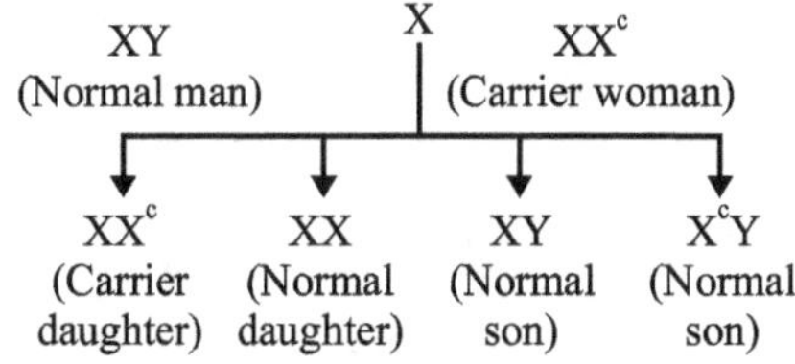

Match the following

6. Match column-I with column-II and find the correct answer.

	Column -I		Column -II
A.	Monoploidy	I.	$2n-1$
B.	Monosomy	II.	$2n+1$
C.	Nullisomy	III.	$2n+2$
D.	Trisomy	IV.	$2n-2$
E.	Tetrasomy	V.	n
		VI.	$3n$

(a) A – V, B – I, C – IV, D – II, E – III
(b) A – V, B – II, C – IV, D – I, E – III
(c) A – VI, B – V, C – III, D – IV, E – II
(d) A – II, B – I, C – III, D – VI, E – V

Assertion & Reason Questions

DIRECTIONS (Qs. 7-10) : *Each of these questions contains an assertion followed by reason. Read them carefully and answer the question on the basis of following options. You have to select the one that best describes the two statements.*

(a) If both Assertion and Reason are correct and the Reason is a correct explanation of the Assertion.
(b) If both Assertion and Reason are correct but Reason is not a correct explanation of the Assertion.
(c) If the Assertion is correct but Reason is incorrect.
(d) If both Assertion and Reason are incorrect.

7. **Assertion:** Deletion and insertion of base pairs of DNA, cause frame-shift mutation.
   Reason: Sickle cell anaemia is a classic example of framshift mutations.

8. **Assertion:** The affected infant with cry-du-chat syndrome has a round, moon-like face, and utter feable, plaintime cries similar to the mewing of cat.
   Reason: Deletion of a part of 21 chromosome produces leukemia, a cancerous malignancy arising in farming tissue.

9. **Assertion:** In haemophilia, a single protein that is a part of the cascade of proteins involved in the clotting of blood is affected.
   Reason: The family pedigree of Queen Victoria shows a numbers of haemophilic discendent as she was carries of the disease.

10. **Assertion:** Grasshopper is an example of XO type of sex determination in which the males have only one x-chromosome besides the autosomes, whereas females have a pair of x-chromosomes.
    Reason: In a number of insects and mammals including man XY type of sex determination is seen where both male and female have same number of chromosome.

Passage/Case Based Questions

DIRECTIONS (Qs. 11-13) : *Read the following passage and answer the questions that follows.*

Some human disorders are inherited and have been previaling in human society since long. Since the controlled crosses are not possible in case of human beings, the study of family history provides an alternative about the inheritance of such disorders.

11. Name the analysis used to study the inheritance of such a disorder.
12. Explain any two human disorders which could be traced by this analysis.
13. Explain the effects of any one of such disorder in the affected individuals.

Very Short Answer Questions

14. What is Barr body ?
15. Give an example of aneuploidy ?
16. What is phenylketonuria ?
17. What is the cause of sickle cell anaemia ?
18. What is haemophilia ?
19. What is pedigree analysis ?
20. What determines sex in humans ?

Short Answer Questions

21. Write 3 postulates of chromosomal theory of inheritance?
22. Significance of chromosomal theory of inheritance.
23. Differentiate between Klinefelter's syndrome and Turner's syndrome.
24. Discuss Down's syndrome.
25. Discuss about phenylketonuria.
26. Sex determination is based on particular chromosomes in both birds and humans. State two points of difference between their mechanisms of sex determination.
27. Why haemophilia is called Royal disease ?

Important Tips & Formulae

Law of Dominance:
- This law states that the characters are controlled by discrete unit called factors and factor occur in pairs. In a dissimilar pair of factors one member of the pair dominates (dominant pair) over the other (recessive).

Law of segregation:
- This law states that the two pairs of alleles get separated or segregated during gamete formation and are randomly distributed in gametes.

Law of independent Assortment:
- This law states that when two pairs of traits are combined in a hybrid, the segregation of one pair of characters is independent of the other pair of characters.

Mendelian Disorder:

Haemophilia
- This is a sex linked recessive disease, which shows its transmission from unaffected carrier female to some of the male progeny.
- In this disease, a single protein that is a part of the cascade of proteins involved in the clotting of blood is affected.
- Due to this, in an affected individual a simple cut will result in non-stop bleeding. The heterozygous female (carrier) for haemophilia may transmit the disease to sons.
- The possibility of a female becoming a haemophilic is extremely rare because mother of such a female has to be at least carrier and the father should be haemophilic (unviable in the later stage of life).
- The family pedigree of Queen Victoria shows a number of haemophilic descendants as she was a carrier of the disease.
- Haemophilia is caused by absence of blood clotting factor VIII and IX and because of this blood clotting is affected.

Sickle-cell anaemia:
- This is an autosome linked recessive trait that can be transmitted from parents to the offspring when both the partners are carrier for the gene (or heterozygous).
- The disease is controlled by a single pair of allele, HbA and HbS. Out of the three possible genotypes only homozygous individuals for HbS (HbSHbS) show the diseased phenotype.
- Heterozygous (HbAHbS) individuals appear apparently unaffected but they are carrier of the disease as there is 50 per cent probability of transmission of the mutant gene to the progeny, thus exhibiting sickle-cell trait.
- The defect is caused by the substitution of Glutamic acid (Glu) by Valine (Val) at the sixth position of the beta globin chain of the haemoglobin molecule.

- The substitution of amino acid in the globin protein results due to the single base substitution at the sixth codon of the beta globin gene from GAG to GUG.
- The mutant haemoglobin molecule undergoes polymerisation under low oxygen tension causing the change in the shape of the RBC from biconcave disc to elongated sickle like structure.

Phenylketonuria :
- This inborn error of metabolism is also inherited as the autosomal recessive trait. The affected individual lacks an enzyme that converts the amino acid phenylalanine into tyrosine.
- As a result of this phenylalanine is accumulated and converted into phenylpyruvic acid and other derivatives. Accumulation of these in brain results in mental retardation.
- These are also excreted through urine because of its poor absorption by kidney.

Chromosomal Disorders:

Down's Syndrome :
- The cause of this genetic disorder is the presence of an additional copy of the chromosome number 21 (trisomy of 21).
- This disorder was first described by Langdon Down (1866). The affected individual is short statured with small round head, furrowed tongue and partially open mouth.
- Palm is broad with characteristic palm crease. Physical, psychomotor and mental development is retarded.

Klinefelter's Syndrome:
- This genetic disorder is also caused due to the presence of an additional copy of X-chromosome resulting into a karyotype of 47, XXY.
- Such an individual has overall masculine development , however, the feminine development (development of breast, i.e., Gynaecomastia) is also expressed.
- Such individuals are sterile. Turner's Syndrome : Such a disorder is caused due to the absence of one of the X chromosomes, i.e., 45 with X0, Such females are sterile as ovaries are rudimentary besides other features including lack of other secondary sexual characters.
- The concept of Incomplete Dominance was given by Karl Corren.
- The Plasma membrane of the Red blood cells has sugar polymers that protrude from its surface and the kind of sugar is controlled by the gene.
- T.H Morgan worked with the tiny fruit flies Drosophila melanogaster because they could be grown on simple synthetic medium in the laboratory and they complete their life cycle in about two days and a single mating could produce a large number of progeny flies.

NCERT Questions

1. Mention the advantages of selecting pea plant for experiment by Mendel.

Sol. Mendel select garden pea (*Pisum Sativum*) as his experimental material because it had the following advantages.

(i) Short life cycle and easy to grow.

(ii) Easy emasculation.

(iii) Seven pairs of contrasting characters easily detectable.

(iv) True breeding/self pollination.

(v) It has perfect bisexual flowers containing both male and female parts. The wers are predeminently self pollinating.

(vi) Because of self fertilization, plants are homozygous. It is therefore, easty to get pure lines for several generations.

2. Differentiate between the following –

(a) Dominant and Recessive

(b) Homozygous and Heterozygous

(c) Monohybrid and Dihybrid.

Sol. (a) The difference between dominance and recessive are :

	Dominance	Recessive
(i)	When a factor (allele) expresses itself in the presence or absence of its recessive factor called dominance.	It can only express itself in the absence of its dominant factor or allele.
(ii)	It forms a complete functional enzyme that perfectly express it.	It forms a incomplete defective enzyme which fails to express itself when present with its dominant allele, i.e., in heterozygous condition.
(iii)	It does not require another similar allele to produce its effect on the Rhino type tall. eq. Tt is tall	It produces its phenotypic effect only in the presence of a similar allele e.g., tt is dwarf.

(b) Differences between homozygous and heterozygous individuals :

	Homozygous	Heterozygous
(i)	They have similar alleles (TT or tt) for a trait.	Have dissimilar alleles (Tt) for a trait.
(ii)	Contains either dominant (TT) or recessive (tt) alleles but not both types (Tt).	Contains both-dominant and recessive alleles (Tt).
(iii)	They are true-breeding for a specific trait and produce progeny having same genotypes and phenotypes on selfing.	They are not true-breeding and produce offspring having three genotypes and mostly two or some time three phenotypes.
(iv)	Only one type of gametes are formed either 'T' or 't' type only, not both.	Produce two types of gametes containing 'T' as well as 't'.

(c)

	Monhybrid	Dihybrid
(i)	It is a cross between two pure organisms in order to study the inheritance of single pain of alleles.	It is a cross between two pure organisms of a species in order to study the inheritance of two pairs of alleles belonging to two different characters.
(ii)	It produces a phenotypic monohybrid ratio of 3:1 in F_2 generation.	It produces a phenotypic dihybrid ratio of $9:3:3$ in F_2 generation.
(iii)	It produces genotypic ratio of $1:2:1$ in F_2 generation.	It produces genotypic ratio of $1:2:1:2:4:2:1:2:1$ in F_2. generation.

3. A diploid organism is heterozygous for 4 loci, how many types of gametes can be produced?

Sol. A diploid organism heterozygous for 4 loci will have the supported genetic constitution YyRr for two characters. The alleles Y–y and R–r will be present on different 4 loci. Each parent will produce four types of gametes – YR, Yr, yR, yr.

4. Explain the Law of Dominance using a monohybrid cross.

Sol. When two different factors (genes) or a pair of contrasting forms of a character are present in an organism, only one expresses itself in the F_1 generation and is termed as dominant while the other remains unexpressed and called recessive factors (gene).

A tall (TT) true breeding plant is crossed with a dwarf (tt) plant. The character of height is represented by 'T' for tall 't' for dwarf are the alternate form as character of height. The F_1 hybrid 'Tt' is Tall, showing that tall is dominant over dwarf while dwarf remains unexpressed in F_1 offspring due to phenomenon of dominance by tall factor or gene.

$$\text{Parents} \quad ♀ \, (TT) \times (tt) \, ♂$$
$$\text{Tall} \quad \text{Dwarf}$$
$$\text{Gametes} \quad (T) \quad (t)$$
$$F_1 \text{ generation} \quad (Tt)$$
$$\text{Tall}$$

In this Tt heterozygous has tall phenotype showing T is dominant over t allele.

5. Define and design a test-cross.

Sol. Crossing of F_1 individual having dominant phenotype with its homozygous recessive parent in called test cross. The test cross is used to determine whether the individuals exhibiting dominant character are homozygous or heterozygous.

$$F_1 \times \text{recessive parent}$$

$$F_1 \text{ generation} \quad (Tt) \quad \times \quad (tt)$$
$$\text{Tall} \quad \text{Dwarf recessive}$$
$$\text{Gametes} \quad (T)(t) \quad (t)(t)$$
$$\text{Offsprings} \quad (Tt)(Tt) \quad (tt)(tt)$$
$$\underline{\text{2 tall}} \quad \underline{\text{2 dwarf}}$$

Ratio – 1 : 1

Test cross helps in establishing hetero/homozygosity of dominant trait.

6. Using a Punnett Square, workout the distribution of phenotypic features in the first filial generation after a cross between a homozygous female and a heterozygous male for a single locus.

Sol.
Parents $♀(TT) \times (Tt)♂$

Gametes $(T)(T) \quad (T)(t)$

F_1 generation

♀ → / ♂ ↓	T	T
T	TT	TT
t	Tt	Tt

Phenotype : All tall

Genotype ratio : TT : Tt
$$2 : 2$$
or $$1 : 1$$

From the Punnett Square it is seen that there is 50% chances of the dominant trait (tall) or recessive trait (dwarf) in either female or male.

7. When a cross is made between tall plant with yellow seeds (TtYy) and tall plant with green seed (Ttyy), what proportions of phenotype in the offspring could be expected to be

(a) tall and green.

(b) dwarf and green.

Sol. A cross between tall plant with yellow seeds (TtYy) & tall plant with green seed (Ttyy) is given below.

Parents → Tall Yellow $\times$ Tall Green
$$\text{Tt Yy} \qquad \text{Tt yy}$$

Gametes → TY, Ty, tY, ty $\quad$ Ty ty

♂ / ♀	Ty	ty
TY	TT Yy (Tall, yellow)	Tt Yy (Tall, yellow)
Ty	Tt yy (Tall, green)	Tt yy (Tall, green)
tY	Tt Yy (Tall, yellow)	tt Yy (Dwarf, yellow)
ty	Tt yy (Tall, green)	tt yy (Dwarf, green)

Phenotype ratio :

(1) Tall and green = 3

(2) Dwarf and green = 1

8. **Two heterozygous parents are crossed. If the two loci are linked what would be the distribution of phenotypic features in F$_1$ generation for a dibybrid cross?**

Sol. Consider 2 characters Blue (B), long (L) seeds of a plant - both characters linked.

Crossing Parents :

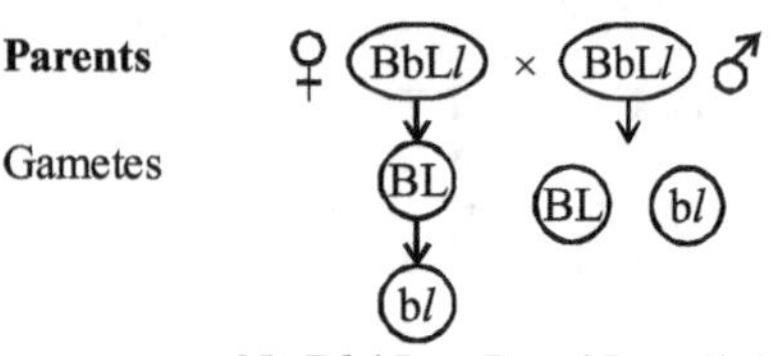

No B*l*, bL as B and L are **linked**

F$_1$ generation

♀♂	BL	b*l*
BL	BBLL	BbL*l*
b*l*	BbL*l*	bb*ll*

Phenotype : BBLL : BbL*l* : BbL*l* : bb*ll*

Blue long   White small

All parental combination, No recombinants.

9. **Briefly mention the contribution of T.H. Morgan in genetics.**

Sol. Thomas Hunt Morgan (1866-1945) is called father of experimental genetics. He was an American scientists, famous for his experimental research with the fruit fly (*Drosophila*) by which he established the chromosome theory of heredity. He discovered presence of gene over chromosomes, chromosome theory of linkage, chromosome mapping, crossing over, criss-cross inheritance & mutability of genes. Morgan's work played a key role in establishing the field of genetics. He received the nobel prize for physiology or Medicine in 1933.

10. **What is pedigree analysis? Suggest how such an analysis, can be useful.**

Sol. Study of the family history about inheritance of a particular trait in several generations is called pedigree analysis. Pedigree analysis helps –

(i) in analysis of transmission of character in family over generation.

(ii) in genetic counselling of disease like haemophilia.

(iii) to identify whether a particular genetic disease is due to recessive gene or a dominant gene.

(iv) to identify the possible origin of the defective gene in the family or in a population.

11. **How is sex determined in human beings?**

Sol. Chromosomal determination of sex in human beings is of XX-XY type. Human beings have 22 pairs of autosomes and one pair of sex chromosomes. The female possess two homomorphic (= isomorphic) sex chromosomes, named XX. The males contain two heteromorphic sex chromosomes, i.e., XY. All the ova formed by female are similar in their chromosome type (22 + X). Therefore, females are homogametic. The male gametes or sperms produced by human males are of two types, gymnosperurus (22 + X) and androsperms (22 + Y). Human males are therefore, heterogametic. Sex of the offspring in determined at the time of fertilization. Fertilization of the egg (22 + X) with a gymnosperm (22 + X) will produce a female child (44 + XX) while fertilization with an androsperm (22 + Y) give rise to male child (44 + XY). As the two types of sperms are produced in equal proportion, there are equal chances of getting a male or female child in a particular mating. As Y-chromosomes determines the male sex of the undividual, it is also called androsome.

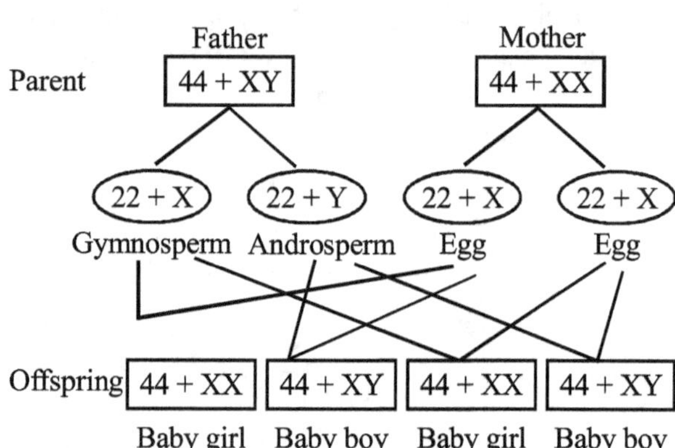

12. **A child has blood group O. If the father has blood group A and mother blood group B, work out the genotypes of the parents and the possible genotypes of the other offsprings.**

Sol. **Parents**

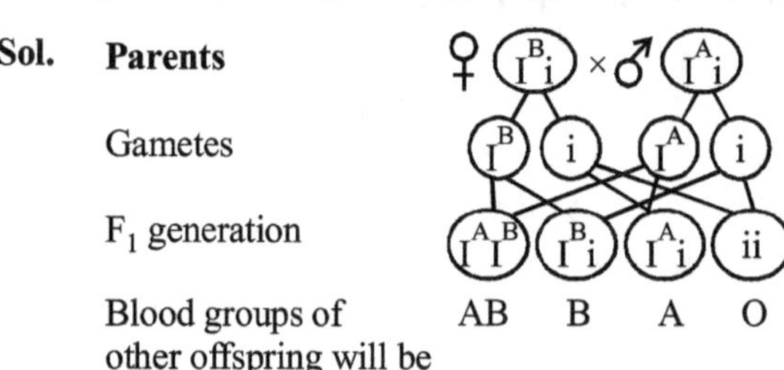

Blood groups of other offspring will be   AB   B   A   O

13. **Explain the following terms with example**

(a) Co-dominance   **(b) Incomplete dominance**

Sol. **(a) Codominance :** Codominance is the phenomenon of two contrasting alleles of the same gene lacking dominant recessive ratio and expressing themselves simultaneously when present together. E.g. ABO blood group system – Human blood group AB is formed when alleles of blood groups A and B are present together ($I^A I^B$). Such RBCs carry both antigen A & B showing that both the alleles are expressing their effect phenotypically & codominant.

(b) Incomplete dominance : Incomplete dominance may be defined as the partial expression of both alleles in a heterozygote so that the phenotype is intermediate between those of two homozyzotes. In this none of the allele is completely dominant, e.g., Pink colour flower in dog flower. In *Mirabilis jalapa* & Snapdragon or dog flowers, there are two types of flower colour in pure state- red & white. When the two types of plant are crossed, the hybrid or plants of F_1 generation have pink flowers. The pink colour apparently appears either due to mixing of red & white colours (incomplete dominance) or expression of a single gene for pigmented flower which produces only pink colour.

14. What is point mutation? Give one example.

Sol. Mutations arising due to change in single base pair of DNA is called point mutation. Eg., sickle cell anaemia, haemophilia.

When heritable alterations occur in a very small segment of DNA molecules i.e., a single nucleoside or nucleotide pair, then these type of mutations are called point mutations (also called as gene mutations). The point mutations may occur due to inversion, substitution (transition and transversion) and frameshift (insertion and detention) type of nucleotide change in the DNA or RNA.

Phenylketonuria is an inborn autosomal, recessive metabolic disorder in which the homozygous recessive individual lacks the enzyme phenylalanine hydroxylase needed to change phenylalanine (amino acid) to tyrosine (animo acid) in liver. It result in hyper phenylalaninemia which is characterised by accumulation and excretion of phenylalanine, phenyl pyruvic acid and related compounds. Lack of the enzyme is due to the abnormal autosomal recessive gene is due to substitution. Affected babies are normal at birth but within a few weeks there is rise (30-50 times) in plasma phenylalanine level which impair brain development. Other symptoms are mental retardation, decreased pigmentation of nair and skin disorder like eczema.

15. Who had proposed the chromosomal theory of the inheritance?

Sol. Chromosomal theory of inheritance was proposed by Sutton and Boveri independently in 1902. The two workers found a close similarity between the transmission of Mendelian hereditary factors (genes) and behaviour of chromosomes during gamete formation and fertilization. They proposed the chromosomes were the carriers of the Mendelian factors. It is the chromosome and not genes which segregate and assert independently during meiosis and recombinant the time of fertilization in the zygote. Chromosome theory of inheritance was expanded by Morghan, Sturtevant and Bridges.

16. Mention any two autosomal genetic disorders with their symptoms.

Sol. Sickle cell anaemia : It occur due to inheritance of a defective allele coding for β-globin. It results in the transformation of HbA into Hbs in which glutamic acid is replaced by valine at six[th] the position in each of two β-chains of haemoglobin. The substitution of amina acid in the globin protein results due to the single base substitution at the sixth codon of the beta globin gone from GAG to GUG. Sickle cell anaemia is a blood disease where the red blood cells be come sickle shaped as compared to normal one. The major characteristic of this disease are anaemia and a tendency of red blood cells to change shape at law oxygen concentration.

Phenylketonuria : It occurs due to absence of phenylalanine hydroxylase enzyme in liver which is essential for the conversion of phenylalanine to tyrosine. As a result of this phenylalanine is accumulated and converted into phenyl pyruvic acid and other derivatives. Mental retardation (due to accumulation of phenylalanine in brain), hypopigmentation of skin & hair, eczema etc, are the symptoms.

Past year Exercise

Very Short Answer Questions

1. Pea flowers produce assured seed sets. Give a reason.

2. Name one autosomal dominant and one autosomal recessive Mendelian disorder in humans.

3. Write the genotype of (i) an individual who is carrier of sickle-cell anaemia gene but apparently unaffected and (ii) an individual affected with the disease.

4. A human being suffering from Down's syndrome shows trisomy of 21st chromosome. Mention the cause of this chromosomal abnormality.

5. Name the event during cell division cycle that results in the gain or loss of chromosome.

6. Mention two contrasting flower related trait studied by Mendel in pea plant experiments.

7. A garden pea plant (A) produced inflated yellow pod and another plant (B) of the same species produced constricted green pods. Identify the dominant traits.

8. Write possible genotypes Mendel got when he crossed F_1-tall plant with a dwarf pea plant.

9. Mention the type of allele that expresses itself only in homozygous state in an organism.

10. A garden pea plant produced axial white flowers another of the same species produced terminal violet flowers. Identify the dominant traits.

11. In a dihybrid cross, when would the proportion of parental gene combinations be much higher than non-parental types, as experimentally shown by Morgan and his group.

12. Mention any two contrasting traits with respects to seeds in pea plant that were studied by Mendel.

13. What are 'true breeding lines' that are used to study inheritance pattern of traits in plants?

14. British geneticist R.C. Punnett developed a graphical representation of a genetic cross called "Punnett Square". Mention the possible result this representation predicts of the genetic cross carried.

Short Answer Questions

15. Why are F_2-phenotypic and genotypic ratios same in a cross between red flowered Snapdragon and white flowered Snapdragon plants? Explain with the help of cross.

16. (i) Why are grasshopper and *Drosophila* said to show male heterogamety? Explain.

(ii) Explain female heterogamety with the help of an example.

17. Explain the sex determination mechanism in humans. How is it different in birds?

18. How test cross helps in identifying the genotype of the organism. Explain.

19. In a dihybrid cross white eyed, yellow bodied female *Drosophila* crossed with red eyed, brown bodied male *Drosophila* produced in F_2- generation 1.3% recombinants and 98.7% progeny with parental type combinations. This observation of Morgan deviated from Mendelian F_2-phenotypic dihybrid ratio. Explain, giving reasons Morgan's observation.

20. Tallness of pea plant is dominant trait, while dwarfness is the alternate recessive trait. When a pure line tall is crossed with a pureline dwarf, what fraction of tall plants in F_2-generation shall be heterozygous? Give reasons.

21. (i) Explain the phenomenon of multiple allelism and codominance taking ABO blood group as an example.

(ii) What is the phenotype of the following.

(i) $I^A i$ (ii) ii

22. A pea plant with purple flowers was crossed with white flowers producing 50 plants with only purple flowers. On selfing, these plants produced 482 plants with purple flowers and 162 with white flowers. What genetic mechanism accounts for these results? Explain.

23. Name a disorder, give the karyotype and write the symptoms where a human male suffers as a result of an additional X-chromosome.

24. How are dominance, codominance and incomplete dominance patterns of inheritance different from each other?

25. During his studies on genes in *Drosophila* that were sex-linked, TH Morgan found F_2-population phenotypic ratio deviated from expected 9 : 3 : 3 : 1. Explain the conclusion he arrived at.

26. Given below is the representation of amino acid composition of the relevant translated portion of β-chain of haemoglobin, related to the shape of human red blood cells.

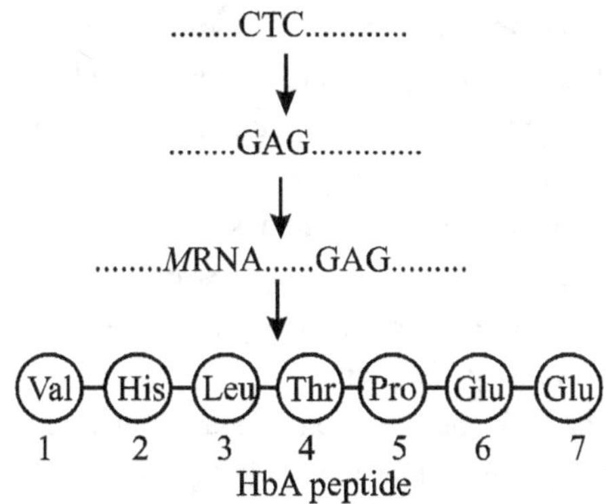

(i) Is this representation indicating a normal human or a sufferer from certain related genetic disease? Give reason in support of your answer.

(ii) What difference would be noticed in the phenotype of the normal and the sufferer related to this gene?

27. Name the phenomenon that leads to situations like 'XO' abnormality in humans. How do humans with 'XO' abnormality suffer? Explain.

28. Why are human females rarely haemophilic? Explain. How do haemophilic patients suffer?

29. A cross between a red flower bearing plant and a white flower bearing plant of *Antirrhinum* produced all plants having pink flowers. Work out a cross to explain how this is possible.

30. Why are human females rarely haemophilic? Explain. How do haemophilic patients suffer?

31. In a typical monohybrid cross the F_2-population ratio is written as 3 : 1 for phenotype but expressed as 1 : 2 : 1 for genotype. Explain with the help of an example.

32. Work out a cross to find the genotype of a tall pea plant. Name the type of cross.

33. In a cross between two tall pea plants, some of the offsprings produced were dwarf. Show with the help of Punett square how this is possible.

34. (a) Why is human ABO blood group gene considered a good example of multiple alleles?

(b) Work out a cross up to F_1 generation only, between a mother with blood group A (Homozygous) and the father with blood group B (Homozygous). Explain the pattern of inheritance exhibited.

35. Human population shows variations in blood groups. Explain the genetic basis for this variation seen in the population.

OR

(a) A normal man marries a normal but carrier colour blind woman. Work out a cross to show the possible genotypes and phenotypes of their progeny.

(b) Why is the 'woman' referred to as a carrier and not colour blind?

36. Using Punnett square show the results of F_2 generation of a dihybrid cross where the parents have contrasting traits with reference to pod colour and seed shape in *Pisum sativum*. Give the phenotype ratio.

37. With reference to flower colour two independent crosses were made, one between pure breed garden pea plants and another between pure breed *Antirrhinum* plants. Write the phenotypes of their F_1 progeny. Justify your answer giving reasons.

38. (a) State the cause and symptoms of Down's syndrome. Name and explain the event responsible for causing this syndrome.

(b) Haemophilia and Thalassemia are both examples of Mendelian disorder, but show difference in their inheritance pattern. Explain how.

39. Differentiate between the following:

(a) Polygenic inheritance and Pleiotropy.

(b) Dominance, Co-dominance and Incomplete dominance.

40. Differentiate between multiple allelism and pleiotropy with the help of an example each.

41.

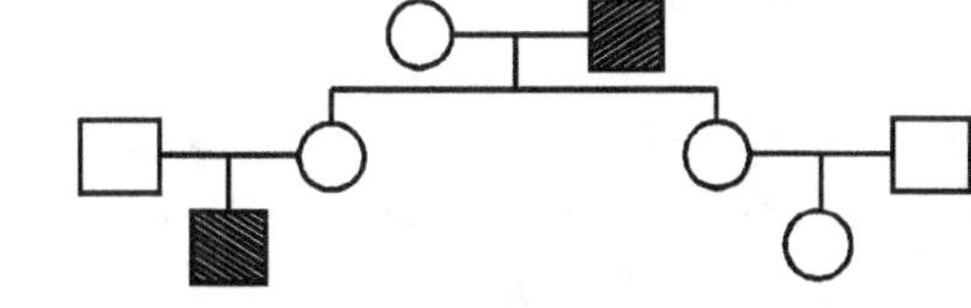

This is the pedigree of a family tracing the movement of the gene for haemophilia. Explain the pattern of inheritance of the disease in the family.

42. In pea plants, the colour of the flower is either violet or white whereas human skin colour shows many gradations. Explain giving reasons how it is possible.

43. In *Snapdragon*, A cross between true breeding red flower (RR) plants and true breeding white flower (rr) plants showed a progeny of plants with all pink flowers.

(a) The appearance of pink flowers is not known as blending. Why?

(b) What is the phenomenon known as ?

44. With the help of one example, explain the phenomena of co-dominance and multiple allelism in human population.

45. Write the scientific name of the fruit-fly. Why did Morgan prefer to work with fruit-flies for his experiments? State any three reasons.

46. Linkage or crossing-over of genes are alternatives of each other. Justify with the help of an example.

47. Why is pedigree analysis done in the study of human genetics? State the conclusions that can be drawn from it.

48. Identify 'a', 'b', 'c', 'd', 'e' and 'f' in the table given below:

No.	Syndrome	Cause	Characteristics of affected individual	Sex Male/ Female/Bot
1	Down's	Trisomy of 21	'a' (i) (ii)	b'
2	'c'	XXY	Overall masculine development	d'
3	Turner's	45 with OX	'e' (i) (ii)	f

49. A cross was carried out between two pea plants showing the contrasting traits of height of the plants. The result of the cross showed 50% parental characters.
    (i) Work out the cross with the help of a Punnett square.
    (ii) Name the type of the cross carried out.

50. How does the gene 'I' control ABO blood groups in humans? Write the effect the gene has on the structure of red blood cells.

OR

Write the types of sex-determination mechanisms the following crosses show. Give an example of each type.
(i) Female XX with Male XO
(ii) Female ZW with Male ZZ

51. A colour-blind child is born to a normal couple. Work out a cross to show how it is possible. Mention the sex of this child.

OR

Mendel published his work on inheritance of characters in 1865, but it remained unrecognised till 1900. Give three reasons for the delay in accepting his work.

52. Women are often blamed for producing female children. Consequently, they are ill-treated and ostracised. How will you address this issue scientifically if you were to conduct an awareness programme to highlight the values involved?

53. A cross between a normal couple resulted in a son who was haemophilic and a normal daughter. In course of time, when the daughter was married to a normal man, to their surprise, the grandson was also haemophilic.

(a) Represent this cross in the form of a pedigree chart. Give the genotypes of the daughter and her husband.

(b) Write the conclusion you draw of the inheritance pattern of this disease.

54. A male honeybee has 16 chromosomes whereas its female has 32 chromosomes. Give one reason.

55. What is a test cross? How can it decipher the heterozygosity of a plant?

56. State of difference between a gene and an allele.

57. State the explain the "Law of independent assortment" in a typical Mendelian dihybrid cross.

58. Compare in any three ways the chromosomal theory of inheritance as proposed by Sutton and Bovery with that of experimental results on pea plant presented by Mendel.

59. Two children, A and B aged 4 and 5 years respectively visited a hospital with a similar genetic disorder. The girl A was provided enzyme-replacement therapy and was advised to revisit periodically for further treatment. The girl, B was, however, given a therapy that did not require revisit for further treatment.
    (a) Name the ailments the two girls were suffering from?
    (b) Why did the treatment provided to girl A required repeated visits?
    (c) How was the girl B cured permanently?

60. Generally it is observed that human males suffer from hemophilia more than that of human females who rarely suffer from it. Explain giving reason.

61. The cytological observations made in a number of insects led to the development of the concept of genetic/ chromosomal basis of sex-determination mechanism. Honey bee is an interesting example to study the mechanism of sex-determination. Study the schematic cross between the male and the female honey bees given below and answer the questions that follow:

(a) Identify the cell divisions 'A" and 'B' that lead to gamete formation in female and male honey bees respectively.

(b) Name the process 'C' that leads to the development of male honey bee (drone).

NCERT Exemplar

Multiple Choice Questions

1. Conditions of a karyotype 2n ±1 and 2n ± 2 are called
   (a) aneuploidy (b) polyploidy
   (c) Allopolyploidy (d) monosomy

2. Distance between the genes and percentage of recombination shows
   (a) a direct relationship
   (b) an inverse relationship
   (c) a parallel relationship
   (d) no relationship

3. In sickle-cell anaemia glutamic acid is replaced by valine. Which one of the following triplet codes for valine ?
   (a) GGG (b) AAG
   (c) GAA (d) GUG

4. Person having genotype $I^A I^B$ would show the blood group as AB. This is because of
   (a) Pleiotropy
   (b) Codominance
   (c) segregation
   (d) incomplete dominance

5. ZZ/ZW type of sex determination is seen in
   (a) Platypus (b) Snails
   (c) Cockroach (d) Peacock

6. Two genes 'A' and 'B' are linked. In a dihybrid cross involving these two genes, the F_1- heterozygote is crossed with homozygous recessive parental type (aa bb). what would be the ratio of offspring in the next generation?
   (a) 1 : 1 : 1 : 1 (b) 9 : 3 : 3 : 1
   (c) 3 : 1 (d) 1 : 1

Assertion & Reason Questions

DIRECTIONS (Qs. 7-8) : *Each of these questions contains an assertion followed by reason. Read them carefully and answer the question on the basis of following options. You have to select the one that best describes the two statements.*

(a) If both Assertion and Reason are correct and the Reason is a correct explanation of the Assertion.
(b) If both Assertion and Reason are correct but Reason is not a correct explanation of the Assertion.
(c) If the Assertion is correct but Reason is incorrect.
(d) If both Assertion and Reason are incorrect.

7. **Assertion:** The genes located on the x-chromosome are called sex-linked genes as x-linked genes and genes present on y-chromosome are described as holandric gene.
   Reason: The number of linkage groups corresponds to the diploid number of chromosomes.

8. **Assertion:** The transfer of genes from one chromosome to another during synapsis is termed as crossing over.
   Reason: Crossing over takes place at 4 strands stage, where each strand represent a chromatid.

Very Short Answer Question

9. A progeny of F_1, is crossed with the homozygous recessive parent. What is this cross called? Work out how is it useful?

Short Answer Question

10. In a mendelian monohybrid cross the F_2 generation shows identical genotypic and phenotypic ratios. What does it tell us about the nature of alleles involved? Justify your answer.

Objective Practice Exercise

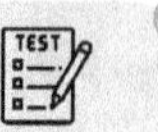

1. Which one of the following traits of garden pea studied by Mendel was a recessive feature?
   (a) Round seed shape
   (b) Axial flower position
   (c) Green seed colour
   (d) Green pod colour

2. The genes controlling the seven pea characters studied by Mendel are now known to be located on _______ different chromosomes?
   (a) Four   (b) Seven
   (c) Six   (d) Five

3. Two crosses between the same pair of genotypes or phenotypes in which the source of the gametes are reversed in one cross is known as
   (a) reverse cross
   (b) test cross
   (c) reciprocal cross
   (d) dihybrid cross

4. In a certain plant, red fruit (R) is dominant over yellow fruit (r) and tallness (T) is dominant over shortness (t). If a plant with RRTt genotype is crossed with a plant rrtt genotype, what will be the percentage of tall plants with red fruits in the progeny?
   (a) 50%   (b) 100%
   (c) 75%   (d) 25%

5. Independent assortment of genes does not take place when
   (a) genes are located on homologous chromosomes
   (b) genes are linked and located on same chromosomes
   (c) genes are located on non homologous chromosomes
   (d) All the above

6. A gene is said to be dominant if
   (a) it expresses its effect only in homozygous state
   (b) it expresses its effect only in heterozygous condition
   (c) it expresses its effect both in homozygous and heterozygous condition
   (d) it never expresses its effect in any conditions

7. In order to find out the different types of gametes produced by a pea plant having the genotype AaBb, it should be crossed to a plant with the genotype
   (a) AABB   (b) AaBb
   (c) aabb   (d) aaBB

8. If Mendel had studied the 7 traits using a plant with 12 chromosomes instead of 14, in what way would his interpretation have been different?
   (a) He would have discovered blending or incomplete dominance
   (b) He would not have discovered the law of independent assortment
   (c) He would have discovered sex linkage
   (d) He could have mapped the chromosome

9. Suppose that in sheep, a dominant allele (B) produces black hair and a recessive allele (b) produces white hair. If you saw a black sheep, you would be able to identify
   (a) its phenotype for hair colour.
   (b) its genotype for hair colour.
   (c) the genotypes for only one of its parents.
   (d) the genotypes for both of its parents.

10. True-breeding plants
   (a) produce the same offspring when crossed for many generations.
   (b) result from a monohybrid cross.
   (c) result from a dihybrid cross.
   (d) result from crossing over during prophase I of meiosis.

11. What is the probability that a cross between a true-breeding pea plant with smooth seeds and a true-breeding pea plant with wrinkled seeds will produce F_1 progeny with smooth seeds?
   (a) 1/2   (b) 1/4   (c) 0   (d) 1

12. Two organisms that are true-breeding for a certain genetic characteristic are mated and their offspring analysed. Which of the following statements about this situation is true?
   (a) Both parents are homozygotes.
   (b) The offspring are either all homozygotes or all heterozygotes.
   (c) The offspring represent the F_1 generation and the gametes produced by the offspring will carry only one allele for this gene.
   (d) All of the above

13. A pea plant that is heterozygous for the flower gene makes gametes. What is the probability that one of its gametes contains the recessive white allele for flower colour?
   (a) 0%   (b) 25%   (c) 50%   (d) 75%

14. Consider a gene that has two alleles and shows complete dominance. When two heterozygotes for this gene breed, they have a 25% chance of producing a homozygous recessive offspring. The next time they breed, what are the chances that they will once again have a homozygous recessive progeny?

(a) 0% (b) 25%

(c) 75% (d) 100%

15. There are three genes a, b, c. Percentage of crossing over between a and b is 20%, b and c is 28% an a and c is 8%. What is the sequence of genes on chromosome?

(a) b, a, c (b) a, b, c

(c) a, c, b (d) None of these

16. The linkage map of X-chromosome of fruit fly has 66 units, with yellow body gene (y) at one end and bobbed hair (b) gene at the other end. The recombination frequency between these two genes (y and b) should be

(a) 100% (b) 66%

(c) > 50% (d) ≤ 50%

17. In man, the A, B, AB, O blood groupings are controlled by a system of multiple alleles. A man of blood group A marries a woman of blood group B and they have one child. Which one of the following statements about the child's blood is correct?

(a) It could only be group A.

(b) It could only be group A or group B.

(c) It could only be group AB.

(d) It could be any of the group A, B, AB and O.

18. Originally, genetic inheritance was thought to be a function of the blending of traits from the two parents. Which exception to Mendel's rules is an example of blending ?

(a) Polygenic inheritance

(b) Incomplete dominance

(c) Codominance

(d) Leiotropism

19. A red-flowered plant crossed with a white-flowered plant of the same species, produced F_1 plants which all had pink flowers.

Self-pollination of the F_1 plants produced and F_2 generation in which 39 plants had red flowers, 83 had pink flowers and 40 had white flowers. What does this experiment demonstrate?

(a) Co-dominance

(b) Continuous variation

(c) A dihybrid cross

(d) Linkage

20. A girl has blood group A and her brother has blood group B. Which combination of genotypes cannot belong to their parents?

	Mother	Father
(a)	$I^A I^A$	$I^B I^O$
(b)	$I^A I^B$	$I^A I^B$
(c)	$I^O I^O$	$I^A I^B$
(d)	$I^B I^O$	$I^A I^O$

21. Which parental phenotypes would produce offspring with blood group phenotypes in the expected ratio of 1 type A : 1 type B?

	Blood group of mother	Blood group of father
(a)	A	B
(b)	AB	AB
(c)	AB	B
(d)	AB	O

22. Two parents, both of blood group A, have a daughter of blood group O. What is the probability that their next child will be a boy who has blood group O?

(a) 0.125 (b) 0.375

(c) 0.50 (d) 0.75

23. A lawyer tells a male client that blood type cannot be used to his advantage in a paternity suit against the client because the child blood, in fact, be the client's, according to blood type. Which of the following is the only possible combination supporting this hypothetical circumstance?

(a) A : B : O

(b) A : O : B

(c) AB : A : O

(d) B : O : A

24. Among white human beings, when individuals with straight hair mate with those with curly hair, wavy-haired children are produced. If two individuals with wavy hair mate, what phenotypes and ratios would you predict among their offspring?

(a) 3 curly : 1 wavy

(b) 1 curly : 1 wavy : 1 straight

(c) 1 straight : 1 curly : 2 wavy

(d) 3 wavy : 1 straight

25. Incomplete dominance occurs when

(a) chromosomes are deleted.

(b) heterozygotes synthesized a reduced amount of an enzyme, producing an intermediate phenotype.

(c) the genes fail to segregate.

(d) the law of independent assortment is upheld.

26. Multiple alleles are present
    (a) at different loci in the same chromosome.
    (b) in different chromosomes.
    (c) at the same locus in one type of chromosomes.
    (d) None of the above.

27. An example of the quantitative trait in man is
    (a) hair colour
    (b) colour of eye
    (c) skin colour
    (d) shape of nose

28. A modified dihybrid mendelian ratio of $9 : 3 : 4$ indicates
    (a) supplementary genes
    (b) complementary genes
    (c) lethal genes
    (d) epistatic genes

29. A woman with normal vision, but whose father was colour blind, marries a colour blind man. Suppose that the fourth child of this couple was a boy. This boy
    (a) may be colour blind or may be of normal vision
    (b) must be colour blind
    (c) must have normal colour vision
    (d) will be partially colour blind since he is heterozygous for the colour blind mutant allele

30. Which of the following is not a hereditary disease?
    (a) Cystic fibrosis
    (b) Thalassemia
    (c) Haemophilia
    (d) Cretinism

31. One of the parents of a cross has a mutation in its mitochondria. In that cross, that parent is taken as a male. During segregation of F_2 progenies that mutation is found in
    (a) one-third of the progenies
    (b) none of the progenies
    (c) all the progenies
    (d) fifty percent of the progenies

32. One child is haemophilic (sex-linked trait), while its fraternal twin brother is normal. Which one of the following informations is most appropriate?
    (a) The mother must have been heterozygous
    (b) The child is a monozygotic twin
    (c) The other child is a female and the father is haemophilic
    (d) The haemophilic child is a male

33. A diseased man marries a normal woman. They have three daughters and five sons. All the daughters were diseased and sons were normal. The gene of this disease is
    (a) sex-linked dominant

(b) sex-linked recessive
(c) sex-linked character
(d) autosomal dominant

34. *Drosophila* flies with XXY genotype are females but in case of humans, such individuals are abnormal males (Klinefelter's syndrome). This indicates that
    (a) The Y chromosome has no role in sex determination
    (b) In *Drosophila*, the Y chromosome is essential for sex determination
    (c) The Y chromosome is male determining in humans
    (d) The Y chromosome is female determining in *Drosophila*

35. Down's syndrome is caused by an extra copy of chromosome number 21. What percentage of offspring produced by an affected mother and a normal father would be affected by this disorder?
    (a) 25%
    (b) 100%
    (c) 75%
    (d) 50%

36. In *Drosophila*, the sex is determined by
    (a) whether the egg is fertilized or develops parthenogenetically
    (b) the ratio of number of X-chromosomes to the sets of autosomes
    (c) X and Y chromosomes
    (d) the ratio of pairs of X-chromosomes to the pairs of autosomes

37. Genes for cytoplasmic male sterility in plants are generally located in
    (a) cytosol
    (b) chloroplast genome
    (c) mitochondrial genome
    (d) nuclear genome

38. In the human ABO blood group system, there are six possible genotypes but only four phenotypes. An explanation of this is that the ABO blood groups are controlled by
    (a) one gene locus with three incompletely dominant (co-dominant) alleles.
    (b) one gene locus with two incompletely dominant (co-dominant) alleles and two recessive alleles.
    (c) one gene locus with two incompletely dominant (co-dominant) alleles are one recessive allele.
    (d) two unlinked gene loci each with two alleles, one dominant and one recessive.

39. What is the pattern of inheritance for a sex-linked allele?

(a) Every affected person has an affected parent.

(b) Unaffected parents can produce children who are affected.

(c) Unaffected mothers have affected sons and daughters who are carriers.

(d) None of the above

40. Sex determination in grasshoppers, humans, and *Drosophila* is similar because

(a) females are hemizygous.

(b) males have one X chromosome and females have two X chromosomes.

(c) all males always have one Y chromosome in all three species.

(d) the ratio of autosomes to sex chromosomes is the same in all three organisms.

41. Across between two tall plants resulted in offspring having few dwarf plants. What would be the genotypes of both the parents?

(a) TT and Tt   (b) Tt and Tt

(c) TT and TT   (d) Tt and tt

42. In a dihybrid cross, If you get 9 : 3 : 3: 1 ratio it denotes that

(a) the alleles of two genes are interacting with each other

(b) it is a multigenic inheritance

(c) It is a case of multiple allelism

(d) The alleles of two genes are segregating independently

43. Which of the following will not result in variations among siblings?

(a) Independent assortment of genes

(b) Crossing over

(c) Linkage

(d) Mutation

44. Mendel's law of independent assortment holds good for genes situated on the

(a) non-homologous chromosomes

(b) homologous chromosomes

(c) extra nuclear genetic element

(d) Same chromosome

45. Occasionally, a single gene may express more than one effect. The phenomenon is called

(a) multiple allelism   (b) mosaicism

(c) pleiotropy   (d) polygeny

46. In a certain taxon of insects some have 17 chromosomes and the others have 18 chromosomes. The 17 and 18 chromosome-bearing organisms are

(a) males and females respectively

(b) females and males, respectively

(c) all males

(d) all females

47. The inheritance pattern of a gene over generations among humans is studied by the pedigree analysis. Character studied in the pedigree analysis is equivalent to

(a) quantitative trait

(b) Mendelian trait

(c) Polygenic trait

(d) maternal trait

48. In the F_2-generation of a Mendelian dihybrid cross the number of phenotypes and genotypes are

(a) phenotypes -4, genotypes-16

(b) phenotypes -9, genotypes -4

(c) Phenotypes-4, genotypes-8

(d) Phenotypes-4, genotypes-9

49. A dwarf pea plant was treated with GA. The plant became tall. The treated plant was then crossed with a homozygous tall pea. The results in F2 are expected to be

(a) all tall

(b) tall and dwarf in 3 : 1 ratio

(c) 50% tall

(d) all dwarf

50. Round seed trait (R) is dominant over wrinkled (r) seed trait in Pea. Heterozygous round seeded plant (Rr) is crossed with wrinkled seeded plant (rr). What is the possibly progeny?

(a) 302 round : 102 wrinkled

(b) 210 round : 95 wrinkled

(c) 105 round : 99 wrinkled

(d) 103 round : 315 wrinkled

Match the following

51. Match column-I with column-II and select the correct answer using the codes given below.

	Column-I		Column-II
A.	ABO blood groups	I.	Dihybrid cross
B.	Law of segregation	II.	Monohybrid cross
C.	Law of Independent assortment	III.	Base pairs substitution
D.	Gene mutation	IV.	Multiple allelism

(a) A – II; B – I; C – IV; D – III

(b) A – IV; B – I; C – II; D – III

(c) A – IV; B – II; C – I; D – III

(d) A – II; B – III; C – IV; D – I

52. Match column-I with column-II and select the correct option from the codes given below.

	Column-I		Column-II
A.	Autosomal	I.	Down's syndrome recessive trait
B.	Sex-linked	II.	Phenylketonuria recessive trait
C.	Metabolic error	III.	Haemophilia linked to autosomal recessive
D.	Additional 21st	IV.	Sickle cell anaemia chromosome

(a) A – II; B – I; C – IV; D – III
(b) A – IV; B – I; C – II; D – III
(c) A – IV; B – III; C – II; D – I
(d) A – III; B – IV; C – I; D – II

Passage Based Questions

DIRECTIONS (Qs. 53-57) : *Following are the passage based questions. Attempt any 4 out of 5 questions.*

Sickle cell anemia is a genetic disorder where the body produces an abnormal hemoglobin called hemoglobin S. Red blood cells are normally flexible and round, but when the hemoglobin is defective, blood cells take on a "sickle" or crescent shape. Sickle cell anemia is caused by mutations in a gene called HBB. It is an inherited blood disorder that occurs if both the maternal and paternal copies of the HBB gene are defective. In other words, if an individual receives just one copy of the defective HBB gene, either from mother or father, then the individual has no sickle cell anemia but has what is called "sickle cell trait". People with sickle cell trait usually do not have any symptoms or problems but they can pass the mutated gene onto their children. There are three inheritance scenarios that can lead to a child having sickle cell anemia:

– Both parents have sickle cell trait
– One parent has sickle cell anemia and the other has sickle cell trait
– Both parents have sickle cell anemia

53. Sickle cell anemia is a/ an __________________ disease.
(a) X linked
(b) autosomal dominant
(c) autosomal recessive
(d) Y linked

54. I f both parents have sickle cell trait, then there is _______ of the child having sickle cell anemia.
(a) 25 % risk
(b) 50 % risk
(c) 75% risk
(d) No risk

55. If both parents have sickle cell trait, then there is _______ of the child having sickle cell trait.
(a) 25 % risk
(b) 50 % risk
(c) 75% risk
(d) No risk

56. If one parent has sickle cell anemia and the other has sickle cell trait, there is __________ that their children will have sickle cell anemia and __________ will have sickle cell trait.
(a) 25 % risk, 75% risk
(b) 50 % risk, 50% risk
(c) 75% risk, 25% risk
(d) No risk

57.

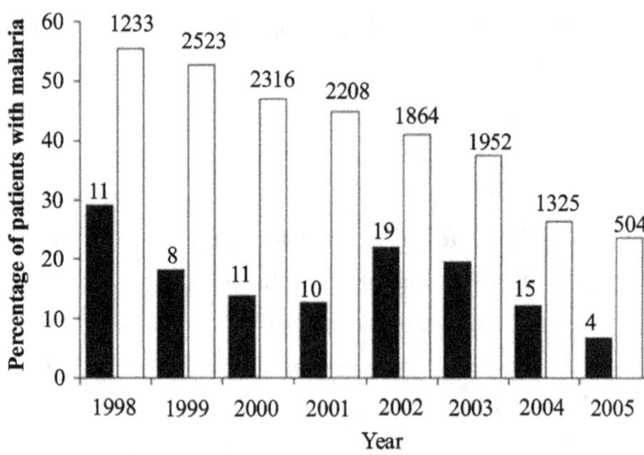

The following statements are drawn as conclusions from the above data (Kenya).

I. Patients with SCD (Sickle Cell Disease) are less likely to be infected with malaria.

II. Patients with SCD (Sickle Cell Disease) are more likely to be infected with malaria.

III. Over the years the percentage of people infected with malaria has been decreasing.

IV. ear 2000 saw the largest percentage difference between malaria patients with and without SCD.

Choose from below the correct alternative.

(a) only I is true
(b) I and IV are true
(c) III and II are true
(d) I and III are true

Chapter Test 

Time : *30 Minutes*   **Max. Marks : *15***

Directions :

- Questions number **1-15** carry **1 mark** each.

1. Three children in a family have blood types O, AB and B respectively. What are the genotypes of their parents?
   (a) $I^A i$ and $I^B i$
   (b) $I^A I^B$ and $i\,i$
   (c) $I^B I^B$ and $I^A I^A$
   (d) $I^A I^A$ and $I^B i$

2. If the blood group of the mother and the child is O and B respectively. Then the person of the following blood group cannot be the father of this child
   (a) O and A
   (b) A, B or O
   (c) AB only
   (d) O only

3. Which of the following crosses will give tall and dwarf pea plants in same proportions?
   (a) TT × tt
   (b) Tt × tt
   (c) TT × Tt
   (d) tt × tt

4. The given figure represents the inheritance pattern of a certain type of traits in humans.

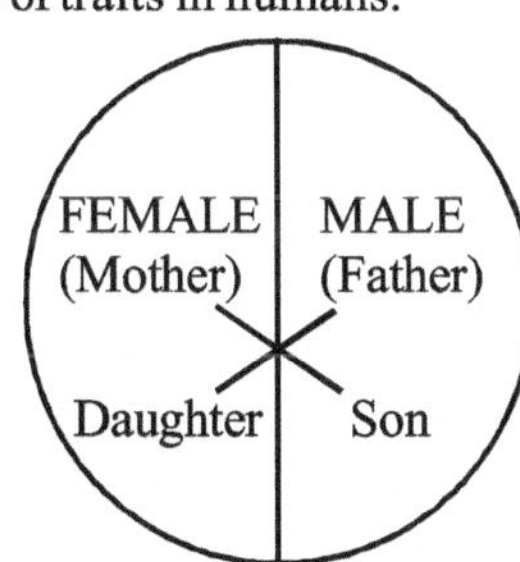

   Which one of the following conditions could be an example of this pattern?
   (a) Thalassemia
   (b) Haemophilia
   (c) Phenylketonuria
   (d) Sickle cell anaemia

5. Match the symbols used in human pedigree analysis (given in column-I) with their name (given in column-II) and choose the correct option.

Column-I		Column-II	
A.	▢—◯	I.	Consanguineous mating
B.	▢═◯	II.	Normal female
C.	◇	III.	Mating
D.	▢—◯ / ■	IV.	Affected female
E.	●	V.	Parents with male child affected with disease
		VI.	Sex unspecified

   (a) A – III, B – I, C – II, D – V, E – IV
   (b) A – II, B – I, C – VI, D – III, E – IV
   (c) A – III, B – IV, C – I, D – V, E – II
   (d) A – III, B – I, C – VI, D – V, E – IV

DIRECTIONS (Qs. 6-7) : *Each of these questions contains an assertion followed by reason. Read them carefully and answer the question on the basis of following options. You have to select the one that best describes the two statements.*

(a) If both Assertion and Reason are correct and the Reason is a correct explanation of the Assertion.
(b) If both Assertion and Reason are correct but Reason is not a correct explanation of the Assertion.
(c) If the Assertion is correct but Reason is incorrect.
(d) If both Assertion and Reason are incorrect.

6. **Assertion:** The percentage of crossing over between two genes is directly proportional to their distance.
   Reason: The unit of crossing over has been termed as Haldone as Centi Morgan (CM).

7. **Assertion:** A homozygous parent produces all gametes that are similar, while a heterozygous one produces two kinds of gametes each having one allele with equal proportional.
   Reason: A hemizygous parent is the one which produces only a single gamete with only one allele.

Passage/Case Based Questions

DIRECTIONS (Qs. 8-12) : *Read the following passage and answer the questions that follows.*

Observe the following schematic representation of determination of sex (xx-xy type mechanism) and answer the question that follows-

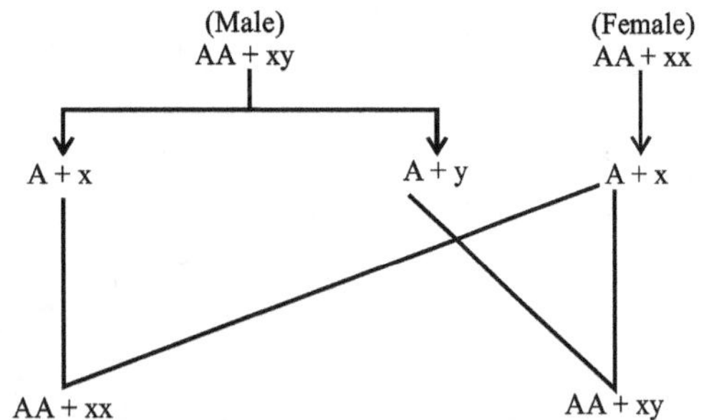

8. In an entity with genetic composition AA + xxy such as Drosophila will be a normal female. In the case of mammals, it will be?
   (a) Turner
   (b) Klinefilter
   (c) Normal female
   (d) Normal male

9. __________ discovered by xy sex chromosome.
   (a) MJD White
   (b) R Brown
   (c) Nettil Stevans
   (d) Mendel

10. This number of Barr bodies are found in a female with xxxy chromosomes
    (a) four
    (b) three
    (c) two
    (d) one

11. If a boy has sexual characters of that of a girl, its genotype would be
    (a) xxy
    (b) xyy
    (c) xo
    (d) xxy

12. The chromosomes accounted for sex determination are referred to as
    (a) Heterosis
    (b) Multiple alleles
    (c) Allosomes
    (d) Autosome

Very Short Answer Questions

13. In which plant co-dominance is reported?
14. Define sex chromosome.
15. Define allele.

Solutions 

Practice Exercise-1 

1. **(d)** Mendel selected Garden of pea as material for his hybridization experiments because of the following reasons:
   (i) Hybridization or crossing in pea is easy.
   (ii) It has bisexual flowers.
   (iii) It has a number of well defined contrasting characters.
   (iv) It shows predominantly self-fertilization.
   (v) It has a short life span.

2. **(d)** It is determined by the ratio of number of X-chromosomes to the number of autosomal sets.

3. **(a)**

4. **(a)** Law of segregation (originated by Gregor Mendel) states that during the production of gametes the two copies of each hereditary factor do not blend or mix up with each other but remains together and segregate (or separate) so that offspring obtains one factor from each parent.

5. **(b)**   6. **(a)**

7. **(c)** In incomple dominace, F_1 hybrids are not related to either of the parents but exhibited a blending of characters of two parents. E.g. 40' clock plant (Mirabilis jalapa), and dog flower (*Antirrhinum majus*).

8. **(b)**

9. **(c)** Assertion is correct but Reason is incorrect.
   Mendel died due to kidney disorder in the year 1884 in the age of 61.

10. **(b)** Assertion and Reason are correct but Reason is not a correct explanation of Assertion.
    Gene is the unit of inheritance which passes from one generation to the other through the gamete.

11. **(a)** Assertion and Reason are correct and the Reason is a correct explanation of Assertion.
    9 purple and 7 white flowers are obtained in sweet pea.

12. **(a)** Assertion and Reason are correct and the Reason is a correct explanation of Assertion.
    When a gene control number of phenotypes that are mostly unrelated, it is said to exhibit pleiotropy.

13. Cross between organism taking only one pair of contrasting characters into consideration is monohybrid cross.

14. Cross between organisms taking two pairs of contrasting character into consideration is called dihybrid cross.

15. First statistical effort to explain biological result framed basis of law of dominance, law of segregation, formed basis for chromosomal theory of inheritance.

16. It is a checker board used to show the result of a cross between two organisms. It depicts both genotypes & phenotypes of the progeny.

17. Dissimilarities between parents and offsprings and between offsprings are called variations.

18. Cross between F_1 generation and recessive parent is called test cross.

19. Establishment of genotype of dominant phenotype.

20. Alfred Sturtevant.

21. Sutton and Boveri in 1902.

22. Seed shape, seed colour, pod shape, plant height.

23. Each gamete is pure for character, it carries one allele for a trait.

24. **Test cross :** Cross between F_1 and recessive parent/to determine genotype of F_1.
    Back cross : Cross between F_1 and any of dominant phenotype parent/need not be a test cross/ to establish. It is used in crop/ homozygosity improvement.

25. **Incomplete dominance**
    - Discovered by Correns in dog flower (*Antirrhinum majus*)
    - Three phenotype RR(red), Pink (Rr), white (rr)
    - R is not completely dominant over r
    - Ratio – Phenotype – Genotypic – 1 : 2 : 1

26. **Codominance**
    - Discovered in ABO blood group system.
    - Both I^A and I^B are dominant.
    - Result in production of AB blood group.
    - I^A and I^B both express their glycoprotein.

27. More than two alternate forms of gene present on the same locus called multiple alleles. There is absence of crossing over in multiple alleles and the mode of inheritance in case of multiple alleles is called multiple allelism. The well known example of multiple allele in human is blood group which also shows condominance. Landsteiner discovered the three blood groups in man (A, B and O). Multiple alleles express different alternatives of the same characters.

28. - A cross between two sets of plants having two pairs of true breeding characters is called dihybrid cross.
    - Round yellow (RRYY) × wrinkled green (rryy)
    - Phenotype ratio – 9 : 3 : 3 : 1
    - Formed basis for law of independent assortment

29. The main postulates of chromosomal theory of inheritance are as follows :
    (i) Chromosomes and genes occur in pair
    (ii) both segregate during meiosis
    (iii) diploid state is restored for both after fertilization.

30. Significance of chromosomal theory of inheritance are as follows :
    (i) Establishment of genes, chromosomes, linkage map formulation.
    (ii) Concept of linkage and recombination.

31. The main difference between linkage and recombination are as follows :

	Linkage	Recombination
1.	Cause of inheritance	Cause of variation
2.	Tendency of genes to stay together	Tendency of genes to segregate
3.	Accounts for parental combination	Accounts for recombinants
4.	Ratio remain fixed	Ratio variable depending on % of recombination
5.	Basis for linkage maps	Basis for gene map of chromosome

1. **(b)** A pair of X chromosomes is present in the female whereas X and Y chromosomes are present in the male. There is an equal possibility of fertilization of the ovum (female gamete containing pair of X chromosomes) with the sperm (male gamete) carrying either X or Y chromosomes. If ovum fertilizes with a sperm carrying X chromosome the zygote develops into the female offspring and the fertilization of ovum with sperm (carrying Y chromosome) results into the male offspring. On this basis, it is evident that only sperm plays an important role to determine the sex of a child.

2. **(c)** The X body of Henking was observed in half of the sperms during spermatogenesis. During his experiments on insects, Henking found the traces of a nuclear structure all through the process of spermatogenesis which he named it as X body. He also observed that, after spermatogenesis, exact half of the sperms received this X body, while the remaining half did not. Later, scientists found out that this X body of Henking was actually a chromosome and hence, named it X-chromosome.

3. **(b)**   4. **(b)**

5. **(b)** In the given cross, disease is passed from carrier female to male progeny, this is known as criss-cross inheritance. The trait which shows criss-cross inheritance is located on the sex chromosome. In XX^C, single recessive gene X^C is present, that does not cause the disease.

6. **(a)** A-V, B-I, C-IV, D-II, E-III

Monoploidy	–	n
Monosomy	–	$2n-1$
Nullisomy	–	$2n-2$
Trisomy	–	$2n+1$
Tetrasomy	–	$2n+2$

7. **(c)** Assertion is correct but Reason is incorrect.
    Sickle cell anaemia is a classic example of mis-dense point mutation.

8. **(b)** Assertion and Reason are correct but Reason is not a correct explanation of Assertion.
    Cry-du-chat syndrome is caused by the deletion in short arm of chromosome number 5.

9. **(b)** Assertion and Reason are correct but Reason is not a correct explanation of Assertion.
    Haemophilia is also called bleeder's disease and royal disease, because many descendants of Queen Victoria, beginning with one of her son's were affected by the disease.

10. **(b)** Assertion and Reason are correct but Reason is not a correct explanation of Assertion.
    In both grasshopper and humans male heterogameity is found and in both cases female homogameity is present.

11. Pedigree Analysis

12. Haemophilia and Thallasemia.

13. Haemophilia is usually an inherited bleeding disorder in which the blood does not clot properly. This can lead to spontaneous bleeding as well as bleeding following injuries or surgery.

14. Inactivated X chromosomes in females.

15. Turner syndrome (X)

16. Phenylketonuria is an Inborn error of metabolism, autosomal recessive trait. It occurs due to lack of enzyme phenylalaninehydroxylase that converts phenylalanine → tyrosine.

17. Substitution of Glutamic acid [Glu] by Valine [Val] at 6th position of β globin chain of haemoglobin molecule.

18. Blood clotting disorder where blood does not clot is known as haemophilia.

19. Analysis of inheritance of a particular trait in family tree over generations is called pedigree analysis.

20. XY sex chromosomes. XY chromosomes in males, XX chromosomes in female.

21. The main postulates of chromosomal theory of inheritance are as follows :
    (i) Chromosomes and genes occur in pair
    (ii) both segregate during meiosis
    (iii) diploid state is restored for both after fertilization.

22. Significance of chromosomal theory of inheritance are as follows :
    (i) Establishment of genes, chromosomes, linkage map formulation.
    (ii) Concept of linkage and recombination.

23. The main difference between Klinefelter's syndrome and Turner's syndrome.

	Klinefelter's syndrome	Turner's syndrome
1.	XXY genotype	XO genotype
2.	Affected male	Affected female
3.	Karyotype has 47 chromosomes	45 chromosomes
4.	Symptoms – Gynaecomastia (enlarged breast) and sterility.	Rudimentary ovaries, under developed breast, have webbed neck and broad chest.

24. **Down's Syndrome**
    – Occur due to Trisomy of 21st chromosome.
    – Characterized with rounded face, flaccid muscle, protruding tongue, broad neck, etc.
    – Also called Mongoloid syndrome.
    – Survivors of down syndrome have higher chances of catching leukaemia & Alzheimers disease.

25. Phenylketonuria is inborn error of metabolism and autosomal recessive trait. In this disorder, the functional enzymes is lacking & cause visible phenotypic changes.

26. Sex determination in organisms is based on the type of sex chromosomes. Two main differences between them are –
    (i) Sex determination in humans is XY type while those in birds is ZW type.
    (ii) In human XY is male, XX is female while in birds ZZ is male, ZW is female.

27. Haemophilia is called royal disease because it was first observed in the royal family of Britain. The family pedigree of Queen Victoria shows a number of descendants suffering from haemophilia as she was carrier.

Past year Exercise

1. Pea flowers produce assured seed sets because they have cleistogamous flowers, which undergo natural self-pollination.

2. Autosomal dominant Mendelian disorder-Huntington's chorea, autosomal recessive Mendelian disorder-Sickle cell anaemia or phenylketonuria.

3. (i) $Hb^A Hb^S$ (ii) $Hb^S Hb^S$

4. Due to non-disjunction, 21st pair of chromosomes fail to separate during oogenesis. Therefore, the egg possesses 24 chromosomes instead of 23. When the egg fuses with a sperm the zygote will have three copies of chromosome 21 causing trisomy.

5. **Aneuploidy -** It is the event during cell division cycle that results in the gain or loss of chromosome.

6. Two contrasting flower traits are
   (i) Flower colour (Violet/White)
   (ii) Flower position (Axial/Terminal)

7. Dominant traits are green and inflated.

8. Tt and tt (in ratios 1:1) is obtained on crossing F_1-tall with dwarf plant.

9. Recessive allele expresses itself only in homozygous state.

10. The dominant trait is axial white flowers and recessive is violet flowers.

11. The proportion of parental gene combination be much higher than non-parental types, when two genes show linkage.

12. Round/Wrinkled = ½, Yellow/Green = ½

13. A true breeding line is the one that has undergone continuous self pollination, shows stable trait inheritance and expression for several generations.

14. Punnett square helps to calculate the probability of all possible genotypes of offspring in a genetic cross.

15. (i) In Snapdragon, the inheritance of flower colour shows incomplete dominance.
    (ii) Neither of the alleles of gene for flower colour is completely dominant over the other and hybrid shows an intermediate phenotype.

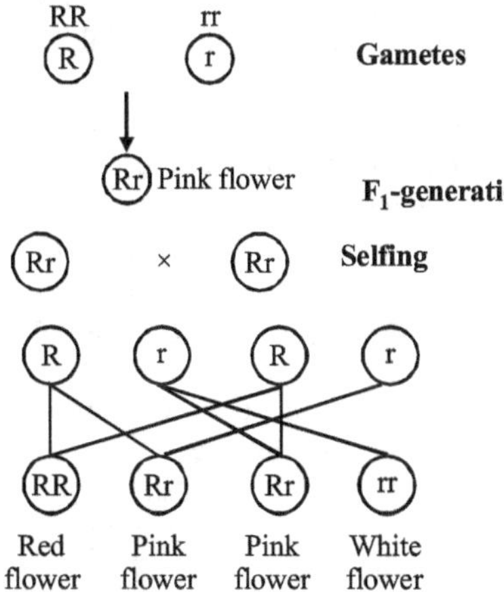

16. (i) *Drosophila* exhibits XY type of sex determination. Males produce two types of sperms, one having X chromosome and one having Y chromosome. Whereas females have only X-type of chromosomes. Grasshoppers exhibit XO type of sex determination. Males produce two types of gametes, one with X chromosome and other with no chromosome. Thus, both show male heterogamety.
    (ii) Female heterogamety is shown by female fowls as they have ZW sex-chromosomes. The ova contains 50% Z-chromosome and other 50% ova have W-chromosome. Hence, they also produce two types of female gametes.

17. Sex determination in humans.
    (i) The males have 22 pair autosomes and a pair of XY-chromosome.
    (ii) The females have 22 pair autosomes and a pair of XX-chromosomes.
    (iii) In males, 50% of sperms carry X-chromosome and other 50% carry Y-chromosomes.
    (iv) In females, all ova contain X-chromosomes.
    (v) The sex of an individual is determined by the type of sperm fertilising the ovum.
    (vi) If the ovum is fertilised by Y-chromosome, the zygote (XY) develops into a male and if the ovum is fertilised by X-chromosome, zygote (XX) develops into a female.

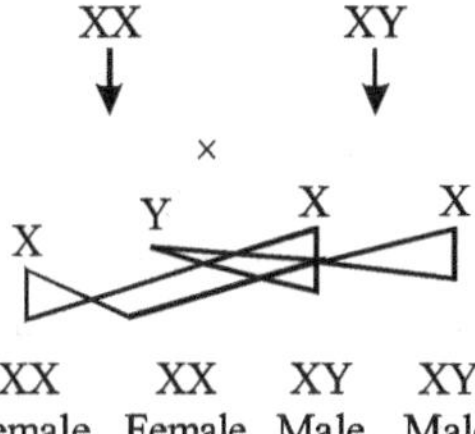

Sex determination in birds
    (i) It is of ZW type.
    (ii) Males are homogametic (ZZ) and females are heterogametic (ZW). The type of ovum fertilised determines the sex of the individual.

18. A test cross is a cross between an organism of unknown genotype and homozygous recessive organism. It helps the breeder to know the genotype of the organism. If the test cross yield offspring of which 50% show the dominant character and 50% show the recessive characters *i.e.*, F_1 ratio is 1 : 1, the individual under test is heterozygous.

19. Morgan saw that when the two genes in a dihybrid cross were situated on the same chromosome, the proportion of parental gene combinations were much higher than the non-parental type. Morgan attributed this due to physical association or linkage of two genes and coined the term linkage to describe this physical association of genes on chromosome and the term recombination to describe the generation of non-parental gene recombinations.

20. (i) When a pureline tall is crossed with a pureline dwarf.

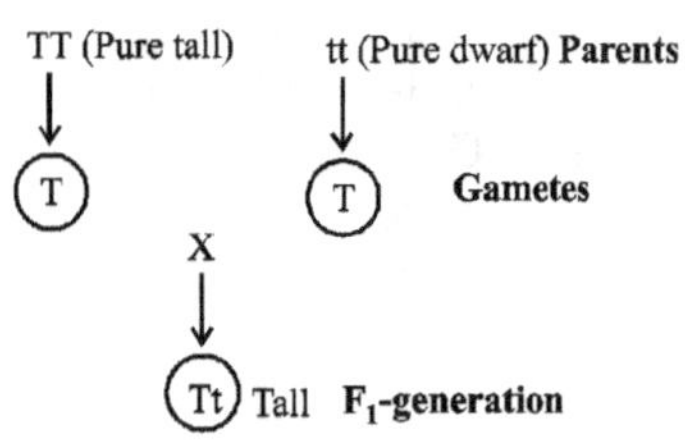

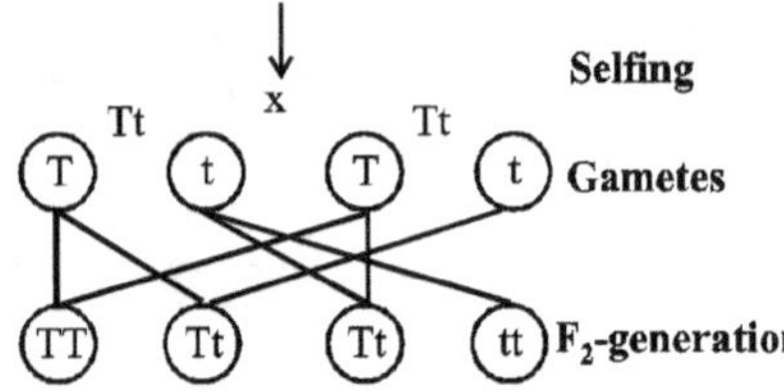

Phenotypic ratio Tall : dwarf
Genotypic ratio   TT : Tt : tt

(ii) Two third of tall progenies are heterozygous because gene for tallness (T) is dominant and also expresses itself in heterozygous condition.

21. (i) **Multiple allelism in ABO blood group**

Multiple allelism is the phenomenon of ocurrence of a gene in more then two allelic forms on the same lows. In case of ABO blood group system, the genes for blood group exists in three allelic form I^A, I^B and I. Co-dominance is the phenomena in which both alleles express themselves when present together. We inherit any two alleles for the blood group. When the genotype is I^AI^B the individual has AB blood group since both I^A and I^B equally influence the formation of antigens A and B.

(ii) **Phenotype** (a) I^Ai – 'A' blood group
(b) ii – 'O' blood group

22.

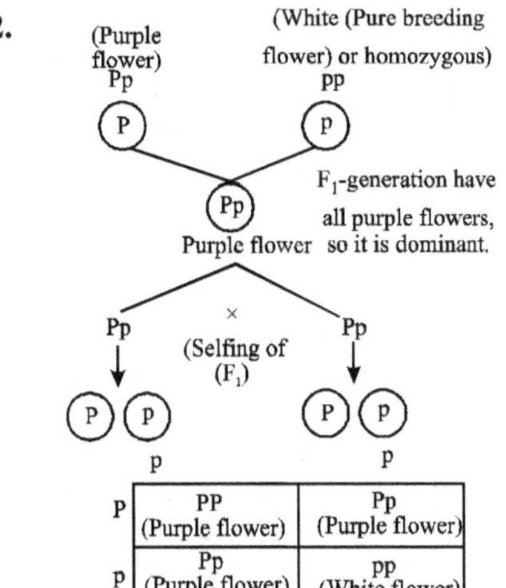

	P	p
P	PP (Purple flower)	Pp (Purple flower)
p	Pp (Purple flower)	pp (White flower)

Purple flowered plants : White flowered plants are in the ratio of 3 : 1.

This result is obtained due to segregation of the alleles at the time of gametogenesis. The alleles remain together in a zygote but during gamete formation they segregate such that the gametes carry only one allele.

23. It is chromosomal disorder called Klinefelter's syndrome, which occurs in males. Human males have XXY sex-chromosome (47 chromosomes) instead of XY.

Symptoms

(i) Sex of the individual is masculine but possess feminine characters.

(ii) Gynaecomastia, *i.e.*, development of breasts.

(iii) Poor beard growth and often sterile.

(iv) feminine pitched voice.

24. Differences between dominance, codominance and incomplete dominance

Dominance	Codominance	Incomplete Dominance
Once allele of a gene expresses itself and suppresses the expression of other allele of the same gene, when they are present together in a hybrid.	Two alleles of a gene are equally dominant and express themselves in the presence of the other.	Neither of the two alleles of a gene completely dominant over the other and the hybrid to intermediate between the two parents.

25. *Conclusion of Morgan's studies are*

(i) Genes were located on the X-chromosomes.

(ii) When the two genes in a dihybrid cross were situated on the same chromosome, the proportion of parental gene combinations were much higher than the non-parental type.

(iii) Morgan stated this association as linkage to describe the physical association of genes on a chromosome.

(iv) Recombination is a term used to describe the generation of non-parental gene combinations.

(v) Morgan also found that some genes were tightly linked (low recombination) and others were loosely linked (high recombination).

26. (i) This representation who are likely to suffer more form the related to the gene represented. The males, the females or both males and females equally? and why? indicates a normal human because (HbA peptide) glutamic acid (Glu) at sixth position of β globin chain of haemoglobin molecule is not substituted by valine.

(ii) The normal individual has biconcave, disc-like RBCs, whereas the sufferer has sickle-shaped RBCs.

(iii) Both males and females are likely to suffer from the disease equally because this is not a sex-linked disease. It is an autosomal-linked recessive trait.

27. (i) XO abnormality is a chromosomal disorder called Turner's syndrome.

(ii) Non-disjunction of chromosome occurs this chromosomal disorder.

(iii) It is the phenomenon of failure of segregation of the members of homologous pairs of chromosomes.

(iv) Such disorder occur due to absence of one X-chromosome, *i.e.*, 45 + XO.

(v) The individual has underdeveloped feminine characters.

(vi) The female is sterile and ovaries are rudimentary.

28. Haemophilia is an X-linked recessive disease therefore, the female having haemophilic allele on single X-chromosome do not produce haemophilic phenotype. The human female are thus rarely haemophilic.

Due to haemophilia the bleeding time in patients increase and blood flow continuously from wound.

29. **Deviation from Mendelism :** Incomplete dominance, a condition where none of the two contrasting alleles or factors is dominant and the expression of the character in a hybrid is intermediate or fine mixture of the expression of two factors (as in homozygous state).

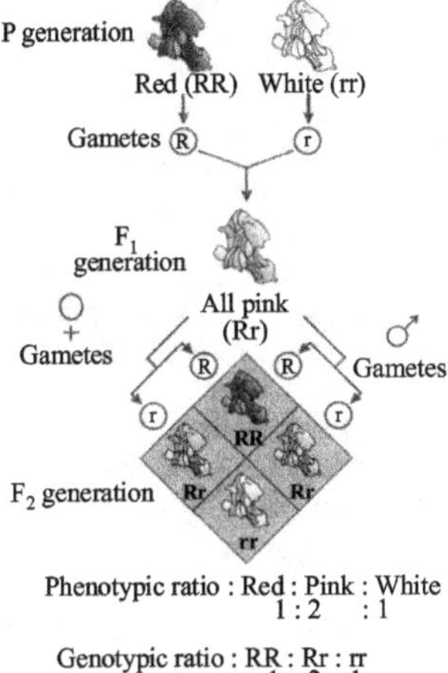

Phenotypic ratio : Red : Pink : White
1 : 2 : 1

Genotypic ratio : RR : Rr : rr
1 : 2 : 1

30. Haemophilia is a sex-linked recessive trait, the gene of which is present on X-chromosome. In females haemophilia appears when both the sex-chromosomes carry its recessive gene $X^h X^h$. Such females die before birth. A woman having a single gene of the trait appear normal but is carrier of the disease XX^h. For sex-linked genes, human males are hemizygous. Therefore $X^h Y$ is haemophiliac man. In haemophilic person, the blood do-not clot, after injury, due to the absence of a blood clotting factor.

31. A monohybrid cross is a cross in which two alternate forms of a single character are taken into consideration. The phenotype and genotypic ratios of F_2 generation can be deduced from the following cross :

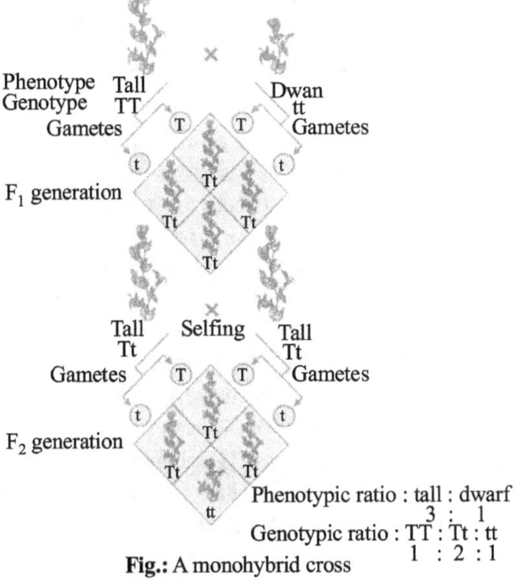

Phenotypic ratio : tall : dwarf
3 : 1
Genotypic ratio : TT : Tt : tt
1 : 2 : 1

Fig.: A monohybrid cross

32. To know the genotype of any organism for any specific trait, the organism is crossed with another organism recessive for that trait. This type of cross is called **test cross.**

Parents

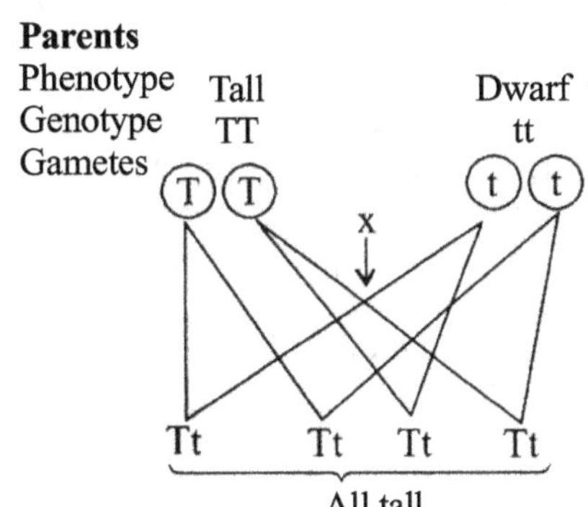

The offspring will be 100% dominant if the individual is homozygous dominant.

Parents

Phenotype   Tall   Dwarf
Genotype   Tt   tt
Gametes   T   t   t   t

Tt   Tt   tt   tt

50% Dominant 50% Recessive

The ratio will be 50% dominant and 50% recessive in case of hybrid or heterozygous individual.

Note : In case of double heterozygous ($RrYy$) crossed with double recessive ($rryy$) the ratio will be 1 : 1 : 1 : 1.

33. Since in the cross involving two tall plants, some of the offspring plants were dwarf, which indicates that both the parent tall plants were heterozygous (Tt and Tt), as the dwarf plant (tt), gets gene/allele for dwarfness from each of the parent.

Parent	Phenotype	Tall	X	Tall
	Genotype	TT		Tt

♀ \ ♂	T	t
T	TT	Tt
t	Tt	tt

Phenotypic ratio : 3 Tall : 1 Dwarf
3 : 1

Genotypic ratio = 1TT : 2 Tt: 1 tt
= 1 : 2 : 1

34. (a) Multiple alleles may be defined as the group of two or more allelomorphs of one gene, only two of which can be present in a diploid cells. The simplest example of multiple alleles is the inheritance of A, B and O blood groups in humans. ABO blood groups are controlled by the gene I. It has 3 multiple alleles (I^A, I^B and i). Out of which any two alleles are found in a person, one from each parent. The allele I^A and I^B, produce blood groups A and B respectively. When both the alleles A and B are present together, the blood group AB is produced. The allele i when homozygous produce the blood group O. Thus, four blood group phenotypes are controlled by six genotypes.

Blood Group (Phenotype)	Genotype
O	ii
A	$I^A I^A$, $I^A i$
B	$I^B I^B$, $I^B i$
AB	$I^A I^B$

Blood Group

(b) **Mother**   Phenotype A (Homozygous)
                    Genotype = $I^A I^A$

    Father   Phenotype = B (Homozygous)
                    Genotype = $I^B I^B$

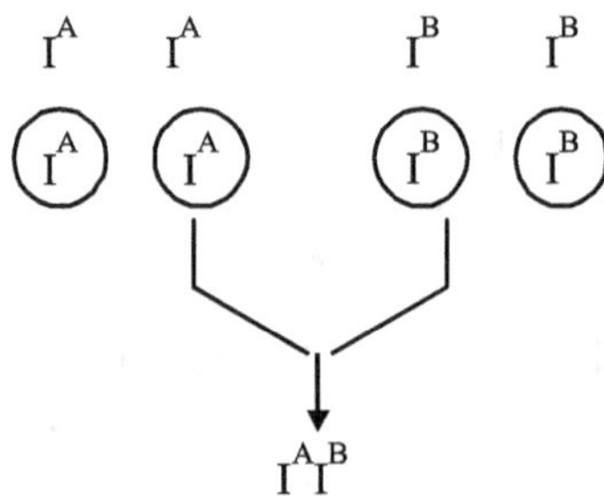

(AB Blood group)

The mother produces ova, with the allele I^A and the father produces the sperms with the allele I^B. The fusion of sperm and ovum result in the offspring with AB blood group ($I^A I^B$). It exhibits Mendelian inheritance which states that the two factors for a trait segregate at the time of gamete formation and again come together at the time of fertilization in the zygote/offspring.

35. In a population, for example a classroom, some students may belong to 'A' blood group, some to 'B', some 'AB' and other 'O' group.

Genetic Basis - Since a character in an organism is determined by a pair of genes/alleles, it means in human beings, the type of blood groups are determined by more than two alternate forms of a gene/alleles, a phenomenon called **multiple alleles.** These alleles are I^A, I^B, I^O or i. These alleles for human blood group show **dominant-recessive** and **codominance effect.** The alleles I^A and I^B are dominant over allele I^O or i, a recessive allele. When both the alleles I^A and I^B are present together, both express independently and show co-dominance.

OR

(a) Progeny of carrier woman for colour blindness and a man with normal vision.

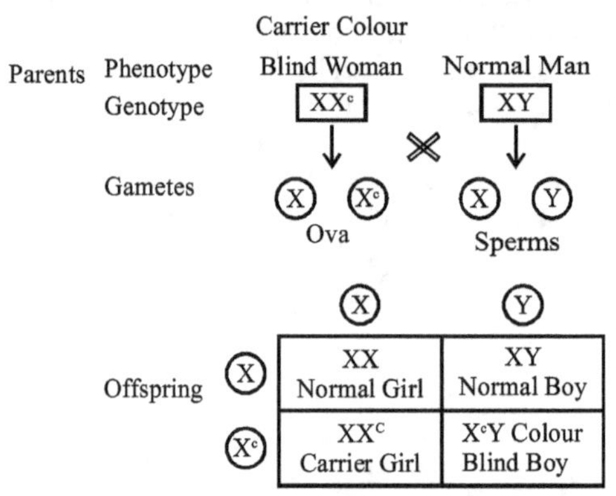

1 Normal Girl (XX) : 1 Carrier Girl (XXᶜ)
1 Normal Boy (XY) : 1 Colour Blind Boy (XᶜY)

(b) For sex-linked characters, the genes of which are present on X-chromosome, a female is carrier when only one of her X-chromosome carry the gene/allele for the disorder and the other X-chromosome carry the normal dominant gene for the trait e.g., XXᶜ (colour blind carrier). The carrier female is otherwise normal phenotypically.

36.

P-generation	Green pod	Yellow pod
Phenotype	`round seeds	wrinkled seeds
Genotype	GGRR	g g r r

Gametes   (GR)   (gr)

          Gg Rr

F_1 generation   (Hybrid green
F_2 generation   pod round seeds)

♀ \ ♂	GR	Gr	gR	gr
GR	GG RR	GGRr	GgRR	GgRr
Gr	GG Rr	GGrr	GgRr	Ggrr
gR	GgRR	GgRr	ggRR	GgRr
gr	GgRr	Ggrr	ggRr	ggrr

F_2 Phenotypic ratio
9 Green round : 3 Green wrinkled : 3 Yellow round : 1 Yellow wrinkled

37. When a cross is made between two pure garden pea plants for colour of flowers, only the dominant colour violet appears in the F_1 progeny, while the recessive colour (white) does not appear. It shows that the allele for violet colour is **completely dominant** over the recessive allele for white colour.

In *Antirrhinum* cross between two pure breeding Red Flower and white flowered plants produce the hybrid F_1 progency all pink in colour. Here none of the two contrasting alleles is dominant and the expression of a character in a hybrid is intermediate. It is called **Incomplete dominance.**

38. (a) Down's syndrome will have 47 chromosomes, with one additional chromosome constituting three copies of chromosome 21 instead of normal two. Such a condition of chromosome addition is called trisomy which arises due to the formation of n+1 male or female gamete and the subsequent fertilisation by a normal n gamete [(n+(n+1)].

Symptoms : (i) Round face, broad forehead (ii) Permanently opened mouth protruding tongue (iii) Projecting lowerlip, shortneck (iv) Flat hands stubby fingers (v) Furrowed tongue (vi) Mongolian type eyelid fold.

Events responsible : This genetic disorder due to autosomal abnormality is a result of non-disjunction of chromosomes of pair 21 and pass in a single egg during oogenesis.

(b) **Haemophilia** is a sex-chromosomal mendelian disorder due to recessive gene mutations of sex-chromosome-X. The pattern of inheritance is criss-cross inheritance *i.e.,* the male passes the character to the same sex offspring-grandsons through the daughters while the female passes the characters to the granddaughters through the sons.

(c) Thalassaemia is an autosomal linked recessively inherited disease, produced due to gene substitution mutation. It results in reduced synthesis of one of a' or $\hat{a}$ - chain of haemoglobin.

They are transmitted to the offspring as per Mendelian principles or laws. In both the male and females, the thalassaemia is controlled by two factors present on the autosomal chromosomes.

While in haemophilia in males the character is controlled by single factor (Hemizygous) present on, X-chromosome.

39. (a) Polygenic inheritance (Quantitative inheritance) is a type of inheritance controlled by three or more genes in which the dominant alleles have cumulative effect, with each dominant allele expressing a part of trait, the full trait being shown only when all the dominant alleles are present.

Pleiotropy is the ability of gene to control multiple phenotypes. The basis of pleiotropy due to the interrelationship between the metabolic pathways that may contribute towards different phenotypes.

(b) (i) **Incomplete dominance** is a condition where none of the two contrasting alleles or factors is dominant and the expression of the character in a hybrid is intermediate or fine mixture of the expression of two factors (as in homozygous state). It is called incomplete dominance.

(ii) **Dominance**, explains that out of two contrasting alleles only one is able to show its effects in the individual/hybrid is called dominant while the other allele which does not show its effect called recessive.

(iii) **Co-dominance** a phenomenon when two alleles able to express themselves independently when present together.

40. If a gene occurs in more than two alternative states or alleles it is known to known as multiple allelism *e.g,* In human being the blood groups A, B, O are determined by 3 alleles – I^A, I^B, I^O or i.

Pleiotropy is the ability of gene to have multiple phenotypic effects because it influences a number of characters simultaneously. For instance white eye mutation in *Drosophila*, lead to depigmentation in many other parts of the body, giving a pleiotropic effect.

41. Th above pedigree analysis shows that the daughters are carriers of haemophilia (XX^h) because father is haemophilic and passes their X/X^h chromosome to their son and daughter. The males always receive X-chromosome from their mother and Y-chromosome from their father. The carrier daughter (XX^h) receives one normal X-chromosome from their mother and the other X^h chromosome from their father. Since the second daughter is also phenotypically normal but carrier (XX^h). It shows that their mother is normal (XX).

This pattern of inheritane of sex-linked diseases is called **criss-cross inheritance** *i.e.* male transfers the sex-linked characters to his grandsons through his daughters.

42. In Pea plants, the colour of flower whether violet or white is determined by a single gene pair. A single gene controls the expression of full trait. A pea plant will have violet colour flower whether it is homozygous (VV) or heterozygous (Vv). There is no variation in the intensity of violet colour. Its inheritance is called as **monogenic inheritance.**

The skin colour in humans shows a **polygenic / quantitative inheritance.** It is a type of inheritance controlled by one or more genes in which the dominant alleles have cumulative/additive effect, with each dominant allele expressing a part or unit of trait and the full trait being shown when all the dominant alleles are present. It is also called multiple factor inheritance.

43. (a) R(dominant allele red colour) is not completely dominant over r (recessive allele white colour) The F_1 generation having pink flowers are selfed, the plants of F_2 generation are of three types – red, pink & white flowered in the ratio of 1:2:1. It is not blending inheritance because parental characters appear in F_2 generation.

(b) The phenomenon is known as incomplete dominance where dominant allele does not completely express itself.

44. ABO blood group in human being is an example of multiple allelism = ½.

ABO blood groups are controlled by the gene I. The gene (I) has three alleles I^A, I^B and i. I^A and I^B are completely dominant over i.

But when I^A and I^B are present together they both express their own types of sugars, this is because of co-dominance.

45. The scientific name of fruit-fly is *Drosophila melanogaster* = ½

(i) The fruit-flies could be grown in simple synthetic medium in the laboratory.

(ii) They complete their life-cycle in about two-weeks.

(iii) There is a clear differentiation of the sexes-the male and female flies are easily distinguishable.

46. Morgan carried out several dihybrid crosses in *Drosophila* to study genes that were sex-linked. He hybridised a yellow bodied, white eyed female was crossed with brown bodied red eyed male and inter crossed their progeny. The F_2 phenotypic ratio of *Drosophila* deviated significantly form Mendel's 9:3:3:1 ratio, the genes for eye colour & body colour are closely located on the 'X' chromosome showing linkage & therefore inherited together, recombinants were formed due to crossing over but at low percentage = ½ × 4.

47. Pedigree analysis is done for the study of inheritance of genetic traits in several generations of a human family in the form of a family tree diagram.
   (i) It helps in genetic counselling to avoid disorders.
   (ii) It shows the origin of a trait and flow of a trait in a family.
   (iii) It is important to know the possibility of a recessive allele that can cause genetic disorders like colour blindness. haemophilia, etc.

48. (a) (i) furrowed tongue (ii) partially open mouth.
   (b) both male and female = ½
   (c) Klinefelter's = ½
   (d) Male = ½
   (e) sterile ovaries / rudimentary ovaries, lack of secondary sexual characters. = ½
   (f) female = ½

49.

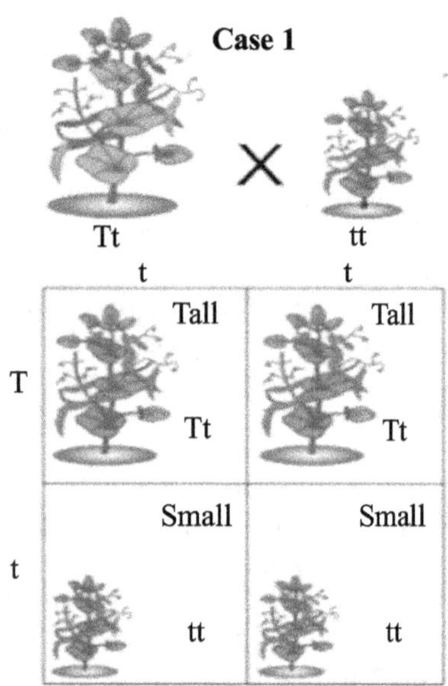

   (ii) The type of cross carried out here is a test cross. It is a cross in which an individual with an unknown dominant phenotype is crossed with an individual (parent) homozygous recessive for that trait. It is used to know whether an individual is homozygous or heterozygous for dominant character.

50. In humans, the ABO blood groups are controlled by a gene called gene 'I'. It has three alleles, namely I^A, I^B and i. A person possesses any two of the three alleles. I^A and I^B dominate over i. But with each other, I^A and I^B are co-dominant.

Allele from Parent 1	Allele from Parent 2	Genotype of offspring	Blood type of offspring
I^A	I^A	$I^A I^A$	A
I^A	I^B	$I^A I^B$	AB
I^A	i	$I^A i$	A
I^B	I^A	$I^A I^B$	AB
I^B	I^B	$I^B I^B$	B
I^B	i	$I^B i$	B
i	i	$i i$	O

These alleles helps to determine the blood group of a person. The plasma membrane of red blood cells has sugar polymers that protrude out from its surface and the kind of sugar is controlled by the gene 'I' of ABO blood group. The alleles I^A and I^B produce A and B types of sugar, while allele i does not produce any sugar.

OR

(i) The type of sex determination mechanism shown in female XX with male XO is male heterogamety.
Example- Grasshopper (Insect) is an example of XO type of sex determination.

(ii) The type of sex determination mechanism shown in female ZW with male ZZ is female heterogamety.
Example- In birds, females have one Z and one W chromosome, whereas males have a pair of Z-chromosomes besides the autosomes.

51. Colour blindness is a sex-linked disease. The gene for this disorder is present on the X chromosome. Hence, it is carried by normal females not expressing the disease. If a colour-blind child is born to a normal couple, then the mother would be the carrier of the disease. The child would be male.
The following cross shows the inheritance of the disorder:

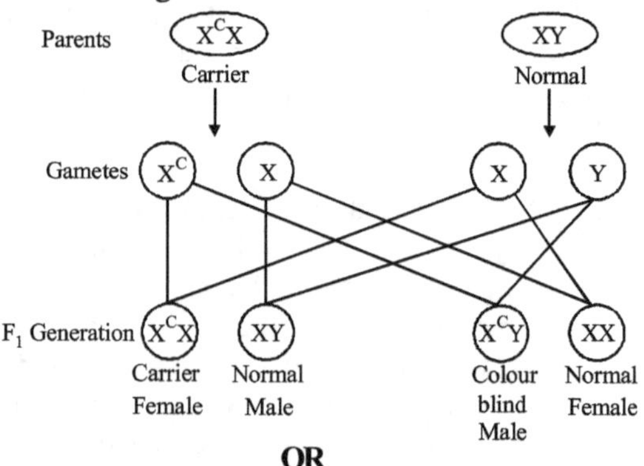

OR

The following are the three reasons that led to the delay in accepting Mendel's work:
(i) Lack of communication and publicity.
(ii) His concept of factors (genes) as discrete units that did not blend with each other was not accepted in the light of variations occurring continuously in nature.
(iii) Mendel's approach to explain biological phenomenon with the help of mathematics was also not accepted.

52. Women are never responsible for determination of the sex of a child. Moreover, it is not appropriate to ill-treat a woman for giving birth to a girl child, as both males and females are equally important for the balance of nature and continuity of our species.

All human-beings have 23 pairs of chromosomes. A human sperm (haploid) has 22 autosomes and one of the two types of sex chromosomes, i.e. either X or Y. On the contrary, human females have 22 autosomes that are exactly same as males and contain two X chromosomes. The sex of an individual is determined by the type of the sex chromosome (X or Y) contained by the sperm that fuses with the ovum. If the fertilising sperm has an X chromosome, then the baby would be a female and if a sperm with Y chromosome fuses with the ovum, it will develop into a male child. Thus, it is evident that it is the genetic makeup of the sperm that determines the sex of the child.

53. (a)

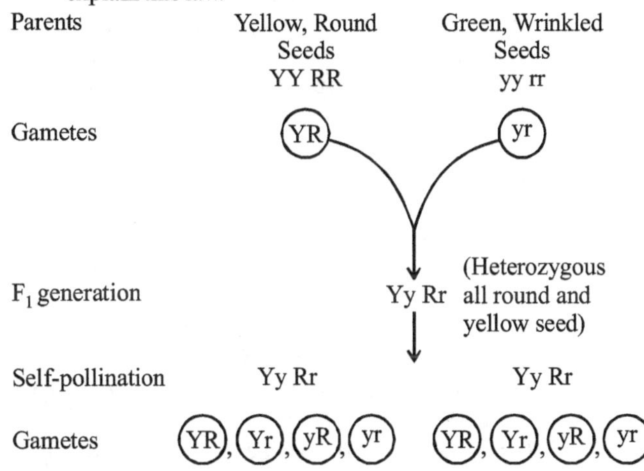

Genotype of daughter- XX^h

Genotype of husband- XY

(b) Haemophilia is a sex-linked recessive disease. Here, it is transmitted from the carrier female to the sons. From the above pedigree chart, it can be observed that the disease is being transmitted from the carrier female to her daughter (carrier) and son (affected). The carrier daughter transmits this disease to the grandson. The inheritance of sex-linked characters from male parent to male grand children through females is called 'criss-cross inheritance.'

54. Male honeybees are born from the unfertilised eggs by the process known as parthenogenesis whereas female honeybees are born from the fertilised egg. Since, unfertilised egg. carries only half the number chromosomes as compared to female honey bee.

55. Test cross is a cross between F1 progeny and its homozygous recessive parent.

This cross determines whether the dominant character is coming from homozygous dominant genotype or heterozygous genotype. (e.g., talness coming from TT of Tt). When TT is crossed with tt, we obtain all Tt (tall) individuals in the progeny. Whereas when Tt is crossed with tt, we obtain Tt (tall) and tt (dwarf) individuals in the progeny. Thus test cross can be used to determine the heterozygosity of the plant.

56. **Gene:** A gene is a unit of inheritance that is transferred from the parent to the offspring. It controls the expression of a character. A gene is a linear piece of DNA present in the nucleus.

Alleles: Alleles are alternative forms of a single gene that lie on the same locus in homologous chromosomes.

57. The law of independent assortment. states that genes of different characters located in different pairs of chromosomes are independent of one another in their segregation during gamete formation. This law was proposed by Mendel based on the results of dihybrid crosses, where inheritance of two traits were considered simultaneously. Independent assortment is not applicable for the genes located on the same chromosomes i.e. linked genes. The following cross between a pure-breeding plant with yellow, round seeds and another pure breeding plant with green, wrinkled seeds, can be taken as an example to explain this law.

	Yellow, Round Seeds	Green, Wrinkled Seeds
Parents	YY RR	yy rr
Gametes	(YR)	(yr)
F₁ generation		Yy Rr (Heterozygous all round and yellow seed)
Self-pollination	Yy Rr	Yy Rr
Gametes	(YR),(Yr),(yR),(yr)	(YR),(Yr),(yR),(yr)

F₂ generation

	YR	Yr	yR	yr
YR	YY RR (yellow, round)	YY Rr (yellow, round)	Yy RR (yellow, round)	Yy Rr (yellow, round)
Yr	YY Rr (yellow, round)	YY rr (yellow, wrinkled)	Yy Rr (yellow, round)	Yy rr (yellow, wrinkled)
yR	Yy RR (yellow, round)	Yy Rr (yellow, round)	yy RR (green, round)	yy Rr (green, round)
yr	Yy Rr (yellow, round)	Yy rr (yellow, wrinkled)	yy Rr (green, round)	yy rr (green, wrinkled)

The Phenotypic ratio is :
Wrinkled yellow and round green are recombinants.
Round yellow and wrinkled green are parental combinations.
The genotypic ratio is :

YYRR	:	YYRr	:	YyRR	:	YyRr	:	YYrr
1	:	2	:	2	:	4	:	1

Yyrr:yy RR	:	yy Rr	:	yy rr
2	:	1	:	2	:	1

In this cross, the factors for colour of seeds and those for shape of seeds have segregated independently and each gamete has one factor for each of these two traits.

58. The chromosomal theory of inheritance given by Sutton and Boveri and experimental results presented by Mendel can be compared in the following ways:
   (i) In a diploid organism, the factors (genes) and chromosomes occur in pairs.
   (ii) Both chromosomes as well as genes segregate at the time of gamete formation such that only one of each pair is transmitted to a gamete. So, a gamete contains only one chromosome of a type and only one of the two alleles of a trait.
   (iii) Each pair of chromosome and gene segregates independent of another pair.
   (iv) The paired condition of both chromosomes as well as Mendelian factors is restored during fertilisation.

OR

   (a) T.H. Morgan studied X-linked genes in *Drosophila* and observed that when the two genes in a dihybrid cross were situated on the same chromosome, the proportion of parental gene combinations is much higher than the non-parental type. He attributed this due to the physical association or linkage of the two genes on a chromosome and coined the term linkage and the term recombination describes the generation of non-parental gene combinations.
   (b) Alfred Sturtevant used the frequency of recombination between gene pairs on the same chromosome as a measure of distance between them and mapped their position on the chromosome.

59. (a) The two girls are suffering from a genetic disorder resulting in adenosine deaminase (ADA) deficiency due to deletion of its gene.
   (b) Girl A was treated by enzyme replacement therapy, in which functional ADA is given to the patient by injection. This technique is not completely curative as it requires repeated infusion.
   (c) Girl B was treated using gene therapy where the gene isolate from marrow cells producing ADA was introduced into cells at an early embryonic stage for a possible permanent cure.

60. Hemophilia is a recessive X-linked genetic disorder. Hemophilia is more common among males than females because males only inherit one X-chromosome. Humans have 22 pairs of autosomal chromosomes and one pair of sex chromosome. There are 46 chromosomes in humans. Females have XX chromosome while males have X and Y chromosome. So, male offspring inherit X-chromosome from their mother and Y-chromosome from their father. Males only have one X-chromosome and if the X-chromosome and this is the reason that males are suffering from haemophilia if the X-chromosome carries mutation. While in females, as they have two X chromosomes, and this is a recessive disorder so females are carrier of this disease and can pass this disorder to male offsprings.

OR

The pattern of inheritance is Incomplete dominance in which the none of the two alleles are dominant over each other. So, when both the alleles are present together intermediate or new phenotypes are formed. Intermediate formed is intermediate between the independent expressions of two alleles.
The phenotypic ratio and genotypic ratio such as 1:2:1 are same in case of incomplete dominance.

61. (a) 'A' Female honeybees are diploid so, the process of meiosis takes place for the gamete formation in female honeybees. While 'B' male honeybees are haploid so, mitosis takes place for the gamete formation in male honeybees.
   (b) Honeybees are classified into three categories such as queen, drone and workers. So, the male honey bees are called drones. The male honey bees or drones are developed from the unfertilized female eggs and this phenomenon is called arrhenotoky. Arrhenotoky is a type of parthenogenesis in which unfertilized eggs are develop into males.

NCERT Exemplar 

1. (a) The changes in chromosome number by additions or deletions of less than a whole set is aneuploidy. In this case organism gains or loses one or more chromosome but not a complete set. Polyploid is defined as the addition of entire set of chromosome. The polyploidy can be tryploidy (3n) tetraploidy (4n), pentaploidy (5n) etc.
   Allopolyploidy is the polyploidy in which chromosome sets are non-homologous. Monosomy is the process in which one chromosome is removed from dipoid set of chromosome $(2n-1)$.

2. (a) Crossing over separates genes aways from each other So, the distance between the genes and percentage of recombination shows and direct relationship, *i.e.*, when genes are close together they have high linkage and exhibit low recombination frequencies, Thus, the other option are wrong as it does not show parallel or inverse relationship.

3. (d) Sickle-cell anaemia is an autosome linked recessive trait which is controlled by a single pair of allele Hb^A and Hb^s only the homozygous individuals for Hbs, *i.e.*, Hb^s Hb^s shows the diseased phenotype. The heterozygous individuals are carriers ($Hb^A Hb^s$). Glutamic acid (Glu) is replaced by valine (Val) at sixth position of β-chain of heamoglobin molecule due to point mutation. This substitution occurs due to the single base substitution of the beta globin gene from GAG (Glu) to GUG (Val).
   Whereas, the other codes GGG, AAG, GAA do not codes for valine.

4. **(b)** The example of codominance is ABO blood grouping in humans. ABO blood groups are controlled by gene I. Gene I consists three alleles I^A, I^B and I^A and I^B are the dominant alleles. When I^A and I^B are present together, both express equally and produce the surface antigens A and B, whereas i is the recessive allele and does not produce any antigen.

The genetic effect of a single gene on multiple phenotypic traits is pleiotropy. Incomplete dominance a genetic term in which does not completely dominate another allele.

The separation of allele during the process of gametogenesis is known as Segregation. This is the basis of reappearance of recessive character in F_2-generation.

5. **(b)** In ZZ/ZW case, the female has heteromorphic (ZW) sex chromosomes. Thus peacock shows ZZ/ZW sex determination type.

In Platypus the sex determination is of XX-XY type. In snails the sex detemination is environmentally induced, while in cockroaches it is of XX-XO types.

6. **(b)** The ratio obtained from a dihydrid cross is 9:3:3:1

Pgener   RRYY   ×   rryy
Lation   (round yellow)   (wrinkled green)
Gametes   RY   ×   ry
f_1 generation
f_2 generation

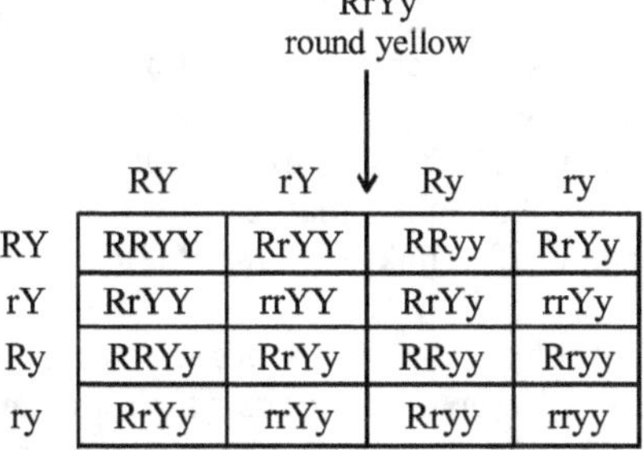

	RY	rY	Ry	ry
RY	RRYY	RrYY	RRyy	RrYy
rY	RrYY	rrYY	RrYy	rrYy
Ry	RRYy	RrYy	RRyy	Rryy
ry	RrYy	rrYy	Rryy	rryy

Phenotypic ratio : round yellow: round green: wrinkled yellow: wrinkled green

9 : 3 : 3 : 1

Phenylketonuria: It is an inborn error of metabolism and also inherited as the autosomal recessive traits.

• The affected individuals lack an enzyme required for the conversion of amino acid phenylalanine into tyrosine.

• So, phenylalanine is accumulated and converted into phenylpyruvic acid and its derivatives.

• So, the accumulation of phenylpyruvic acid & its derivatives in the brain results in mental retardation.

7. **(c)** Assertion is correct but Reason is incorrect.
The number of linkage groups corresponds to the haploid number of chromosomes.

8. **(a)** Assertion and Reason are correct and the Reason is a correct explanation of Assertion.
Crossing over takes place in pachytene stage of prophase I of meiotic division.

9. When a progeny of F_1 is crossed with the homozygous recessive parent, it is called test cross. Such a cross is useful to determine the genotype of an unknown *i.e.*, whether it is heterozygous, or homozygous dominant for the trait.

10. In a monohybrid cross, starting with parents which homozygous dominant and homozygous recessive, F_1 would be heterozygous for the trait and would express the dominant allele. But in case of incomplete dominance, a monohybrid cross shows the result as follows.

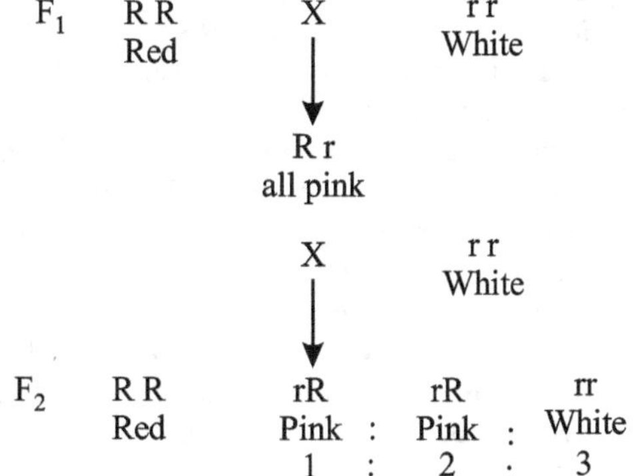

Phenotypic ratio
Genotypic ratio

Here the genotypic and phenotypic ratios are the same. So, we can conclude that when genotypic and phenotypic ratios are the same, the alleles show incomplete dominance.

Objective Practice Exercise 

1. **(c)** Yellow seed colour is dominant over green seed colour.

2. **(a)** The seven traits are now know to be present on 4 chromosomes. But they do not shown linkage, because of large distances between them on the chromosome.

3. **(c)** Dihybrid cross is made between individuals having contrasting traits in order to study the inheritance of two pairs of alleles. Test cross is a back cross between individual with a dominant trait and its recessive parent to know whether the individual is homozygous or heterozygous for the trait.

4. **(a)** Parent :   RRTt × rrtt

Gametes :   (RT),   (Rt),   (rt)

Offspring :   RrTt   Rrtt
          tall with red fruit   tall with yellow fruit
Ratio = 1 : 1

5. **(b)** Independent assortment of genes takes place only when they are located on separate non-homologous chromosomes. Where two or more than two genes are located on same chromosome, independent assortment will not be possible.

6. **(c)** A dominant gene would lead to the expression of its phenotype irrespective of the fact whether its allelic gene is dominant or recessive.

7. **(c)** In order to find out the gamete or the genotype of an unknown individual, scientists perform a test cross. In test cross, the individual in question is crossed with the homozygous recessive parent.

8. **(b)** If Mendel had studied a plant with 12 chromosomes, he would have encountered linked genes, and hence he would not have arrived at the principle of independent assortment

9. **(a)** Black is the phenotype of the sheep. Without further information, you cannot identify the genotype of a black sheep because it could be either BB or Bb. The possible genotypes of the parents of a black sheep could be BB × BB, BB × Bb, Bb × bb, or Bb × Bb. Thus, there is no one single genotype for either parent.

10. **(a)** Monohybrid and dihybrid crosses produce heterozygous individuals; true-breeding individuals are always homozygous.

11. **(d)** This is an example of a monohybrid cross. All of the F_1 progeny would have smooth seeds. (The F_1 generation would all have the genotype Ss, producing the phenotype of smooth seeds because the smooth allele, S, is dominant to the wrinkled allele, s).

12. **(d)** Given that both parents are true-breeding, the cross must be either AA × AA, AA × aa, or aa × aa. If you work out these crosses, you will see that all of the possible answers are true for each possible situation.

13. **(c)** Heterozygotes can make two kinds of gametes, each with equal probability.

14. **(b)** Each conception is an independent event, so the probabilities remain the same each time.

15. **(a)**

<pre>
       +—————————————+————+
   b ——————→ 20 ←——— a ←——→ c
          units   8 units

   +——————————————————————————————+
              28 units
</pre>

Percent crossing over between two genes is proportional to the distance between them.

16. **(b)** Mapping of genes on chromosomes is based on the assumption that genes are arranged on the chromosome and that the percentage of crossing over (recombination frequency) between two genes is an index of their distance apart. Distances between genes is expressed as map units, where, one map unit is defined as 1 per cent recombination.

17. **(d)**

	Possibility 1 :	Possibility 2:
Blood group	A × B	A × B
Genotype :	$I^A I^A \times I^B I^B$	$I^A I^O \times I^B I^O$
Gametes :	$I^A I^B$	$I^A\ I^O\ \ I^B\ I^O$
Child's		
Blood group :	AB	AB, A, B or O

18. **(b)** Incomplete dominance results in the progeny's expressing an intermediate form of the two parental alleles. (In a cross between red-flowered plants and white-flowered plants, the expression of pink-flowered plants would be a "blend" of the parental traits). Co-dominance is not an example of blending because both alleles are fully expressed in the individual.

19. **(a)** The alleles for red and white flowers are co-dominant, resulting in pink flowers when both are present in the genotype.

20. **(a)** If the mother has blood group $I^A I^A$ and the father has blood group $I^B I^O$, then their children can only have genotypes $I^A I^B$ or $I^A I^O$, which have the phenotypes blood group AB and blood group A respectively.

21. **(d)** The mother would have genotype $I^A I^B$ and the father would have genotype $I^O I^O$. Thus, the two genotypes possible for their offspring would be $I^A I^O$ and $I^B I^O$, with equal probability. Hence, the expected phenotypes would be 1 type A : 1 type B.

22. **(a)** The probability of the next child being a boy is 0.5, the probability that the child has blood group O is 0.25. Hence, the probability that the next child will be a boy with blood group O is $0.5 \times 0.25 = 0.125$. These probabilities are independent of the sex and blood group of the first child.

23. **(a)**   24. **(c)**   25. **(b)**   26. **(c)**   27. **(c)**

28. **(a)**

29. **(a)** Since the woman's father was colour blind. She would be a carrier of the colour blindness gene. When she marries a colour blind man. Their progeny could be

Parent	$X^c X$	×	$X^c Y$		
	Carrier		Colour blind		
	Woman		Man		
Progeny	$X^c X^c$		$X^c Y$	$X X^c$	XY
	Colour			Carrier	
	blind son			daughter	

30. **(d)** Cystic fibrosis : It is a common disorder of caucasian race in which thick and more salty mucus blocks the respiratory tract. The homozygous recessive condition produces the defective protein which regulates chloride transport channel.

Cretinism : In this disorder, the physical growth, mental growth and sexual growth in children is retarded. Such a dwarf and sterile child is called a cretin. It is due to hyposecretion of thyroid hormones.

Thalassemia : Due to defective production of α or β chains of haemoglobin, autosomal recessive.

Haemophilia : Sex linked disorder due to defective recessive gene.

31. **(b)** Mitochondria is an organelle present in the cytoplasm. A zygote receives its cytoplasm from the female parent gamete. Hence, in the given question, the F_2 progenies do not receive the mitochondrial genome from the male parent and mutation is not passed to progenies.

32. **(a)** The mother must have been a haemophilic carrier $(X^h X)$. One of the twins would have inherited the normal X chromosome and the other would have received the X chromosome carrying the gene for haemophilia.

33. **(a)** Sex linked disorders follow criss-cross inheritance pattern where affected father passes on the gene to their daughters. The daughters receive one of their X - chromosome from their fathers.

34. **(c)** In human, the Y chromosome bears the androgenic factor or the male determining factor. Whereas, in *Drosophila*, the ratio of sex chromosomes to autosomes is the factor determining sex of the individual.

35. **(d)** 50% of ova will have (n + 1) chromosome which would, on fertilisation, yield abnormal zygotes $(n + 1) + (n) = 2n + 1$.

36. **(b)** Calvin Bridges demonstrated that in *Drosophila*, the sex is determined by ratio of the number of X chromosomes to the sets of autosomes.

37. **(a)** Male sterility in plants can be controlled by nuclear genes or cytoplasm or by both. Three different mechanisms for control of male sterility in plants are :

(i) Genetic male sterility; (ii) Cytoplasmic male sterility; (iii) Cytoplasmic genetic male sterility. In Maize, the genes for cytoplasmic control of male sterility are located in cytoplasm.

38. **(c)** The A, B and O blood groups occur on one gene locus, where A and B are co-dominant, and O is the recessive allele. It is expressed only when present in the homozygous condition.

39. **(c)** The most common sex-linked alleles are X-linked and are passed from a mother to her son (since the mother always donates one of her X chromosome to her son and the father always donates his Y chromosome to his son). Daughters can also receive the X-linked allele from their mothers, but the father donates the other X chromosome, so daughters can be carriers.

40. **(b)** In these three species, females have two X chromosomes and males have one X chromosome. The ratio of X chromosomes to autosomes is important (and different in each organism) in *Drosophila* and grasshoppers, but not in humans. In all three species, males have one Y chromosome, but the Y chromosome is required for male fertility, not for *Drosophila* to be male (in *Drosophila*, male flies can be XO).

41. **(b)** The F_1 plants of genotype Tt are self-pollinated. (both tall (T) but with dwarf (t) alleles).

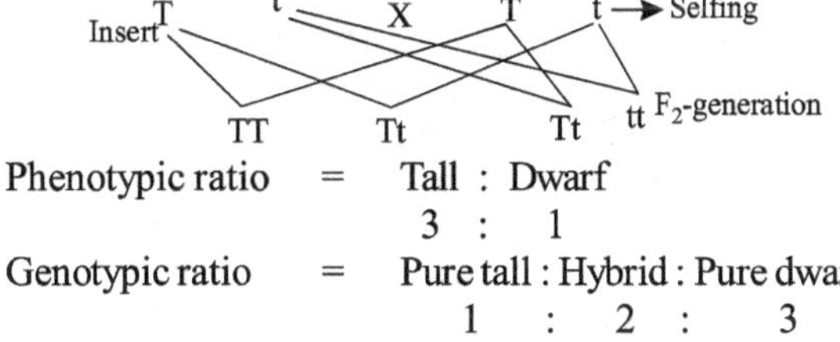

Phenotypic ratio   =   Tall : Dwarf
                             3 : 1
Genotypic ratio   =   Pure tall : Hybrid : Pure dwarf
                             1   :   2   :   3

42. **(d)** Alleles of two genes are segregeting independently. Mendel explained by crossing a pea plant with round and yellow seeds and one with wrinkled and green ones.

All F_1 hybrids give yellow and round seeds. Since yellow colour is dominant over the green and the round shape is dominant over the winkled.

When the F_1- hybrid plants are crossed to each or allowed to self fertilise, and F_2- generation form as represented in the following figure

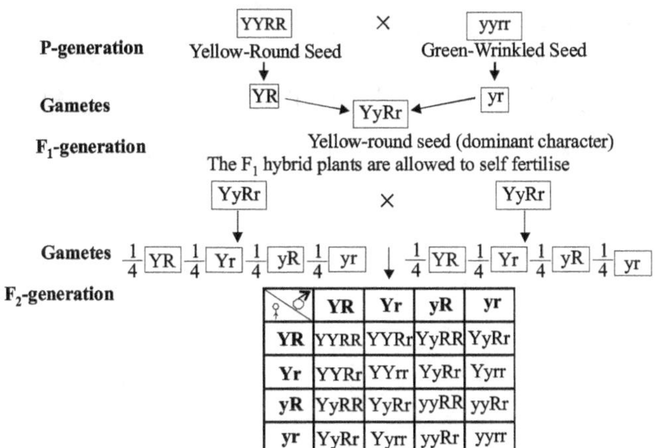

Phenotypic ratio – 9 : 3 : 3 : 1

The outcome of the dihybrid cross make it very clear that segregation of the seed colour is independent of the seed shape and both the parental and new combinations of the characters appear in the F_2 offspring, *i.e.*, assortment of genes of one pair is independnet of the other pair.

43. **(c)** Linkage will not result in variations among sibling. Morgan carried out several dihybrid crosses in Drosophila to study genes related to sex-linked.

He came to know that the genes were located on the X-chromosome and also observed that when the two genes in a dihybrid cross were situated on the same chromosome, the proportion of parental gene combinations were much higher than the non-parental type.

It indicates that due to the physical association of the two genes, no variation will occur among siblings. Independent assortment of genes means that allele pair transmitted to offspring is independent on one another.

The exchange of genetic material between homologous chromosomes is crossing over. It is one of the final phases of genetic recombination. Mutation is the sudden inheritable change in genetic material of an organism which transfers to next generation.

44. **(a)** **Non-homologous Chromosome :** The law of independent assortment holds true as long as two different genes are on separate chromosomes. When the genes are on separate chromosome, the two alleles of one gene (A and a) will segregate into gametes independently of the two alleles of the other gene (B and b).

45. **(c)** Pleotropy is a phenomenon in which a single gene may express more than one trait. Sometimes, one trait will be very evident and other will be less evident, *e,g.*, a gene for white eye in Drosophila also affect the shape of organs is male responsible for sperm storage as well as other structures.

Multiple allelism is a series of three or more alternative or allelic forms of a gene, that can occupy the same locus.

Mosaicism is the occurrence of cells that differ in their genetic component from other cells of the body.

Polygeny refers to a single characteristics that is controlled by more than two genes. (It is also known as multifactorial inheritance).

46. **(a)** In certain insects, such as cockroach, and some roundworms, the Y-chromosome is missing so that the male has only one sex chromosome, *i.e.* 'X' condition in the male is XO (O means absence of one sex chromosome) and in the female it is XX., thus males showing 17 chromosome while females show 18 chromosome.

47. **(b)** Mendelian inheritance in human is gained by analysis of family pedigrees or the results of matings that have already occured. We may be able to predict how the trait is inherited by analysing a pedigree.

It acts as visual tool for documenting the biological relationship in families and to determine the mode of inheritance (dominant, recessive etc.) related to genetic disease. Whereas quantitative trait polygenic trait and material traits are not studied by pedigree analysis.

Continous traits are often measured and given a quantitative value, they are a often referred as quantitative traits. *e.g.* crop yield weight gain in animals IQ, etc.

Polygenic traits are another exception to Mendel's rule, which occurs when a traits is controlled by more than one gene. This means that each dominant allele adds to the expression of the next dominant allele.

The traits inherited and expressed from the maternal parent to the subsequent offsprings are **maternal traits**.

48.   **(d)**   Mendelian dihybrid cross

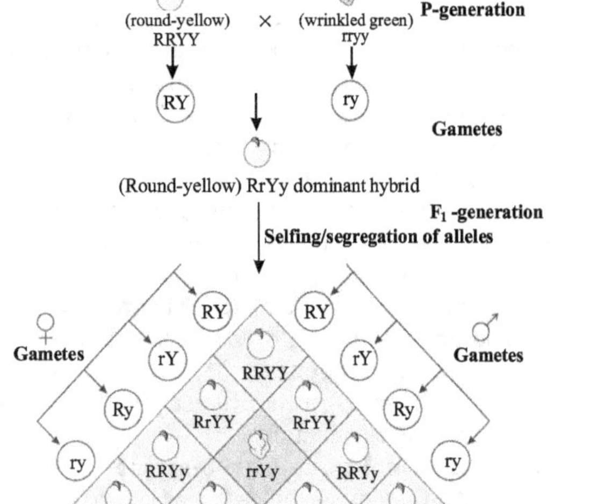

Phenotypic ratio   Round-yellow : Round-green : Wrinkled-yellow : Wrinkled-green
$$9 \ : \ 3 \ : \ 3 \ : \ 1$$
4 (phenotypes)

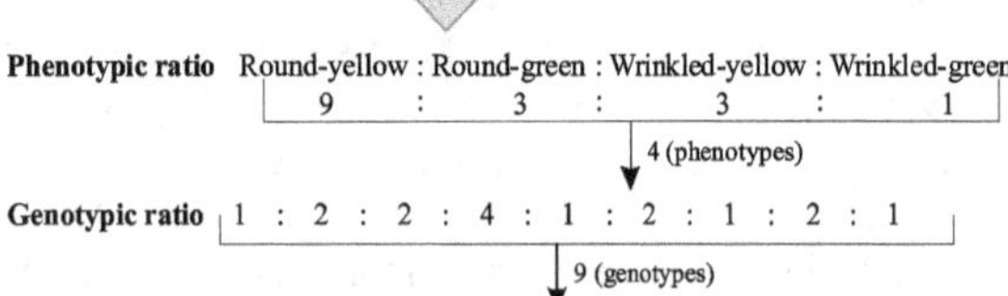

Genotypic ratio $1 : 2 : 2 : 4 : 1 : 2 : 1 : 2 : 1$

9 (genotypes)

Results of a dihybrid cross where the two parents differed in two pairs of contrasting traits : seed colour and seed shape

Other combination do not show dihybrid cross ratio of Mendelian inheritance.

49.   **(b)**   **50.**   **(c)**

51.   **(c)**   ABO blood group is an example of multiple allelisms because of presence of more than two alleles (I^A, I^B and i) of a gene. They are produced due to repeated mutation of the same gene but in different directions. Law of segregation can be explained with the help of monohybrid cross.. Law of independent assortment can be explained with the help of dihybrid cross. Law of independent assortment states that allele pairs, which are independent of one another, separate independently during the formation of gametes. Gene

mutation is a permanent alteration in the DNA sequence. Mutations range in size; they can affect anywhere from a single DNA building block (base pair) to a large segment of a chromosome that includes multiple genes.

52.   **(c)**   Sickle cell anaemia is an autosomal recessive trait. Haemophilia is a sex linked recessive trait. Metabolic error linked to autosomal recessive: Phenylketonuria. Phenylketonuria is an inherited disease due to faulty metabolism of phenylalanine. The affected individual lacks an enzyme that converts the amino acids phenylalanine into tyrosine. It is characterized by the presence of phenyl ketones in the urine and usually first noted by signs of mental retardation in infancy. Down's syndrome occurs due to presence of an Additional 21st chromosomes.

53.   **(c)**   **54.**   **(a)**   **55.**   **(b)**   **56.**   **(b)**

57.   **(d)**

Chapter Test

1.   **(a)**   Parents having genotype I^Ai and I^Bi have children of the following blood group type – O, AB, and B.

2.   **(a)**   In the absence of 'B' allele, the B-antigen cannot develop in the child.

3.   **(b)**

4.   **(b)**   The inheritance pattern of a particular trait shown in the given picture results in haemophilia. Haemophilia is a group of inherited blood disorders in which the blood does not clot properly. It is caused by a fault in one of the genes that determine how the body makes blood clotting factor VIII or IX. These genes are located on the X-chromosome. Haemophilia appears only in human male which can be transferred to their grandson through their carrier daughter (Criss-cross inheritance).

5.   **(d)**

6.   **(b)**   Assertion and Reason are correct but Reason is not a correct explanation of Assertion.

One unit of map (cm) is therefore, equivalent to 1% of crossing over.

7.   **(b)**   Assertion and Reason are correct but Reason is not a correct explanation of Assertion.

Homizygous condition is found in gametes are haploid organisms.

8.   **(b)**   **9.**   **(b)**   **10.**   **(b)**   **11.**   **(a)**

12.   **(c)**

13.   Snapdragon or *Antirrhinum*.

14.   Chromosomes which determines the sex of on individual.4 X & Y sex chromosomes are present in humans and Z & W in birds.

15.   Genes code for a pair of contrasting character is known as allele.

5 Molecular Basis of Inheritance

Molecular basis of Inheritance

Nucleic acid

DNA

RNA

DNA as a genetic material

mRNA
also known as messenger RNA. It is 5% of total RNA. Its life span is 1-4 min. It is the longest RNA

rRNA
It is 80% of total RNA. Base sequence is similar in all. It is synthesized in NOR of DNA. It is also most stable and are called Ribozyme

tRNA
It is 15% of total RNA and small in all RNA 20 tRNA are present in a cell. It aquires clover leaf structure.

Human genome project
Different individual have different DNA sequence to find out the DNA sequence of genome genetic engineering techniques were used in year 1990

Applications

DNA finger printing
It was developed by Dr. Alec. Jefrey in 1984. DNA sequences differ from one individual to another. This is a technique generally using repeated sequence in human genome that produces a unique pattern for every individual

Replication
Formation of New DNA from old DNA. It is a semiconservative method.

Transcription
Copying of genetic information from strand of DNA to RNA

Translation
Process of polymerisation of amino-acids to form polypeptide.

Protein synthesis

Griffith's experiment
He carried experiment with streptococcus pneumoniae infect to mice smooth and rough strains were used, S-train was virulent and R was non-virulent S + R infected mice died transfer of genetic material S $\rightarrow$ R. That was DNA.

Harshey and Chase
With T_2 phage which attached on E. Coli. Viruses were grown containing radioactive sulphur and phosphorous. (32p) virus caused radioactivity in E.Coli. due to DNA transfer.

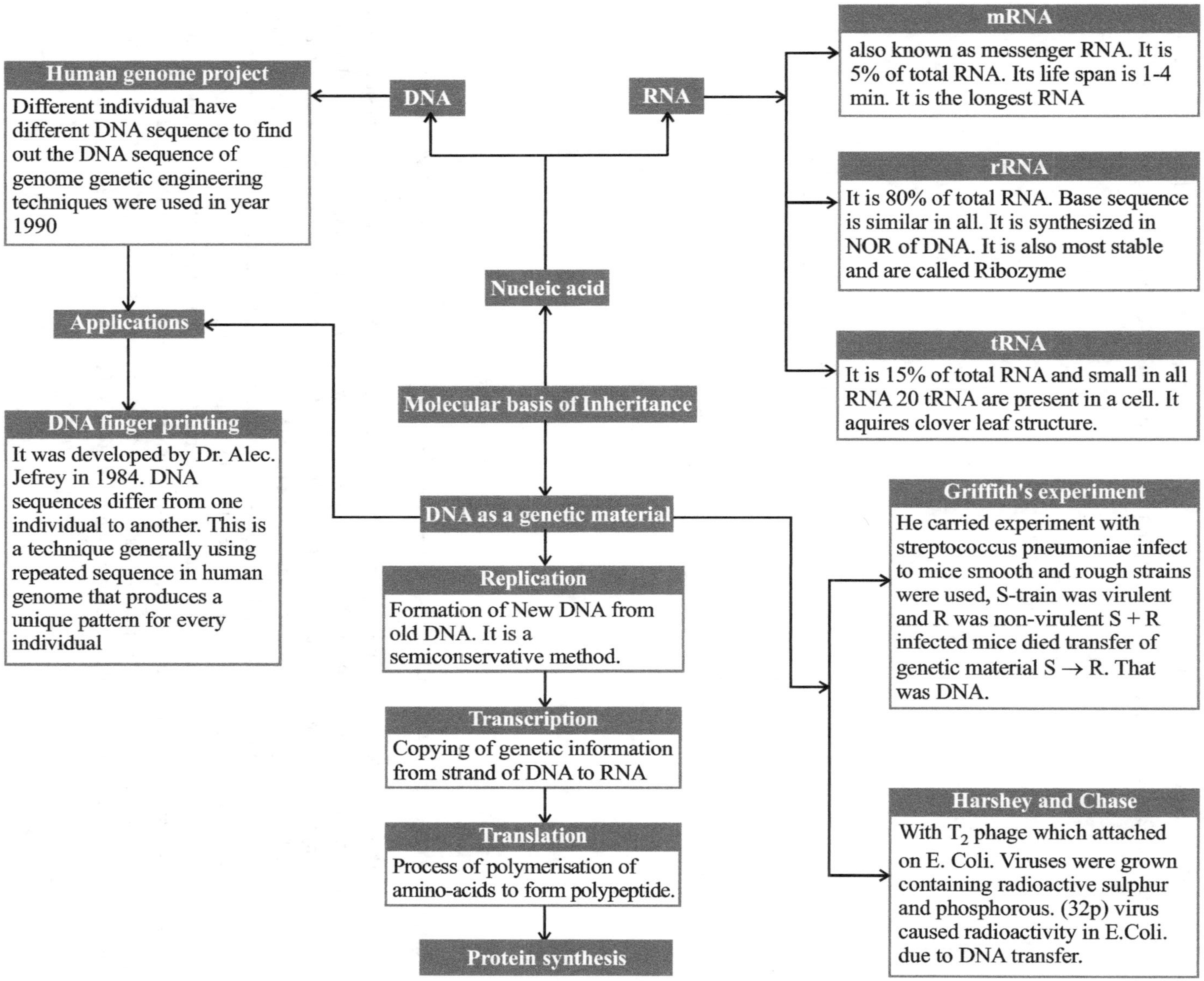

Topic 1   DNA, RNA as a Genetic Material

Genetic material is that subtance which not only control the formation and expression of traits in an organism but can replicate and pass on from a cell to its daughter cell or from one generation to next. Nucleic acids are the building blocks of genetic material. These are long polymers of nucleotides. DNA (deoxyribonucleic acid) and RNA (ribonucleic acids) are two types of nucleic acids, found in living systems. RNA is the main genetic material in retroviruses.

DNA (Deoxyribonucleic Acid)

DNA is a long chain polymer of deoxyribonucleotides. The length of DNA is defined as number of nucleotides present in it. This also is the characteristics of an organism. For example, a bacteriophage known as $\phi \times 174$ has 5386 nucleotides, bacteriophage lambda has 48502 base pair (bp), *Escherichia coli* has 4.6×10^6 bP, and haploid content of human DNA is 3.3×10^9 bp.

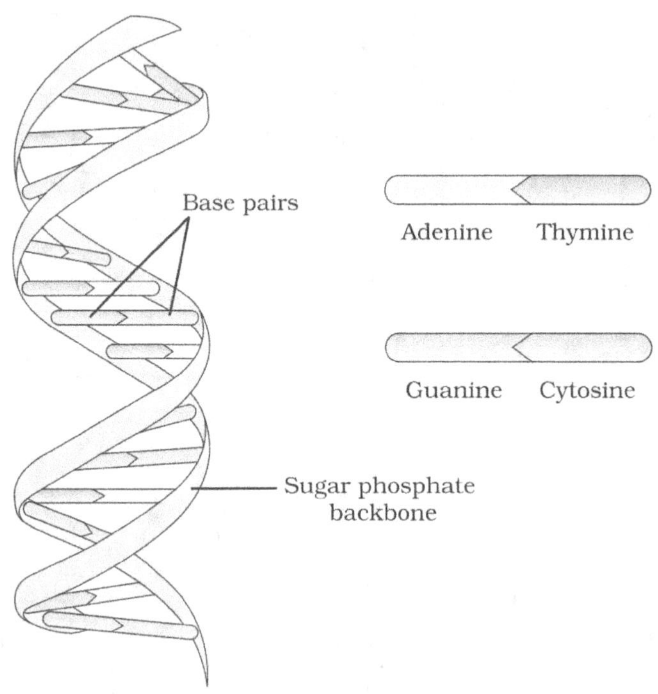

Fig. DNA double helix

Nucleotide is made up of 3 chemical groups $\rightarrow \underbrace{\text{A nitrogen base moiety} + \text{pentose sugar}}_{\text{Nucleoside}} + \text{phosphate group}$

Nitrogenous base are of two types – purines (9 membered double rings with nitrogen at 1, 3, 7 & 9th positions) and pyrimidines (6 membered rings with nitrogen at 1 and 3rd position). Purines are of two types – adenine (A) and guanine (G) and pyrimidines are of three types – thymine (T), cytosine (C) and uracil (U). A characteristics that differentiate DNA from RNA is that DNA contains all of the nitrogen bases except uracil and RNA contains all of the nitrogen bases except thymine. Pentose sugar is deoxyribose in DNA and ribose in RNA. Nucleotides constituting the DNA are called deoxyribonucleotides. Nitrogen base link to phosphate sugar through   N-glycoside linkage and form nucleotides. DNA molecule is composed of four types of nucleotides (AMP, GMP, CMP, TMP) The backbone of a DNA strand/chain is build up of alternate deoxyribose & phosphoric acid groups. The phosphate group is connected to carbon 5' of the sugar residue of its own nucleotide & carbon 3' of the sugar residue of the next nucleotide by phosphodiester bonds. Phosphate groups provides acidity to the nucleic acids because at least one of its side group is free to dissociate. Nitrogen bases lie at right angles to the longitudinal axis of the DNA chains.

DNA as acidic substance was discovered in nucleus by **Friedrich Meischer** in 1869 and called **nuclein**. **Wilkins-Franklin** carried out X ray diffraction (X-ray crystallography) on the basis of which **Watson and Crick** suggested 3-D structure of DNA in 1953. Normal DNA double helix is 20Å wide, has 10 bp in one complete turn of helix covering 34 Å in length and is called right handed B-DNA. When it is subjected to excess salt and relative humidity lower than 92%, it undergoes transition forming, A, C and D conformations. A-DNA has 11, C has 9.33 and D has 8 bp/turn of helix. The 2 strands of DNA double helix separate upon heating (around 80°C) due to breaking of H bonds between the strands. This phenomenon is called melting of DNA.

FEATURES OF 3-DIMENSIONAL DOUBLE HELICAL STRUCTURE OF DNA

DNA is composed of 2 strands wound around each other to form a double helix, with base inside and sugar phosphate backbone on outside. 2 DNA strands are organized in antiparallel and complementary arrangement [i.e., 2 strands run in opposite orientation (one in 5' – 3' and allies in 3' – 5')]. The bases of 2 strands form hydrogen bond with each other. Adenine pairs with thymine with 2 hydrogen bonds and guanine pairs with cytosine with three hydrogen bonds. A = T, G $\equiv$ C is called complementary base pairing that makes sequencing possible if template strand sequence is known. The helix is generally right handed i.e. its turn run clockwise looking along the helix axis. The pitch of helix is 3.4 nm (1 nm = 10^{-9}m) and there are 10bp in each turn. Distance between 2 bp in helix = 0.34 nm. where as diameter of helix is 20 Å. One base pair stacks one another in staircase arrangement that causes structural stability to helical structure.

G : C, A : T base pair form the most stable conformation both from steric considerations and from the point of view of maximizing hydrogen bond formation. **Erwin Chargaff** (1950) found that purine and pyrimidine content of DNA are equal. According to Chargaff the percentage of adenine (A) is equal to percentage of thymine (T) and the percentage of guanine (G) is equal to the percentage of cytosine (C). The percentage of A + G equals to 50% & the percentage of T + C equals to 50%. These relationships are called **Chargaffs' rule**.

Quantitatively A = T & C = G or $\dfrac{A}{T} = \dfrac{C}{G} = 1$. Chargaff rule also states that A + G = T + C or A + C = G + T.

The concept of central dogma in molecular biology was proposed by **Francis Crick** (1958). It proposes unidirectional or one way flow of information from DNA to RNA & then to protein.

$$\text{DNA} \xrightarrow{\text{Transcription}} \text{mRNA} \xrightarrow{\text{Translation}} \text{Polypeptide (protein)}$$

Temin reported that retroviruses or retro transposons operates a central dogma reverse flow of information or teminism inside the host cells in which the entire process is catalyzed by reverse transcriptase. This is represented as

$$\text{RNA} \longrightarrow \text{DNA} \longrightarrow \text{mRNA} \longrightarrow \text{Protein}$$

Packaging of DNA Nelix

The average distance between the two adjacent are pairs is 0.34 mm (0.34 × 10^{-9} m or 3.4 Å) The number of base pairs in Escherichia cali is 4.6 × 10^6. The total length of its DNA is 1.36 mm. Similarly, 6.6 × 10^9bp of two human genome i.e., diploid cell will have DNA length of 2.2 metres. The long sized DNA are accomodated in small areas (about 1 um in E.coli and 5 µ m nucleus in human being) only through packing or compaction. In prokaryotes DNA lies in cytoplasm. It is super coiled (coiled and recoiled) with the help of RNAs and non histone basic proteins like polyamines, The compacted mass of DNA is called nucleoid or prochromosome.

Eukaryotic DNA Packaging

DNA is organized into bead structure called **nucleosome**. There is a set of positively charged, basic proteins called **histones** which are rich in basic amino acids – lysine and arginine. They have positively charged side chains. Histones organize into unit of 8 molecules called histone octamer. Negatively charged DNA is wrapped around this positively charged octamer to form nucleosome. One histone octamer has 8 histones. DNA packaging is best explained by – **Solenoid model**. There are 5 classes of histone called H1, H2a, H2b, H3 and H4. Out of which whereas H1, H2a & H2b are rich in lysine and H3 & H4 are rich in arginine. Most conserved are histones H_3 and H_4, H_1 is least conserved. Four of than H_2A, H_2B, H_3 and H_4 occus in pairs. One nucleosome (DNA + histone octamer) attaches to other nucleosome with the help of linker DNA associated with H1 protein. Histone octamer has 2 molecule each of histone H2a, H2b, H3 and H4. DNA takes 1.8 left handed turns around octamer. Overall packaging solid is 7, which means DNA length is shortened about seven fold by winding around nucleosome.

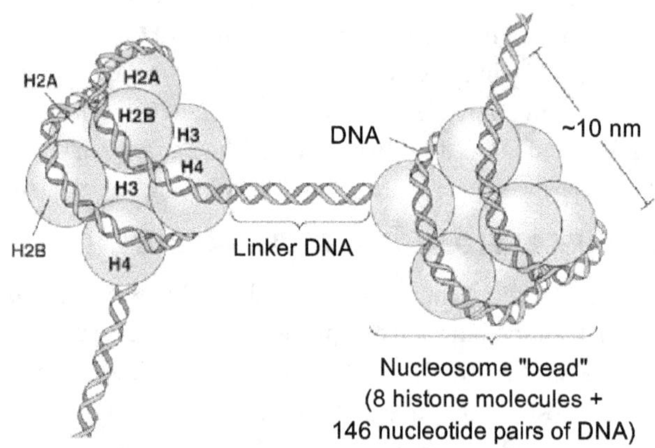

Fig. : Nucleosome structure

A typical nucleosome contains 200 bp of DNA helix. Nucleosome forms chromatin in the form of bead on string. Chromatin condense/super coil at metaphase stage to form chromosomes. Packaging of chromatin to chromosomes occurs with the help of additional set of proteins called NHC (non-histone chromosomal) proteins.

NHC are high molecular weight protein having amino acids - tyrosine & tryptophan. On the basis of packaging, chromatin is classified into 2 types – euchromatin and heterochromatin.

(1) Euchromatin

    (i)   Transcriptionally active.

    (ii) Loosely packed, rich in gene concentration.

    (iii) Lightly stained.

(2) Heterochromatin

    (i) Transcriptionally inactive.

    (ii) Densely packed.

    (iii) Darkly stained.

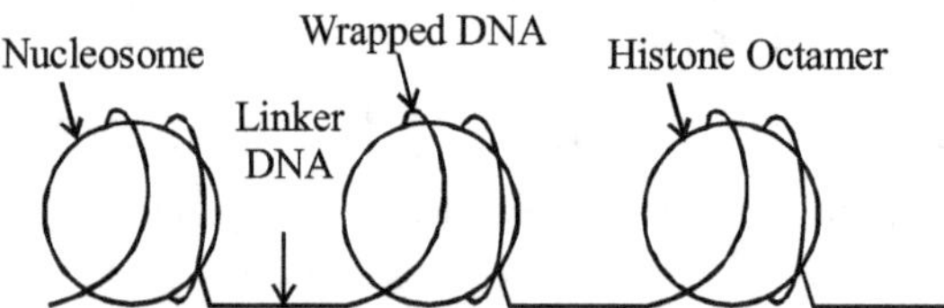

Fig. : Bead on a string-structure of chromatin

Order of packaging is as follows :

DNA → Histone Octamer → Nucleosome → 6 nucleosome → Solenoid → 7 solenoid → 30 nm fibre → Chromatin → Protein scaffold/nuclear matrix → Radial loops → packaging → Chromosome.

ESTABLISHMENT OF DNA AS GENETIC MATERIAL

Frederick Griffith (in 1928), a British Medical officer described the phenomenon of bacterial transformation. He carried out experiment with *Streptococcus pneumoniae* (bacterium causing pneumonia) which is used to infect mice. It has 2 types of colonies on culture plate – S (smooth due to mucous polysaccharide which makes it infective) and R (rough strain, mucous polysaccharide absent).

Steps of experiment are –

(i)   S strain (Virulent) → injected into mice → Mice die

(ii)   R strain (Non-virulent) → injected into mice → Mice survive

(iii) S strain (Heat killed) → injected into mice → Mice survive

(iv) S strain (Heat killed) + R strain (Live) → injected into mice → Mice die

By using S Strain (heat killed) and R strain (live) it was concluded that R strain has been transformed by some material of S strain which makes R strain virulent and enable to synthesize smooth polysachharide. This must be due to transfer of genetic material from S → R strain.

Establishment of Biochemical Nature of Transforming Genetic Material

Ostwald Avery, Colin Macleod and Mc Carty in 1933-34 revealed the chemical nature of the transforming substance to be DNA. They purified DNA, RNA, Protein from heat killed S strain to see which of them could transform R cells $\rightarrow$ S cells. They also observed that protein digesting enzyme (Protease) and RNA digesting (RNase) have no effect on transformation whereas digestion of DNA with DNase would not cause transformation. This finding established that transforming genetic material is DNA.

Hershey-Chase experiment

Hershey & Chase (1962) discovered that DNA is the genetic material of bacteriophage. Infection of bacteria with virus called bacteriophage. Hershey & Chase experimented with T_2 phage which attacks the bacterium *E. coli*. Some virus made to grow on culture containing radioactive sulphur and some on radioactive phosphorus. They have these finding :

(i) Virus $\rightarrow$ Radioactive phosphorus containing culture plate $\rightarrow$ Radioactive DNA
(ii) Virus $\rightarrow$ Radioactive sulphur containing culture plate $\rightarrow$ Radioactive protein coat.
(iii) Radioactively labelled sulphur virus $\rightarrow$ *E. coli* bacteria infection $\rightarrow$ No radioactivity in Bacteria
(iv) Radioactively labelled phosphorus virus $\rightarrow$ Infection of *E. coli* $\rightarrow$ Radioactivity in *E. coli*.

These findings indicated that protein did not enter the bacteria from the viruses but DNA from virus particle enters bacteria as genetic material because of which radioactivity is discovered in bacteria.

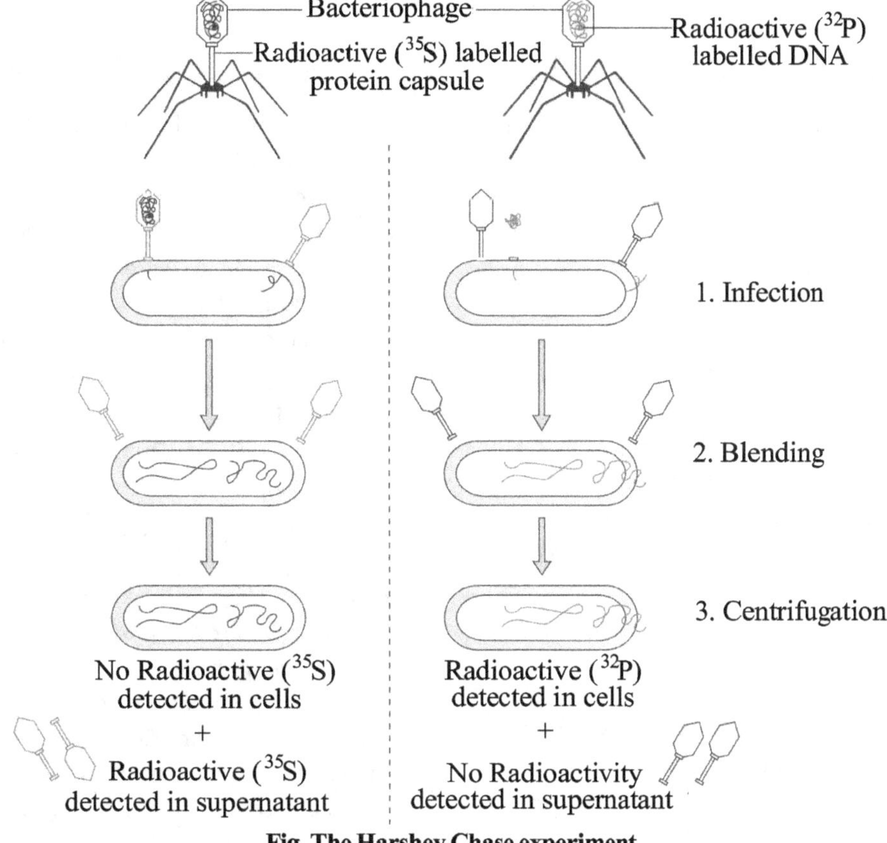

Fig. The Harshey Chase experiment

Properties of Genetic Material

Genetic material must fulfil the following criteria :
(i) Stably inheritable.
(ii) Chemically and structurally stablity.
(iii) Stably replicable (undergo replication).
(iv) Should undergo evolution (mutation/recombination/variation).
(v) Should follow Mendel's laws of inheritance.

Stability of DNA Over RNA

Base pairing/Stacking/Complementarity makes DNA structurally and chemically stable. Specificity of base pairing/denaturation – Separation of 2 DNA strands in heat conditions. renaturation – Restoring of DNA double strands in restored conditons. 2' OH group present at every nucleotide in RNA is reactive group which is prone to nucleophilic attack and makes RNA labile and unstable. RNA has been proved to work in enzymatic fashion – named as ribozyme, and hence proving it be to be more reactive. Presence of thymine instead of uracil in DNA makes it additionally stable, helping in DNA repair and making it suitable as genetic material. DNA is preferred for storage of genetic information and RNA is more suitable for transmission of genetic information in central dogma. First nucleic/genetic material from evolutionary point of view is thought to be RNA because

(i)   It is catalytic as ribozyme [catalyzing post transcriptional tRNA modifications]

(ii)   Self splicing intron I/III class.

(iii)   Single stranded and has 2' OH reactive group.

(iv)   Single stranded RNA could have given rise to double stranded DNA which is found to be more stable and less suspectible to mutation.

Practice Exercise-1

Multiple Choice Questions

1. The scientists involved in discovery of DNA as chemical basis of heredity were
    (a) Hershey and Chase
    (b) Griffith and Avery
    (c) Avery, Mac Leod and McCarty
    (d) Watson and Crick

2. Information flow or central dogma of modern biology is
    (a) RNA → Proteins → DNA
    (b) DNA → RNA → RNA
    (c) RNA → DNA → Proteins
    (d) DNA → RNA → Proteins

3. In Meselson and Stahl's experiments, heavy DNA was distinguished from normal DNA by centrifugation in
    (a) CsOH gradient
    (b) $^{14}NH_4Cl$
    (c) $^{15}NH_4Cl$
    (d) CsCl gradient

4. If a double stranded DNA has 20% of cytosine, what will be the percentage of adenine in it?
    (a) 20%   (b) 40%
    (c) 30%   (d) 60%

5. In some viruses, RNA is present instead of DNA indicating that
    (a) their nucleic acid must combine with host DNA before replication.
    (b) they cannot replicate.
    (c) there is no hereditary information.
    (d) RNA can act to transfer heredity.

Match the following

6. Match the column-I with column-II and select the correct combination from the given options.

	Column - I		Column - II
A.	Griffith	I.	Nucleoid
B.	Hershey and Chase	II.	Active chromatin
C.	Prokaryotic DNA	III.	Transduction
D.	Euchromatin	IV.	Transformation

(a) A – II; B – I; C – III; D – IV
(b) A – III; B – I; C – IV; D – II
(c) A – IV; B – III; C – I; D – II
(d) A – II; B – III; C – I; D – IV

Assertion & Reason Questions

DIRECTIONS (Qs. 7-10) : *Each of these questions contains an assertion followed by reason. Read them carefully and answer the question on the basis of following options. You have to select the one that best describes the two statements.*

(a) If both Assertion and Reason are correct and the Reason is a correct explanation of the Assertion.

(b) If both Assertion and Reason are correct but Reason is not a correct explanation of the Assertion.

(c) If the Assertion is correct but Reason is incorrect.

(d) If both Assertion and Reason are incorrect.

7. **Assertion :** DNA acts as the genetic material in most of the organisms.

    Reason : RNA though it also acts as a genetic material in some organisms, mostly functions as a messenger.

8.   **Assertion :** A bacteriophage known as $\phi \times 174$ has 5,386 nucleus, bacteriophage lambda has 48,502 base pairs (bp) and erichia coli has $4.6 \times 10_6$ bp.

   Reason : The diploid content of human DNA is 3.3×10^9 bp.

9.   **Assertion :** DNA as an acidic substance present in nucleus was first identified by Friedrich Meischer in 1869 and he named it as nuclein'.

   Reason : In 1953, James Watson and Francis Crick based on the X-ray diffraction data produced by Maurice Wilkins and Rosalind Franklin, proposed a very simple but famous Double Heli model for the structure of DNA.

10.   **Assertion :** According to the Chargaff's rule, for a double stranded DNA, the ratio between Adenine and Thymine and Guanine and Cytosine are constant and equals one.

   Reason : Both the DNA strands are said to be complementary to each other and therefore if the sequence of bases in one strand is known then the sequence in other strand can be predicted.

Passage/Case Based Questions

DIRECTIONS (Qs. 11-12) : *Read the following passage and answer the questions that follows.*

During an arguement between two biology students, Roamn said that during the course of evdution, DNA was choren over RNA because the former has stable structure and is less readive as compared to the later. Ajay was not convinced and said that RNA was the first genetic material in organism.

11.   Give an evidence that RNA was the first genetic material.

12.   Do human contains RNA ? If yes, mention its function

Very Short Answer Questions

13.   Difference between DNA and RNA.
14.   Define nucleosome.
15.   What is base pairing rule of Watson and Crick model ?
16.   What are raw materials for DNA synthesis ?
17.   What is proof reading in DNA synthesis ?
18.   Define genetic material.
19.   How is first ribonucleotide different from others in RNA chain?
20.   What is satellite DNA?

Short Answer Questions

21.   Why mRNA is called heterogenous RNA (hnRNA) ?
22.   Why, a base pairing is always between certain purine and pyrimidine ?
23.   How the double helical model of DNA discovered?
24.   How the nitrogenous bases are paired in DNA?
25.   What do you understand by antiparallel DNA strands ?

Topic 2   Replication, Transcription and Translation 

REPLICATION

DNA replication or DNA synthesis is the process of copying a double stranded DNA prior to cell division. Semiconservative replication of chromosome was found by Taylor (1957) in *Vicia Faba* using ir-radiated thymidine. Replication of DNA is found to be semiconservative and its experimental proof has been provided by Meselson and Stahl by conducting following experiment :

(i)   Culturing *E.coli* for many generations in N^{15} containing culture.

(ii) N^{15} was incorporated as nitrogenous base in newly synthesized DNA.

(iii)   Heavy DNA separated from normal by centrifugation in CsCl (cesium chloride) density gradient.

(iv)   Culturing of DNA from *E.coli* cells having N^{15} in medium with N^{14}.

(v)   Extraction of DNA from *E.coli* cells in step (d) and to measure density of ds DNA in CsCl centrifugation.

(vi)   Cycles repeated for another 40 minutes in normal culture.

Results of Experiment :

Meselson and Stahl were able to extract the bacterial DNA and centrifuge it in caesium chloride solution. Depending on the mass of the molecule, the DNA would settle out at a particular point in the tube. The 15N bacteria were then transferred to a growth medium containing the normal, lighter isotope of nitrogen, 14N have they reproduced by cell division. Extracts of DNA from the first generation off spring were shown to have a lower density, since half the DNA was made up of the original stand containing 15N and the other half was made up of the new stand containing 14N. At succeeding generation times, the DNA extracts were formed to have a lower proportion of 15N as more 14N was incorporated into the bacterial DNA. This was the conclusive evidence for the semi conservative method of DNA replication.

DNA extracted after recycling of procedure produced 2 types of DNA– hybrid and light.

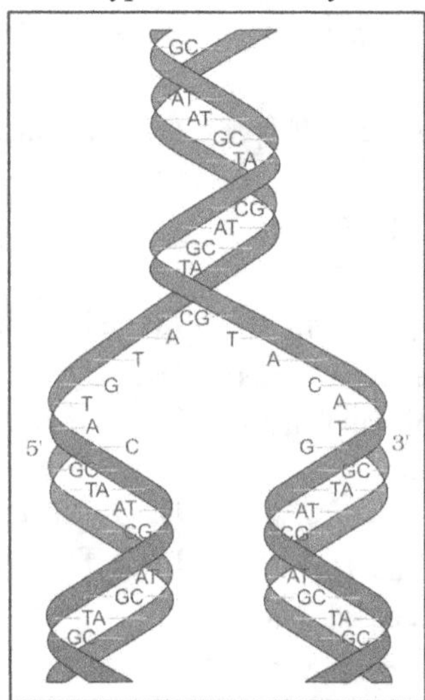

**Fig. Watson Crick model
for semiconservative DNA replication**

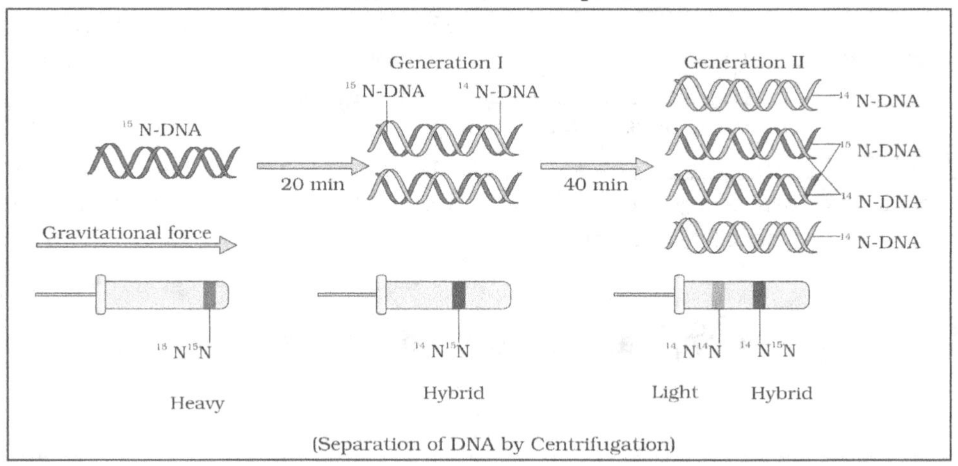

Fig. Messelson and Stahl's Experiment

Mechanism of DNA Replication

(i)   DNA polymerase is responsible for the template directed polymerisation of deoxyribonucleotide triphosphate. It is of 3 types :
    (a)   DNA polymerase I – DNA synthesis in $5' \rightarrow 3'$ direction + $3' \rightarrow 5'$ and $5' \rightarrow 3'$ exonuclease activity.
    (b)   DNA polymerase II – Catalyze $5' \rightarrow 3'$ synthesis + $3' \rightarrow 5'$ exonuclease activity.
    (c)   DNA polymerase III – DNA repair after replication completes.

(ii)   DNA polymerase I from *E.coli* catalyzes the stepwise addition of deoxyribonucleotides to 3' OH end of DNA chain.
    $(DNA)_n$ residues + dNTP $\rightarrow (DNA)_{n+1}$ + PPi.

Requirements of Enzyme are

(i)   All four dNTPs (dATP, dGTP, dTTP and dCTP), Mg^{2+}.
(ii)   DNA template to be copied by DNA polymerase.
(iii)   A primer with a free 3' OH end that enzyme can be extended by enzyme.

Steps of Replication

(i)   DNA replication occurs during S phase of cell cycle and require template and DNA polymerase along with primer.
(ii)   DNA double helix is unwound by helicase enzyme and single stranded (ss) DNA is stabilized by SSB-single stranded binding protein.

(iii)   DNA topoisomerase I allows the helix to unwind without causing extensive rotation of the chromosome.

(iv)   DNA topoisomerase II separates the 2 daughter DNA circles following replication.

(v)   DNA replication begins at a specific site called ori (origin) which has recognition site for DNA polymerase, which also provides site for attachment of RNA primer.

(vi)   The enzyme which form RNA from DNA are called RNA polymerase. The synthesis of RNA primer is brought about by enzyme primase.

(vii)   In bacterial chromosome, replication starts at a single origin and both strands of a double helix serve as template for DNA synthesis which proceeds outwards in both directions from single origin (i.e., it is bidirectional).

(viii)   Region of DNA undergoing replication forms replication bubble/replication eye having 2 replicating forks moving in opposite direction around DNA circle.

(ix)   dsDNA is antiparallel, one strand runs in 5'-3' direction and its complementary runs in 3'-5'. New DNA strand is made against each template strand. DNA polymerase makes DNA only in 5'-3' direction. So are template strand with 3'-5' orientation, new DNA strand is made in continuous piece in correct 5'-3' direction. This DNA is called **leading strand**.

(x)   On template strand which has 5' → 3' orientation, DNA polymerase synthesizes short pairs of new DNA (about 1000 nucleotide long) in 5' → 3' direction and then joins these piece together. These small fragments are called **okazaki fragments** and new DNA strand made in this discontinuous manner is called **lagging strand**. Okazaki fragments are joined by means of DNA ligase.

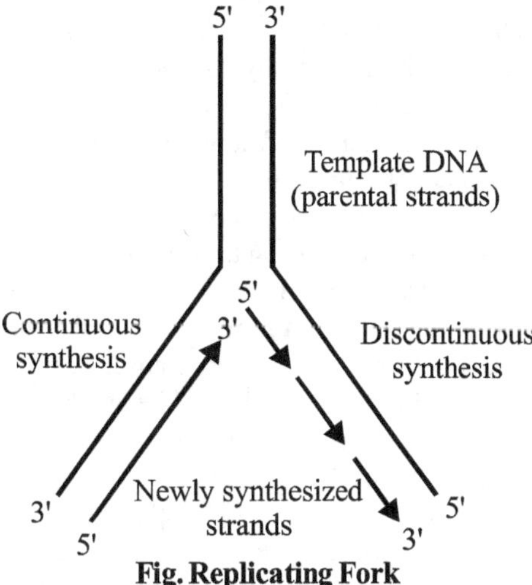

Fig. Replicating Fork

TRANSCRIPTION

Process of copying genetic information from one strand of DNA to RNA is called **transcription**. At a time only one DNA strand is being transcribed into RNA. The strand of DNA with polarity 3' → 5' act as template strand and the DNA strand with polarity 5' → 3' act as coding strand.

e.g.   3' – ATGCATGCATGCATGC – 5' → template strand.

5' – TACGTACGTACGTACG – 3' → coding strand.

Transcription is carried out by DNA dependent RNA polymerase. Transcription unit is the segment of deoxyribonucleic acid between the sites of initiation & termination of transcription. Transcription unit has 3 regions in the DNA.

(i)   A promoter – where RNA polymerase binds.

(ii)   A structural gene – which will undego transcription.

(iii)   A terminator – a site where transcription will end.

In eukaryotes, the RNA produced originally is processed (by splicing) to produce mRNA, segments of gene represented in mRNA are called **exons** whereas the ones not represented is called **introns**. Introns usually contains palindromic base sequence and constitutes junk/satellite DNA.

Gene : A gene is defined as the functional unit of inheritance. DNA sequence coding for a polypeptide is a cistron. Structural gene that codes for one polypeptide as in eukaryotes is called **monocistronic**. Structural gene that codes for more than one polypeptide as in prokaryotes is called **polycistronic**.

Split gene : Structural gene that has coding/expressed sequences called exons alternating with intervening sequences called introns are called spilt genes eg. eukaryotic genes.

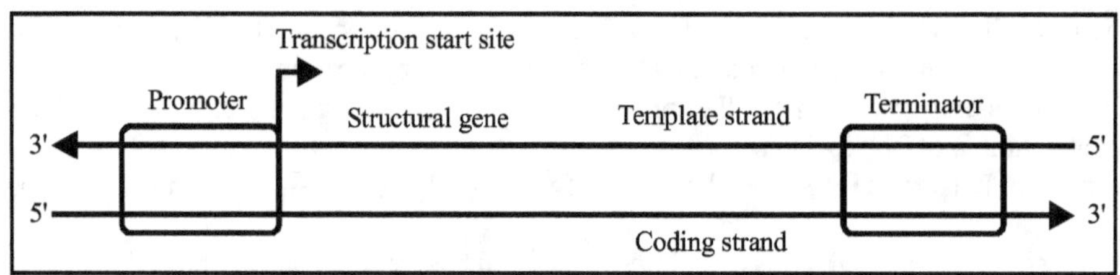

Fig. Schematic structure of a transcription unit

Types of RNA & Process of Transcription

Ribonucleic and (RNA) was the first genetic material. It is a non hereditary nucleic acid except in some viruses (retro viruses). RNA is a polymer of ribonucleotide & is made up of pentose ribose sugar, phosphoric acid & nitrogenous base (A, U, C, G). The 2' OH group of ribonucleotides is a reactive group, that makes RNA as a catalyst. It is evident that essential life process such as metabolism, translation, splicing etc, have evolved around RNA, even before DNA has evolved as a genetic material. In RNA also, each nucleotide has three components as in DNA. The nitrogen bases are of two types: -

Purines — (Adenine and Guanine)

Pyrimidines — (Cytosine and uracil)

The sugar is ribose which has an additional OH group on the 2' – position. The nucleosides and nucleotides are called ribonucleosides and ribonucleotides respectively. The RNA may be mainly of two types – genetic & non-genetic. **Genetic RNA** are seen in most of the plant viruses & some animal viruses. The genetic RNA carries the genetic message and is capable of self replication. It is called RNA dependent RNA synthesis. On the basis of molecular size & function, three forms of non genetic RNA are :

(i)   mRNA (messenger RNA) – provides template for translation.

(ii)   tRNA (transfer RNA) – brings aminoacids and reads genetic code.

(iii)   rRNA (ribosomal RNA) – structural and catalytic role during translation.

RNA processing : In prokaryotes, mRNA transcribed from protein coding genes requires no modification prior to translation. In fact, many mRNA molecules begin to translate even before RNA synthesis has finished. Ribosomal RNA (rRNA) and transfer RNA (tRNA) are synthesized as precursor molecule that do not require post-transcriptional processing.

RNA transcription requires enzyme RNA polymerase, DNA template, all four types of ribonucleoside triphosphates (ATP, GTP, CTP and UTP), divalent metal ions Mg^{2+} or Mn^{2+} as cofactor, rho (ρ) factor etc. RNA polymerase can initiate transcription at specific DNA sequences known as promoters. It then produces an RNA chain which is complementary to the DNA strand used as template. RNA polymerase has five polypeptides – σ, β, β', α and ω. Chain of β, β', α & ω constitute the core enzyme. σ or sigma factor recognises the promoter region while the remaining core enzymes takes part in transcription. Rho factor helps in elongation and termination of the RNA synthesis. Core enzyme contains polymerization catalytic unit within β subunit. The first nucleotide in RNA transcript is usually pppG and pppA. RNA polymerase then synthesize rRNA in 5' → 3' direction, using ATP, CTP, GTP, UTP as precursor.

Transcription Bubble :

(i)   Region of unwound DNA undergoing transcription.

(ii)   RNA transcript forms a transient DNA-RNA hybrid then pulls away from template as transcription proceeds.

(iii)   DNA is wound ahead of transcription bubble and after the transcription complex has passed, DNA rewinds.

Transcription continues till a termination sequence in form of GC rich/palindromic region is reached. DNA made from this palindrome is self complementary and basepair internally to form hairpin structure. Termination sequence is located downstream/towards 3' end of coding strand.

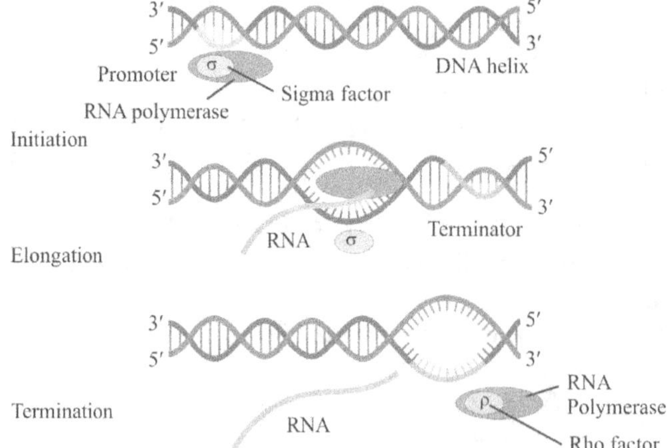

Fig. Process of Transcription in Bacteria

Differences between Prokaryotic and Eukaryotic Transcription

RNA Polymerase of one type in prokaryotes coding for all 3 types of RNA. RNA polymerase are of 3 types –

RNA Polymerase I → transcribes rRNA (28S, 18S, 5.8S)

RNA Polymerase II → transcribes mRNA (hnRNA-Heterogenous RNA)

RNA Polymerase III → transcribes tRNA, 5S rRNA and SnRNA (small nuclear RNAs)

Transcription and translation takes place in same compartment (there is no separate cytosol and nucleus in bacteria). So transcription and translation are coupled in bacteria where as in eukaryotes transcription and translation occur in nucleus and cytosol respectively and thus compartmentalized. RNA produced in bacteria/prokaryotes do not undergo extensive processing whereas pre mRNA, rRNA and tRNA in eukaryotes undergo extensive processing.

In prokaryotes : No splitting event takes place. But in eukaryotes – primary transcript has both exons and introns and introns are non functional. Now it is subjected to process called splicing where introns are removed and exons are joined in defined manner.

Capping : All unusual nucleotide (methyl guanosine triphosphate) is added to 5' end of hnRNA.

Tailing : Adenylate residues [200-300] are added at 3' end of a template in independent manner. It is fully processed hnRNA, now called mRNA which is transported out of nucleus for translation.

RNA splicing : Intron sequences are removed by process known as splicing and ligates the ends of exon sequences together.

RNA editing : The sequence of an mRNA molecule may be changed after synthesis and processing by RNA editing.

Example : In *Trypanosoma* mitochondrial RNA, half of uridines in final mRNA are acquired after editing.

Table : Difference in prokaryotic and Eukoyti type of transcription

	Prokaryotic transcription	Eukaryotic transcription
1.	It occurs in contact with cytoplasm	It occurs inside the nucleus.
2.	There is no specific period for its occurrence	Major part of transcription occurs in G1 and G2 phases.
3.	It is coupled to translation	Transcription and translation are spacially separated.
4.	Products of transcription become effective	Products of transcription come out of the nucleus for functioning in cytoplasm.
5.	There is only one RNA polymerase	There are three types of RNA polymerase
6.	RNA polymerase does not have separate transcription factors.	Transcription factors are involved in recognition of promotor site
7.	mRNA is generally polycistronic	mRNA is generally monocistronic
8.	Splicing is generally not required	In most of the cases splicing is required for removing intervening sequences.

GENETIC CODE

Transfer of genetic information from a polymer of nucleotides to a polymer of amino acids is called translation.. This is accomplished with the help of genetic code which is row of three consecutive nucleotides – coding for 20 amino acids. Codon exists on mRNA, corresponding anticodon on tRNA and protein synthesis and elongation occurs in rRNA.

Salient Features of Genetic Code are –

(i) **Triplet nature :** 64 possible codons are there. 61 code for 20 amino acids and 3 do not code for any amino acid. These are called **stop codon – UAA, UAG, UGA.**

(ii) **Start codon :** These are codons which code for initiating amino acid for protein chain. **AUG** codes for methionine. It is first codon to be read by ribosome in mRNA.

(iii) **Degeneracy of codon :** One amino acid is coded by several codons. As a result of degeneracy, a mutation that changes only a single nucleotide in DNA, changes a single nucleotide in corresponding mRNA, has no effect on amino acid sequence of the encoded polypeptide.

(iv) **Wobble position :** During protein synthesis, each codon is recognized by a triplet of base, called anticodon, in a specific tRNA molecule. Each base in codon pairs with its complementary base in anticodon. However, the pairing of 3rd base of codon is less stringent than rest of 2 bases. This 3rd position is called wobble position.

(v) **Universality of code :** All living organism use the same code except some mitochondrial mRNA codons.

(vi) **Reading frame :** Since the sequence of mRNA molecule is read in group of three nucleotides [codon] from 5' end, it can be read in three possible reading frame. Usually there is only one reading frames include several termination (stop) codons.

First Position →   Second Position   ← Third Position

	U	C	A	G	
U	UUU Phe UUC Phe UUA Leu UUG Leu	UCU Ser UCC Ser UCA Ser UCG Ser	UAU Tyr UAC Tyr UAA Stop UAG Stop	UGU Cys UGC Cys UGA Stop UGG Trp	U C A G
C	CUU Leu CUC Leu CUA Leu CUG Leu	CCU Pro CCC Pro CCA Pro CCG Pro	CAU His CAC His CAA Gin CAG Gin	CGU Arg CGC Arg CGA Arg CGG Arg	U C A G
A	AUU Ile AUC Ile AUA Ile AUG Met	ACU Thr ACC Thr ACA Thr ACG Thr	AAU Asn AAC Asn AAA Lys AAG Lys	AGU Ser AGC Ser AGA Arg AGG Arg	U C A G
G	GUU Val GUC Val GUA Val GUG Val	GCU Ala GCC Ala GCA Ala GCG Ala	GAU Asp GAC Asp GAA Glu GAG Glu	GGU Gly GGC Gly GGA Gly GGG Gly	U C A G

Fig. : The Codons for the various Amino Acids

Reading frame 1 : UUA UGA GCG CUA AAC – Not possible
               Leu Stop* Ala Leu Asn

Reading frame 2 : U UAU GAG CGC UAA AU – Not possible
                 Tyr Glu Arg Stop*

Reading frame 3 : UU AUG AGC GCU AAA U – Produces functional protein
                 Met Ser Ala Lys

(vii) **Overlapping genes :** Usually one sequence of base encodes only a single protein, however in some bacteriophage DNA, genes overlap, with each gene being in a different reading frame. This is overlapping gene.

(viii) **Open reading frame :** DNA sequence that has run of codon starting with codon ATG and ending with TGA, TAA, TAG. These runs of codons are called ORF and they identify coding regions.

(ix) **Continuity of codons :** Codons are read in mRNA in a continuous fashion, there are no punctuations.

(x) **Specificity of codon :** One codon codes for only one amino acid.

Genetic code was deciphered by many researches such as Khorana, Nirenberg and Mothali. Out of 64 codons, UAA, UAG and UGA are chain termination codons and as they do not code for any amino acid, so also called non sense codons. Genetic code is continuous, commaless, degenerate, triplet with third position being wobble and specific.

tRNA : The Adapter Molecule

tRNA is intermediate between reading of codons on mRNA and formation of amino acid chain for protein. tRNA is also called adaptor or supernatant RNA, soluble RNA (sRNA). Adapter role was assigned to tRNA by **Francis Crick**. The first person to determine the base seguance of a tRNA molecule was Robert Kolley. tRNA has 4 arms, folded into clover leaf like structure and amino acid acceptor branch. Clover leaf 2° structure is due to internal base pairing.

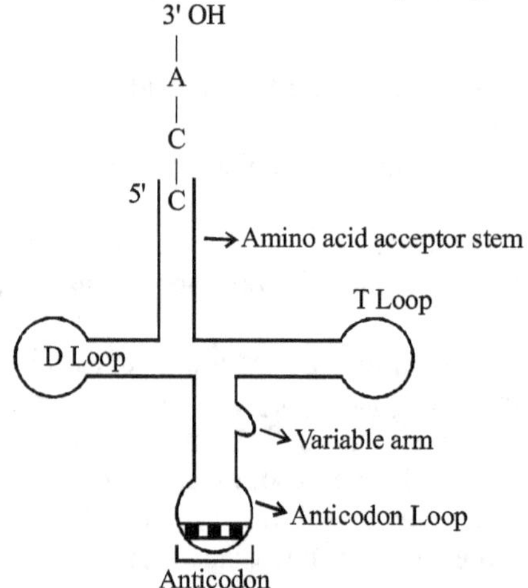

Fig. : Structure of t-RNA

Structure of tRNA :

(i) **Anticodon arm** contains in its loop 3 nucleotides of anticodon which will form base pair with complementary codon in mRNA during translation.

(ii) **D/DHU arm** with **D loop** contains dihydrouracil – an unusual pyrimidine.

(iii) **T/T$_\psi$ C arm :** Pseudouracil (ψ) in sequence T ψ C.

(iv) **Variable/arm :** With 3-21 nucleotide.

(v) **Amino acid acceptor stem :** Site where amino acid attaches at 3'OH group of 3'-CCA sequence.

3 D structure of tRNA was proposed by **S. H. Kim** in 1973. tRNA helps to transport amino acids from the surrounding cytoplasm to the site of protein synthesis.

TRANSLATION

The process of decoding of the message from mRNA to protein with the help of tRNA, ribosome and enzyme is called translation (protein synthesis). The main step in protein synthesis are **activation, initiation, elongation & termination** of polypeptide chain. During translation, mRNA is read in 5' → 3' direction and aminoacyl tRNA carry specific amino acid and recognises the corresponding codons in tRNA with amino acid. It requires ATP activate tRNA and form aminoacyl tRNA.

Initiation of Protein Synthesis :

It requires initation factors. Prokaryotes has 70 S ribosome and eukaryotes has 80 S ribosome. Each ribosome has 3 binding sites for tRNA :

A site – Incoming amino acyl tRNA binds.

P site – tRNA linked to growing polypeptide chain is bound.

E site – Which bind diacylated tRNA to be release from ribosome.

Steps :

(i) Formation of initiation complex 30 S ribosome + mRNA + initiation factors + tRNA → initiator charged

(ii) Addition of 80 S ribosomal sub unit

(iii) tRNA is base paired to AUG initiator codon (start codon) at P site.

Elongation :

Amino acyl tRNA binding : Acylated tRNA corresponding to 2nd codon binds to A site as ribosome in presence of elongation factor, using GTP.

Peptide bond formation : Formation of peptide bond between C terminal of amino acyl tRNA at **P** site and amino acyl tRNA at **A site**.

Translocation : Deacyclated tRNA moves from P → E site. Dipeptidyl tRNA moves A → P site. Ribosome moves along mRNA for next codons in A site.

> A = Acceptor site
> P = Peptidyl site
> E = Exit site

The cycle is repeated till all the codon have been exposed to A-site. The tRNA released comes back to cytoplasm to pick up another amino acid.

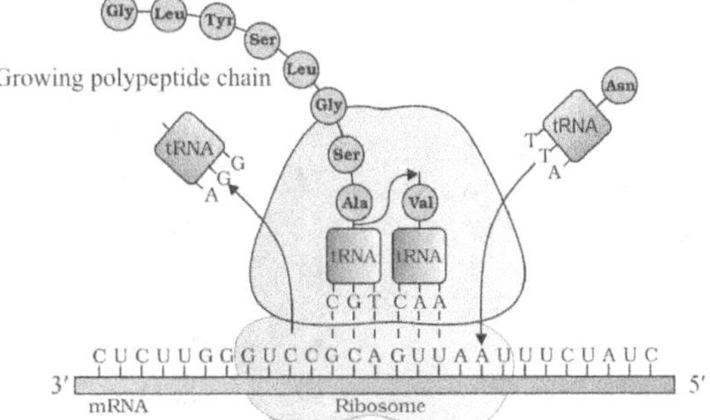

Fig. Translation

Termination

When one of 3 termination/stop codons [UAG, UAA and UGA] are positioned in A site, for which there are no tRNA, termination of translation occurs in presence of release factor (RF) which causes cleaving of bond between polypeptide and tRNA in P site. Polypeptide leaves ribosome followed by mRNA and now tRNA ready to start next cyle of translation. Ribosomes attached to RER synthesize proteins which are translocated through the lumen of ER. After synthesis the protein may be incorporated in membrane or may be secreted from the cell.

Practice Exercise-2

Multiple Choice Questions

1. Genetic code is
   (a) triplet, universal, ambiguous and degenerate.
   (b) triplet, universal, non-ambiguous and non-degenerate.
   (c) triplet, universal, non-ambiguous and degenerate.
   (d) triplet, universal, ambiguous and non-degenerate.

2. Which one of the following group of codons is called as degenerate codons?
   (a) UAA, UAG and UGA
   (b) GUA, GUG, GCA, GCG and GAA
   (c) UUC, UUG, CCU, CAA and CUG
   (d) UUA, UUG, CUU, CUC, CUA and CUG

3. A DNA strand with the sequence AACGTAACG is transcribed. What is the sequence of the mRNA molecule synthesized ?
   (a) AACGTAACG
   (b) UUGCAUUGC
   (c) AACGUAACG
   (d) TTGCATTGC

Match the following

4. Match the codons given column I with their respective amino acids given in column II and choose the correct answer.

Column-I (Codons)		Column-II (Amino acids)
A.	UUU	I. Serine
B.	GGG	II. Methionine
C.	UCU	III. Phenylalanine
D.	CCC	IV. Glycine
E.	AUG	V. Proline

   (a) A – III; B – IV; C – I; D – V; E – II
   (b) A – III; B – I; C – IV; D – V; E – II
   (c) A – III; B – IV; C – V; D – I; E – II
   (d) A – II; B – IV; C – I; D – V; E – III

5. Match the enzymes (given in column I) with their function (given in column II) and choose the correct combination from the given options.

Column-I		Column-II
A.	Helicase	I. Joining of nucleotides
B.	Gyrase	II. Opening of DNA
C.	Primase	III. Unwinding of DNA
D.	DNA polymerase III	IV. RNA priming

   (a) A – II; B – I; C – III; D – IV
   (b) A – II; B – I; C – IV; D – III
   (c) A – IV; B – III; C – I; D – II
   (d) A – II; B – III; C – IV; D – I

Assertion & Reason Questions

DIRECTIONS (Qs. 6-9) : *Each of these questions contains an assertion followed by reason. Read them carefully and answer the question on the basis of following options. You have to select the one that best describes the two statements.*

   (a) If both Assertion and Reason are correct and the Reason is a correct explanation of the Assertion.
   (b) If both Assertion and Reason are correct but Reason is not a correct explanation of the Assertion.
   (c) If the Assertion is correct but Reason is incorrect.
   (d) If both Assertion and Reason are incorrect.

6. **Assertion :** During DNA replication, both the parental strands as template for the synthesis of new daughter strands.
   Reason : The Okazaki fragments are formed on the parent? which runs in 5' → 3' direction and proves discontinuous? synthesis.

7. **Assertion :** A transcription unit in DNA is defined primarily by three regions in the DNA, viz, a promoter, the structural and a terminator.
   Reason : The promoter is located towards 5' end of the structural gene and it is a DNA sequence that provides binding site DNA polymerase.

8. **Assertion :** The process of translation requires transfer of genetic information from a polymer of nucleotides to a polymer of amino acids.
   Reason : Har Gobind Khorana synthesised RNA molecules with defined combination of bases, viz, homopolymers and copolymers.

9. **Assertion :** In capping, an unusual nucleotide (methyl guanosine triphosphate) is added to the 5' end of hnRNA and this step is catalysed by the enzyme guanyl transferase.
   Reason : In trailing, 20-30 adenylate residues are added at 3' end in a template independent manner and it is catalysed by the enzyme poly A polymerase.

Very Short Answer Questions

10. What is function of tRNA ?
11. How many bases code for one amino acid ?
12. A polypeptide of 600 amino acids will be coded by how many bases of mRNA ?
13. Out of 64 possible codon, how many are start and stop codons ?
14. If sequence of codon of mRNA is CGU, CGC, CGA, CGG, AGA, AGG give DNA sequence for it.
15. Are there any base triplet that code for amino acid and also start signal ? Name them.
16. What is a transcription unit ?
17. What are 2 functions of DNA polymerase ?
18. Where and when does replication occur ?
19. In which directions leading and lagging strand synthesized?
20. What does the Association of a m-RNA with several ribosonues is called?

Short Answer Questions

21. What is significance of mutation?
22. Give reason why genetic codes are triplet code ?

23. How does RNA polymerase bind to DNA during transcription ?

24. Why replication of DNA in eukaryotes starts at many points of origin and in both direction ?

25. Certain mutations are called silent mutation. Why?

26. Why 3rd base in codon is called wobble position?

27. What are the functions of mRNA and tRNA ? Which anticodons will be required to recognize following codons?

   (i)   AAU   (ii)   UAU
   (iii) CGA   (iv) GCA

28. Certain molecular processes are given in column (A) Give the term to these processes in column (B) after selecting them from the following terms: Recombination, gene regulation, prokaryotic, transcription, eukaryotic transcription, translation, replication, gene transfer, DNA fingerprinting

Column A	Column B
(i) DNA ⟶ DNA	
(ii) DNA ⟶ hnDNA	
(iii) mRNA ⟶ Protein	
(iv) Repressor protein + Operator ⟶ No transcription	

29. What do you understand by degeneracy of genetic code?

Topic 3   Regulation of gene Expression

REGULATION OF GENE EXPRESSION

Gene expression is the mechanism at the molecular level by which a gene is able to express itself in the phenotype of an organisms. In eukaryotes, the regulation could be exerted at–

(i) Transcriptional level (formation of primary transcript).

(ii) Processing level (RNA splicing) level.

(iii) Transport of mRNA from nucleus to cytoplasm.

(iv) Translational level.

Mostly genes are regulated at transcriptional level. Many protein coding genes in bacteria are regulated together in operon which serve as transcriptional unit that are coordinately regulated.

GENE EXPRESSION IS OF THREE TYPES :

Inducible, constitutive and repressible. Regulation can also be under negative or positive control. The genes in a cell are expressed to perform a particular function or a set of functions. For example if an enzyme called betagalactosidase is synthesised by *E. Coli* it is used to catalyse the hydrolysis of a disaccharide, lactose into galactose and glucose, the bacteria use them as a source. of energy. Hence, if the bacteria do not have lactose around them to be utilised for energy source, they would no longer require the synthesis of the enzyme betagalactosidase. Therefore, in simple terms it is the metabolic, physiological or environmental conditions that regulate the expression of genes. The development and differentiation of embryo into adult organisms are also a result of the coordinated regulation of expression of several sets of genes. One of the best studied example of gene expression is **lac operon**. Model of lac operon was suggested by Jacob and Monod in 1961.

Inducible enzyme

E.coli makes little of these 3 enzymes. However when lactose is available, it causes a large and coordinated increase in amount of each enzyme. Thus each enzyme is called inducible enzyme and process is called induction. Inducer is an metabolizable compound that turns on transcription of inducible gene. Operons are segments of genetic material (DNA) which function as regulated units or unit that can be switched on or switched off. In lac operon, a polycistronic structural gene is regulated by a common promoter & regulatory genes.

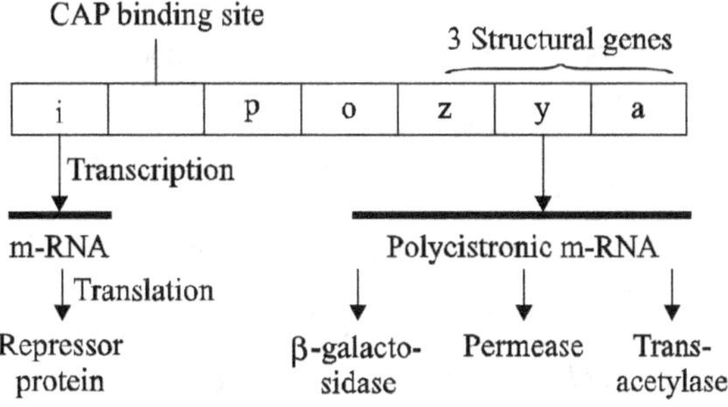

It consists of one regulatory gene (the i gene) & three structural genes (*Z, Y & A*). The i gene codes for the repressor of the lac operon. Structural genes produces 3 enzymes for the degradation of lactose to glucose & galactose. *Z* produces β-galactosidase for splitting lactose into glucose & galactose. Y-produces β-galactoside permease (membrane bound proteins) which is required in entry of the lactose/galactose. A produces β-galactoside transacetylase enzyme that transfers an acetyl group from acetyl CoA to β-galactosides. **Structural genes** are genes that code for the primary structure of proteins/enzyme to be regulated.

Operator gene : DNA sequence that regulates transcription of the structural genes.

Regulator gene : Encodes a protein that recognizes operon sequence.

Mechanism of Regulation of Lac Operon

Few molecules of β-galactosidase in cell before induction converts lactose to allolactose which turns on transcription of these three genes in the lac operon. Allolactose is an inducer for the lac operon model. The repressor of operon is synthesized from I gene. The repressor protein binds to operator region of the operon and prevents RNA polymerase from transcribing the operon. Transcription and formation of mRNA occurs in absence of repressor and presence of inducer (Lactose). RNA polymerase binds at the promotor region that lies upstream of structural genes. Regulation of the operon by repressor is called as **negative regulation** as it decreases expression of structural gene. **Positive control** of gene expression is when the regulatory protein binds to DNA and increases rate of transcription. In this case the regulating protein is called an activator.

HUMAN GENOME PROJECT (HGP)

HGP established whole genome of human with the help of genetic engineering techniques, cloning techniques and bioinformatics. It was an ambitious international project which began in 1990. The goal of projects are :

(i)   To develop ways of mapping the human genome at increasing fine level of expression.

(ii)   To store this information in database and develop tools for data analysis.

(iii)   To address the ethical, legal and social issues [ELSI] that may arise from the project.

This was project coordinated by U.S. Department of Energy and National Institute of Health. The Wellcome trust (U.K.) became a major partner with contribution from Japan, France, Germany, China and others.

SALIENT FEATURES OF HUMAN GENOME

(i)   The human genome contains 3164.7 millions of nucleotides (bp).

(ii)   The size of the genes varies an everage gene consists of 3000 bases, while the largest gous days trophin cainsts of 2.4 million bases.

(iii)   The total number of genes is estimated at 30,000 and 99.9% of the nucleotides are the some in all humans.

(iv)   The functions of over 50% of the discovered genes are not known.

(v)   Only less than 2% of the genome codes for proteins.

(vi)   Repetitive sequences make up a large portion of the human genome.

(vii)   Repetitive sequences throw light on chromosome structive dynamics and Evolution, though they are thought to have no direct coding functions.

(viii) Chromosome No. 1 has 2968 genes (the maximum) and the y-chromosome has 231 gene (the last).

(ix)   Scientist have identified about 1.4 million locations where DNA differs in single base in human beings these are called single nucleotide polymorphism (SNPs, pronounced as snips).

Implications of Human Genome Project (HGP)

(i)   Prepared sequencing more than 1200 genes that are responsible for common cardiovascular ailments, endocrine disease like diabetes, neurological disorder like Alzheimer, deadly coma and many more.

(ii)   HGP holds a key to design drugs, genetically modified diets and finding our genetic identity.

(iii)   Many non-human model organisms such as bacteria, yeast, *Caenorhabolitis elegans* (a free living non pathogenie nematode), *Drosophila* (fruit fly), plants (rice and *Arabidopies*) have also been sequenced.

DNA FINGERPRINTING

The technique of DNA finger printing was processed and reflected by British geneticist Dr. Alec Jeffrey in 1984. It is a technique for identifying individuals, generally using repeated sequences (repetitive DNA) in the human genome that produces a pattern of band that is unique for every individuals.

Principle of DNA Fingerprinting

(i)   Every individual organism is unique. DNA sequences has some specific regions in DNA called repetitive DNA → which are short stretch repeated many times.

(ii)   These short nucleotide repeats vary in number from person to person and are called variable number of tandem repeat (VNTR). The VNTR of 2 persons may be of same length and sequence at certain sites, but vary at others.

(iii) A child might inherit a chromosome with 6 tandem repeats from mother and six tandem repeated 4 times from father. This is an example of DNA polymorphism. Polymorphism arised due to mutation.

(iv) VNTR/Satellite DNA/repetitive DNA are distinguished as different peaks from bulk genomic DNA during density gradient centrifugation. Bulk DNA forms a major peak and other satellite DNA makes small peaks.

(v) VNTR belongs to class of satellite DNA referred to as minisatellite size of VNTR varies from 1 → 20 bp.

(vi) Pattern of VNTR probe hybridisation in autoradiogram gives many bands of different size.

(vii) These pattern differ from individual to individual except in case of monozygotic twins.

Techniques for DNA Fingerprinting

DNA fingerprints can be prepared from extremely minute amounts of blood, semen, hair bulb or any other cells of the body. The major steps:

(i) DNA is cut into fragments with site recognising restriction enzymes for restriction fragments length analysis.

(ii) If the content of DNA is limited, DNA can be amplified by making many copies of it using PCR or polymerase chain reaction.

(iii) DNA is cut into fragments with site recognising restriction enzymes for restriction fragment length analysis.

(iv) Chopped DNA fragments are introduced and passed through electrophoresis setup containing agarose polymer gel. The separated fragments can be visualised by staining them with a dye that fluoresces under ultra violet radiations.

(v) Double - stranded DNA is then split into single-stranded DNA using alkaline chemicals.

(vi) Separated DNA sequences are transferred from gel onto a nitrocellulose or nylon membrane (Southern blotting).

(vii) The nylon sheet is then immersed in a bath and probes or markers that are radioactive synthetic DNA segments of known sequences are added. The probes target a specific nucleotide sequence, which is complementory to UNTR sequences and hybridise them.

(viii) Lastly, x-ray film is exposed to the nylon sheet containing radioactive probes. Dark bonds develop at the probe sites. Thus hybridised fragments are detected by autoradiography.

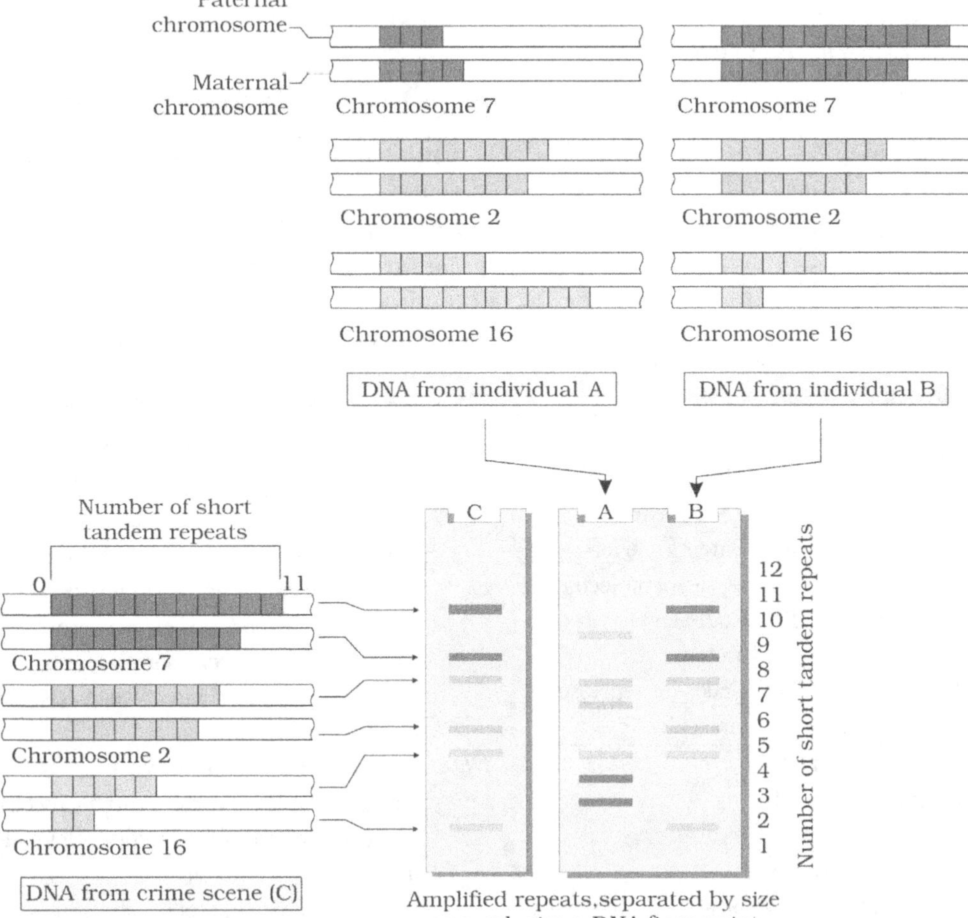

Fig. Schematic representation of DNA fingerprinting : Few representative chromosomes have been shown to contain different copy number of VNTR. For the sake of understanding different colour schemes have been used to trace the origin of each band in the gel. The two alleles (paternal and maternal) of a chromosome also contain different copy numbers of VNTR. It is clear that the banding pattern of DNA from crime scene matches with individual B, and not with A.

Application of DNA Fingerprinting

(i)   Identification of criminals in forensic laboratories.

(ii)   Determination of paternity in disputes/legal cases.

(iii)   Verification of migrants from one country to another.

(iv)   Identification of racial groups to map biological evolution.

Practice Exercise-3

Multiple Choice Questions

1. Which process is used for amplication or multiplication of DNA for finger printing ?

   (a) Polymerse chain reaction (PCR)

   (b) Nesslerisation

   (c) Southern blotting

   (d) Northern blotting

2. Polymorphism in DNA sequence

   (a) is the basis of genetic mapping of human genome.

   (b) arises due to mutation.

   (c) is the basis of DNA finger printing.

   (d) All of the above

3. SNP which is pronounced as "snips" stands for

   (a) Small Nuclear Protein

   (b) Single Nucleotide Particle

   (c) Single Nucleotide Polymorphism

   (d) Small Nicking Points

Match the following

4. Match the column-I with column-II and choose the correct combination from the given options.

	Column - I		Column - II
A.	Operator site	I.	Binding site for RNA polymerase
B.	Promoter site	II.	Binding site for repressor molecule
C.	Structural gene	III.	Codes for enzyme protein
D.	Regulator gene	IV.	Codes for repressor molecules

   (a) A – II; B – I; C – III; D – IV

   (b) A – II; B – I; C – IV; D – III

   (c) A – IV; B – III; C – I; D – II

   (d) A – II; B – III; C – I; D – IV

5. Match the steps of protein by synthesis given in column-I with their feature given in column-II and select the correct combination from the given options.

	Column - I		Column - II
A.	Termination	I.	Aminoacyl tRNA synthetase
B.	Translation	II.	Okazaki fragments
C.	Transcription	III.	GTP dependent release factor
D.	DNA replication	IV.	RNA polymerase

   (a) A – II; B – I; C – III; D – IV

   (b) A – III; B – I; C – IV; D – II

   (c) A – IV; B – III; C – I; D – II

   (d) A – II; B – III; C – I; D – IV

Assertion & Reason Questions

DIRECTIONS (Qs. 6-9) : *Each of these questions contains an assertion followed by reason. Read them carefully and answer the question on the basis of following options. You have to select the one that best describes the two statements.*

(a) If both Assertion and Reason are correct and the Reason is a correct explanation of the Assertion.

(b) If both Assertion and Reason are correct but Reason is not a correct explanation of the Assertion.

(c) If the Assertion is correct but Reason is incorrect.

(d) If both Assertion and Reason are incorrect.

6. **Assertion :** Lactose is the substrate for the enzyme beta galactosidase and it regulates switching on and off of lac operon, hence it is termed as inducer.

   Reason : The repressor of the operon is synthesised from the gene and the repressor protein binds to the operator region of the operon and prevents RNA polymerase from transcribing the operon.

7. **Assertion :** In the lactose operon, the z gene codes for beta galactosidase which is primarily responsible for the hydrolyases of the disaccharide, lactose into its monomeric units, galactose and glucose.

   Reason : The y gene codes for permease, which increases permeability of the cell to β-galactosides and the *a* gene encode a transacetylase.

8. **Assertion :** The technique of DNA fingerprinting was intially developed by Alec jeffreys.
    Reason : The DNA fingerprinting technique involved southern blot hybridisation using radiolabelled VNTR as probe.

9. **Assertion :** The Human Genome Project was a 13-year project coordinated by the U.S. Department of Energy and the National Institute of Health.
    Reason : During the early years of the HGP, the Welcome Trust (U.K.) became a major partner; additional contribution came from Japan, France, Gemany, China and others.

Very Short Answer Questions

10. In which technique variable tendem repeats (VNTRs) are analysed?

11. Can DNA be amplify in vitro also ?

Short Answer Questions

12. Define operon.

13. What is the organization of *lac* operon.

14. List 3 goals of Human Genome Project?

15. Give uses of DNA fingerprinting ?

Important Tips & Formulae

Packaging of DNA Helix:

- In prokaryotes, such as, E. coli, though they do not have a defined nucleus, the DNA is not scattered throughout the cell. DNA (being negatively charged) is held with some proteins (that have positive charges) in a region termed as 'nucleoid'.
- The DNA in nucleoid is organised in large loops held by proteins.
- In eukaryotes, this organisation is much more complex. There is a set of positively charged, basic proteins called histones.
- A protein acquires charge depending upon the abundance of amino acids residues with charged side chains.
- Histones are rich in the basic amino acid residues lysines and arginines.
- Both the amino acid residues carry positive charges in their side chains.
- Histones are organised to form a unit of eight molecules called as histone octamer. The negatively charged DNA is wrapped around the positively charged histone octamer to form a structure called nucleosome.
- A typical nucleosome contains 200 bp of DNA helix. Nucleosomes constitute the repeating unit of a structure in nucleus called chromatin, thread-like stained (coloured) bodies seen in nucleus.
- The nucleosomes in chromatin are seen as 'beads-on-string' structure when viewed under electron microscope (EM).
- The beads-on-string structure in chromatin is packaged to form chromatin fibers that are further coiled and condensed at metaphase stage of cell division to form chromosomes.
- The packaging of chromatin at higher level requires additional set of proteins that collectively are referred to as Non-histone Chromosomal (NHC) proteins.
- In a typical nucleus, some region of chromatin are loosely packed (and stains light) and are referred to as euchromatin.
- The chromatin that is more densely packed and stains dark are called as Heterochromatin. Euchromatin is said to be transcriptionally active chromatin, whereas heterochromatin is inactive.

Difference between DNA and RNA:

- Due to the presence of 2'-OH group at every nucleotide in RNA is a reactive group and makes RNA labile and easily degradable.
- It makes RNA more reactive and catalytic.
- The presence of thymine in place of uracil provides extra stability to the DNA.
- Both DNA and RNA have ability to mutate but RNA being unstable mutate at a faster rate.
- Viruses having RNA genome and having shorter life span mutate and evolve faster.

- Polymorphism refers to the variation at genetic level arises due to mutations.
- DNA fingerprinting involves Southern Blot hybridisation using radiolabelled VNTRs as a probe.
- VNTRs stands for Variable number Tandem repeats and it belongs to a class of satellite DNA called as mini-satellite. The number of repeats shows very high degree of polymorphism.
- Adenine forms two hydrogen bonds with thymine from opposite strand whereas guanine is bonded with cytosine with three H-bonds.

Central Dogma:

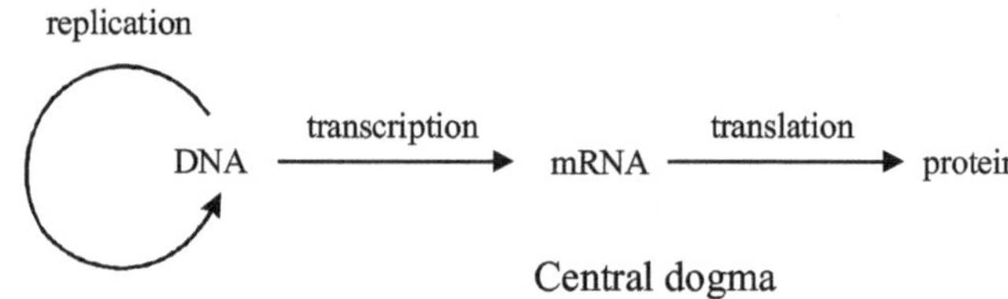

Central dogma

- In case of some viruses such as reteroviruses, the flow of information is in reverse direction that is from RNA to DNA.
- Taylor and his colleags in 1958 experimentally proved that DNA in chromosome replicate semiconservatively by using radioactive thymidine to detect distribution of newly synthesised DNA in the chromosomes was performed on Vicia faba (faba beans).
- The RNA polymerase II transcribes precursor of mRNA, the heterogeneous nuclear RNA (hnRNA).
- The primary transcript contains both the exon and introns.
- Introns are non-functional part of RNA.
- **Splicing** is the process of removal of introns from primary transcript (hnRNA) and exons are joined by DNA ligase.
- hnRNA undergo two additional processing called as capping and tailing.
- In capping an unusual nucleotide (methyl guanosine triphosphate) is added to the 5'-end of hnRNA.
- In tailing, adenylate residues (200-300) are added at 3'-end in a template independent manner.
- It is the fully processed hnRNA, now called mRNA, that is transported out of the nucleus for translation.
- Insertion or deletion of three or its multiple bases insert or delete one or multiple codon hence one or multiple amino acids, and reading frame remains unaltered from that point onwards. Such mutations are referred to as **frame-shift insertion or deletion mutations**.
- Sickle cell anaemia is caused because of point mutation results in a change of single base pair in the gene for beta globin chain that results in the change of amino acid residue glutamate to valine.

- The concept of Lac Operon was given by Francois Jacob and Jacque Monad.
- The lac operon consists of one regulatory gene (the i gene - here the term i does not refer to inducer, rather it is derived from the word inhibitor) and three structural genes (z, y, and a).
- The i gene codes for the repressor of the lac operon.
- The z gene codes for beta-galactosidase (?-gal), which is primarily responsible for the hydrolysis of the disaccharide, lactose into its monomeric units, galactose and glucose.
- The y gene codes for permease, which increases permeability of the cell to ?-galactosides.
- The a gene encodes a transacetylase.
- Hence, all the three gene products in lac operon are required for metabolism of lactose.
- Regulation of lac operon by repressor is referred to as negative regulation. Lac operon is under control of positive regulation as well.

Human Genome Project:
- Human Genome Project (HGP) was called a mega project.
- Human genome is said to have approximately 3 x 109 bp,
- HGP was closely associated with the rapid development of a new area in biology called as Bioinformatics.

Goals of HGP:
Some of the important goals of HGP were as follows:
- Identify all the approximately 20,000-25,000 genes in human DNA;
- Determine the sequences of the 3 billion chemical base pairs that make up human DNA;
- Store this information in databases;
- Improve tools for data analysis;
- Transfer related technologies to other sectors, such as industries;
- Address the ethical, legal, and social issues (ELSI) that may arise from the project.

The commonly used hosts were bacteria and yeast, and the vectors were called as BAC (bacterial artificial chromosomes), and YAC (yeast artificial chromosomes).
Salient Features of Human Genome
Some of the salient observations drawn from human genome project are as follows:
- The human genome contains 3164.7 million nucleotide bases.
- The average gene consists of 3000 bases, but sizes vary greatly, with the largest known human gene being dystrophin at 2.4 million bases.
- The total number of genes is estimated at 30,000-much lower than previous estimates of 80,000 to 1,40,000 genes. Almost all (99.9 per cent) nucleotide bases are exactly the same in all people.
- The functions are unknown for over 50 per cent of discovered genes.
- Less than 2 per cent of the genome codes for proteins.
- Repeated sequences make up very large portion of the human genome.
- Repetitive sequences are stretches of DNA sequences that are repeated many times, sometimes hundred to thousand times. They are thought to have no direct coding functions, but they shed light on chromosome structure, dynamics and evolution.
- Chromosome 1 has most genes (2968), and the Y has the fewest (231).
- Scientists have identified about 1.4 million locations where singlebase DNA differences (SNPs - single nucleotide polymorphism, pronounced as 'snips') occur in humans. This information promises to revolutionise the processes of finding chromosomal locations for disease-associated sequences and tracing human history.
- DNA fingerprinting involves identifying differences in some specific regions in DNA sequence called as repetitive DNA, because in these sequences, a small stretch of DNA is repeated many times.

NCERT Questions

1. **Group the following as nitrogenous bases and nucleosides: Adenine, Cytidine, Thymine, Guanosine, Uracil and Cytosine.**

Sol. Nitrogenous Base – Adenine, Uracil and Cytosine, Thymine; Nucleosides – Cytidine, guanosine.

2. **If a double stranded DNA has 20 per cent of cytosine, calculate the per cent of adenine in the DNA.**

Sol. In a DNA molecule, the number of cytosine molecule is equal to guanine molecules & the number of adenine molecules are equal to thymine molecules. As a result, if a double stranded DNA has 20% of cytosine, it has 20% of guanine. The remaining 60% includes both adenine & thymine which are in equal amounts. So, the percentage of adenine is 30%.

3. **If the sequence of one strand of DNA is written as follows:**
5'–ATGCATGCATGCATGCATGCA T G C–3'
Write down the sequence of complementary strand in 5' → 3' direction.

Sol. 5'–G C A T G C A T G C A T G C A T G C A T G C A T–3'.

4. **If the sequence of the coding strand in a transcription unit is written as follows:**
5'-ATGCATGCATGCATGCATGCATGCATGC-3'
Write down the sequence of mRNA.

Sol. mRNA: 5'–A U G C A U G C A U G C A U G C A U G C A U G C A U G C–3'.

5. **Which property of DNA double helix led Watson and Crick to hypothesise semi-conservative mode of DNA replication? Explain.**

Sol. Complementary base pairing property of DNA double helix led Watson and Crick to hypothesise semi-conservative mode of DNA replication. Watson & Crick observed that the nitrogenous bases are in complementary pairing in two strands of double helix of DNA molecule. Such an arrangement of DNA molecule led them to hypothesize the semi conservative mode of replication of DNA.

6. **Depending upon the chemical nature of the template (DNA or RNA) and the nature of nucleic acids synthesized from it (DNA or RNA), list the types of nucleic acid polymerases.**

Sol. The types of nucleic acid polymerase required for syntheis of DNA and RNA are:

(i) DNA dependent DNA polymerase – It helps in replication of DNA

(ii) RNA dependent DNA polymerase – It helps in synthesis of DNA from RNA (reverse transcription)

(iii) DNA dependent RNA polymenase - It helps in synthesis of RNA from DNA (trancription)

In eukaryotes there are at least three RNA polymerases in addition to those found in cell organelles.

RNA polymerase I transcribes rRNA (28s, 18s, and 5.85s)

- RNA polymerase II transcribes the precursor of mRNA called heterogeneous nuclear RNA (hn RNA)

-RNA polymerase III transcribes tRNA, 5SrRNA and Sn RNAs.

7. **How did Hershey and Chase differentiate between DNA and protein in their experiment while proving that DNA is the genetic material?**

Sol. Alfred Hershey and Martha Chase (1952) worked with viruses that infect bacteria called bacteriophages. In 1952, they chose a bacteriophage known as T_2 for their experimental material. They decided to see which of the bacteriophage components proteins or DNA entered bacterial cells & directed reproduction of the virus.

The bacteriophage attaches to the bacteria and its genetic material then enters the bacterial cell. The viral genome take over bacterial cellular machinery and directs to replicate viral genome and subsequently manufactures more virus particles. Hershey and Chase worked to discover whether it was protein or DNA from the viruses that entered the bacteria.

They grew some viruses on a medium that contained radioactive phosphorus and some others on medium that contained radioactive sulphur. Viruses grown in the presence of radioactive phosphorus contained radioactive DNA but not radioactive protein because DNA contains phosphorus but protein does not. Similarly, viruses grown on radioactive sulphur contained radioactive protein but not radioactive DNA because DNA does not contain sulphur.

Radioactive phages were allowed to attach to *E. coli* bacteria. Then, as the infection proceeded, the viral coats were removed from the bacteria by agitating them in a blender. The virus particles were separated from the bacteria by spinning them in a centrifuge.

Bacteria which was infected with viruses that had radioactive DNA were radioactive, indicating that DNA was the material that passed from the virus to the bacteria. Bacteria that were infected with viruses that had radioactive proteins were not radioactive. This indicates that proteins did not enter the bacteria from the viruses. DNA is therefore the genetic material that is passed from virus to bacteria.

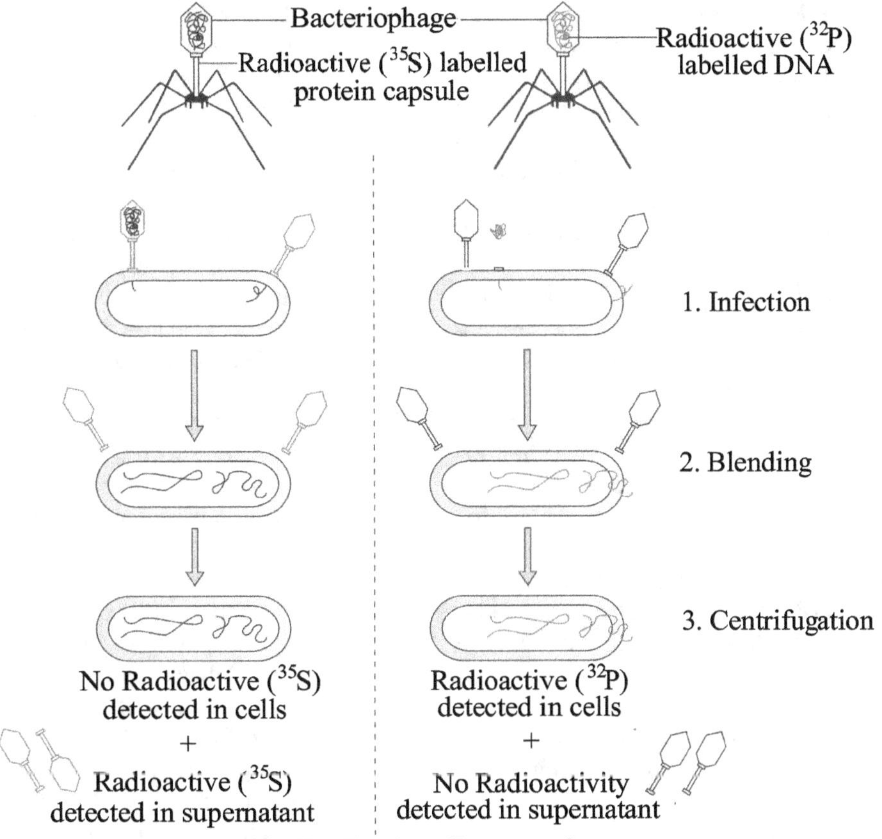

Fig. The Harshey-Chase experiment

8. **Differentiate between the followings:**
   (i) **Repetitive DNA and Satellite DNA**
   (ii) **mRNA and tRNA**
   (iii) **Template strand and Coding strand**

Sol. (i) The main differences between repetitive DNA and satellite DNA are as following :

	Repetitive DNA	**Satellite DNA**
(i)	It occurs in introns	It occurs at telomeres
(ii)	It has junk DNA	It has useful DNA
(iii)	It has evolutionary significance	It maintains structure of chromosome
(iv)	It has palindromes	It has hexanucleotide repeats
(v)	It is basis of DNA fingerprinting	It is basis of human genome project

(ii) The main difference between mRNA and tRNA are as following :

	mRNA (Messanger RNA)	**tRNA (transfer RNA)**
(i)	It has coding sequences.	It is a acceptor molecule.
(ii)	It have codons.	It has anticodons.
(iii)	It is a linear structure.	It is a folded structure.
(iv)	It carries information for amino acid sequence.	It carries amino acid from cell cytoplasm to ribosome.

(iii) The main difference between template strand and coding strand are as follows :

Template strand	**Coding strand**
2 strands of DNA have opposite polarity and DNA dependent RNA polymerase catalyze polymerization in only one direction, that is 5' → 3', the strand that has polarity 3' → 5' acts as template.	The strand with polarity 5' → 3' and the sequence same as RNA (except thymine at place of uracil is displaced) during transcription. This strand is called coding strand. All reference point in transcription is made with coding strand.

9. **List two essential roles of ribosome during translation.**

Sol. Protein synthesis occurs over the ribosomes and so they are called protein factories.

Ribosomes usually form rosette or helical groups during active protein synthesis. They are known as polyribosomes or polysomes (Rich, 1963). The different ribosomes of a polysomes are held together by a strand of messenger RNA - Polyribosomes helps to produce a number of copies of the some polypeptide.

A eukaryotic ribosome has a groove at the junction of the two submits. From this groove, a tunnel extends through the large subunit and opens into a canal of the endoplasmic reticulum. The polypeptides are synthesized in the groove between the two ribosomal submits and pass through the tunnel of the large submit into the endoplasmic reticulum. While in the groove, the developing polypeptides is protected from the cellular enzymes.

10. **In the medium where *E. coli* was growing, lactose was added, which induced the *lac* operon. Then, why does lac operon shut down some time after addition of lactose in the medium?**

Sol. Because lactose gets metabolized as a result of induction of lac operon and it is the inducer of lac operon.

11. **Explain (in one or two lines) the function of the followings:**

(a) **Promoter**   **(b)** **tRNA**

(c) **Exons**

Sol. **Promoter :** Site of attachment of RNA polymerase.

tRNA : Acceptor molecules for amino acid

Exons : Coding sequences of hnRNA.

12. **Why is the Human genome project called a mega project?**

Sol. Human genome project is called a mega project because

(i)   it generated a lot of data related to human genome.

(ii)   it generated lot of information in the form of sequence annotation.

(iii) it was carried out in number of labs and coordinated on extensive scale.

13. **What is DNA fingerprinting? Mention its application.**

Sol. DNA fingerprinting is identification of difference in specific region of DNA sequences based on DNA polymorphism, repetitive DNA and satellite DNA.

Application of DNA fingerprinting : Settling, paternity disputes and identity of criminal by different DNA profiles in forensic laboratories.

14. **Briefly describe the following:**

(i) **Transcription**   **(ii)** **Polymorphism**

(iii) **Translation**   **(iv)** **Bioinformatics**

Sol. **(i)** **Transcription :** It is the process of copying genetic information from sense stand of the DNA into RNA or the formation of RNA (ribonucleic acid) over DNA template. It is meant for taking the coded information from DNA to the site where it is required for protein synthesis. Principles of complementarity is used even in transcription. The exception is that uracil is incorporated instead of Theymine opposite adenine of template. Only a segment of DNA is transcribed and that only one of the two strands is copied. The segment of DNA that takes part in transcription is called transcription unit. It has three components (i) a promoter, (ii) the structural gene and (iii) a terminator.

(ii) **Polymorphism :** It is a variation at genetic level which arises due to mutations. The polymorphism in DNA sequences is the basis of genetic mapping of human genome as well as DNA finger printing. If an inheritable mutation is observed in a population at high frequency, it is referred to as DNA polymorphism.

(iii) **Translation :** It is the mechanism by which the triplet base sequence of mRNA guides the linking of a specific sequence of amino acid to form a polypeptide chain (protein) or ribosomes in the cell cytoplasm All the protein that a cell needs are synthesized by the cell within itself. The raw material required in protein synthesis are ribosomes, amino acids, m RNA, tRNAs and aminoacyl tRNA synthetase. Mechanism of protein synthesis involves following steps.

- Activation of amino acids

-Charging or amino acylation of tRNA

-Initiation

-Elongation

-Termination

The ribosomes more along the mRNA 'reading each codon in turn. Molecules of transfer RNA (tRNA), each bearing a particular-amino acid, are bought to their correct position along the mRNA. In this way amino acids are assembled in the correct sequence to form the polypeptide chain.

(iv) **Bioinformatics :** Computational method of handling and analyzing biological databases. Bioinformatics is the combination of biology and information technology. Basically, bioniformatics in a recently developed science using information to understand biological phenomenon. It broadly involves the computational tools and methods used to manage, analyse and manipulate volumes of biological data.

Past year Exercise

1. Meselson and Stahl carried out centrifugation in $CsCl_2$ density gradient to separate:
   (a) DNA from RNA
   (b) DNA from protein
   (c) the normal DNA from $^{15}N-DNA$
   (d) DNA from tRNA

2. Mention the role of the codons AUG and UGA during protein synthesis.

3. Name the enzyme involved in continuous replication of DNA strand. Mention the polarity of the template strand.

4. Mention the contribution of genetic maps in human genome project.

5. Mention any two ways in which Single Nucleotide Polymorphisms (SNPs) identified in human genome, can bring out revolutionary changes in biological and medical sciences.

6. Name the positively charged protein around which the negatively charged DNA wrapped.

7. State the role of transposons in silencing of mRNA in eukaryotic cells.

8. Name the enzyme and state its property that is responsible for continuous and discontinuous replication of the two strands of a DNA molecule.

9. Name the specific components and the linkages between them that form deoxyguanosine.

10. Which one of an intron and an exon is the reminiscent of antiquity?

11. Which one is tailed with adenylate residues between 3' end and 5' end of hn RNA?

12. Name the enzyme that joins the small fragments of DNA of a lagging strand during DNA replication.

13. Name the specific components and the linkage between them that form deoxyadenosine.

14. Why is secondary immune response more intense than the primary immune response in humans?

15. Mention how does DNA polymorphism arise in a population.

16. How is repetitive/satellite DNA separated from bulk genomic DNA for various genetic experiments?

17. What is a cistron ?

18. Retroviruses have no DNA. However, the DNA of the infected host cell does possess viral DNA. How is it possible ?

19. Answer the questions based on the dinucleotide shown below.

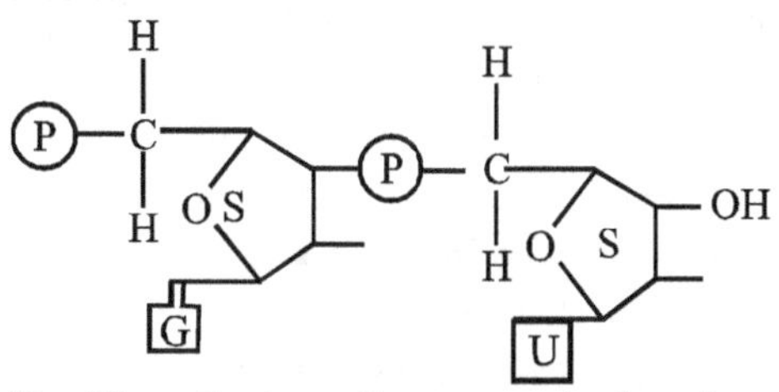

   (i) Name the type of sugar guanine base is attached to.
   (ii) Name the linkage connecting the two nucleotides.
   (iii) Identify the 3' end of the dinucleotide. Give a reason for your answer.

20. Draw a schematic representation of a dinucleotide. Label the following.
   (i) The component of a nucleotide
   (ii) 5' end
   (iii) N-glycosidic linkage
   (iv) Phosphodiester linkage

21. The following is the flow chart highlighting the steps in DNA fingerprinting technique. Identify A, B, C, D, E and F.

   Isolation of DNA from blood cell
   ↓
   Cutting DNA by A
   ↓
   Separation of DNA fragments by electrophoresis using B
   ↓
   Transfer (blotting) of fragments to C gel
   ↓
   DNA's split into single strands
   ↓
   Introduction of labelled D probes
   ↓
   E of single strands with D
   ↓
   Detection of banding pattern by F

22. Explain the role of regulatory gene in a *lac* operon. Why is regulation of *lac* operon called negative regulation?

23. (i) How many codons code for amino acids and how many do not?

(ii) Explain the following giving one example of each.
   (a) Unambiguous and specific codon
   (b) Degeneration codon
   (c) Universal codon
   (d) Initiator codon

24. Mention the role of ribosome in peptide bond formation. How does ATP facilitate it?

25. State the dual role of deoxyribonucleoside triposphates during DNA replication.

26. (i) Name the enzyme that catalyses the transcription of *hn*RNA.
   (ii) Why does the *hn*RNA needs to undergo changes? List the changes *hn*RNA undergoes and where in the cell such changes take place.

27. (i) Name the scientist who called *t*RNA an adapter molecule.
   (ii) Draw a clover leaf structure of *t*RNA showing the following
   (a) Tyrosine attached to its amino acid site.
   (b) Anticodon for this amino acid in its correct site (codon for tyrosine is UCA).
   (iii) What does the actual structure of *t*RNA look like?

28. How do histones acquire positive charge?

29. Write the full form of VNTR. How is VNTR different from 'Probe'?

30. Unambiguous, universal and degenerate are some of the terms used for the genetic code. Explain the salient features of each of them.

31. Draw a neat labelled sketch of a replicating fork of DNA.

32. (i) Name the enzyme responsible for the initiation transcription of *t*RNA and the amino acid, the *t*RNA gets linked with.
   (ii) Explain the role of initiator *t*RNA in of protein synthesis.

33. (i) Construct a complete transcription unit with promoter and terminator on the basis of hypothetical template strand given below.

$$\text{A T G C A T G C A T A C}$$
$$\longleftarrow$$

   (ii) Write the RNA strand transcribed from the above transcription unit along with its polarity

34. (i) Name the enzyme responsible for transcription of *t*RNA and amino acid, the initiator *t*RNA gets linked with.
   (ii) Explain the role of initiator *t*RNA in initiation of protein synthesis.

35. How are the structural genes activated in *lac* operon in *E.coli*?

36. In a maternity clinic, for some reasons the authorities are not able to hand over the two new-borns to their

respective real parents. Name and describe the technique that you would suggest to sort out the matter.

37. A burglar in a huff forgot to wipe off his blood-stains from the place of crime where he was involved in a theft and fight. Name the technique which can help in identifying the burglar from the blood stains. Describe the technique.

38. (a) Explain DNA polymorphism as the basis of genetic mapping of human genome.
   (b) State the role of VNTR in DNA fingerprinting.

39. Describe the structure of a RNA polynucleotide chain having four different types of nucleotides.

40. Why is DNA considered a better genetic material?

41.

i	p	o	x	y	a

Given above is a schematic representation of the *lac* operon in *E.coli*. What is the significant role of '*i*' gene is switching on or off the operon?

42.

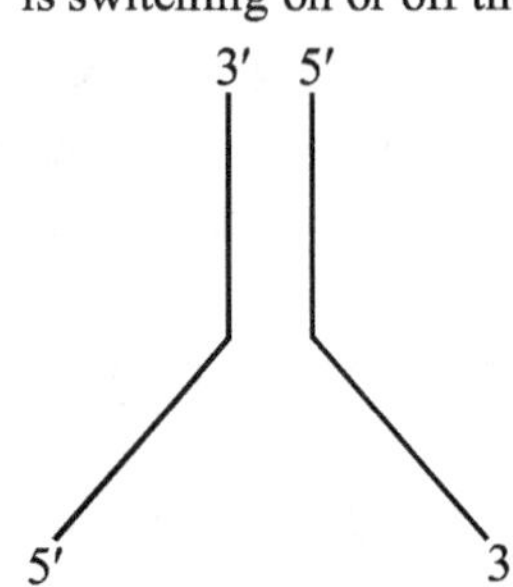

(a) Identify the structure shown above.
(b) Redraw the structure as a replicating fork and label the parts.
(c) Write the source of energy for this replication and list the enzymes involved in this process.
(d) Mention the difference in the synthesis based on the polarity of the two template strands.

43.

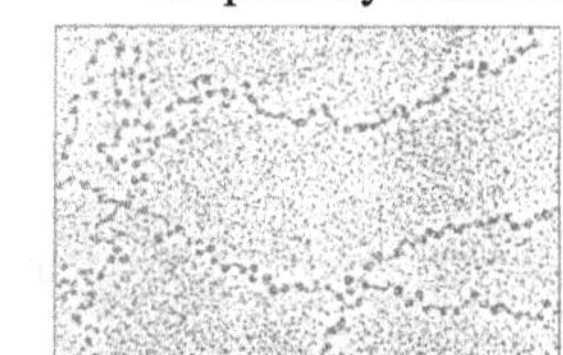

Shown above is the Electron Micrograph (E.M.) picture of "beads-on-string".

(a) Identify and explain the detailed structure of a bead with the help of a labelled diagram.
(b) Describe packaging of "beads-on-string" in a eukaryotic cell.

44. Given below are the sequence of nucleotides in a particular mRNA and amino acids coded by it:

UUUAUGUUCGAGUUAGUGUAA

Phe – Met – Phe – Glu – Leu – Val

Write the properties of genetic code can be and that cannot be correlated from the above given data.

45. State the difference between the structural genes in a Transcription Unit of Prokaryotes and Eukaryotes.

46. Explain the two factors responsible for conferring stability to double helix structure of DNA.

47. (i) Name the scientist who suggested that the genetic code should be made of a combination of three nucleotides.

    (ii) Explain the basis on which he arrived at this conclusion.

48. Suggest a technique to a researcher who needs to separate fragments of DNA.

49. Discuss the role the enzyme DNA ligase plays during DNA replication.

50. Give an example of an autosomal recessive trait in humans. Explain its pattern of inheritance with the help of a cross.

51. Following are the features of genetic codes. What does each one indicate? Stop codon; Unambiguous codon; Degenerate codon; Universal codon

52. (a) Write the features that a biomolecule must fulfil to be able to act as a genetic material.

    (b) DNA and RNA are both genetic materials. Which one of the two is more stable and why?

OR

(a) Explain Hardy-Weinberg Principle on the basis of the algebraic equation $p^2 + 2pq + q^2 = 1$.

(b) How do gene migration and genetic drift affect this genetic equilibrium?

53. (a) Write the contributions of the following scientists in deciphering the genetic code.

    George Gamow: Hargobind Khorana; Marshall Nirenberg; Severo Ochoa

    (b) State the importance of a Genetic code in protein biosynthesis.

54. Explain how the biochemical characterization (nature) of "Transforming Principle' was determined, which was not defined from Griffith's experiments.

55. In an agricultural field there is a prevalence of the following organisms and crop diseases which are affecting the crop yield badly :

    (a) Write rust   (b) Leaf and stripe rust

    (c) *Black rot*   (d) *Jassids*

    Recommend the varieties of crops the farmers should grow to get rid of the existing problem and thus improve the crop yield.

NCERT Exemplar

Multiple Choice Questions

1. Which of the following statements is the most appropriate for sickle-cell anaemia?
   (a) It cannot be treated with iron supplements
   (b) It is molecular disease
   (c) It confers resistance to acquiring malaria
   (d) All of the above

2. One of the following is true, with respect to AUG
   (a) It codes for methionine only
   (b) It is also an initiation codon
   (c) It code for methionine in both prokaryotes and eukaryotes
   (d) All of the above

3. The first genetic material could be
   (a) Protein   (b) Carbohydrates
   (c) DNA   (d) RNA

4. With regard to mature mRNA in eukaryotes
   (a) exons and introns do not appear in the mature RNA
   (b) exons appear but introns do not appear in the mature RNA
   (c) introns appear but exons do not appear in the mature RNA
   (d) Both exons and introns appear in the mature RNA

5. The human chromosome with the highest and least number of genes in them are respectively
   (a) chromosome 21 and Y   (b) chromosome 1 and X
   (c) chromosome 1 and Y   (d) chromosome X and Y

Match the following

6. Match the following genes of the Lac operon with their respective products:

   (A) i gene   (i) b-galactosidase
   (B) z gene   (ii) Permease
   (C) a gene   (iii) Repressor
   (D) y gene   (iv) Transacetylase

   Select the **correct** option.

	(A)	(B)	(C)	(D)
(a)	(i)	(iii)	(ii)	(iv)
(b)	(iii)	(i)	(ii)	(iv)
(c)	(iii)	(i)	(iv)	(ii)
(d)	(iii)	(iv)	(i)	(ii)

Assertion & Reason Questions

DIRECTIONS (Qs. 7-8) : *Each of these questions contains an assertion followed by reason. Read them carefully and answer the question on the basis of following options. You have to select the one that best describes the two statements.*

(a) If both Assertion and Reason are correct and the Reason is a correct explanation of the Assertion.

(b) If both Assertion and Reason are correct but Reason is not a correct explanation of the Assertion.

(c) If the Assertion is correct but Reason is incorrect.

(d) If both Assertion and Reason are incorrect.

7. **Assertion :** A molecule that can act as genetic material should be able to express itself in the form of Mendalian characters.

   Reason : The genetic material should be stable enough not to change with different stage of cycle, age or with change physiology of the organs.

8. **Assertion :** Histone are organised to form a unit of eight molecule called as histone octamer body.

   Reason : The negatively charged DNA is wrapped around the positively charged histone oclamer to form a structure called Nucleosome.

Very Short Answer Questions

9. "Genes contain the information that is required to express a particular trait." Explain.

Short Answer Questions

10. Retrovirus do not follow central dogma. Comment.

11. What are the functions of (i) methylated guanosine cap, (ii) poly-A "tail" in a mature on RNA?

Objective Practice Exercise

Multiple Choice Questions

1. Degeneration of a genetic code is attributed to the
   (a) third member of a codon
   (b) first member of a codon
   (c) second member of a codon
   (d) entire codon

2. Crossing over that results in genetic recombination in higher organisms occurs between
   (a) sister chromatids of a bivalent
   (b) non-sister chromatids of a bivalent
   (c) two daughter nuclei
   (d) two different bivalents

3. The following ratio is generally constant for a given species

   (a) $\dfrac{A+G}{C+T}$ (b) $\dfrac{T+C}{G+A}$

   (c) $\dfrac{G+C}{A+T}$ (d) $\dfrac{A+C}{T+G}$

4. Eukaryotic chromosomes
   (a) are circular and contain origin and terminator sequences.
   (b) are linear and have origins and telomeres.
   (c) contain coding and non-coding sequences.
   (d) Both (b) and (c)

5. The ends of eukaryotic chromosomes
   (a) are single-stranded and must be bound by transcription complexes.
   (b) are highly repetitive sequences that hold replicated chromosomes together.
   (c) shorten every time a cell divides.
   (d) require telomerase to move to other sites in the chromosome.

6. Chromatin structure must be altered in order for gene expression to occur because
   (a) condensed chromatin is replicated but not transcribed.
   (b) condensed chromatin makes most DNA sequence inaccessible to the transcription complex.
   (c) decondensed chromatin has more nucleosomes per DNA molecule.
   (d) heterochromatin is actively transcribed and euchromatin is not transcribed.

7. A sample of DNA from an unknown organism is analyzed and found to contain histone proteins, more than 2 billion base pairs, and large segments of noncoding DNA. From this information, one can conclude that the organism is
   (a) a bacterium
   (b) an animal
   (c) a plant
   (d) some kind of eukaryotic organisms

8. Which of the following parts of a DNA molecule are held together by hydrogen bonds?
   (a) The carbons within the sugar–phosphate group.
   (b) The carbons within the nitrogen-containing bases.
   (c) Nucleotide bases on opposite strands of the helix.
   (d) Successive nucleotides within a single strand of the helix.

9. Even though you and your brothers or sisters are all humans, odds are that each of you has a somewhat different genetic makeup. The molecular basis for this inherited genetic variation
   (a) is related to the difference in the DNA nucleotide sequence of your genes.
   (b) depends on whether protein or DNA is used as the hereditary material.
   (c) depends on whether adenine pairs with thymine or guanine.
   (d) is the result of errors in the DNA replication process.

10. The primary reason DNA was first thought to be a poor candidate for the hereditary material was that
    (a) Griffith's experiments showed that protein, not DNA, caused transformation.
    (b) viruses lack DNA yet still pass genetic information between generations.
    (c) DNA was believed to have a simple chemical structure with little variability.
    (d) the work of Hershey and Chase showed that protein was the genetic material.

11. Consider Griffith's experiments on transformation in *Streptococcus pneumoniae*. Now imagine that you are extending these experiments by injecting a mixture of heat-killed strain R bacteria and live strain S bacteria into a mouse. The result will be that the mouse will _______, and you will find live strain _______ bacteria in its blood.

   (a) die; R   (b) live; R

   (c) die; S   (d) live; S

12. A murder has occurred, and you are asked to help solve it. The police bring you a sample from the crime scene of what they believe is the killer's DNA and ask you for a chemical analysis. Your study of this sample reveals the presence of adenine, thymine, ribose, and uracil, leading you to conclude that the sample is

   (a) pure DNA.

   (b) pure RNA.

   (c) probably a mixture of DNA and RNA.

   (d) probably a mixture of rRNA and mRNA.

13. Prior to mutation, a sequence of DNA reads GAGCCTATGCCAGTA. After the mutation, the sequence reads GAGCGTACGCCATTA. Which of the following best explains the change in DNA that has occurred?

   (a) There was a single base deletion.

   (b) There was a single base substitution.

   (c) There were multiple base deletions.

   (d) There were multiple base substitutions.

14. Experiments by Avery, McLeod, and McCarty supported DNA as the genetic material by showing that

   (a) both protein and DNA samples provided the transforming factor.

   (b) DNA was not complex enough to be the genetic material.

   (c) only samples with DNA provided activity.

   (d) even though DNA was molecularly simple, it provided adequate variation to act as the genetic material.

15. Chargaff's rules of base pairing states that

   (a) the ratio of purines to pyrimidmes is roughly equal in all tested organisms.

   (b) the ratio of A to T is roughly equal in all tested organisms.

   (c) the ratio of A + T and G + C is roughly equal in all tested organisms.

   (d) Both (a) and (b)

16. A small segment of DNA contains the base sequence CGT. If an mRNA transcript is made that includes this DNA sequence, what will be the anticodon on the tRNA that will bind to the corresponding mRNA codon for this DNA triplet?

   (a) CGT   (b) GCA

   (c) CGU   (d) GCT

17. A functional piece of mRNA has 66 codons. The maximum number of amino acids that could be present in the protein coded for by this mRNA would be 66.

18. A triplet base sequence in DNA reads ATT. What will be the corresponding mRNA codon, tRNA anticodon, and amino acid called by this DNA?

   (a) TAA; UTT; methionine

   (b) TAA; AUU; no amino acid (= stop codon)

   (c) UAA; AUU; no amino acid (= stop codon)

   (d) CGG; GCC; alanine

19. The primary function of DNA polymerase is to

   (a) add nucleotides to the growing daughter strand.

   (b) seal nicks along the sugar-phosphate backbone of the daughter strand.

   (c) unwind the parent DNA double helix.

   (d) prevent reassociation of the denatured parent DNA strands.

20. The lagging daughter strand of DNA is synthesized in what appears to be the "wrong" direction. This synthesis is accomplished by

   (a) ligating (connecting) short Okazaki fragments that are synthesized in short spurts in the "right" direction.

   (b) primase.

   (c) using multiple primers and DNA polymerase I.

   (d) Both (a) and (b)

21. RNA primers are necessary in DNA synthesis because

   (a) DNA polymerase can only add to an existing strand of nucleotides.

   (b) DNA polymerase can only add to an existing DNA strand.

   (c) DNA primase is the first enzyme in the replication complex.

   (d) All of the above

22. Proofreading and repair occur

   (a) at anytime during or after synthesis of DNA.

   (b) only before DNA methylation occurs.

   (c) only in the presence of DNA polymerase.

   (d) only in the presence of an excision repair mechanism.

23. When a molecule of DNA replicates without error, each of the resulting molecules contains
   (a)   the same amount of A as T.
   (b)   the same amount of G as C.
   (c)   one new strand and one old strand.
   (d)   All of the above.

24. Transcriptional regulation
   (a)   is highly efficient at completely preventing transcription
   (b)   allows the cell to only produce proteins that are needed at the time
   (c)   can be induced by a repressor protein
   (d)   All of these

25. What does "*lac*" refer to in what we call the *lac* operon?
   (a)   *Lac* insect
   (b)   Lactose
   (c)   Lactase
   (d)   The number 1,00,000

26. In negative operon
   (a)   co-repressor binds with repressor
   (b)   co-repressor does not bind with repressor
   (c)   co-repressor binds with inducer
   (d)   cAMP have negative effect on *lac* operon

27. If the gene encoding the *lac* repressor is mutated so that it can no longer bind the operator, will transcription of that operon occur?
   (a)   Yes, but only when lactose is present.
   (b)   No, because RNA polymerase is need to transcribe the genes.
   (c)   Yes, because the operator will not be bound by repressor and RNA polymerase can transcribe the *lac* operon.
   (d)   No, because cAMP levels are low when the repressor is nonfunctional.

28. If the gene encoding the *trp* repressor is mutated such that it can no longer bind tryptophan, will transcription of the *trp* operon occur?
   (a)   Yes, because the *trp* repressor can only bind the *trp* operon and block transcriptional initiation when it is bound to tryptophan.
   (b)   No, because this mutation does not affect the part of the repressor that can bind the operator.
   (c)   No, because the *trp* operon is repressed only when tryptophan levels are high.

   (d)   Yes, because the *trp* operon can allosterically regulate the enzymes needed to synthesize the amino acid tryptophan.

29. Transcriptional regulation in prokaryotes can occur by
   (a)   a repressor binding an operator and preventing transcription.
   (b)   an activator binding upstream from a promoter and positively affecting transcription.
   (c)   different promoter sequences binding RNA polymerase more tightly, resulting in more effective transcriptional initiation.
   (d)   All of the above

30. Post–transcriptional regulation includes
   (a)   binding of repressor on silencer regions.
   (b)   transport of messenger RNA into the cytoplasm.
   (c)   decreasing messenger RNA stability in the cytoplasm.
   (d)   Both (b) and (c)

31. Which of the following is the first thing that happens when a signal molecule acts on a target cell?
   (a)   A transcription factor acts on the DNA.
   (b)   The signal molecule binds to RNA.
   (c)   A new protein is made in the target cell.
   (d)   The signal molecule binds to a receptor.

32. Which process is used for amplication or multiplication of DNA for finger printing?
   (a)   Polymerse chain reaction (PCR)
   (b)   Nesslerisation
   (c)   Southern blotting
   (d)   Northern blotting

33. Polymorphism in DNA sequence
   (a)   is the basis of genetic mapping of human genome.
   (b)   arises due to mutation.
   (c)   is the basis of DNA finger printing.
   (d)   All of the above

34. Which of the following is **Not** a goal of the human genome project?
   (a)   To sequence the genomes of selected model organisms.
   (b)   To eliminate all diseases.
   (c)   To consider social, ethical and legal aspects of genetic information.
   (d)   To develop computational tools for analyzing sequence information.

35. In addition to the human genome sequence, draft or finished genome sequences existed for eight model organisms by 2002. Which of the following organisms are not the part of that group of eight model organisms?

(a) *Saccharomyces cerevisiae*

(b) *Drosophila melanogaster*

(c) *Oryza sativa*

(d) *Quercus rubra*

36. Each individual has a unique DNA fingerprinting as individuals differ in

(a) number of minisatellites on chromosome.

(b) location of minisatellites on chromosome.

(c) size of minisatellites on chromosome.

37. Satellite DNA

(a) is classified in many categories such as micro-satellites, minisatellites, etc. on the basis of base composition length of segments and number of repetitive units.

(b) normally does not code for any protein.

(c) shows polymorphism.

(d) All of the above

38. In a DNA strand the nucleotides are linked together by

(a) glycosidic bonds

(b) phosphodiester bonds

(c) peptide bonds

(d) hydrogen bonds

39. Nucleoside differs from a nucleotide. It lacks the :

(a) base   (b) sugar

(c) Phosphate group   (d) Hydroxyl group

40. Both deoxyribose and ribose belong to a class of sugars called

(a) Trioses   (b) hexoses

(c) Pentoses   (d) Polysaccharides

41. The fact that a purine always paired base through hydrogen bonds with a pyrimidine base leads to, in the DNA double helix.

(a) the antiparallel nature

(b) the semiconservative nature

(c) uniform width throughout DNA

(d) uniform length in all DNA

42. The net electric charge on DNA and histones is

(a) both positive   (b) both negative

(c) both (a) and (b)   (d) zero

43. Who amongst the following scientists had no contribution in the development of the double helix model for the structure of DNA ?

(a) Rosalind franklin   (b) Maurice Wilkins

(c) Erwin Chargaff   (d) Meselson and Stahl

44. Which of the following steps in transcription is catalysed by RNA polymerase ?

(a) Initiation   (b) Elongation

(c) Termination   (d) All of these

45. Control of gene expression takes place at the level of

(a) DNA- replication   (b) transcription

(c) Translation   (d) None of these

46. Which was the last human chromosome to be compeletely sequenced?

(a) chromosome 1   (b) chromosome 11

(c) chromosome 21   (d) chromosome X

47. Regulatory proteins are the accessory proteins that interact with RNA polymerase and affect its role in transcription. Which of the following statements is correct about regulatory protein?

(a) They only increase expression

(b) They only decrease expression

(c) They interact with RNA polymerase but do not affect the expression

(d) They can act both as activators and as repressors

48. Discontinuous synthesis of DNA occurs in one strand, because

(a) DNA molecule being synthesised is very long

(b) DNA dependent DNA polymerase catalyses polymerisation only in one direction $(5' \rightarrow 3')$

(c) It is a more efficient process

(d) DNA ligase has to have a role

49. Which of the following are the functions of RNA?

(a) It is carrier of genetc information from DNA to ribosomes synthesising polypeptide

(b) It carries amino acids to ribosomes

(c) It is a constituent of ribosomes

(d) All of the above

50. While analysing the DNA of an organism a total number of 5386 nucleotides were found out of which the proportion of different bases were Adenine = 29% Guanine = 17% Cytosine = 32%, Thymine = 17%. Considering the Chargaffs rule it can be concluded that

(a) it is double-stranded circular DNA

(b) it is single-stranded DNA

(c) it is a double-linear DNA

(d) No conclusion can be drawn

Match the following

51. Match column-I with column-II and select the correct combination from the given options.

Column-I		Column-II	
A.	Sigma factor	I.	5' – 3'
B.	Capping	II.	Initiation
C.	Tailing	III.	Termination
D.	Coding strand	IV.	5' end
		V.	3' end

(a) A – III; B – V; C – IV; D – II
(b) A – II; B – IV; C – V; D – I
(c) A – II; B – IV; C – V; D – III
(d) A – III; B – V; C – IV; D – I

52. Match column-I (Scientists) with column-II (Discoveries) and select the correct options.

Column-I (Scientists)		Column-II (Discoveries)	
A.	Alec Jeffreys	I.	*Lac* operon
B.	F. Sanger	II.	Automated DNA sequences
C.	Jacob and Monod	III.	DNA finger printing
D.	Avery, Mc Leod	IV.	Transforming principle and McCarty

(a) A – II; B – III; C – IV; D – I
(b) A – III; B – II; C – I; D – IV
(c) A – III; B – II; C – IV; D – I
(d) A – I; B – II; C – III; D – IV

Chapter Test

Time : *30 Minutes*   **Max. Marks : *15***

Directions :

- Questions number **1-15** carry **1 mark** each.

1. Evolution was termed RNA world due to discovery of
   (a) absence of RNAs in some cells.
   (b) genomic RNA.
   (c) RNA enzymes.
   (d) synthesis of proteins by *m*RNA, *t*RNA and rRNA

2. What is the main function of tRNA in relation to protein synthesis ?
   (a) Initiates transcription
   (b) Inhibits protein synthesis.
   (c) Identifies amino acids and transport them to ribosomes.
   (d) proof reading.

3. *Escherichia coli* fully labelled with ^{15}N is allowed to grow in ^{14}N medium. The two strands of DNA molecule of the first generation bacteria have
   (a) different density and do not resemble with their parent DNA.
   (b) different density but resemble with their parent DNA.
   (c) same density and resemble with their parent DNA.
   (d) same density but do not resemble with their parent DNA.

4. During infection of *E. coli* cells by bacteriophage T_2,
   (a) proteins are the only phage components that actually enter the infected cell.
   (b) both proteins and nucleic acids enter the cell.
   (c) only proteins from the infecting phage can also be detected in progeny phage.
   (d) only nucleic acids enter the cell.

5. Match the column-I with column-II and choose the correct combination from the given options.

	Column - I		Column - II
A.	Operator site	I.	Binding site for RNA polymerase
B.	Promoter site	II.	Binding site for repressor molecule
C.	Structural gene	III.	Codes for enzyme protein
D.	Regulator gene	IV.	Codes for repressor molecules

   (a) A – II; B – I; C – III; D – IV
   (b) A – II; B – I; C – IV; D – III
   (c) A – IV; B – III; C – I; D – II
   (d) A – II; B – III; C – I; D – IV

DIRECTIONS (Qs. 6-7) : *Each of these questions contains an assertion followed by reason. Read them carefully and answer the question on the basis of following options. You have to select the one that best describes the two statements.*

(a) If both Assertion and Reason are correct and the Reason is a correct explanation of the Assertion.
(b) If both Assertion and Reason are correct but Reason is not a correct explanation of the Assertion.
(c) If the Assertion is correct but Reason is incorrect.
(d) If both Assertion and Reason are incorrect.

6. **Assertion :** The two chains of DNA are coiled in a right handed fashion and the pitch of helix is 3-4 min

   Reason : There are roughly 10 bp in each turn and the distance between bp in a helix approximately equal to 0.34n m

7. **Assertion :** During the initiation of of translation, amino acids are tRNA–a process commonly called as charging of tRNA or aminoacylation of tRNA.

   Reason : The ribosome consists of structural RNAs and about 80 different proteins.

Passage/Case Based Questions

DIRECTIONS (Qs. 8-12) : *Read the following passage and answer the questions that follows.*

Observe the diagram given below and answer the questions that follows

     P   i   P   O   Z   Y   a

8. LAC operan is an example of
   (a) only postive regulation
   (b) only negative regulation
   (c) both positive and negative regulation
   (d) cometines positive sometimes negative

9. Which of these arts as an induces of the law operon?

   (a) Allolactose (b) lactose

   (c) Galactose (d) Glucose

10. The sequence of the structural gene in the lac operon is

    (a) Lac Z – Lac Z – Lac Y

    (b) Lac Z – Lac Y – Lac A

    (c) Lac Z – Lac A – Lac Y

    (d) Lac A – Lac Y – Lac Z

11. Lac operon will be turned on when

    (a) Lactose is less than glucose

    (b) Lactose is less in the medium

    (c) Lactose is more than glucose

    (d) Glucose is enough in the medium

12. In Lac operon, the gene product of Lac A gene is

    (a) Beta – galactoside permease

(b) Beta – galactosidase trans acetylase

(c) beta galactosidase

(d) Beta – galactosidase isomerase.

Very Short Answer Questions

13. Formation of peptide bond is catalyzed by __________.

14. DNA replication requires primer. Why?

15. __________ in RNA is replaced by thymine in DNA.

Solutions

1. **(c)** The scientists involved in the discovery of DNA as chemical basis of heredity were Avery, Mac Leod and McCarty. They expanded the work of Griffith on the process of transformation.

2. **(d)** Central dogma term was proposed by Crick (1958). It proposes unidirectional or one way flow of information from DNA to RNA and then to protein (polypeptide).

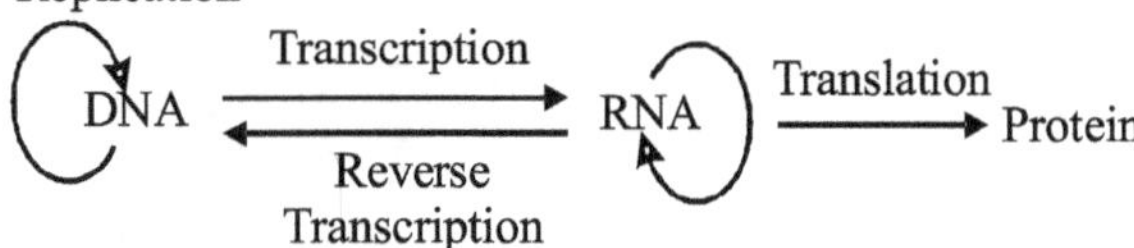

3. **(d)** In Meselson and Stahl's experiments, heavy DNA was distinguished from normal DNA by centrifugation in CsCl gradient. When DNA is mixed with caesium chloride it will settle down at a particular height in centrifugation and heavier one higher up.

4. **(c)** The purines and pyrimidines are always in equal amounts as per chargaff's rule. So, if cytosine is 20%, the thymine will be 30% and thymine is equal to adenine. Then the percentage of adenine will be 30%.

5. **(d)** RNA and DNA both are genetic material and carry genetic information from one generation to other. A virus is a small parasite that cannot reproduce by itself. Most viruses have either RNA or DNA as their genetic material. Once a virus infects a susceptible cell, it can direct the cell machinery to produce more viruses.

6. **(c)** Griffith described the phenomenon of bacterial transformation. Hershey and Chase discovered that RNA is the genetic material of bacteriophage. Prokaryotic DNA is also called nucleoid. Nucleoid is an irregularly-shaped region within the cell of a prokaryote (unicellular organisms) that contains all or most of the genetic material. Euchromatin is a chromosome material and comprises the most active portion of the genome within the cell nucleus. It does not stain strongly except during cell division and represents the major genes and is involved in transcription.

7. **(b)** Assertion and Reason are correct but Reason is not a correction explanation of Assertion.
    DNA and RNA are the two types of nucleic acids found in living systems.

8. **(c)** Assertion is correct but Reason is incorrect.
    The haploid content of human DNA is 3.3×10^9 bp.

9. **(b)** Assertion and Reason are correct but Reason is not a correction explanation of Assertion.
    Wilkins, watson and crick get the Nobel prize for deciphering the double helical model of DNA

10. **(b)** Assertion and Reason are correct but Reason is not a correction explanation of Assertion.
    The base pairing confess a very unique property to the pelynucleotide chain.

11. RNA is the first genetic material in cells becauses RNA is capable of both storing genetic information and catalyzing chemical reactions, also it has the tendency of self-replication.

12. Yes, RNA is present in humans. RNA carries out a blood range of functions from translating gentic information into the molecular machines and the structure of the cell to regulating the activity of genes during development, cellular differentiation and changing environments.

13. DNA is deoxyribose nucleic acid and RNA is ribonucleic acid. DNA has thymine which is replaced by uracil in RNA negatively charged.

14. Positively charged histone octamer wrapped around by DNA to form a structure called nucleosome.

15. According Watson and Crick model, adenine pairs with thymine and cytosine pairs with guanine.

16. Deoxyribose sugar, phosphate group and nitrogenous bases.

17. Removal of incorrect bases during replication by DNA polymerase enzyme.

18. A substance which stores biological information, transfer it to next generation and express it in offspring.

19. First ribonucleotide in RNA is triphosphate, rest are monophosphate.

20. Part of DNA which contains repeated sequences is called satellite DNA.

21. The precusor RNA or primary transcript with both exon and intron sequences is heterogeneous nuclear RNA which undergoes splicing and processing to form mRNA.

22. The space of 20 Å between two sugar phosphate backbones of DNA can accomodate only one purine and one pyrimidine because, 2 purines would be too large and 2 pyrimidines would be too close to form hydrogen bonds.

23. The double helical model of DNA was proposed by Watson and Crick in 1953. The work was based on the X-ray diffraction data produced by Wilkins and Franklin.

24. The nitrogenous bases in DNA are paired through hydrogen bonds forming base pairs. Adenine forms two hydrogen bonds with thymine and guanine forms three hydrogen bonds with cytosine.

25. The two strands of DNA are antiparallel i.e., they run parallel in opposite directions. The one chain runs in 5' → 3' direction while other runs in 3' → 5' direction.

Practice Exercise-2 

1. **(c)** Genetic code is the depiction of codon by which the information in RNA is decoded in a polypeptide chain. The information is transferred in the form of triplet of bases coding for one amino acid. It is triplet, universal, non-ambiguous and degenerate in nature.

2. **(a)** Degenerate codons (also called as non - sense codons or terminator codons) do not code for any amino acids. Three types of degenerate codons are UAG (amber), UAA (ochre) and UGA (opal).

3. **(b)** When a DNA strand with the sequence AACGTAACG is transcribed, the resultant sequence of the mRNA molecule synthesized is UUGCAUUGC. This is based on the paring of nitrogenous bases - adenine pairs with thymine (in DNA) and uracil (in RNA) and guanine with cytosine.

4. **(a)** A-III, B-IV, C-I, D-V, E-II

UUU	–	Phenylalanine
GGG	–	Glycine
UCU	–	Serine
CCC	–	Proline
AUG	–	Methionine

5. **(d)** Helicase is an enzyme which unwinds the DNA strand by breaking the H - Bonding present between the nucleotide pairs. Gyrase catalyzes the breaking and rejoining of bonds linking adjacent nucleotides in circular DNA to generate supercoiled DNA helices. The synthesis of RNA primer is done by primase enzyme. DNA polymerase III is involved in the synthesis of DNA from its deoxyribonucleoside triphosphate precursors.

6. **(b)** Assertion and Reason are correct but Reason is not a correction explanation of Assertion.

The oka zaki fragments are finally joined by the enzyme DNA ligase.

7. **(b)** Assertion and Reason are correct but Reason is not a correction explanation of Assertion.

It is the presence of a promoter in a transcription unit that also define the template and coding strands

8. **(b)** Assertion and Reason are correct but Reason is not a correction explanation of Assertion.

A homopolymer has all the same type of monomers attached to each, whereas a co-polymer has two types of monomers attached together.

9. **(c)** Assertion is correct but Reason is incorrect.

In tailing 200-300 adenylate residues are added at 3'end in a template independent manner.

10. Adapter molecule bearing anticodon and amino acid.

11. Set of 3 nitrogenous bases i.e., triplet codon.

12. 600 × 3 = 1800 bases of mRNA because set of triplet nucleotides i.e., codon code for an amino acid.

13. 2 start codon (AUG) and GUG 3 stop codons (UAA, UAG, UGA).

14. GCA, GCG, GCT, GCC, TCT, TCC.

15. Yes, AUG and GUG.

16. Bases of DNA sense strand from promotor to terminator sites.

17. Catalyse synthesis of DNA and proof reading.

18. In nucleus, during 'S' phase of cell cycle in eukaryotes, in cytoplasm and continuously in prokaryotes.

19. Leading strand – 5' → 3'

Lagging strand – 3' → 5'

20. Polysomes.

21. Mutation allows adaptation and evolution to occur in species.

22. Singlet and doublet codes are insufficient as these can specify only 4 and 16 amino acid respectively out of 20.

23. It binds to a region of DNA called promotor that is recognized by sigma subunit of the enzyme RNA polymerase.

24. (i) To compensate for slow rate of replication (1-2 μm/minute).

(ii) Long size of chromosome.

25. Silent mutation are those which :

(i) Occur at 3rd base position of codon.

(ii) Do not alter expression of the genes.

26. Named after discoverer, the first 2 bases of tRNA anticodon pairs specifically with first 2 bases of mRNA codons, but 3rd base can pair with unusual bases (wobble hypothesis).

27. **mRNA :** Carries codons, specify sequence of amino acids in protein.

tRNA : Carry anticodon, adapter molecule for charged amino acid.

Anticodons :

(i) AAU → UUA

(ii) UAU → AUA

(iii) CGA → GCU

(iv) GCA → CGU

28. **Column B**

(i) Replication

(ii) Transcription

(iii) Translation

(iv) Gene regulation

29. In genetic code some amino acids are coded by more than one codon. It is degeneracy of genetic code.

Practice Exercise-3

1. **(a)** Polymerase chain reaction (PCR) is a process used for the amplification (copy - small segments) of DNA. It is a technique for enzymatically replicating DNA without using living organisms, such as *E. coli* or yeast. It is commonly used in the medical and biological research labs for a variety of tasks, like detection of hereditary diseases, the identification of genetic fingerprints, diagnosis of infectious diseases, cloning of genes, paternity testing etc.

2. **(d)** Polymorphism in DNA sequence is a variation at genetic level. It arises due to mutation and is the basis of genetic mapping of human genome as well as of DNA fingerprinting.

3. **(c)** Single nucleotide polymorphism (SNP) is the most common type of genetic variation among people. Each SNP represents a difference in a single DNA building block, called a nucleotide. For example, a SNP may replace the nucleotide cytosine (C) with the nucleotide thymine (T) in a certain stretch of DNA.

4. **(a)** Operator site gives passages to RNA polymerase moving from the promoter to structural gene. Promoter site is the initiation point for transcription and the site for binding of RNA polymerase. Structural gene determines the amino acid sequence on the segment of DNA molecule. Regulator gene controls the activity of operator gene by producing repressor molecules.

5. **(b)** GTP dependent release factor is involved in the termination. Termination requires the activities of three release factors R_1, R_2, R_3. A release factor allows for the termination of translation by recognizing the termination codon or stop codon in an mRNA sequence. Amino acyl tRNA synthetase is an enzyme which plays an important role in translation during protein synthesis. This enzyme is responsible for the specific amino acylation of tRNA. Transcription is the process of transferring the information stored in DNA into a new molecule of mRNA through the synthesis of RNA over the DNA template. Transcription is carried out with the help of an RNA polymerase enzyme and a number of accessory proteins (called transcription factors). RNA polymerase enzyme is responsible for copying a DNA sequence into an RNA sequence. DNA replication is the process in which a double-stranded DNA molecule is copied to produce two identical DNA molecules. Okazaki fragments are short, newly synthesized DNA fragments that are formed on the lagging (or discontinuous) template strand during DNA replication.

6. **(b)** Assertion and Reason are correct but Reason is not a correction explanation of Assertion.

All the three gene products in *lac* operon are requird for metabolism of lactose.

7. **(b)** Assertion and Reason are correct but Reason is not a correction explanation of Assertion.

In the presence of an inducer, such as lactose or allolactosc, the repressor is inactivated by interaction with the inducer. This allows RNA polymerase access to the promoter and transcription proceeds.

8. **(a)** Assertion and Reason are correct and the Reason is a correction explanation of Assertion.

In the DNA fingerprinting technique, satellite DNA acts as probe that shows very high degree of polymorphism. It was called as Variable Number of Tandem Repeats (VNTR).

9. **(b)** Assertion and Reason are correct but Reason is not a correction explanation of Assertion.

The human Genome project was started in 1990 and was completed in 2003.

10. DNA finger printing.

11. Yes, PCR.

12. A group of genes including an operator, a common promotor and one or more structural genes that are controlled as a unit to produce messenger RNA (mRNA).

13. The *lac* operon consists of one regulatory gene (the i gene – here the term i does not refer to inducer, rather it is derived from the word inhibitor) and three structural genes (z, y and a). The i gene codes for the repressor of the lac operon. The z gene codes for beta-galactosidase (β-gal), which is primarily responsible for the hydrolysis of the disaccharide, lactose into its monomeric units, galactose and glucose. They gene codes for permease, which increases permeability of the cell to β-galactosides. The *a* gene encodes of transacetylase.

14. (i) Identification of 20,000-25,000 genes in human DNA.

(ii) Determination of sequence of 3 billion base pairs in human DNA.

(iii) Storing information to cure genetic diseases.

15. Uses of DNA finger printing are :

(i) Settling paternity disputes.

(ii) Establishing identity of migrants.

(iii) Establishment of criminals in forensic science laboratory.

Past year Exercise 

1. (c) The Meselson and Stahl carried out centrifugation in $CsCl_2$ density gradient for separation the normal DNA from ^{15}N DNA. The normal DNA was extracted from the culture one generation after the transfer ^{15}N to ^{14}N medium which has hybrid or intermediate density.

2. The codon AUG initiates protein synthesis whereas the codon UGA stops protein synthesis.

3. DNA polymerase is the enzyme involved in continuous replication of DNA strand.

4. Genetic maps have played an important role in sequencing of genes, DNA fingerprinting, tracing human history, chromosomal location for disease associated sequence.

5. (i) By tracing human history.
   (ii) By finding chromosomal locations for disease associated sequences.

6. Histones are the positively charged proteins.

7. Transposons, also unknown as 'jumping genes' are mobile genetic elements, which can become integrated at different sites in the genome. They can disrupt gene expression. In most of eukaryotes, transposons are retrotransposons which undergo transcription to form ds-RNA that initiate RNA interference and thus silencing the m-RNA of the nematode specific genes. As a result, the parasite could not infest, multiply and survive in a transgenic host expressing RNA interference.

8. **Name of enzyme :** DNA Polymerase
   Property : DNA polymerase help in the formation of a new strand in a continuous fashion over the template strand with $3' \rightarrow 5'$ polarity and in discontinuous fashion over the template strand with polarity $5' \rightarrow 3'$. The discontinuous synthesized fragments are later joined by enzyme DNA ligase. The new strand has always $5' \rightarrow 3'$ polarity. DNA polymerase, always polymerise nucleotide in $5' \rightarrow 3'$ direction over the template.

9. (a) **Components :** Deoxyribose sugar and the nitrogen base-guanine
   (b) **Linkage :** Nitrogen base is attached by its N-atom at 1 position by N-glycosidic bond.

10. The primary transcript in case of eukaryotes contain both the transcripts of exons and introns. The introns are removed and exons are joined in a defined order by a process called **Splicing.** The presence of introns is reminiscent of antiquity.

11. The 3' end of hn RNA is tailed with polyadenylate residue.

12. DNA ligase joins okazaki fragments to form a continuous DNA strand.

13. **Components :** N-base adenine (a purine) + deoxyribose sugar.
    Linkage : N-glycosidic linkage.

14. When our body exposed to an antigen the body will store immune cells, which have a memory of past infections. This means that when a secondary infection occurs the body will defend itself by producing the same antibody that was produced to defend against the antigen previously. This means the secondary response is more quicker and intense.

15. Polymorphism (variation at genetic level) arises due to mutations. In DNA polymorphism more than one variant (allele) at a locus occurs in human population with a frequency greater then 0.01. It can also be introduced by genetic drift.

16. Repetitive/Satellite DNA are distinguished as different peaks from bulk genomic DNA during density gradient centrifugation. Bulk DNA forms a major peak and other satellite DNA makes small peaks.

17. Cistron is that segment of DNA which specifies synthesis of a polypeptide.

18. After attacking the host cell, retrovirus enters into macrophages (as in case of HIV) where RNA genome of the virus replicates to form viral DNA with the help of enzyme reverse transcriptase. This viral DNA gets incorporated into the host cell's DNA and directs the infected cells to produce more viruses. The macrophages continue to produce virus and works as a HIV factory. Hence, the infected host cell possesses viral DNA.

19. (i) Pentose sugar or deoxyribose sugar.
    (ii) Two nucleotides are linked through $3' - 5'$ phosphodiester linkage to form a dinucleotide.
    (iii) The polymer has a free $3' - OH$ group which is referred to as $3' -$ end of polynucleotide chain.

20. Schematic representation of a dinucleotide.

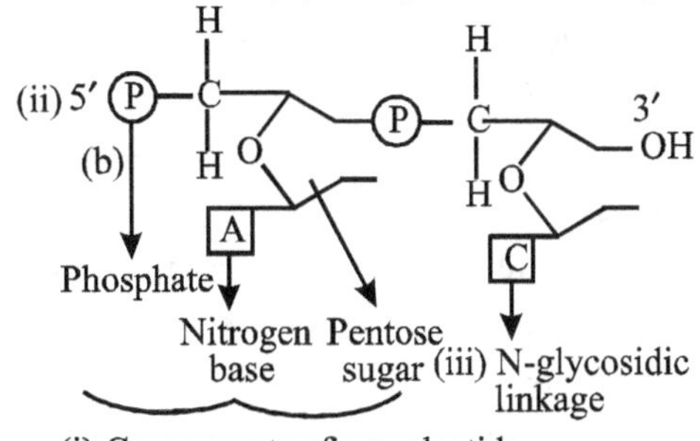

Fig : A dinucleotide

21. A – Restriction endonuclease
    B – Ethidium bromide
    C – Agarose
    D – VNTR
    E – A piece
    F – Autoradiography

22. The *lac* operon consists of one regulatory gene and three structural gene (z, y and a). The i gene codes for the repressor of the *lac* operon. If repressor protein binds to operator region of operon, it prevents RNA polymerase from transcribing the operon. Whereas, in presence of lactose (inducer) the repressor become inactivated due to interaction with inducer.

    This allow RNA polymerase access to promoter and transcription proceeds. Regulation of *lac* operon is negative, it can be visualised as regulation of enzymes synthesis by its substrate. Regulation of *lac* operon by repressor is referred to as negative regulation.

23. (i) 61 codons codes for amino acids and 3 codons do not code for any amino acids. These function as stop codons.

    (ii) (a) Unambiguous and specific – codon codes for only one amino acid, so it is unambiguous and specific, *e.g.*, GGA.

    (b) Some amino acids are coded by more than one codon, so, the code is degenerate, e.g., UUV

    (c) Codon is nearly universal. Some exceptions to the rule are mitochondrial codon and in some protozoan, *e.g.*, UUV

    (d) Initiator codon. AUG has dual function. It codes for methionine and also acts as initiator.

24. Ribosomes are main cellular site for protein synthesis. They also act as catalyst (235 rRNA) in prokaryotes for formation of peptide bonds. ATP provides energy for activation of amino acids.

25. (i) The deoxyribonucleoside triphosphates act as substrates for polymerisation.

    (ii) These also serve as energy source in the form of ATP and GTP.

26. (i) RNA polymerase II catalyses the transcription of *hn*RNA.

    (ii) *hn*RNA undergoes changes because it contains introns and exons and is non-functional. Changes in *hn*RNA are

    (a) Splicing occurs in which introns are removed and the exons are joined together in a definite order.

    (b) Capping occurs, in which an unusual nucleotide, methyl guanosine triphosphate is added to the 5′ end of *hn*RNA.

    (c) Tailing occurs, in which about 200-300 adenylate residues are added to the 3′ end of *hn*RNA.

    (d) All these processes occur inside the nucleus.

27. (i) Francis Crick.

    (ii) 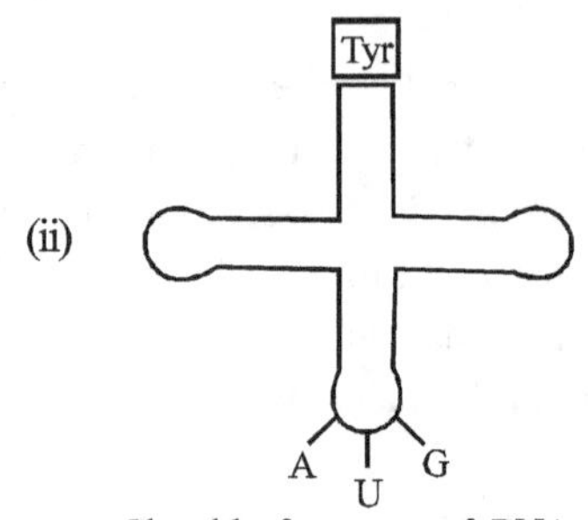

    Clovel leaf structure of *t*RNA

    (iii) The actual structure of *t*RNA looks like inverted L.

28. Histone proteins acquire positive charge depending upon the abundance of amino acids residues, *i.e.*, lysine and arginines, with charged side chains. Both these amino acids carry positive charges in their side chains.

29. VNTR -Variable Number Tandem Repeat. Differences between VNTR and Probe

VNTR	Probe
It is a class of satellite DNA, where a small sequence is arranged tandemly in many copy numbers.	It is a radioactivity labelled VNTR, used for hybridization with DNA segments.

30. (i) Genetic code is 'unambiguous' means one codon codes for one amino acid, hence genetic code is unambiguous and specific.

    (ii) Genetic code is 'universal' as a codon codes for the same particular amino acid in all organisms from human to bacteria.

    (iii) Genetic code is degenerate because some amino acids are coded by more than one codons.

31. The replication fork of DNA

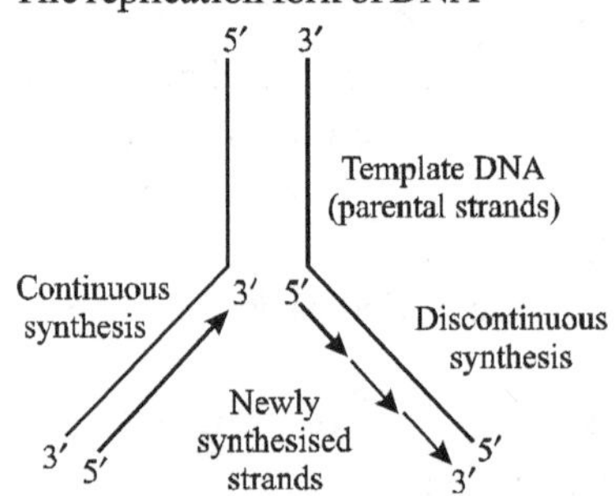

    Replicating fork of DNA

32. (i) RNA pol III is responsible for transcription of *t*RNA and the initiator *t*RNA gets linked with the aminoacid methionine.

    (ii) The initiator tRNA, which is charged with amino acid methionine, reaches the smaller subunit of ribosome. Its anticodon UAC recognises the codon AUG on mRNA and binds by forming complementary base pairs. The large subunit of ribosome joins the smaller subunit and initiates translation

33. (i) Transcription unit

(ii) RNA transcribed

U A C G U A C G U A T G
5'   mRNA   3'

34. (i) RNA polymerase transcribe *t*RNA and methionine is amino acid.

(ii) The initiator *t*RNA binds to the amino acids methionine, at its amino acid acceptor site.

It has anticodon loop, which has anticodon for methionine, *i.e.*, UAC, it recognis the start codon (AUG) at P site and binds to it according to complementarity of bases.

35. *Lac* operon consist of an operator, which control all structural gene as a unit. A regulatory gene (*i* gene), three structural genes (z, y, a) which codes for enzymes. A promoter, where RNA polymerase binds for transcription. The regulatory genes codes for a repressor protein and repressor has high affinity for the operator region and prevent RNA polymerase from transcribing the structural gene *i.e.*, the *lac* operon is switched off or inactive.

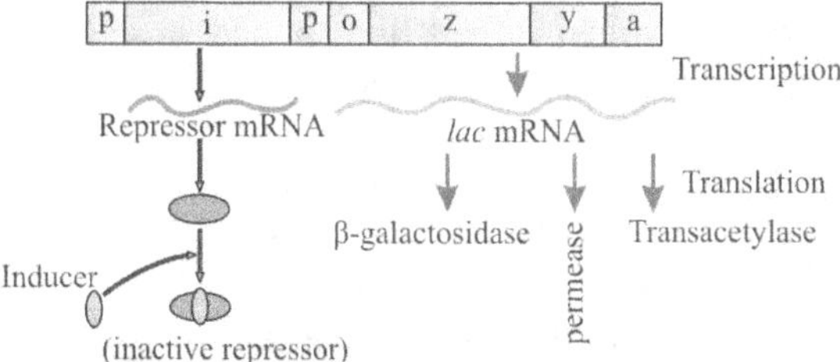

Lac operon in presence of inducer

When inducer (lactose) is added it binds with repressor protein and inactivate it. This allow RNA polymerase access to promoter and transcription proceeds.

36. **DNA fingerprinting** is the technique by which the real parentage of the two new-born babies can be established.

(i) **Alec Jeffreys** used satellite DNA as probes for DNA fingerprinting because of high degree of polymorphism. It was called variable number of tandem repeats (VNTR). VNTR are mini-satellite with numbers of repeat showing very high degree of polymorphism and size varies from 0.1 to 20 kb.

(ii) **Southern-blot hybridization technique includes :**

    (a) **Extraction :** Isolation of DNA from cells in a high speed centrifuge.

    (b) **Amplification :** Many copies of extracted DNA are made by PCR-technique.

    (c) **Digestion** of DNA by restriction endonuclease.

    (d) **Separation** of DNA fragments by electrophoresis.

    (e) **Southern Blotting** transferring (blotting) of separated DNA fragments to synthetic membranes such as nitrocellulose or nylon.

    (f) **Hybridization** using labelled VNTR probe

    (g) **Autoradiography :** Detection of hybridized DNA by autoradiography.

(iii) After hybridisation, autoradiography shows many brands of different sizes. These bands give a characteristic pattern for an individual DNA. Paternity dispute can be solved by comparing the pattern of DNA bands of the new born baby with that of mother/ father.

37. DNA finger printing is the technique by which the burglar can be identified from the blood-stains found from the place of crime by comparing DNA bands of the blood with his DNA bands.

For techqniue see Q. 21 of 1st set (All India)

38. (a) An inheritable mutation on that is observed in a population at high frequency, it is referred to as **DNA polymorphism**. In DNA sequence is the basis of genetic mapping of human genome as well as of DNA fingerprinting. DNA polymorphism are the variations at genetic level which arise due to mutation.

Allelic variation is described as DNA polymorphism, if more than one variant (allele) at a locus occurs in human population with a frequency greater than 0.01.

Satellite DNA is classified into many categories depending on length, base composition (A : T rich or G : C rich) and number of repetitive units such as micro-satellites and mini-satellites

These sequences show high degree of polymorphism and form the basis of DNA fingerprinting. They do not code for any protein. Polymorphism is a very important identification tool in forensic application. Secondly, as polymorphism is inheritable from parent to children, it forms basis of paternity testing, in case of disputes. Thirdly, it is the basis of genetic mapping in humans.

(b) Short nucleotide repeats in the DNA are very specific in each individual and vary in number from person to person but are inherited. These are called the **'Variable Number Tandem Repeats' (VNTRs)**. These are also called **"minisatellites"**.

Role of VNTR in DNA fingerpriting : DNA fingerprinting technique for identifying individuals generally using repeated sequences in the human genome that produces a pattern of bands that is unique for every individuals. Each individual inherits these repeats from his/her parents which are used as **genetic markers** in a personal identity test.

For example, a child might inherit a chromosome with six tandem repeats from the mother ad the same tandem repeated four times in the homologous chromosome inherited from the father. The half of VNTR alleles of the child resemble that of the mother and half that of the father.

39. **RNA or ribonucleic acid** is normally a single stranded structure. It functions as carrier of coded genetic or hereditary information from DNA to cytoplasm for taking part in protein and enzyme synthesis. It contains 70-12000 ribonucleotides joined end to end. It is made up of pentose ribose sugar, phosphoric acid & nitrogenous base. The axis or backbone is formed of alternate residues of phosphate and ribose sugar.

$$S—P—S—P—S—P—S—P$$
$$C \qquad A \qquad U \qquad G$$

Fig. A segment of RNA showing arrangement of its components
Phosphate combines with carbon 5' of its sugar and carbon 3' of next sugar similar to the arrangement found in DNA strand. Nitrogen bases are attached to sugars at carbon 1' of the latter. There are four types of nitrogen bases Two types of purines :
Adenine (A), guanine (G).
Two types of pyrimidines :
Cytosine (C) and uracil (U).
There are many types of RNAs and out of these rRNA, mRNA and tRNA are major classes of RNAs that are involved in gene expression.

40. DNA is a better genetic material because (a) instead of 2-OH group of sugar there is only H and further (b) thymine in place of uracil (c) being double stranded, it is preferred for storage of gentic information.

41. Repressor protein synthesised by *i*-gene combine with inducer (lactose) to form **inactive repressor** which does not bind to operator gene and RNA polymerase from promoter gene moves to the structural genes to help in transcription. In the absence of lactose, repressor binds to the operator gene which is switched off and RNA polymerase cannot move from promoter gene and thus there is no transcription.

42. (a) Replicating Fork
(b)

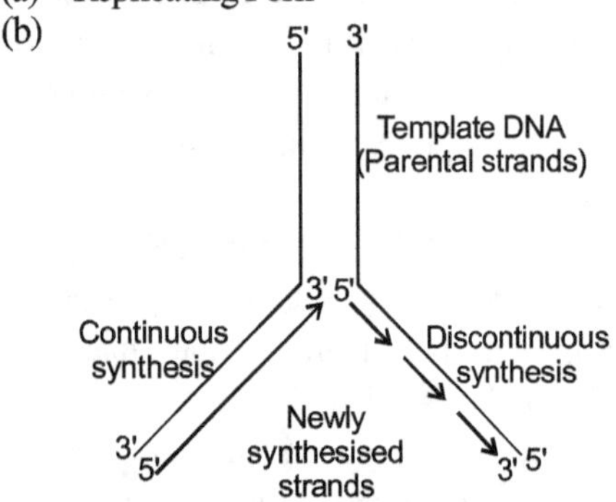

Fig. Replicationg fork

(c) Activiated deoxyribonucleotide triphosphate act as substrate and also provide energy for polymerisation reaction, similar to ATP.

List of enzymes
(i) Helicases : Unzips the two strands of DNA
(ii) Single stranded DNA binding proteins : Stablise single strands
(iii) Topoisomerases : Release tension in the uncoiled part by nicking resealing straightened DNA strands.
(iv) RNA polymerase Primase : for primer synthesis
(v) DNA polymerase (Prokaryotes) have three major types of DNA polymerases III, II and I)
(d) On the template strand with 3' - 5' polarity, the sythesis of new strand is continuous while in the other template strand with 5'-3' polarity the synthesis of new strand is in discontinuous fashion forming okazaki fragments.

43. (a) Identification : Chromatin (a stained thread like body) The beads-on-string are called Nucleosome which consists of a core of positively charged histone octamer, a unit of eight molecules of histone protein. Histones are rich in basic amino acid residue, lysine and arginine with positive charges on their side chains. The negatively charged DNA is wrapped around the Nucleosomes are linked by H-1 histone proteins to form the repeating units-beads on string, a coiled thread like stained structure called chromatin fibres in the nucleus.

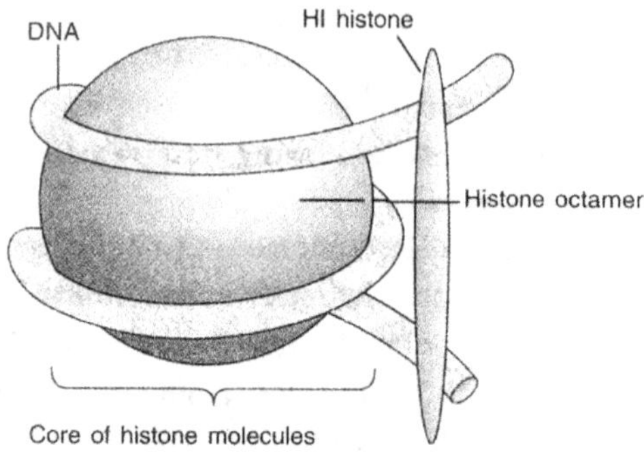

Fig. Nucleosome

(b) Nucleosomes constitute the repeating units in beads on string structure called chromatin. The chromatin is packaged to form chromatin fibres which further undergo coiling, overcoiling and supercoiling and condensed at metaphase stage of cell division to form structures called chromosomes. The packaging of chromatin at higher levels occur by non-histone chromosomal (NHC) proteins. In a typical non-dividing nuclues, chromatin consists of Euchromatin (loose, light stained transcriptionally active) and Heterochromatin condensed, dark-stained inactive).

44. **mRNA :** UUU AUG UUC GAG UUA GUG UAA

Amino acids : Phe – Met – Phe – Glu – Leu – Val – Stop codon.

Properties of genetic code that can be correlated

(i) **Triplet code :** Three adjacent bases constitute a codon, specifies a particular amino acid in a polypeptide.

(ii) **Commaless :** Genetic code is continuous

(iii) **Non-overlapping code :** A nitrogen base is a constituent of only one codon.

(iv) **Non-ambiguous codon :** One codon species, one amino acid and not any other.

(v) **Stop codon :** Polypeptide chain termination is signalled by three termination codon *e.g.* UAA.

Properties that cannot be correlated

(i) **Start signal/Initiation codon**

(ii) AUG (methionine) or GUG (valine)

(iii) Universal Code.

(iv) **Related Codons** Amino acids with similar properties have related codons.

(v) Degeneracy of code.

45. Differences between prokaryotic and eukaryotic transcription.

(a) RNA produced in bacteria/prokaryotic do not undergo extensive processing whereas pre mRNA, rRNA and tRNA in eukaryotes undergo extensive processing.

(b) In prokaryotes, no splitting event takes place. But in eukaryotes–primary transcript has both exons and introns are non-functional. Now it is subjected to process called splicing where introns are removed and exons are joined in defined manner.

46. The two factors responsible for conferring stabiltiy to double helix structure of DNA are:

(i) Hydrogen bonding between the nitrogenous bases A on one chain is joined to T on the other hand by 2 hydrogen bonds, C on one chain is linked to G on the other chain by 3 hydrogen bonds.

(ii) The bases project inward at planes approximately perpendicular to the long axis of the molecule, and are therefore, stacked one above the other.

47. (i) George Gamow suggested that the genetic code should be made up of a combination of three nucleotides.

(ii) He proposed that if 20 amino acids are to be coded by 4 bases, then the code should be made up of three nucleotides. ($4^2 = 16$), which is less than 20. So, the codon was proposed to be triplet. A permutation combination of 4^3 ($4 \times 4 \times 4$) would generate 64 codons; generating many more codons than required.

48. Gel electrophoresis is a technique that can be used to separate DNA fragments. Being negatively charged. DNA fragments get separated according to their size as they move towards the anode under the influence of an electric field.

49. During replication, the synthesis of a new strand of DNA at a leading parent DNA strand is continuous. However, it is discontinuous at the lagging strand in the form of DNA segments. These DNA segments are known as Okazaki fragments. These fragments are later joined with the help of the enzyme DNA ligase.

50. Sickle cell anaemia is an example of autosomal recessive trait in humans. The genes responsible for this disease are located on autosomes. This disease is only expressed if both the copies are defective. People with a single defective copy of the gene are clinically normal; however, they can pass on this defective gene to their subsequent generations.

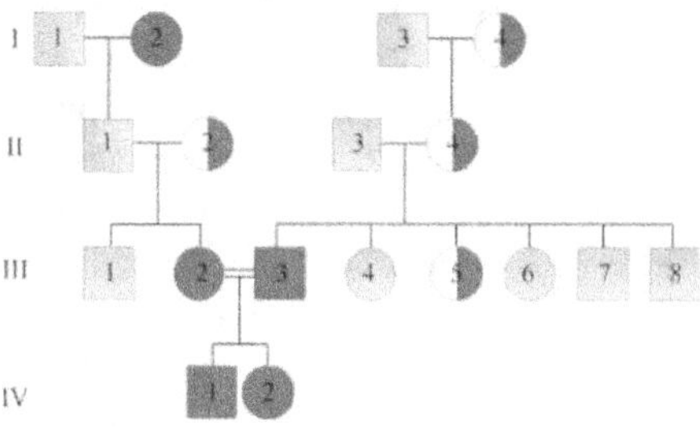

51. **The features of genetic code are as follows:**

Stop codon - Indicates termination of translation, also the stop codons do not code for any amino acid

Unamibiguous codon - Indicates that each codon codes for only one amino acid.

Degenerate codon - Indicates that more than one codon can code for a specific one amino acid

Universal codon - Indicates that one codon codes for the same amino acid in all species.

52. (a) The features that biomolecules must fulfil as a genetic material are as follows:

- Ability to replicate means a biomolecule should have an ability to generate replica.

- Stability means a biomolecule should be chemically and structurally stable.

- Mutation means a biomolecule should provide a scope for slow changes which is required for evolution.

- Expression means a biomolecule should be able to express itself in the form of 'Mendelian characters'.

(b) DNA is more stable because of the presence of thymine that provides extra stability to the DNA.

OR

(a) The algebraic equation $p^2 + q^2 + 2pq = 1$ is a binomial expansion of $(p + q)^2$. This algebraic equation represents the Hardy-Weinberg's principle that is used to calculate the genetic variation of a population at equilibrium. The Hardy-Weinberg principle states that the allele frequencies in a population are stable and which is remains constant from one generation to another generation.

So, p represents the frequency of allele A, q represents the frequency of allele a, p^2 represents the frequency of AA (homozygous) individuals in a population. Whereas q^2 represents the frequency of aa and 2pq represents the frequency of Aa (heterozygous) individuals. It also indicates that the sum of all the allelic frequencies is equal to one.

(b)   Gene migration refers to the movement of the alleles from one population to another that result in inbreeding between the members of the two population. So, the removal of alleles from one population or addition of alleles into another population is called gene migration. While genetic drift which is also called 'Swell Wright Effect'. Genetic drift is random in allele frequencies. It results in elimination of alleles or fixation of the other alleles in the population.

53.   (a)   Genetic code is the biochemical basis of heredity consisting of codons in DNA and RNA that determine the specific amino acid sequence in proteins and appear to be uniform for nearly all known forms of life.

Importance of genetic code in protein biosynthesis: Genetic code is important because it provides information encoded in genetic material (DNA or RNA sequences) to be translated into proteins (amino acid sequences) by living cells. All organisms on Earth utilise proteins in chemical reactions to facilitate physiological functions. Differences in genetic code result in different proteins, and thus different genetic variations in organisms.

(b)   The contribution of the scientists in deciphering the genetic code

S. No.	Scientists	Contributions
1	George Gamow	George Gamow coined the term genetic code. Theoretically he proposed a triplet genetic code.
2	Hargobind Khorana	Synthesised a chain of alternate nucleotide GUGUGUGUGU. He found that it stimulated synthesis of a peptide having alternate valine-cysteine-valine-cysteine.
3	Marshall Nierenberg	Discovered the first "triplet"— a sequence of three bases of DNA that codes for one of the twenty amino acids that serve as the building blocks of proteins.
4	Severo Ochoa	Determined the direction of the genetic code. He prepared a number of nucleotide co-polymers and deciphered several codons. He discovered the enzyme named Severo Ochoa enzyme which is a polynucleotide phosphorylase. This enzyme is helpful in polymerising RNA with definedsequences in a template-independent manner.

54.   Transforming Principle : In 1928, Frederick Griffith, in a series of experiments with *Streptococcus pneumoniae* (bacterium responsible for pneumonia), witnessed a miraculous transformation in the bacteria. During the cource of his experiment, a living organism (bacteria) had changed in physical form. He concluded that the R strain bacteria had somehow been tranformed by the heat - killed S strain bacteria. Some 'transforming principle', transferred from the heat - killed S strain, had enabled the R strain to synthesise a smooth polysaccharide coat and become virulent. This must be due to the transfer of the genetic material. However, the biochemical nature of genetic material was not defined from his experiments. Oswald Avery, Colin MacLeod and Maclyn McCarty worked to determine the biochemical nature of 'tranforming principle' in Griffith's experiment. They purified biochemicals (proteins , DNA, RNA, etc.) from the heat - killed S cells to see which ones could transform live R cells into S cells. They discoveredf that DNA alone from S bacteria caused R bacteria to become transformed. They also discovered that protein - digesting enzymes (proteases) and RNA - digesting enzymes (RNases) did not affect transformation, so the transforming substance was not a protein or RNA. Digestion with DNase did inhibit transformation, suggesting that the DNA caused the transformation. They concluded that DNA is the hereditary material, but not all biologist were convinced.

55.

S.No.	Crop Disease/Organism	Resistant Crop Variety
A	White rust	Pusa Swarnim
B	Leaf and stripe rust	Himgiri
C	Black rot	Pusa Shubhra
D	Jassids	Pusa Sem 2

Above mentioned crop varieties should be grown by the farmers to get rid of the existing problem and thus improve the crop yield because they are resistant to the given crop diseases or organisms.

NCERT Exemplar

1.   **(d)**   Sickel-cell anaemia is an autosome linked recessive trait. Only the homozygous individuals for Hb^s, *i.e.*, Hb^s Hb^s show the diseased phenotype. The heterozygous individuals (Hb^s / Hb^A) are carriers.

It is also known that heterozygous, having both types of haemoglobin. It shows resistance to malaria infection because the body targets the *P. falciparum* (protozoan) infected cells for destruction of RBC.

2. **(d)** Polypeptide synthesis is signalled by two initiation codons commonly AUG or methionine codon and rarely GUG or valine codon. Since there are 64 triplet codons and only 20 amino acids, the insertion of some amino must get influenced by more than one codon.

   Only tryptophan (UGG) and methonine (AUG) are specified by single codons. AUG codes for methionine in both prokaryotes and eukaryotes.

3. **(d)** The first genetic material was considered as RNA. There are now enough evidence to suggest that essential life processes (such as metabolism, translation, splicing etc.) evolved around RNA.

   It acts as a genetic material as well as catalyst (there are some important biochemical reactions in living systems that are catalysed by RNA catalysts and not by protein enzymes). But, RNA being a catalyst was reactive and hence unstable and not by protein enzymes) but, RNA being a catalyst was reactive and hence unstable.

   Therefore, DNA has evolved from RNA with chemical modifications that make it more stable.

4. **(b)** The coding sequence or expressed sequences are defined exons. The exons appear in mature or processed RNA and are interrupted by introns or intervening sequence which do not appear in mature or processed RNA.

5. **(c)** In human chromosome 1 has highest genes (2968 approx.) and the Y has the fewest (231 aprox). genes

6. **(c)** Lac operon consist of one regulatory genes (i gene) and three structural genes (z, y, and a).
   - i gene codes for Repressor.
   - z gene codes for Beta-galactosidase.
   - y gene codes for Permease.
   - a gene codes for Transacetylase.

7. **(b)** Assertion and Reason are correct but Reason is not a correction explanation of Assertion.

   Stability as one of the properties of genetic material was very evident in Griffith's transforming principle' itself that heat, which killed the bacteria, atleast did not destroy some of the properties of genetic material.

8. **(b)** Assertion and Reason are correct but Reason is not a correction explanation of Assertion.

   Histone octamer is made up of two units each or H2A, H2B, H3 and H4. The nucleosomes in chromatin are seen as 'beads-on-string'.

9. The genes present in an organism show a particular trait by way of forming certain product. This is facilitated by the process of transcription and translation (according to central dogma of genetics).

10. Genetic material of retrovirus is RNA. At the time of synthesis of protein, RNA is 'reverse transcribed' to its complementary DNA first, which is opposite to the central dogma. Hence, retrovirus are not known to follow central dogma.

11. Methylated Guanine cap helps in binding of mRNA to smaller ribosomal sub-unit during initiation of translation. Poly–A tail provides longevity to mRNA's life. Tail length and longevity of mRNA are positively correlated.

12. Use of ^{15}N will be inappropriate because method of detection of ^{35}p and ^{15}N is different (^{32}p being a radioactive isotope while ^{15}N is not radioactive but is the heavier isotope of Nitrogen). Even if ^{15}N was radioactive then its presence would have been detected both inside the cell (^{15}N incorporated as nitrogenous base in DNA) as well as in the supernatant because ^{15}N would also get incorporated in amino group of amino acids in proteins). Hence the use of ^{15}N would not give any conclusive results.

Objective Practice Exercise 

1. **(a)** According to the Wobble hypothesis, tRNA anticodon has the ability to wobble at its 5′end by pairing with even non-complementary base of mRNA codon. It corresponds to third base degeneracy of the codons.

2. **(b)** Crossing over occurs between non–sister chromatids of two homologous chromosomes. Homologous chromosomes form bivalent. Crossing over occurs between chromosomes in a nucleus.

3. **(c)** According to Chargaff purines and pyrimidines are in equal amounts. Purine (adenine) is equimolar with pyrimidine (thymine) and purine (guanine) is equimolar with pyrimidine (cytosine). Base ratio is specific for species.

4. **(d)** Prokaryotic chromosomes are circular and contain termination sequences.

5. **(c)** The ends of eukaryotic chromosomes are bound by telomerases not transcription factors. Centromeres not telomeres hold the newly replicated chromosomes together. Transposons do not require telomerase to move to other sites on chromosomes.

6. **(b)** Nucleosomes condense the DNA. Heterochromatin is transcriptionally inactive, while euchromatin is transcriptionally active.

7. **(d)** These three clues are all characteristics of eukaryotic DNA, but we have no information that permits us to decide from which kingdom of eukaryotes the sample came.

8. **(c)** Hydrogen bonds connect the bases on opposite strands of the DNA molecule, which is the reason that the helix can be unwound and separated relatively easily. All other bonds in file molecule are covalent.

9. **(a)** The fundamental factor that makes one individual different from another is the specific sequence of DNA bases in our genes.

10. **(c)** Since the building blocks of DNA were thought to be structurally simple and few number, biologists prior to the 1940s thought that only proteins could have the necessary complexity and diversity to be the hereditary material.

11. **(c)** Since strain R bacteria do not harm the mouse, this experiment is the equivalent of injecting the virulent strain S only. Thus the mouse will die, and you will find living strain S bacteria in its blood.

12. **(c)** The available evidence indicates that both DNA and RNA are present in the sample. The logic here is that thymine is unique to DNA, and both ribose and uracil are found only in RNA. With this evidence, however, you can say nothing about the types of RNA present in the sample, or whether the sample is actually from the killer.

13. **(d)** Since the total number of bases is the same, either no deletions or insertions occurred, or an equal number of each must have occurred. In this case, however, simply comparing each strand base-for-base shows that the more likely, explanation is that multiple substitutions took place along the sequence.

14. **(c)** These researchers were able to isolate nearly pure DNA samples. It was only these samples that provided transformation activity.

15. **(d)** Chargaff found that the relative ratios of purine to pyrimidines were equal. Adenine and guanine are purines and cytosine and thymine are pyrimidines; therefore, ratios of adenine and thymine should be equal. Chargaff also found that there is no conserved ratio between specific pairs (*e.g.*, $A + T$ and $G + C$).

16. **(c)** A DNA triplet of CGT would yield an mRNA codon of GCA. The complementary tRNA anticodon would therefore be CGU.

17. **(b)** False, A functional strand of mRNA must have a start and a stop codon. The start codon often also codes for the amino acid methionine, which may or may not end up being a part of the final protein. However, the stop codon would not code for an amino acid. Thus, with 66 codons in the mRNA, there could be as many as 65 amino acids in the protein product.

18. **(c)** The complementary base-pairing rules of DNA-to-RNA and RNA-to-RNA give the codon and anticodon. Recall also that there is no thymine in RNA; uracil and adenine are complementary bases for RNA.

19. **(a)** DNA polymerase adds nucleotides to an existing nucleotide strand.

20. **(d)** Okazaki fragments are short pieces of newly synthesized DNA. The production of each of these fragments is dependent on a beginning RNA primer. The small fragments are ultimately ligated connected together to form the lagging strand.

21. **(a)** DNA polymerase cannot initiate the building of a nucleotide strand; it can only add to an existing strand. Thus, RNA primers are necessary to begin DNA synthesis.

22. **(a)** For the integrity of DNA to be maintained, repair mechanisms must be active during synthesis, modification, and utilization of DNA.

23. **(d)** All of these will be true if the DNA molecule replicates correctly.

24. **(b)**

25. **(b)** Lactose operon in *E.coli* is a catabolic pathway in which the structural genes remain switched off unless the inducer (Lactose) is present in the medium.

26. **(a)** In negative (repressible) operon, the repressor co-repressor complex binds with the operator. The free repressor cannot bind to the operator.

27. **(c)** If the *lac* repressor is non functional, it cannot bind the operator site and transcription of the *lac* operon will occur at all times, whether or not lactose is present.

28. **(a)** If the repressor can no longer bind tryptophan, then it cannot bind the operator and transcription of the *trp* operon will always be on, whether tryptophan levels in the cell are high or low.

29. **(d)** Option *a* refers to the *lac* and *trp* repressors, option *b* to the CRP protein, and option *c* refers to promoter that have different transcriptional efficiencies.

30. **(d)**

31. **(d)** The first effect of any signal molecule must involve the binding of the molecule to a receptor.

32. **(a)** Polymerase chain reaction (PCR) is a process used for the amplification (copy - small segments) of DNA. It is a technique for enzymatically replicating DNA without using living organisms, such as *E. coli* or yeast. It is commonly used in the medical and biological research labs for a variety of tasks, like detection of hereditary diseases, the identification of genetic fingerprints, diagnosis of infectious diseases, cloning of genes, paternity testing etc.

33. **(d)** Polymorphism in DNA sequence is a variation at genetic level. It arises due to mutation and is the basis of genetic mapping of human genome as well as of DNA fingerprinting.

34. **(b)** Human genome project was launched in the year 1990. It is an international scientific research project having the goal to determine the sequence of base pairs which make up human DNA, and to identify and map all of the genes of the human genome.

35. (d) Many non-human model organisms such as bacteria, *Saccharomyces cerevisiae* (yeast), *Caenorhabditis elegans* (a free living non-pathogenic nematode) *Drosophila* (the fruit fly), plants (*Oryza sativa* and *Ararbidopsis thalliana*), etc. have also been sequences.

36. (d) Minisatellites are inherently unstable and susceptible to mutation at a higher rate than other sequences of DNA. Thus, due to difference in number, location and size of minisatellites on chromosomes, each individual has a unique DNA fingerprint.

37. (d) Satellite DNA is a portion of DNA consisting of short, repeating sequences of nucleotide pairs near the region of the centromere. Normally it does not code for any protein but shows polymorphisms. It is classified in many categories like micro- or minisatellites based on the composition, length of segments and number of repetitive units.

38. (b) In a DNA strand the nucleotides are linked together by 3'–5' phosphodiester linkage (bonds) to form a dinucleotide. To form a polynucleotide chain, more nucleotides can be joined.

39. (c) A nitrogenous base is attached to the pentose sugar by an N-glycosidic linkage to form a nucleoside, i.e., Nucleoside = Nitrogen base + Pentose sugar. When a phosphate group is attached to the 5'-OH of a nucleoside through phosphodiester linkage, a nucleotide is formed, *i.e.* Nucleotide = Nitrogen base + Pentose sugar + phosphate (PO_4)

So, a nucleoside differs from a nucleotide as it lacks the phosphate group.

40. (c) Both deoxyribose and ribose belong to the class pentoses as it contains '5' carbon atoms.

41. (a) The diameter of the strand always constant due to a pairing of purine (adenine and guanine) and pyrimidine (cytosine and thymine). The specific bonding gives uniformity and keep strands together.

42. (c) DNA consists of a nitrogenous base, pentose sugar and phosphate group. Due to the presence of phosphate group $\left(PO_4^{3-} \right)$, DNA has negative charge

Histones are rich in the basic amino acid lysines and arginines, that carry positive charges in their side chains, Therefore, histones are positively charged.

43. (d) In 1953 **James Watson** and **Francis Crick**, based on the X-ray diffraction data produced by **Maurice Wilkins** and **Rasalind Franklin** proposed a double helix model of DNA.

Erwin chargaff observed that, in double-stranded DNA, the ratios between adenine and thymine and guanine and cytosine are constant and equal. **Matthew Meselson** and **franklin stahl** in 1958 performed experiments on *E. Coli* to prove that DNA replicates semiconservatively. But had no contribution it the development of double helix model.

44. (b) The DNA dependent RNA polymerase helps in elongation of DNA by catalysing the polymerisation in only one direction, *i.e.*, $5' \to 3'$.

45. (b) Considering that gene expression results in the formation of a polypeptide, and can be regulated at several levels. In eukaryotes, the regulation could be at transcriptional level (formation of primary transcript, processing level (regulation of splicing), transport of mRNA from nucleus to the cytoplasm and translational level.

While, in prokaryotes control of the rate of transcriptional initiation is the predominant site for control of gene expression.

46. (a) Chromosome 1 was the last completed chromosome, sequenced two decades after the beginning of the human Genome project (hGP). It is for the largest human chromosome.

47. (d) Regulatory sequences (proteins) control the functions of structural genes and are called regulatory genes. The important regulatory genes are promoters, terminators, operators and repressor.

To regulate the process of transcription, trancription factors (a sequence of specific DNA-binding factor) alone or with other proteins. promoter (as on activator) or stop as a repress or the binding site of RNA polymerase to DNA.

48. (b) DNA polymerase adds deoxyribonucleotides to the free 3'- end of the growing polynucleote chain so that replication of the $3' \to 5'$ strand of the DNA molecule is continuous (growth of the new strand occurs in $5' \to 3'$ direction)

Since, DNA dependent DNA polymerase catalyses polymerisation only in one direction $(5' \to 3')$ discontinuous synthesis of DNA occurs in the other strand.

49. (d) rRNA, mRNA and tRNA are major classes of RNAs which are involved in gene expression. rRNAs bind protein molecules and give rise to ribosomes.

mRNA carries coded information for translation into polypeptide formation.

tRNA is called soluble or adaptor RNA that carries amino acids to mRNA during protein synthesis.

50. (b) According to chargaff's rules of base pairing
(i) The amount of adenine is always equal to the amount of thymine and the amount of guanine is always equal to the amount of cytosine.

(ii) Adenine is joined to thymine with two hydrogen bonds and guanine is jointed to cytosine by three hydrogen bonds.

(iii) The ratio of adnine to thymine and that of guanine to cytosine is always equal to one.

i.e., $\dfrac{A}{T} = \dfrac{G}{C} = 1$

In the given organism, the DNA is not following the Chargaff's rule, hence it can be concluded that it is a single-stranded DNA not double-stranded.

51. **(b)** Sigma factor is associated with the initiation of transcription. Sigma factor confers the specificity of RNA synthesis at the promoter region. Capping involves the addition of unusual nucleotide at the 5' end of hn RNA. Tailing involves the addition of adenylate residues at 3' end in a template independently. Coding strand (also called leading strand) is a strand synthesized by an enzyme in continuous piece in 5' - 3' direction.

52. **(b)** Alec Jeffreys developed techniques for DNA finger printing and DNA profiling. These techniques are now used worldwide in forensic science. F. Sanger worked on protein sequencing and DNA sequencing and got Noble prize for the same. Jacob and Monad proposed the lac (lactose) operon. Avery, McLeod and McCarty expanded the work of Griffith on the process of transformation.

Chapter Test 

1. **(c)**

2. **(c)** tRNA (or transfer RNA) is a single stranded RNA molecule which brings amino acid and reads the genetic code in the process of transcription. It helps decode a messenger RNA (mRNA) sequence into a protein. It functions at specific sites in the ribosome during translation, which is a process that synthesizes a protein from a mRNA molecule.

3. **(a)** Messelson and Stahl (1958) cultured (*Escherichia coli*) bacteria in a culture medium containing ^{15}N. After these had been replicated for a few generations in the medium both the strands of their DNA contained ^{15}N as constituents of purines and pyrimidines. When these bacteria with ^{15}N were transferred in cultural medium containing ^{14}N, it was found that DNA separated from fresh generation of bacteria possesses one strand heavier than the other. The heavier strand represents the parental strand and lighter one is the new one synthesized from the culture indicating semi conservative mode of DNA replication.

4. **(d)** The experiment conducted by Hershey and Chase proved that DNA is the genetic material and that during infection of *E. coli* cells by bacteriophage T2, only nucleic acids (DNA or RNA) enter the cell. Nucleic acids from the head pass through the hollow tail and enter the bacterial cell. The remainder of the phage remains on the outside of the bacterium as "ghost".

5. **(a)** Operator site gives passages to RNA polymerase moving from the promoter to structural gene. Promoter site is the initiation point for transcription and the site for binding of RNA polymerase. Structural gene determines the amino acid sequence on the segment of DNA molecule. Regulator gene controls the activity of operator gene by producing repressor molecules.

6. **(b)** Assertion and Reason are correct but Reason is not a correction explanation of Assertion.

The plane of one base pair stacks over the other in double helix.

7. **(b)** Assertion and Reason are correct but Reason is not a correction explanation of Assertion.

In its inactive stats, ribosome exists as two submits viz a large submit and a small submit. Theb cellula factory responsible for regnthesizing proteins in the ribosoml.

8. **(c)**   9. **(a)**   10. **(b)**   11. **(c)**

12. **(b)**

13. Peptidyl transferase.

14. DNA polymerase can not initially synthesis of new DNA strand, but can catalyze growth of chain.

15. Uracil.

www.ingramcontent.com/pod-product-compliance
Lightning Source LLC
Chambersburg PA
CBHW060114120726
48003CB00009B/2627